Behavior Analysis with Machine Learning Using R

Chapman & Hall/CRC
The R Series

Recently Published Titles

Statistical Inference via Data Science: A ModernDive into R and the Tidyverse
Chester Ismay and Albert Y. Kim

Reproducible Research with R and RStudio, Third Edition
Christopher Gandrud

Interactive Web-Based Data Visualization with R, plotly, and shiny
Carson Sievert

Learn R: As a Language
Pedro J. Aphalo

Using R for Modelling and Quantitative Methods in Fisheries
Malcolm Haddon

R For Political Data Science: A Practical Guide
Francisco Urdinez and Andres Cruz

R Markdown Cookbook
Yihui Xie, Christophe Dervieux, and Emily Riederer

Learning Microeconometrics with R
Christopher P. Adams

R for Conservation and Development Projects: A Primer for Practitioners
Nathan Whitmore

Using R for Bayesian Spatial and Spatio-Temporal Health Modeling
Andrew B. Lawson

Engineering Production-Grade Shiny Apps
Colin Fay, Sébastien Rochette, Vincent Guyader, and Cervan Girard

Javascript for R
John Coene

Advanced R Solutions
Malte Grosser, Henning Bumann, and Hadley Wickham

Event History Analysis with R, Second Edition
Göran Broström

Behavior Analysis with Machine Learning Using R
Enrique Garcia Ceja

For more information about this series, please visit: https://www.crcpress.com/Chapman--HallCRC-The-R-Series/book-series/CRCTHERSER

Behavior Analysis with Machine Learning Using R

Enrique Garcia Ceja

CRC Press
Taylor & Francis Group
Boca Raton London New York

CRC Press is an imprint of the
Taylor & Francis Group, an **informa** business
A CHAPMAN & HALL BOOK

First edition published 2022
by CRC Press
6000 Broken Sound Parkway NW, Suite 300, Boca Raton, FL 33487-2742

and by CRC Press
2 Park Square, Milton Park, Abingdon, Oxon, OX14 4RN

CRC Press is an imprint of Taylor & Francis Group, LLC

Library of Congress Cataloging-in-Publication Data

Names: Garcia Ceja, Enrique, author.
Title: Behavior analysis with machine learning using R / Enrique Garcia Ceja.
Description: First edition. | London ; Boca Raton : CRC Press, 2022. | Includes bibliographical references and index. | Summary: "Behavior Analysis with Machine Learning Using R introduces machine learning and deep learning concepts and algorithms applied to a diverse set of behavior analysis problems. It focuses on the practical aspects of solving such problems based on data collected from sensors or stored in electronic records. The included examples demonstrate how to perform common data analysis tasks such as: data exploration, visualization, preprocessing, data representation, model training and evaluation. All of this, using the R programming language and real-life behavioral data. Even though the examples focus on behavior analysis tasks, the covered underlying concepts and methods can be applied in any other domain. No prior knowledge in machine learning is assumed. Basic experience with R and basic knowledge in statistics and high school level mathematics are beneficial. Features: Build supervised machine learning models to predict indoor locations based on WiFi signals, recognize physical activities from smartphone sensors and 3D skeleton data, detect hand gestures from accelerometer signals, and so on. Program your own ensemble learning methods and use Multi-View Stacking to fuse signals from heterogeneous data sources. Use unsupervised learning algorithms to discover criminal behavioral patterns. Build deep learning neural networks with TensorFlow and Keras to classify muscle activity from electromyography signals and Convolutional Neural Networks to detect smiles in images. Evaluate the performance of your models in traditional and multi-user settings. Build anomaly detection models such as Isolation Forests and autoencoders to detect abnormal fish behaviors. This book is intended for undergraduate/graduate students and researchers from ubiquitous computing, behavioral ecology, psychology, e-health, and other disciplines who want to learn the basics of machine learning and deep learning and for the more experienced individuals who want to apply machine learning to analyze behavioral data"-- Provided by publisher.
Identifiers: LCCN 2021028230 (print) | LCCN 2021028231 (ebook) | ISBN 9781032067049 (hardback) | ISBN 9781032067056 (paperback) | ISBN 9781003203469 (ebook)
Subjects: LCSH: Behavioral assessment--Data processing. | Task analysis--Data processing. | Machine learning. | R (Computer program language)
Classification: LCC BF176.2 .G37 2022 (print) | LCC BF176.2 (ebook) | DDC 155.2/8--dc23/eng/20211006
LC record available at https://lccn.loc.gov/2021028230
LC ebook record available at https://lccn.loc.gov/2021028231

ISBN: 978-1-032-06704-9 (hbk)
ISBN: 978-1-032-06705-6 (pbk)
ISBN: 978-1-003-20346-9 (ebk)

DOI: 10.1201/9781003203469

Publisher's note: This book has been prepared from camera-ready copy provided by the authors.

Typeset in LM Roman
by KnowledgeWorks Global Ltd.

To My Family,

who have put up with me despite my bad behavior.

Contents

List of Figures

Welcome

This book aims to provide an introduction to machine learning concepts and algorithms applied to a diverse set of behavior analysis problems. It focuses on the practical aspects of solving such problems based on data collected from sensors or stored in electronic records. The included examples demonstrate how to perform several of the tasks involved during a data analysis pipeline such as: data exploration, visualization, preprocessing, representation, model training/validation, and so on. All of this, using the **R** programming language and real-life datasets.

Some of the content that you will find here includes, how to:

- Build **supervised machine learning** models to predict indoor locations based on Wi-Fi signals, recognize physical activities from smartphone sensors and 3D skeleton data, detect hand gestures from accelerometer signals, and so on.
- Use **unsupervised learning** algorithms to discover criminal behavioral patterns.
- Program your own **ensemble learning** methods and use multi-view stacking to fuse signals from heterogeneous data sources.
- Train **deep learning** models such as *neural networks* to classify muscle activity from electromyography signals and *Convolutional Neural Networks* to detect smiles in images.
- **Evaluate the performance** of your models in *traditional* and *multi-user* settings.
- Train **anomaly detection** models such as *Isolation Forests* and *autoencoders* to detect abnormal fish trajectories.
- And much more!

The accompanying source code for all examples is available at `https://github.com/enriquegit/behavior-crc-code`. The book itself was written in

R with the `bookdown` package[1] developed by Yihui Xie[2]. The front cover and comics were illustrated by Vance Capley[3].

About the Front Cover

The front cover depicts two brothers (Biås and Biranz) in what seems to be a typical weekend. They are exploring and enjoying nature as usual. What they don't know is that their lives are about to change and there is no turning back. Suddenly, Biranz spots a strange object approaching them. As it makes its way out of the rocks, its entire figure is revealed. The brothers have never seen anything like that before. The closest similar image they have in their brains is a hand-sized carnivorous plant they saw at the botanical garden during a school visit several years ago. Without any warning, the creature releases a load of spores into the air. Today, the breeze is not on the brothers' side and the spores quickly enclose them. After seconds of being exposed, their bodies start to paralyze. Moments later, they can barely move their pupils. The creature's multiple stems begin to inflate and all of a sudden, multiple thorns are shot. Horrified and incapable, the brothers can only witness how the thorns approach their bodies and they can even hear how the air is being cut by the sharp thorns. At this point, they are only waiting for the worst. After some seconds, it seems that they haven't felt any impact. Has time just stopped? No – the thorns were repelled by what appears to be a bionic dolphin emitting some type of ultrasonic waves. However, one of the projectiles managed to dodge the sound defense and is heading directly to Biås. While flying almost one mile above sea level, an eagle aims for the elusive thorn and destroys it with surgical precision. But the creature keeps being persistent with its attacks. Will the brothers escape from this crossfire battle?

[1] https://CRAN.R-project.org/package=bookdown

[2] https://twitter.com/xieyihui

[3] http://www.vancecapleyart.com/

About the Author

Enrique is a Data Scientist at Optimeering. He was previously a Researcher at SINTEF, Norway. He worked as a postdoc at the University of Oslo and obtained his PhD from Tecnólogico de Monterrey University, México. He also worked as a software engineer at Huawei. For the last 11 years, he has been conducting research on behavior analysis using machine learning. Feel free to contact him for any questions, comments, and feedback.

e-mail: e.g.mx [at] ieee.org

Twitter: `https://twitter.com/e_g_mx`

website: `http://www.enriquegc.com`

Preface

Automatic behavior monitoring technologies are becoming part of our everyday lives thanks to advances in sensors and machine learning. The automatic analysis and understanding of behavior are being applied to solve problems in several fields, including health care, sports, marketing, ecology, security, and psychology, to name a few. This book provides a practical introduction to machine learning methods applied to behavior analysis with the R programming language. No previous knowledge in machine learning is needed. You should be familiar with the basics of R and some knowledge in basic statistics and high school-level mathematics would be beneficial. Even though the exercises focus on behavior analysis tasks, the covered machine learning underlying concepts and methods can be easily applied in any other domain.

Supplemental Material

The supplemental material consists of examples' code, shiny apps, and datasets. The source code for the examples and the shiny apps can be downloaded from `https://github.com/enriquegit/behavior-crc-code`. Instructions on how to set up the code, run shiny apps, and get the datasets are in Appendix A. A reference for all the utilized datasets is in Appendix B.

Conventions

DATASET names are written in uppercase italics. Functions are referred to by their name followed by parenthesis (omitting their arguments), for example: `myFunction()`. Class labels are written in italics and between single quotes: *'label1'*. The following icons are used to provide additional contextual information:

Provides additional information and notes.

Important information to consider.

Provides tips and good practice recommendations.

Lists the R scripts and files used in the corresponding section.

Interactive shiny app available. Please see Appendix A for instructions on how to run shiny apps.

The folder icon will appear at the beginning of a section (if applicable) to indicate which scripts were used for the corresponding examples.

Acknowledgments

I want to thank Ketil Stølen and Robert Kabacoff who reviewed the book and gave me valuable suggestions.

I want to thank Michael Riegler, Darlene E., Jaime Mondragon y Ariana, Viviana M., Linda Sicilia, Ania Aguirre, Anton Aguilar, Gagan Chhabra, Aleksander Karlsen, 刘爽, Ragnhild Halvorsrud, Tine Nordgreen, Petter Jakobsen, Jim Tørresen, my former master's and PhD. advisor Ramon F. Brena, and my former colleagues at University of Oslo and SINTEF.

I want to thank Vance Capley who brought to life the front cover and comic illustrations, Francescoozzimo who drew the comic for chapter 10, and Katia Liuntova who animated the online front cover. The examples in this book rely heavily on datasets. I want to thank all the people that made all their datasets used here publicly available. Thanks to Yihui Xie who developed the `bookdown` R package with which this book was written.

Thanks to Rob Calver, Vaishali Singh, and the CRC Press team who helped me during the publishing process.

I want to thank all the music bands I listened to during my writing-breaks: Lionheart, Neaera, Hatebreed, Sworn Enemy, Killswitch Engage, As I Lay Dying, Lamb of God, Himsa, Slipknot, Madball, Fleshgod Apocalypse, Bleeding Through, Caliban, Chimaira, Heaven Shall Burn, Darkest Hour, Demon Hunter, Frente de Ira, Desarmador, Después del Odio, Gatomadre, Rey Chocolate, ill niño, Soulfly, Walls of Jericho, Arrecife, Corcholata, Amon Amarth, Abinchova, Fit for a King, Annisokay, Sylosis, Meshuggah.

1

Introduction to Behavior and Machine Learning

In the last years, machine learning has surged as one of the key technologies that enables and supports many of the services and products that we use in our everyday lives and is expanding quickly. Machine learning has also helped to accelerate research and development in almost every field including natural sciences, engineering, social sciences, medicine, art and culture. Even though all those fields (and their respective subfields) are very diverse, most of them have something in common: They involve living organisms (cells, microbes, plants, humans, animals, etc.) and living organisms express behaviors. This book teaches you machine learning and data-driven methods to analyze different types of behaviors. Some of those methods include supervised, unsupervised, and deep learning. You will also learn how to explore, encode, preprocess, and visualize behavioral data. While the examples in this book focus on behavior analysis, the methods and techniques can be applied in any other context.

This chapter starts by introducing the concepts of *behavior* and *machine learning*. Next, basic machine learning terminology is presented and you will build your first classification and regression models. Then, you will learn how to evaluate the performance of your models and important concepts such as *underfitting*, *overfitting*, *bias*, and *variance*.

1.1 What Is Behavior?

Living organisms are constantly sensing and analyzing their surrounding environment. This includes inanimate objects but also other living entities. All of this is with the objective of making decisions and taking actions, either consciously or unconsciously. If we see someone running,

DOI: 10.1201/9781003203469-1

we will react differently depending on whether we are at a stadium or in a bank. At the same time, we may also analyze other cues such as the runner's facial expressions, clothes, items, and the reactions of the other people around us. Based on this aggregated information, we can decide how to react and behave. All this is supported by the organisms' sensing capabilities and decision-making processes (the brain and/or chemical reactions). Understanding our environment and how others behave is crucial for conducting our everyday life activities and provides support for other tasks. But, **what is behavior**? The Cambridge dictionary defines behavior as:

> *"the way that a person, an animal, a substance, etc. behaves in a particular situation or under particular conditions".*

Another definition by dictionary.com is:

> *"observable activity in a human or animal".*

The definitions are similar and both include humans and animals. Following those definitions, this book will focus on the automatic analysis of human and animal behaviors however, the methods can also be applied to robots and to a wide variety of problems in different domains. There are three main reasons why one may want to analyze behaviors in an automatic manner:

1. **React.** A biological or an artificial agent (or a combination of both) can take actions based on what is happening in the surrounding environment. For example, if suspicious behavior is detected in an airport, preventive actions can be triggered by security systems and the corresponding authorities. Without the possibility to automate such a detection system, it would

be infeasible to implement it in practice. Just imagine trying to analyze airport traffic by hand.

2. **Understand.** Analyzing the behavior of an organism can help us to understand other associated behaviors and processes and to answer research questions. For example, Williams et al. [2020] found that *Andean condors* the heaviest soaring bird (see Figure 1.1), only flap their wings for about 1% of their total flight time. In one of the cases, a condor flew $\approx$ 172 km without flapping. Those findings were the result of analyzing the birds' behavior from data recorded by bio-logging devices. In this book, several examples that make use of inertial devices will be studied.

FIGURE 1.1 Andean condor. (Hugo Pédel, France, Travail personnel. Cliché réalisé dans le Parc National Argentin Nahuel Huapi, San Carlos de Bariloche, Laguna Tonchek. Source: Wikipedia (CC BY-SA 3.0) [https://creativecommons.org/licenses/by-sa/3.0/legalcode]).

3. **Document and Archive.** Finally, we may want to document certain behaviors for future use. It could be for evidence purposes or maybe it is not clear how the information can be used now but may come in handy later. Based on the archived information, one could gain new knowledge in the future and use it to react (take decisions/actions), as shown in Figure 1.2. For example, we could document our nutritional habits (what do we eat, how often, etc.). If there is a health issue, a specialist could use this historical information to make a more precise diagnosis and propose actions.

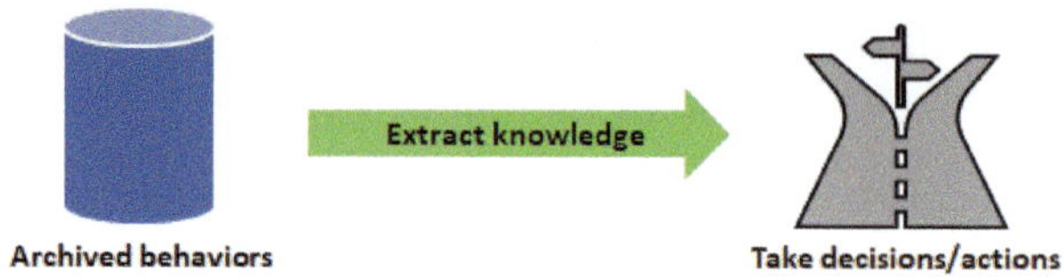

FIGURE 1.2 Taking decisions from archived behaviors.

Some behaviors can be used as a proxy to understand other behaviors, states, and/or processes. For example, detecting body movement behaviors during a job interview could serve as the basis to understand stress levels. Behaviors can also be modeled as a composition of lower-level behaviors. In chapter 7, a method called *Bag of Words* that can be used to decompose complex behaviors into a set of simpler ones will be presented.

In order to analyze and monitor behaviors, we need a way to observe them. Living organisms use their available senses such as eyesight, hearing, smell, echolocation (bats, dolphins), thermal senses (snakes, mosquitoes), etc. In the case of machines, they need *sensors* to accomplish or approximate those tasks, for example color and thermal cameras, microphones, temperature sensors, and so on.

The reduction in the size of sensors has allowed the development of more powerful wearable devices. *Wearable devices* are electronic devices that are worn by a user, usually as accessories or embedded in clothes. Examples of wearable devices are smartphones, smartwatches, fitness bracelets, actigraphy watches, etc. These devices have embedded sensors that allow them to monitor different aspects of a user such as activity levels, blood pressure, temperature, and location, to name a few. Examples of sensors that can be found in those devices are accelerometers, magnetometers, gyroscopes, heart rate, microphones, Wi-Fi, Bluetooth, Galvanic skin response (GSR), etc.

Several of those sensors were initially used for some specific purposes. For example, accelerometers in smartphones were intended to be used for gaming or detecting the device's orientation. Later, some people started to propose and implement new use cases such as activity recognition [Shoaib et al., 2015] and fall detection. The magnetometer, which measures the earth's magnetic field, was mainly used with map applications to determine the orientation of the device, but later, it was found that it can also be used for indoor location purposes [Brena et al., 2017].

In general, wearable devices have been successfully applied to track different types of behaviors such as physical activity, sports activities, location, and even mental health states [Garcia-Ceja et al., 2018c]. Those devices generate a lot of raw data, but it will be our task to process and analyze it. Doing it by hand becomes impossible given the large amounts of data and their variety. In this book, several *machine learning* methods will be introduced that will allow you to extract and analyze different types of behaviors from data. The next section will begin with an introduction to machine learning. The rest of this chapter will introduce the required machine learning concepts before we start analyzing behaviors in chapter 2.

1.2 What Is Machine Learning?

You can think of *machine learning* as a set of computational algorithms that *automatically* find useful patterns and relationships from data. Here, the keyword is *automatic*. When trying to solve a problem, one can hard-code a predefined set of rules, for example, chained if-else conditions. For instance, if we want to detect if the object in a picture is an *orange* or a *pear*, we can do something like:

```
if(number_green_pixels > 90%)
  return "pear"
else
  return "orange"
```

This simple rule should work well and will do the job. Imagine that now your boss tells you that the system needs to recognize *green apples* as well. Our previous rule will no longer work, and we will need to include additional rules and thresholds. On the other hand, a machine learning algorithm will automatically learn such rules based on the updated data. So, you only need to update your data with examples of *green apples* and "click" the re-train button!

The result of *learning* is *knowledge* that the system can use to solve new instances of a problem. In this case, when you show a new image to the system, it should be able to recognize the type of fruit. Figure 1.3 shows this general idea.

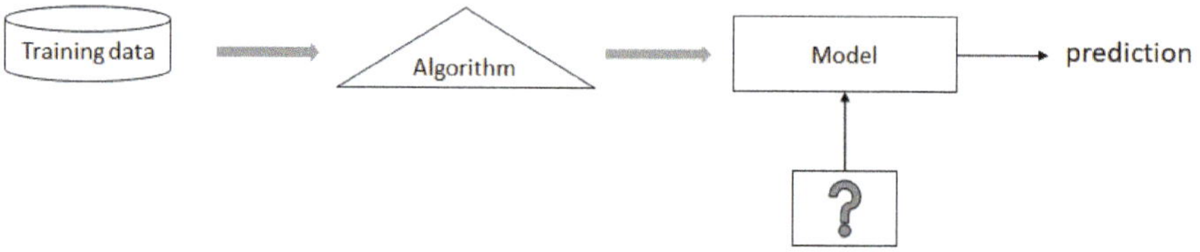

FIGURE 1.3 Overall Machine Learning phases. The '?' represents the new unknown object for which we want to obtain a prediction using the learned model.

For more formal definitions of machine learning, I recommend you check [Kononenko and Kukar, 2007].

Machine learning methods rely on three main building blocks:

- **Data**
- **Algorithms**
- **Models**

Every machine learning method needs **data** to learn from. For the example of the fruits, we need examples of images for each type of fruit we want to recognize. Additionally, we need their corresponding output types (labels) so the algorithm can learn how to associate each image with its corresponding label.

Not every machine learning method needs the expected output or labels (more on this in the Taxonomy section 1.3).

Typically, an **algorithm** will use the **data** to learn a **model**. This is called the learning or training phase. The learned **model** can then be used to generate predictions when presented with new data. The data used to train the models is called the **train set**. Since we need a way to test how the model will perform once it is deployed in a real setting (in production), we also need what is known as the **test set**. The test set is used to estimate the model's performance on data it has never seen before (more on this will be presented in section 1.6).

1.3 Types of Machine Learning

Machine learning methods can be grouped into different types. Figure 1.4 depicts a categorization of machine learning 'types'. This figure is based on [Biecek et al., 2012]. The x axis represents the certainty of the labels and the y axis the percent of training data that is labeled. In the previous example, the labels are the names of the fruits associated with each image.

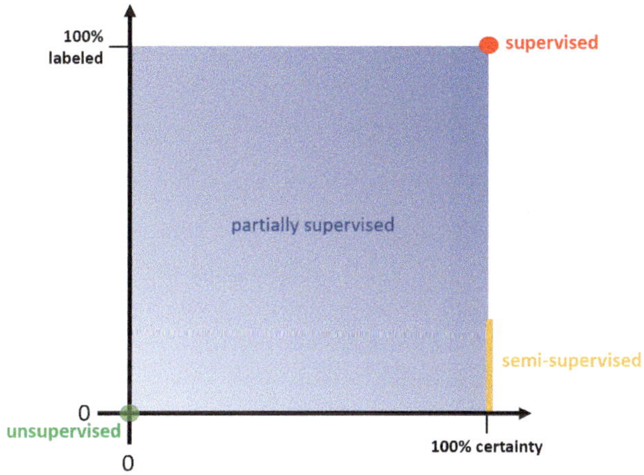

FIGURE 1.4 Machine learning taxonomy. (Adapted from Biecek, Przemyslaw, et al. "The R package bgmm: mixture modeling with uncertain knowledge." *Journal of Statistical Software* 47.i03 (2012). (CC BY 3.0) [`https://creativecommons.org/licenses/by/3.0/legalcode`]).

From the figure, four main types of machine learning methods can be observed:

- **Supervised learning.** In this case, 100% of the training data is labeled and the certainty of those labels is 100%. This is like the fruits example. For every image used to train the system, the respective label is also known and there is no uncertainty about the label. When the expected output is a category (the type of fruit), this is called **classification**. Examples of classification models (a.k.a classifiers) are decision trees, k-Nearest Neighbors, Random Forest, neural networks, etc. When the output is a real number (e.g., temperature), it is called

regression. Examples of regression models are linear regression, regression trees, neural networks, Random Forest, k-Nearest Neighbors, etc. Note that some models can be used for both classification and regression. A supervised learning problem can be formalized as follows:

$$f(x) = y \tag{1.1}$$

where f is a function that maps some input data x (for example images) to an output y (types of fruits). Usually, an **algorithm** will try to *learn* the best **model** f given some **data** consisting of n pairs (x, y) of examples. During learning, the algorithm has access to the expected output/label y for each input x. At *inference time*, that is, when we want to make predictions for new examples, we can use the learned model f and feed it with a new input x to obtain the corresponding predicted value y.

- **Semi-supervised learning.** This is the case when the certainty of the labels is 100% but not all training data are labeled. Usually, this scenario considers the case when only a very small proportion of the data is labeled. That is, the dataset contains pairs of examples of the form (x, y) but also examples where y is missing $(x, ?)$. In supervised learning, both x and y must be present. On the other hand, semi-supervised algorithms can learn even if some examples are missing the expected output y. This is a common situation in real life since labeling data can be expensive and time-consuming. In the fruits example, someone needs to tag every training image manually before training a model. Semi-supervised learning methods try to extract information also from the unlabeled data to improve the models. Examples of some semi-supervised learning methods are self-learning, co-training, and tri-training. [Triguero et al., 2013].
- **Partially-supervised learning.** This is a generalization that encompasses supervised and semi-supervised learning. Here, the examples have uncertain (*soft*) labels. For example, the label of a fruit image instead of being an *'orange'* or *'pear'* could be a vector $[0.7, 0.3]$ where the first element is the probability that the image corresponds to an orange and the second element is the probability that it's a pear. Maybe the image was not very clear, and these are the beliefs of the person tagging the images encoded as probabilities. Examples of models that

can be used for partially-supervised learning are mixture models with belief functions [Côme et al., 2009] and neural networks.

- **Unsupervised learning.** This is the extreme case when none of the training examples have a label. That is, the dataset only has pairs $(x, ?)$. Now, you may be wondering: If there are no labels, is it possible to extract information from these data? The answer is *yes*. Imagine you have fruit images with no labels. What you could try to do is to automatically group them into meaningful categories/groups. The categories could be the types of fruits themselves, i.e., trying to form groups in which images within the same category belong to the same type. In the fruits example, we could infer the true types by visually inspecting the images, but in many cases, visual inspection is difficult and the formed groups may not have an easy interpretation, but still, they can be very useful and can be used as a preprocessing step (like in vector quantization). These types of algorithms that find groups (hierarchical groups in some cases) are called **clustering methods**. Examples of clustering methods are k-means, k-medoids, and hierarchical clustering. Clustering algorithms are not the only unsupervised learning methods. Association rules, word embeddings, and autoencoders are examples of other unsupervised learning methods. *Note*: Some people may claim that word embeddings and autoencoders are not fully unsupervised methods but for practical purposes, this is not relevant.

Additionally, there is another type of machine learning called **Reinforcement Learning (RL)** which has substantial differences from the previous ones. This type of learning does not rely on example data as the previous ones but on stimuli from an agent's environment. At any given point in time, an agent can perform an action which will lead it to a new state where a *reward* is collected. The aim is to learn the sequence of actions that maximize the reward. This type of learning is not covered in this book. A good introduction to the topic can be consulted here[1].

This book will mainly cover supervised learning problems and more specifically, classification problems. For example, given a set of wearable sensor readings, we want to predict contextual information about a given user such as location, current activity, mood, and so on. Unsupervised

[1] `http://www.scholarpedia.org/article/Reinforcement_learning`

learning methods (clustering and association rules) will be covered in chapter 6 and autoencoders are introduced in chapter 10.

1.4 Terminology

This section introduces some basic terminology that will be helpful for the rest of the book.

1.4.1 Tables

Since data is the most important ingredient in machine learning, let's start with some related terms. First, data needs to be stored/structured so it can be easily manipulated and processed. Most of the time, datasets will be stored as *tables* or in R terminology, *data frames*. Figure 1.5 shows the classic `mtcars` dataset[2] stored in a data frame.

The columns represent *variables* and the rows represent *examples* also known as *instances* or *data points*. In this table, there are 5 variables *mpg*, *cyl*, *disp*, *hp* and the *model* (the first column). In this example, the first column does not have a name, but it is still a variable. Each row represents a specific car model with its values per variable. In machine learning terminology, rows are more commonly called *instances* whereas in statistics they are often called *data points* or *observations*. Here, those terms will be used interchangeably.

Figure 1.6 shows a data frame for the `iris` dataset which consists of different kinds of plants [Fisher, 1936]. Suppose that we are interested in predicting the *Species* based on the other variables. In machine learning terminology, the variable of interest (the one that depends on the others) is called the *class* or *label* for classification problems. For regression, it is often referred to as y. In statistics, it is more commonly known as the *response*, *dependent*, or y variable, for both classification and regression.

In machine learning terminology, the rest of the variables are called *features* or *attributes*. In statistics, they are called *predictors*, *independent*

[2]mtcars dataset `https://stat.ethz.ch/R-manual/R-patched/library/datasets/html/mtcars.html` extracted from the 1974 Motor Trend US magazine.

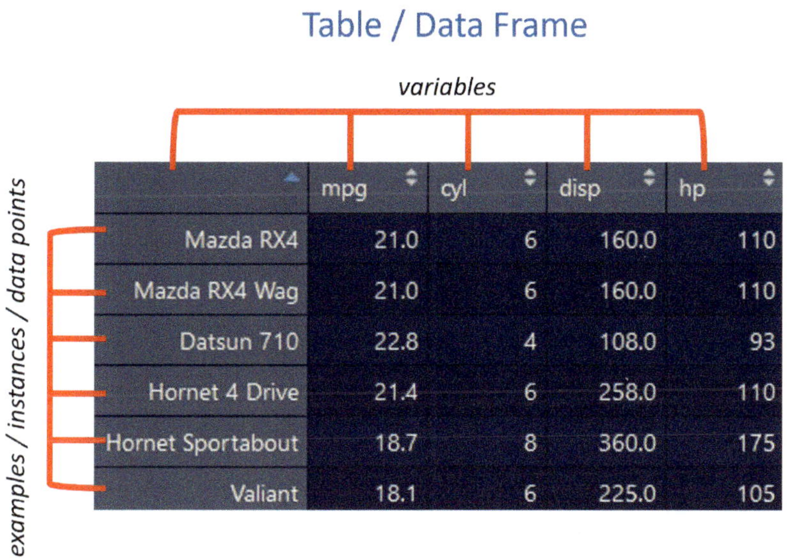

FIGURE 1.5 Table/Data frame components. Source: Data from the 1974 Motor Trend US magazine.

variables, or just X. From the context, most of the time it should be easy to identify dependent from independent variables regardless of the used terminology. The word **feature vector** is also very common in machine learning. A feature vector is just a structure containing the features of a given instance. For example, the features of the first instance in Figure 1.6 can be stored as a feature vector $[5.4, 3.9, 1.3, 0.4]$ of size 4. In a programming language, this can be implemented with an array.

1.4.2 Variable Types

When working with machine learning algorithms, the following are the most commonly used variable types. Here, when I talk about variable types, I do not refer to programming-language-specific data types (int, boolean, string, etc.) but to more general types regardless of the underlying implementation for each specific programming language.

- **Categorical/Nominal:** These variables take values from a discrete set of possible values (categories). For example, the categorical variable *color* can take the values *'red'*, *'green'*, *'black'*, and so on. Categorical variables do not have an ordering.

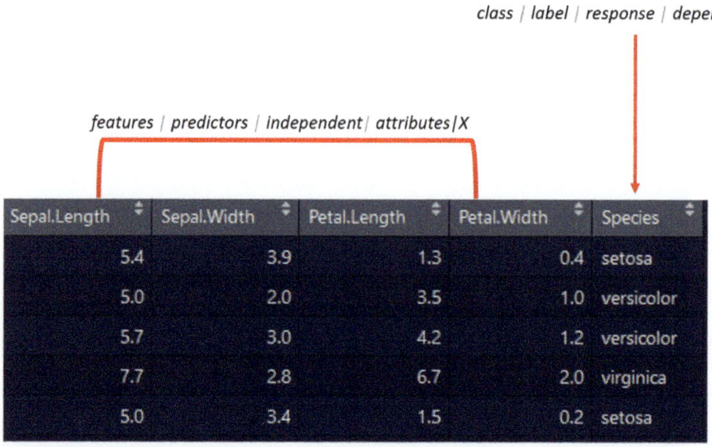

Sepal.Length	Sepal.Width	Petal.Length	Petal.Width	Species
5.4	3.9	1.3	0.4	setosa
5.0	2.0	3.5	1.0	versicolor
5.7	3.0	4.2	1.2	versicolor
7.7	2.8	6.7	2.0	virginica
5.0	3.4	1.5	0.2	setosa

FIGURE 1.6 Table/Data frame components (cont.). Source: Data from Fisher, Ronald A., "The Use of Multiple Measurements in Taxonomic Problems." *Annals of Eugenics* 7, no. 2 (1936): 179–88.

- **Numeric:** Real values such as height, weight, price, etc.
- **Integer:** Integer values such as number of rooms, age, number of floors, etc.
- **Ordinal:** Similar to categorical variables, these take their values from a set of discrete values, but they do have an ordering. For example, low $<$ medium $<$ high.

1.4.3 Predictive Models

In machine learning terminology, a *predictive model* is a model that takes some input and produces an output. *Classifiers* and *Regressors* are predictive models. I will use the terms classifier/model and regressor/model interchangeably.

1.5 Data Analysis Pipeline

Usually, the data analysis pipeline consists of several steps which are depicted in Figure 1.7. This is not a complete list but includes the most common steps. It all starts with the data collection. Then the data exploration and so on, until the results are presented. These steps can be followed in sequence, but you can always jump from one step to another one. In fact, most of the time you will end up using an iterative approach by going from one step to the other (forward or backward) as needed.

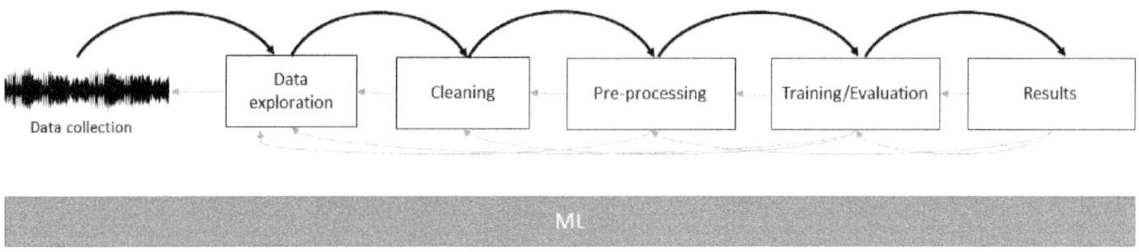

FIGURE 1.7 Data analysis pipeline.

The big gray box at the bottom means that machine learning methods can be used in all those steps and not just during training or evaluation. For example, one may use dimensionality reduction methods in the *data exploration* phase to plot the data or classification/regression methods in the *cleaning* phase to impute missing values. Now, let's give a brief description of each of those phases:

- **Data exploration.** This step aims to familiarize yourself and understand the data so you can make informed decisions during the following steps. Some of the tasks involved in this phase include summarizing your data, generating plots, validating assumptions, and so on. During this phase you can, for example, identify outliers, missing values, or noisy data points that can be cleaned in the next phase. Chapter 4 will introduce some data exploration techniques. Throughout the book, we will also use some other data exploratory methods but if you are interested in diving deeper into this topic, I recommend you check out the "Exploratory Data Analysis with R" book by Peng [2016].

- **Data cleaning.** After the data exploration phase, we can remove the identified outliers, remove noisy data points, remove variables that are not needed for further computation, and so on.

- **Preprocessing.** Predictive models expect the data to be in some structured format and satisfying some constraints. For example, several models are sensitive to class imbalances, i.e., the presence of many instances with a given class but a small number of instances with other classes. In fraud detection scenarios, most of the instances will belong to the normal class but just a small proportion will be of type *'illegal transaction'*. In this case, we may want to do some preprocessing to try to balance the dataset. Some models are also sensitive to feature-scale differences. For example, a variable *weight* could be in kilograms but another variable *height* in centimeters. Before training a predictive model, the data needs to be prepared in such a way that the models can get the most out of it. Chapter 5 will present some common preprocessing steps.

- **Training and evaluation.** Once the data is preprocessed, we can proceed to train the models. Furthermore, we also need ways to evaluate their generalization performance on new unseen instances. The purpose of this phase is to try, and fine-tune different models to find the one that performs the best. Later in this chapter, some model evaluation techniques will be introduced.
- **Interpretation and presentation of results.** The purpose of this phase is to analyze and interpret the models' results. We can use performance metrics derived from the evaluation phase to make informed decisions. We may also want to understand how the models work internally and how the predictions are derived.

1.6 Evaluating Predictive Models

Before showing you how to train a machine learning model, in this section, I would like to introduce the process of **evaluating** a predictive model, which is part of the data analysis pipeline. This applies to both classification and regression problems. I'm starting with this topic because it will be a recurring one every time you work with machine learning. You will also be training a lot of models, but you will need ways to validate them as well.

Once you have trained a model (with a training set), that is, finding the best function f that maps inputs to their corresponding outputs, you may want to estimate how good the model is at solving a particular problem when presented with examples it has never seen before (that were not part of the training set). This estimate of how good the model is at predicting the output of new examples is called the **generalization performance**.

To estimate the generalization performance of a model, a dataset is usually divided into a *train set* and a *test set*. As the name implies, the train set is used to train the model (learn its parameters) and the test set is used to evaluate/test its generalization performance. We need independent sets because when deploying models in the wild, they will be presented with new instances never seen before. By dividing the dataset into two subsets, we are simulating this scenario where the test set instances were never seen by the model at training time so the performance estimate will be more accurate rather than if we used the same set to train and then to evaluate the performance. There are two main validation methods that differ in the way the dataset is divided into train and test sets: *hold-out validation* and *k-fold cross validation*.

1) Hold-out validation. This method randomly splits the dataset into train and test sets based on some predefined percentages. For example, randomly select 70% of the instances and use them as the train set and use the remaining 30% of the examples for the test set. This will vary depending on the application and the amount of data, but typical splits are 50/50 and 70/30 percent for the train and test sets, respectively. Figure 1.8 shows an example of a dataset divided into 70/30.

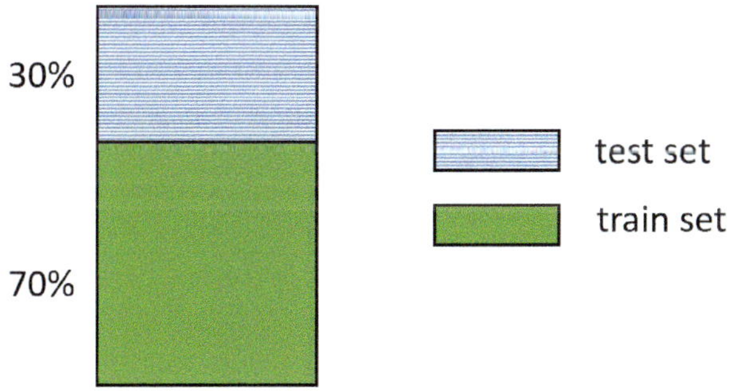

FIGURE 1.8 Hold-out validation.

Then, the train set is used to train (fit) a model, and the test set to evaluate how well that model performs on new data. The performance can be measured using performance metrics such as the *accuracy* for classification problems. The accuracy is the percent of correctly classified instances.

It is a good practice to estimate the performance on both, the train and test sets. Usually, the performance on the train set will be better since the model was trained with that very same data. It is also common to measure the performance computing the error instead of accuracy. For example, the percent of misclassified instances. These are called the *train error* and *test error* (also known as the *generalization error*), for both the train and test sets, respectively. Estimating these two errors will allow you to 'debug' your models and understand if they are underfitting or overfitting (more on this in the following sections).

2) k-fold cross-validation. Hold-out validation is a good way to evaluate your models when you have a lot of data. However, in many cases, your data will be limited. In those cases, you want to make efficient use of the data. With hold-out validation, each instance is included either in the train or test set. k-fold cross-validation provides a way in which instances take part in both, the test and train set, thus making more efficient use of the data.

This method consists of randomly assigning each instance into one of k folds (subsets) with approximately the same size. Then, k iterations are performed. In each iteration, one of the folds is used to test the model while the remaining ones are used to train it. Each fold is used once as the test set and $k-1$ times as part of the train set. Typical values for k are 3, 5, and 10. In the extreme case where k is equal to the total number of instances in the dataset, it is called leave-one-out cross-validation (LOOCV). Figure 1.8 shows an example of cross-validation with $k=5$.

The generalization performance is then computed by taking the average accuracy/error from each iteration.

Hold-out validation is typically used when there is a lot of available data and models take significant time to be trained. On the other hand, k-fold cross-validation is used when data is limited. However, it is more computational intensive since it requires training k models.

Validation set.

Most predictive models require some hyperparameter tuning. For example, a k-Nearest Neighbors model requires to set k, the number of neighbors. For decision trees, one can specify the maximum allowed

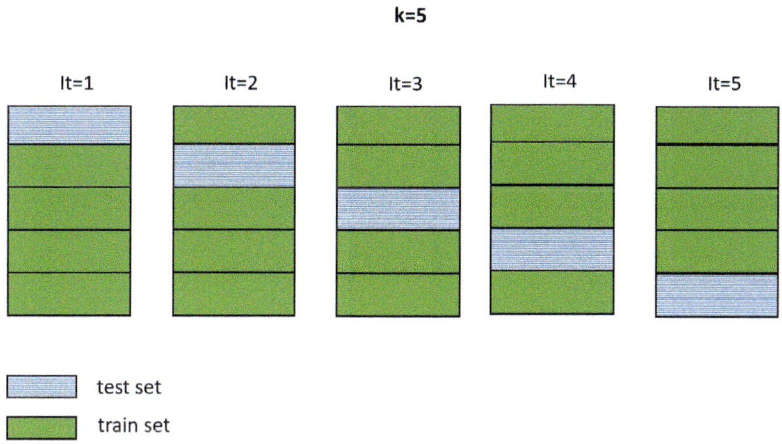

FIGURE 1.9 k-fold cross validation with k=5 and 5 iterations.

tree depth, among other hyperparameters. Neural networks require even more hyperparameter tuning to work properly. Also, one may try different preprocessing techniques and features. All those changes affect the final performance. If all those hyperparameter changes are evaluated using the test set, there is a risk of *overfitting* the model. That is, making the model very specific to this particular data. Instead of using the *test set* to fine-tune parameters, a *validation set* needs to be used instead. Thus, the dataset is randomly partitioned into three subsets: **train/validation/test** sets. The *train set* is used to train the model. The *validation set* is used to estimate the model's performance while trying different hyperparameters and preprocessing methods. Once you are happy with your final model, you use the *test set* to assess the final generalization performance and this is what you report. The **test set is used only once**. Remember that we want to assess performance on unseen instances. When using *k-fold cross validation*, first, an independent test set needs to be put aside. Hyperparameters are tuned using cross-validation and the test set is used at the very end and just once to estimate the final performance.

When working with multi-user systems, we need to additionally take into account between-user differences. In those situations, it is advised to perform extra validations. Those multi-user validation techniques will be covered in chapter 9.

1.7 Simple Classification Example

simple_model.R

So far, a lot of terminology and concepts have been introduced. In this section, we will work through a practical example that will demonstrate how most of these concepts fit together. Here you will build (from scratch) your first classification and regression models! Furthermore, you will learn how to evaluate their generalization performance.

Suppose you have a dataset that contains information about felines including their maximum speed in km/hr and their specific type. For the sake of the example, suppose that these two variables are the only ones that we can observe. As for the types, consider that there are two possibilities: *'tiger'* and *'leopard'*. Figure 1.10 shows the first 10 instances (rows) of the dataset.

speed	class
48.60231	tiger
50.58418	leopard
52.63359	leopard
47.48848	tiger
55.96977	leopard
58.10348	leopard
53.47864	leopard
49.88309	leopard
54.02068	leopard
48.46697	tiger

FIGURE 1.10 First 10 instances of felines dataset.

This table has 2 variables: *speed* and *class*. The first one is a numeric variable. The second one is a categorical variable. In this case, it can take two possible values: *'tiger'* or *'leopard'*.

This dataset was synthetically created for illustration purposes, but I promise you that hereafter, we will mostly use real datasets!

The code to reproduce this example is available in the *'Introduction to Behavior and Machine Learning'* folder in the script file `simple_model.R`. The script contains the code used to generate the dataset. The dataset is stored in a data frame named `dataset`. Let's start by doing a simple exploratory analysis of the dataset. More detailed exploratory analysis methods will be presented in chapter 4. First, we can print the data frame dimensions with the `dim()` function.

```
# Print number of rows and columns.
dim(dataset)
#> [1] 100   2
```

The output tells us that the data frame has 100 rows and 2 columns. Now we may be interested to know how many of those correspond to *tigers*. We can use the `table()` function to get that information.

```
# Count instances in each class.
table(dataset$class)
#> leopard   tiger
#>      50      50
```

Here we see that 50 instances are of type *'leopard'* and also that 50 instances are of type *'tiger'*. In fact, this is how the dataset was intentionally generated. The next thing we can do is to compute some summary statistics for each column. R already provides a very convenient function for that purpose. Yes, it is the `summary()` function.

```
# Compute some summary statistics.
summary(dataset)
#>      speed            class
#>  Min.   :42.96   leopard:50
#>  1st Qu.:48.41   tiger  :50
#>  Median :51.12
```

```
#>  Mean   :51.53
#>  3rd Qu.:53.99
#>  Max.   :61.65
```

Since *speed* is a numeric variable, `summary()` computes some statistics like the mean, min, max, etc. The *class* variable is a factor. Thus, it returns row counts instead. In R, categorical variables are usually encoded as factors. It is similar to a string, but R treats factors in a special way. We can already appreciate that with the previous code snippet when the summary function returned class counts.

There are many other ways in which you can explore a dataset, but for now, let's assume we already feel comfortable and that we have a good understanding of the data. Since this dataset is very simple, we won't need to do any further data cleaning or preprocessing.

Now, imagine that you are asked to build a model that is able to predict the type of feline based on the observed attributes. In this case, the only thing we can observe is the *speed*. Our task is to build a function that maps speed measurements to classes. That is, we want to be able to predict the type of feline based on how fast it runs. According to the terminology presented in section 1.4, *speed* would be a **feature** variable and *class* would be the **class** variable.

Based on the types of machine learning methods presented in section 1.3, this one is a **supervised learning** problem because for each instance, the class is available. And, specifically, since we want to predict a category, this is a **classification** problem.

Before building our classification model, it would be worth plotting the data. Figure 1.11 shows the speeds for both tigers and leopards.

Here, I omitted the code for building the plot, but it is included in the script. I also added vertical dashed lines at the mean speeds for the two classes. From this plot, it seems that leopards are faster than tigers (with some exceptions). One thing we can note is that the data points are grouped around the mean values of their corresponding classes. That is, most of the tiger data points are closer to the mean speed for tigers and the same can be observed for leopards. Of course, there are some exceptions where an instance is closer to the mean of the opposite class. This could be because some tigers may be as fast as leopards. Some leopards may also be slower than the average, maybe because they are newborns

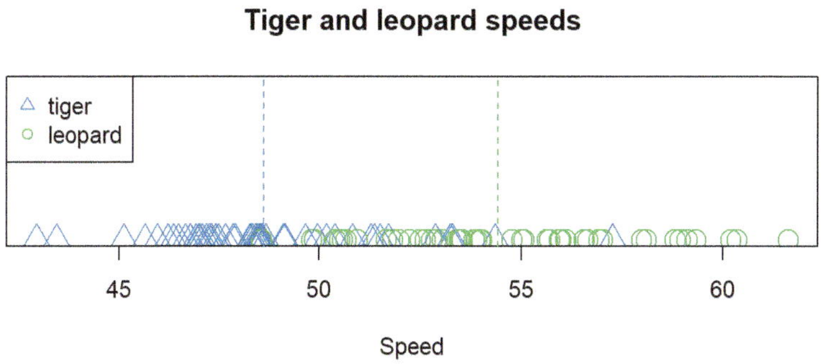

FIGURE 1.11 Feline speeds with vertical dashed lines at the means.

or they are old. Unfortunately, we do not have more information, so the best we can do is use our single feature *speed*. We can use these insights to come up with a simple model that discriminates between the two classes based on this single feature variable.

One thing we can do for any new instance we want to classify is to compute its distance to the 'center' of each class and predict the class that is the closest one. In this case, the center is the mean value. We can formally define our model as the set of n centrality measures where n is the number of classes (2 in our example).

$$M = \{\mu_1, \dots, \mu_n\} \tag{1.2}$$

Those centrality measures (the class means in this particular case) are called the **parameters** of the model. Training a model consists of finding those optimal parameters that will allow us to achieve the best performance on new instances that were not part of the training data. In most cases, we will need an **algorithm** to find those parameters. In our example, the algorithm consists of simply computing the mean speed for each class. That is, for each class, sum all the corresponding speeds and divide them by the number of data points that belong to that class.

Once those parameters are found, we can start making predictions on new data points. This is called *inference* or *prediction*. In this case, when a new data point arrives, we can predict its class by computing its distance to each of the n centrality measures in M and return the class of the closest one.

The following function implements the training part of our model.

```
# Define a simple classifier that learns
# a centrality measure for each class.
simple.model.train <- function(data, centrality=mean){

  # Store unique classes.
  classes <- unique(data$class)

  # Define an array to store the learned parameters.
  params <- numeric(length(classes))

  # Make this a named array.
  names(params) <- classes

  # Iterate through each class and compute its centrality measure.
  for(c in classes){

    # Filter instances by class.
    tmp <- data[which(data$class == c),]

    # Compute the centrality measure.
    centrality.measure <- centrality(tmp$speed)

    # Store the centrality measure for this class.
    params[c] <- centrality.measure
  }

  return(params)
}
```

The first argument is the training data and the second argument is the centrality function we want to use (the mean, by default). This function iterates each class, computes the centrality measure based on the speed, and stores the results in a named array called `params` which is then returned at the end.

Most of the time, training a model involves feeding it with the training data and any additional **hyperparameters** specific to each model. In this case, the centrality measure is a hyperparameter and here, we set it to be the *mean*.

The difference between **parameters** and **hyperparameters** is that the former are learned during training. The **hyperparameters** are settings specific to each model that can be defined before the actual training starts.

Now that we have a function that performs the training, we need another one that performs the actual inference or prediction on new data points. Let's call this one `simple.classifier.predict()`. Its first argument is a data frame with the instances we want to get predictions for. The second argument is the named vector of parameters learned during training. This function will return an array with the predicted class for each instance in `newdata`.

```
# Define a function that predicts a class
# based on the learned parameters.
simple.classifier.predict <- function(newdata, params){

  # Variable to store the predictions of
  # each instance in newdata.
  predictions <- NULL

  # Iterate instances in newdata
  for(i in 1:nrow(newdata)){

    instance <- newdata[i,]

    # Predict the name of the class which
    # centrality measure is closest.
    pred <- names(which.min(abs(instance$speed - params)))

    predictions <- c(predictions, pred)
  }
```

```
  return(predictions)
}
```

This function iterates through each row and computes the distance to each centrality measure and returns the name of the class that was the closest one. The distance computation is done with the following line of code:

```
pred <- names(which.min(abs(instance$speed - params)))
```

First, it computes the absolute difference between the speed and each centrality measure stored in `params` and then, it returns the class name of the minimum one. Now that we have defined the training and prediction procedures, we are ready to test our classifier!

In section 1.6, two evaluation methods were presented. *Hold-out* and *k-fold cross-validation*. These methods allow you to estimate how your model will perform on new data. Let's start with *hold-out validation*.

First, we need to split the data into two independent sets. We will use 70% of the data to train our classifier and the remaining 30% to test it. The following code splits `dataset` into a `trainset` and `testset`.

```
# Percent to be used as training data.
pctTrain <- 0.7

# Set seed for reproducibility.
set.seed(123)

idxs <- sample(nrow(dataset),
               size = nrow(dataset) * pctTrain,
               replace = FALSE)

trainset <- dataset[idxs,]

testset <- dataset[-idxs,]
```

The `sample()` function was used to select integer numbers at random from 1 to n, where n is the total number of data points in `dataset`. These randomly selected data points are the ones that will go to the train set. The `size` argument tells the function to return 70 numbers which correspond to 70% of the total since `dataset` has 100 instances.

The last argument `replace` is set to `FALSE` because we do not want repeated numbers. This ensures that any instance only belongs to either the train or the test set. **We don't want an instance to be copied into both sets.**

Now it's time to test our functions. We can train our model using the `trainset` by calling our previously defined function `simple.model.train()`.

```
# Train the model using the trainset.
params <- simple.model.train(trainset, mean)

# Print the learned parameters.
print(params)
#>    tiger  leopard
#> 48.88246 54.58369
```

After training the model, we print the learned parameters. In this case, the mean for *tiger* is 48.88 and for *leopard*, it is 54.58. With these parameters, we can start making predictions on our test set! We pass the test set and the newly-learned parameters to our function `simple.classifier.predict()`.

```
# Predict classes on the test set.
test.predictions <- simple.classifier.predict(testset, params)

# Display first predictions.
head(test.predictions)
#> [1] "tiger"   "tiger"   "leopard" "tiger"   "tiger"   "leopard"
```

Our predict function returns predictions for each instance in the test set.

We can use the `head()` function to print the first predictions. The first two instances were classified as tigers, the third one as leopard, and so on.

But how good are those predictions? Since we know what the true classes are (also known as **ground truth**) in our test set, we can compute the performance. In this case, we will compute the accuracy, which is the percentage of correct classifications. Note that we did not use the class information when making predictions, we only used the *speed*. We pretended that we didn't have the true class. We will use the true class only to evaluate the model's performance.

```
# Compute test accuracy.
sum(test.predictions == as.character(testset$class)) /
  nrow(testset)
#> [1] 0.8333333
```

We can compute the accuracy by counting how many predictions were equal to the true classes and divide them by the total number of points in the test set. In this case, the test accuracy was 83.0%. **Congratulations! you have trained and evaluated your first classifier.**

It is also a good idea to compute the performance on the same train set that was used to train the model.

```
# Compute train accuracy.
train.predictions <- simple.classifier.predict(trainset, params)
sum(train.predictions == as.character(trainset$class)) /
  nrow(trainset)
#> [1] 0.8571429
```

The *train accuracy* was 85.7%. As expected, this was higher than the *test accuracy*. Typically, what you report is the performance on the *test set*, but we can use the performance on the *train set* to look for signs of over/under-fitting which will be covered in the following sections.

1.7.1 k-fold Cross-validation Example

Now, let's see how k-fold cross-validation can be implemented to test our classifier. I will choose a $k = 5$. This means that 5 independent sets are going to be generated and 5 iterations will be run.

```
# Number of folds.
k <- 5

set.seed(123)

# Generate random folds.
folds <- sample(k, size = nrow(dataset), replace = TRUE)

# Print how many instances ended up in each fold.
table(folds)
#> folds
#>  1  2  3  4  5
#> 21 20 23 17 19
```

Again, we can use the `sample()` function. This time we want to select random integers between 1 and k. The total number of integers will be equal to the total number of instances n in the entire dataset. Note that this time we set `replace = TRUE` since $k < n$, so this implies that we need to pick repeated numbers. Each number will represent the fold to which each instance belongs to. As before, we need to make sure that each instance belongs only to one of the sets. Here, we are guaranteeing that by assigning each instance a single fold number. We can use the `table()` function to print how many instances ended up in each fold. Here, we see that the folds will contain between 17 and 23 instances.

k-fold cross-validation consists of iterating k times. In each iteration, one of the folds is selected as the test set and the remaining folds are used to build the train set. Within each iteration, the model is trained with the train set and evaluated with the test set. At the end, the average accuracy across folds is reported.

```
# Variables to store accuracies on each fold.
test.accuracies <- NULL
train.accuracies <- NULL

for(i in 1:k){
  testset <- dataset[which(folds == i),]
  trainset <- dataset[which(folds != i),]

  params <- simple.model.train(trainset, mean)
  test.predictions <- simple.classifier.predict(testset, params)
  train.predictions <- simple.classifier.predict(trainset, params)

  # Accuracy on test set.
  acc <- sum(test.predictions ==
               as.character(testset$class)) /
    nrow(testset)

  test.accuracies <- c(test.accuracies, acc)

  # Accuracy on train set.
  acc <- sum(train.predictions ==
               as.character(trainset$class)) /
    nrow(trainset)

  train.accuracies <- c(train.accuracies, acc)
}

# Print mean accuracy across folds on the test set.
mean(test.accuracies)
#> [1] 0.829823

# Print mean accuracy across folds on the train set.
mean(train.accuracies)
#> [1] 0.8422414
```

The test mean accuracy across the 5 folds was $\approx$ 83% which is very similar to the accuracy estimated by hold-out validation.

Note that in section 1.6 a **validation set** was also mentioned. This one is useful when you want to fine-tune a model and/or try different preprocessing methods on your data. In case you are using hold-out validation, you may want to split your data into three sets: train/validation/test sets. So, you train your model using the train set and estimate its performance using the validation set. Then you can fine-tune your model. For example, here, instead of the mean as centrality measure, you can try to use the median and measure the performance again with the validation set. When you are pleased with your settings, you estimate the final performance of the model with the test set *only once*.

In the case of k-fold cross-validation, you can set aside a test set at the beginning. Then you use the remaining data to perform cross-validation and fine-tune your model. Within each iteration, you test the performance with the validation data. Once you are sure you are not going to do any parameter tuning, you can train a model with the train and validation sets and test the generalization performance using the test set.

One of the benefits of machine learning is that it allows us to find patterns based on data freeing us from having to program hard-coded rules. This means more scalable and flexible code. If for some reason, now, instead of 2 classes we needed to add another class, for example, a *'jaguar'*, the only thing we need to do is update our database and retrain our model. We don't need to modify the internals of the algorithms. They will update themselves based on the data.

We can try this by adding a third class *'jaguar'* to the dataset as shown in the script `simple_model.R`. It then trains the model as usual and performs predictions.

1.8 Simple Regression Example

simple_model.R

As opposed to classification models where the aim is to predict a category, **regression models predict numeric values**. To exemplify this, we can use our felines dataset but instead try to predict *speed* based on the type of feline. The *class* column will be treated as a **feature** variable and *speed* will be the **response variable**. Since there is only one predictor, and it is categorical, the best thing we can do to implement our regression model is to predict the mean speed depending on the class.

Recall that for the classification scenario, our learned parameters consisted of the means for each class. Thus, we can reuse our training function `simple.model.train()`. All we need to do is to define a new predict function that returns the speed based on the class. This is the opposite of what we did in the classification case (return the class based on the speed).

```
# Define a function that predicts speed
# based on the type of feline.
simple.regression.predict <- function(newdata, params){

  # Variable to store the predictions of
  # each instance in newdata.
  predictions <- NULL

  # Iterate instances in newdata
  for(i in 1:nrow(newdata)){

    instance <- newdata[i,]

    # Return the mean value of the corresponding class stored in params.
    pred <- params[which(names(params) == instance$class)]
```

```
    predictions <- c(predictions, pred)
  }

  return(predictions)
}
```

The `simple.regression.predict()` function iterates through each instance in `newdata` and returns the mean speed from `params` for the corresponding class.

Again, we can validate our model using *hold-out validation*. The train set will contain 70% of the instances and the remaining will be used as the test set.

```
pctTrain <- 0.7
set.seed(123)
idxs <- sample(nrow(dataset),
               size = nrow(dataset) * pctTrain,
               replace = FALSE)

trainset <- dataset[idxs,]
testset <- dataset[-idxs,]

# Reuse our train function.
params <- simple.model.train(trainset, mean)

print(params)
#>    tiger  leopard
#> 48.88246 54.5836
```

Here, we reused our previous function `simple.model.train()` to learn the parameters and then print them. Then we can use those parameters to infer the speed. If a test instance belongs to the class *'tiger'* then return 48.88. If it is of class *'leopard'* then return 54.58.

```
# Predict speeds on the test set.
test.predictions <-
  simple.regression.predict(testset, params)

# Print first predictions.
head(test.predictions)
#> 48.88246 54.58369 54.58369 48.88246 48.88246 54.58369
```

Since these are numeric predictions, we cannot use accuracy as in the classification case to evaluate the performance. One way to evaluate the performance of regression models is by computing the **mean absolute error (MAE)**. This measure tells you, on average, how much each prediction deviates from its true value. It is computed by subtracting each prediction from its real value and taking the absolute value: $|predicted - realValue|$. This can be visualized in Figure 1.12. The distances between the true and predicted values are the errors and the MAE is the average of all those errors.

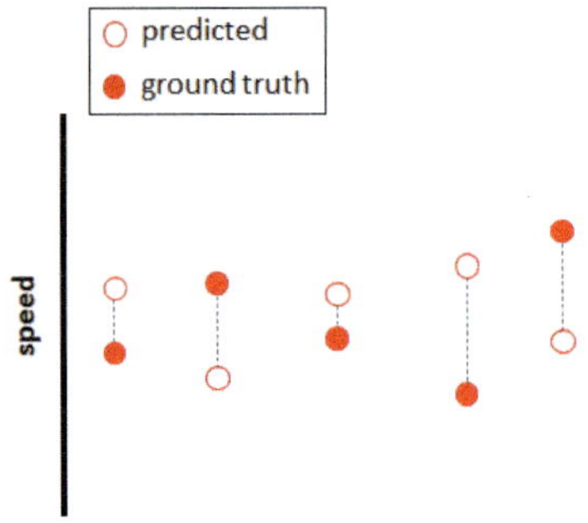

FIGURE 1.12 Prediction errors.

We can use the following code to compute the MAE:

```
# Compute mean absolute error (MAE) on the test set.
mean(abs(test.predictions - testset$speed))
#> [1] 2.562598
```

The MAE on the *test set* was 2.56. That is, on average, our simple model had a deviation of 2.56 km/hr with respect to the true values, which is not bad. We can also compute the MAE on the *train set*.

```
# Predict speeds on the train set.
train.predictions <-
  simple.regression.predict(trainset, params)

# Compute mean absolute error (MAE) on the train set.
mean(abs(train.predictions - trainset$speed))
#> [1] 2.16097
```

The MAE on the *train set* was 2.16, which is better than the *test set* MAE (small MAE values are preferred). **Now, you have built, trained, and evaluated a regression model!**

This was a simple example, but it illustrates the basic idea of regression and how it differs from classification. It also shows how the performance of regression models is typically evaluated with the MAE as opposed to the accuracy used in classification. In chapter 8, more advanced methods such as neural networks will be introduced, which can be used to solve regression problems.

In this section, we have gone through several of the data analysis pipeline phases. We did a simple exploratory analysis of the data and then we built, trained, and validated the models to perform both classification and regression. Finally, we estimated the overall performance of the models and presented the results. Here, we coded our models from scratch, but in practice, you typically use models that have already been implemented and tested. All in all, I hope these examples have given you the feeling of how it is to work with machine learning.

1.9 Underfitting and Overfitting

From the felines classification example, we saw how we can separate two classes by computing the mean for each class. For the two-class problem, this is equivalent to having a decision line between the two means (Figure 1.13). Everything to the right of this decision line will be closer to the mean that corresponds to *'leopard'* and everything to the left to *'tiger'*. In this case, the classification function is a vertical line. During learning, the position of the line that reduces the classification error is searched for. We implicitly estimated the position of the line by finding the *mean values* for each of the classes.

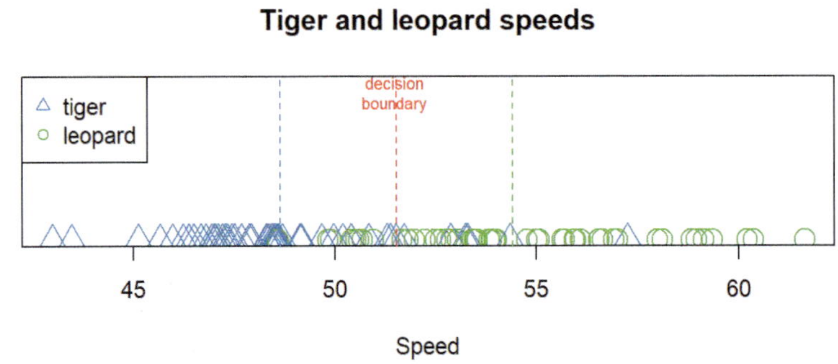

FIGURE 1.13 Decision line between the two classes.

Now, imagine that we do not only have access to the *speed* but also to the felines' *age*. This extra information could help us reduce the prediction error since age plays an important role in how fast a feline is. Figure 1.14 (left) shows how it will look like if we plot *age* in the x-axis and *speed* in the y-axis. Here, we can see that for both, tigers and leopards, the *speed* seems to increase as *age* increases. Then, at some point, as *age* increases the *speed* begins to decrease.

Constructing a classifier with a single vertical line as we did before will not work in this 2-dimensional case where we have 2 predictors. Now we will need a more complex decision boundary (function) to separate the two classes. One approach would be to use a line as before but this time we allow the line to have a slope (angle). Everything below the line is classified as *'tiger'* and everything else as *'leopard'*. Thus, the learning phase involves finding the line's *position* and its *slope* that achieves the smallest error.

Figure 1.14 (left) shows a possible decision line. Even though this function is more complex than a vertical line, it will still produce a lot of misclassifications (it does not clearly separate both classes). This is called **underfitting**, that is, the model is so simple that it is not able to capture the underlying data patterns.

Let's try a more complex function, for example, a curve. Figure 1.14 (middle) shows that a curve does a better job at separating the two

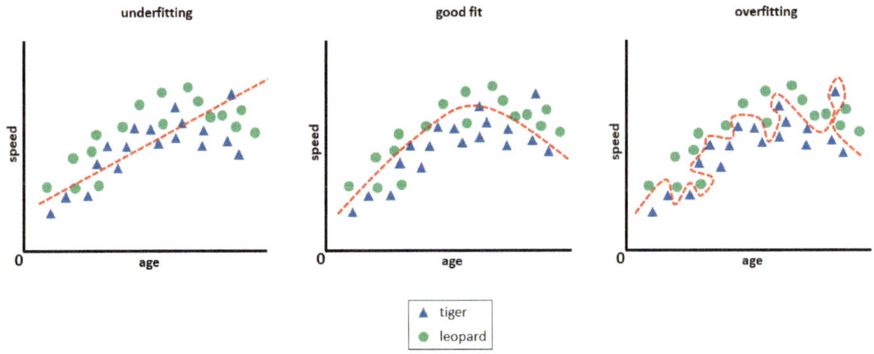

FIGURE 1.14 Underfitting and overfitting.

classes with fewer misclassifications but still, 3 leopards are misclassified as tigers and 1 tiger is misclassified as leopard. Can we do better than that? Yes, just keep increasing the complexity of the decision function.

Figure 1.14 (right) shows a more complex function that was able to separate the two classes with 100% accuracy or equivalently, with a 0% error. However, there is a problem. This function learned how to accurately separate the *training data*, but it is likely that it will not do as well with a new *test set*. This function became so specialized with respect to this particular data that it failed to capture the overall pattern. This is called **overfitting**. In this case, the model 'memorizes' the train set instead of finding general patterns applicable to new unseen instances. If we were to choose a model, the best one would be the one in the middle. Even if it is not perfect on the train data, it will do better than the other models when evaluated on new test data.

Overfitting is a common problem in machine learning. One way to know if a model is overfitting is by checking if the error in the train set is low while it is high on a new set (can be a test or validation set). Figure 1.15 illustrates this idea. Too-simple models will produce a high error for both, the train and validation sets (underfitting). As the complexity of the model increases, the errors on both sets are reduced. Then, at some point, the complexity of a model becomes so high that it gets too specific on the train set and fails to perform well on a new independent set (overfitting).

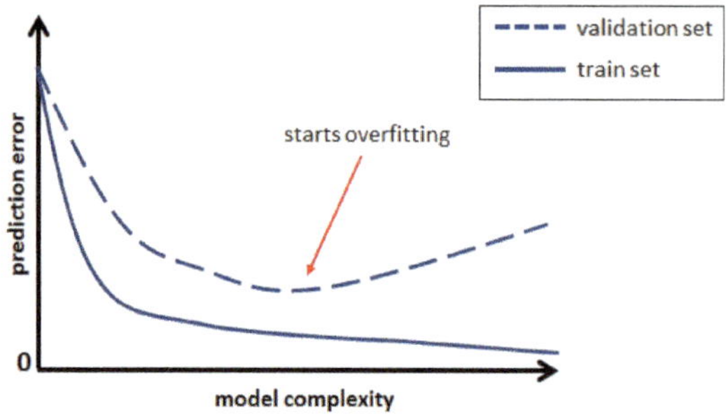

FIGURE 1.15 Model complexity vs. train and validation error.

In this example, we saw how *underfitting* and *overfitting* can affect the generalization performance of a model in a classification setting but the same can occur in regression problems.

There are several methods that aim to reduce overfitting, but many of them are specific to the type of model. For example, with decision trees (covered in chapter 2), one way to reduce overfitting is to limit their depth or build ensembles of trees (chapter 3). Neural networks are also highly prone to overfitting since they can be very complex and have millions of parameters. In chapter 8, several techniques to reduce the effect of overfitting will be presented.

1.10 Bias and Variance

So far, we have seen how to train predictive models and evaluate how well they do on new data (test/validation sets). The main goal is to have predictive models that have a low error rate when used with new data. Understanding the source of the error can help us make more informed decisions when building predictive models. The *test error*, also known as the *generalization error* of a predictive model can be decomposed into three components: bias, variance, and noise.

Noise. This component is inherent to the data itself and there is nothing we can do about it. For example, two instances having the same values in their features but with a different label.

Bias. How much the average prediction differs from the true value. Note the *average* keyword. This means that we make the assumption that an infinite (or very large) number of train sets can be generated and for each, a predictive model is trained. Then we average the predictions of all those models and see how much that average differs from the true value.

Variance. How much the predictions change for a given data point when training a model using a different train set each time.

Bias and variance are closely related to underfitting and overfitting. High variance is a sign of overfitting. That is, a model is so complex that it will fit a particular train set very well. Every time it is trained with a different train set, the *train error* will be low, but it will likely generate very different predictions for the same test points and a much higher *test error*.

Figure 1.16 illustrates the relation between overfitting and high variance with a regression problem.

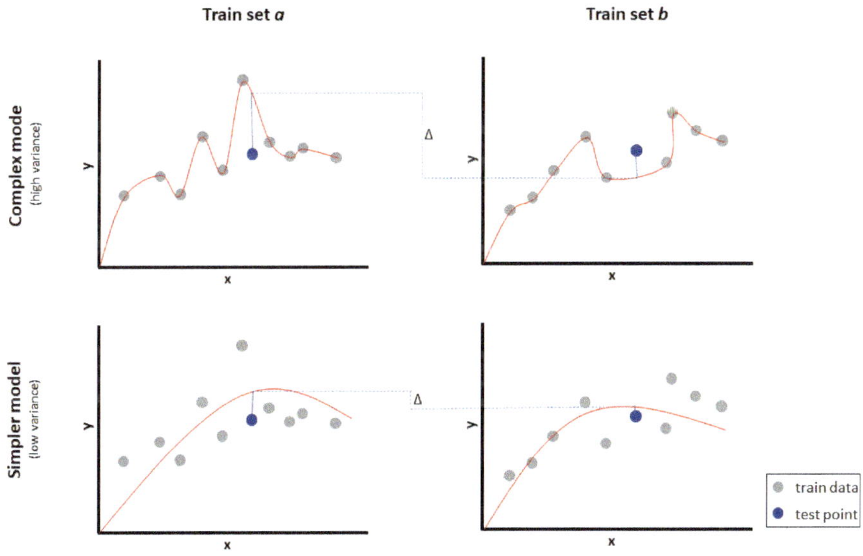

FIGURE 1.16 High variance and overfitting.

Given a feature x, two models are trained to predict y: i) a *complex model* (top row), and ii) a *simpler model* (bottom row). Both models are fitted with two training sets (a and b) sampled from the same distribution. The complex model fits the train data perfectly but makes very different predictions (big Δ) for the same test point when using a different train set. The simpler model does not fit the train data so well but has a smaller Δ and a lower error on the test point as well. Visually, the function (red curve) of the complex model also varies a lot across train sets whereas the shapes of the simpler model functions look very similar.

On the other hand, if a model is too simple, it will underfit causing *highly biased* results without being able to capture the input-output relationships. This results in a high *train error* and in consequence, a high *test error* as well.

A formal definition of the error decomposition is explained in the book "The elements of statistical learning: data mining, inference, and prediction" [Hastie et al., 2009].

1.11 Summary

In this chapter, several introductory machine learning concepts and terms were introduced and they are the basis for the methods that will be covered in the following chapters.

- **Behavior** can be defined as *"an observable activity in a human or animal"*.
- Three main reasons of why we may want to analyze behavior automatically were discussed: **react**, **understand**, and **document/archive**.
- One way to observe behavior automatically is through the use of sensors and/or data.
- **Machine Learning** consists of a set of computational algorithms that automatically find useful patterns and relationships from data.
- The three main building blocks of machine learning are: **data**, **algorithms**, and **models**.
- The main types of machine learning are **supervised learning**, **semi-supervised learning**, **partially-supervised learning**, and **unsupervised learning**.
- In R, data is usually stored in data frames. Data frames have variables (columns) and instances (rows). Depending on the task, variables can be **independent** or **dependent**.
- A **predictive model** is a model that takes some input and produces an output. *Classifiers* and *regressors* are predictive models.
- A data analysis pipeline consists of several tasks including data collection, cleaning, preprocessing, training/evaluation, and presentation of results.
- Model evaluation can be performed with **hold-out validation** or **k-fold cross-validation**.
- **Overfitting** occurs when a model 'memorizes' the training data instead of finding useful underlying patterns.
- The test error can be decomposed into **noise**, **bias**, and **variance**.

WHERE ARE WE?
BIÅS
BIRANZ
YOU ARE IN THE TOWER AND I AM THE DIRECTOR. EAGLE AND DOLPHIN SAVED YOU BUT THEY DIDN'T MAKE IT.
" THEY PASSED THEIR POWERS ON TO YOU. HERE YOU WILL LEARN HOW TO CONTROL THEM. "
1 YEAR LATER
WELL DONE. YOU ARE DECREASING THAT MEAN ABSOLUTE ERROR.
LET'S TRY A NEW SETTING TO MAKE SURE YOU ARE NOT OVERFITTING.
SORRY TO INTERRUPT THE TRAINING BUT I'VE JUST RECEIVED A REPORT OF A STRANGE OBJECT 300 KM FROM HERE.
1 # Define function.
2 simple.model.train <- function(data, centrality =mean){
3 classes <- unique (data$class)
WE'LL TAKE CARE OF THAT.
TO BE CONTINUED.
behavior.enriquegc.com

2

Predicting Behavior with Classification Models

In the previous chapter, the concept of **classification** was introduced along with a simple example (feline-type classification). This chapter will cover more in depth concepts on classification methods and their application to behavior analysis tasks. Moreover, additional **performance metrics** will be introduced. This chapter begins with an introduction to **k-Nearest Neighbors (k-NN)** which is one of the simplest classification algorithms. Then, an example of k-NN applied to indoor location using Wi-Fi signals is presented. This chapter also covers **Decision Trees** and **Naive Bayes** classifiers and how they can be used for activity recognition based on smartphone accelerometer data. After that, **Dynamic Time Warping (DTW)** (a method for aligning time series) is introduced, together with an example of how it can be used for hand gesture recognition.

2.1 k-Nearest Neighbors

k-Nearest Neighbors (k-NN) is one of the simplest classification algorithms. The predicted class for a given *query instance* is the most common class of its k nearest neighbors. A *query instance* is just the instance we want to make predictions on. In its most basic form, the algorithm consists of two steps:

1. Compute the distance between the *query instance* and all *training instances*.
2. Return the most common class label among the k nearest training instances (neighbors).

This is a type of *lazy-learning* algorithm because all the computations take place at prediction time. There are no parameters to learn at

DOI: 10.1201/9781003203469-2

training time! The training phase consists only of storing the training instances so they can be compared to the query instance at prediction time. The hyper-parameter k is usually specified by the user and depends on each application. We also need to specify a *distance function* that returns small distances for similar instances and big distances for very dissimilar instances. For numeric features, the **Euclidean distance** is one of the most commonly used distance function. The Euclidean distance between two points can be computed as follows:

$$d(p,q) = \sqrt{\sum_{i=1}^{n} (p_i - q_i)^2} \tag{2.1}$$

where p and q are n-dimensional feature vectors and i is the index to the vectors' elements. Figure 2.1 shows the idea graphically (adapted from the k-NN article[1] in Wikipedia). The query instance is depicted with the '?' symbol. If we choose $k = 3$ (represented by the inner dashed circle) the predicted class is *'square'* because there are two squares but only one circle. If $k = 5$ (outer dotted circle), the predicted class is *'circle'*.

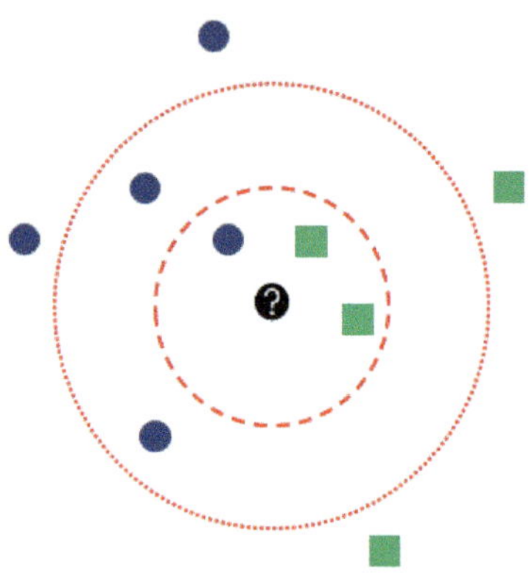

FIGURE 2.1 k-NN example for $k = 3$ (inner dashed circle) and $k = 5$ (dotted outer circle). (Adapted from Antti Ajanki AnAj. Source: Wikipedia (CC BY-SA 3.0) [https://creativecommons.org/licenses/by-sa/3.0/legalcode]).

Typical values for k are small odd numbers like $1, 2, 3, 5$. The k-NN algorithm can also be used for regression with a small modification:

[1] https://en.wikipedia.org/wiki/K-nearest_neighbors_algorithm

Instead of returning the majority class of the nearest neighbors, return the mean value of their response variable. Despite its simplicity, k-NN has proved to perform really well in many tasks including time series classification [Xi et al., 2006].

2.1.1 Indoor Location with Wi-Fi Signals

`indoor_classification.R indoor_auxiliary.R`

You might already have experienced some troubles with geolocation services when you are inside a building. Part of this is because GPS technologies do not provide good indoors-accuracy due to several sources of interference. For some applications, it would be beneficial to have accurate location estimations inside buildings even at room-level. For example, in domotics and localization services in big public places like airports or shopping malls. Having good indoor location estimates can also be used in behavior analysis such as extracting trajectory patterns.

In this section, we will implement k-NN to perform indoor location in a building based on Wi-Fi signals. For instance, we can use a smartphone to scan the nearby Wi-Fi access points and based on this information, determine our location at room-level. This can be formulated as a classification problem: Given a set of Wi-Fi signals as input, predict the location where the device is located.

For this classification problem, we will use the *INDOOR LOCATION* dataset (see Appendix B) which was collected with an Android smartphone. The smartphone application scans the nearby access points and stores their information and label. The label is provided by the user and represents the room where the device is located. Several instances for every location were recorded. To generate each instance, the device scans and records the MAC address and signal strength of the nearby access points. A delay of 500 ms is set between scans. For each location, approximately 3 minutes of data were collected while the user walked in the specific room. Figure 2.2 depicts the layout of the building where the data was collected. The data has four different locations: *'bedroomA'*, *'bedroomB'*, *'tvroom'*, and the *'lobby'*. The lobby (not shown in the layout) is at the same level as bedroom A but on the first floor.

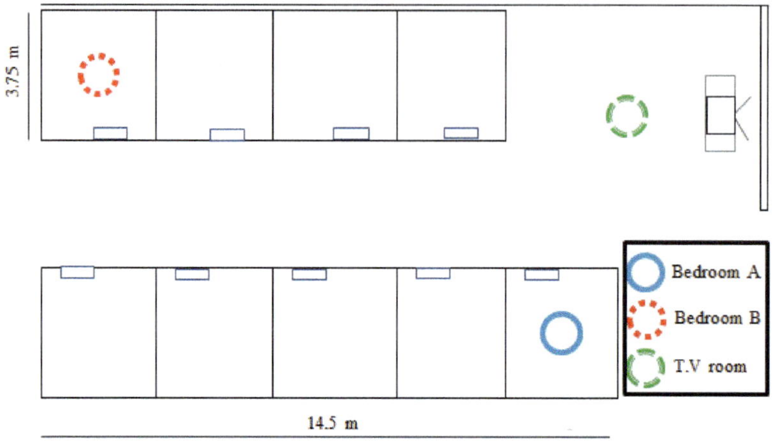

FIGURE 2.2 Layout of the apartments building. (Adapted by permission from Springer: Lecture Notes in Computer Science, Contextualized Hand Gesture Recognition with Smartphones, Garcia-Ceja E., Brena R., Galván-Tejada C.E., 2014, `https://doi.org/10.1007/978-3-319-07491-7_13`).

Table 2.1 shows the first rows of the dataset. The first column is the class. The `scanid` column is a unique identifier for the given Wi-Fi scan (instance). To preserve privacy, MAC addresses were converted into integer values. Every instance is composed of several rows. For example, the first instance with `scanid=1` has two rows (one row per mac address). Intuitively, the same location should have similar MAC addresses across scans. From the table, we can see that at *bedroomA* access points with MAC address 1 and 2 are usually found by the device.

Since each instance is composed of several rows, we will convert our data frame into a list of lists where each inner list represents a single instance with the class (`locationId`), a unique id, and a data frame with the corresponding access points. The example code can be found in the script `indoor_classification.R`.

```
# Read Wi-Fi data
df <- read.csv(datapath, stringsAsFactors = F)

# Convert data frame into a list of lists.
# Each inner list represents one instance.
```

TABLE 2.1 First rows of wi-fi scans.

locationid	scanid	mac	signalstrength
bedroomA	1	1	−88.50
bedroomA	1	2	−91.00
bedroomA	2	1	−88.00
bedroomA	2	2	−90.00
bedroomA	3	1	−87.62
bedroomA	3	2	−90.00
bedroomA	4	2	−90.25
bedroomA	4	1	−90.00
bedroomA	4	3	−91.00

```
dataset <- wifiScansToList(df)

# Print number of instances in the dataset.
length(dataset)
#> [1] 365

# Print the first instance.
dataset[[1]]
#> $locationId
#> [1] "bedroomA"
#>
#> $scanId
#> [1] 1
#>
#> $accessPoints
#>   mac signalstrength
#> 1   1          -88.5
#> 2   2          -91.0
```

First, we read the dataset from the csv file and store it in the data frame `df`. To make things easier, the data frame is converted into a list of lists using the auxiliary function `wifiScansToList()` which is defined in the script `indoor_auxiliary.R`. Next, we print the number of instances in the dataset, that is, the number of lists. The dataset contains 365 instances.

The 365 was just a coincidence, the data was not collected every day during one year but in the same day. Next, we extract the first instance with `dataset[[1]]`. Here, we see that each instance has three pieces of information. The class (locationId), a unique id (scanId), and a set of access points stored in a data frame. The first instance has two access points with MAC addresses 1 and 2. There is also information about the signal strength, though, this one will not be used.

Since we would expect that similar locations have similar MAC addresses and locations that are far away from each other have different MAC addresses, we need a distance measure that captures this notion of similarity. In this case, we cannot use the Euclidean distance on MAC addresses. Even though they were encoded as integer values, they do not represent magnitudes but unique identifiers. Each instance is composed of a set of n MAC addresses stored in the `accessPoints` data frame. To compute the distance between two instances (two sets) we can use the *Jaccard distance*. This distance is based on element sets:

$$j(A, B) = \frac{|A \cup B| - |A \cap B|}{|A \cup B|} \tag{2.2}$$

where A and B are sets of MAC addresses. A **set** is an unordered collection of elements with no repetitions. As an example, let's say we have two sets, S_1 and S_2:

$$S_1 = \{a, b, c, d, e\}$$
$$S_2 = \{e, f, g, a\}$$

The set S_1 has 5 elements (letters) and S_2 has 4 elements. $A \cup B$ means the **union** of the two sets and its result is the set of all elements that are either in A or B. For instance, the union of S_1 and S_2 is $S_1 \cup S_2 = \{a, b, c, d, e, f, g\}$. The $A \cap B$ denotes the **intersection** between A and B which is the set of elements that are in both A and B. In our example, $S_1 \cap S_2 = \{a, e\}$. Finally the vertical bars $||$ mean the **cardinality** of the set, that is, its number of elements. The cardinality of S_1 is $|S_1| = 5$ because it has 5 elements. The cardinality of the union of the two sets $|S_1 \cup S_2| = 7$ because this set has 7 elements.

In R, we can implement the Jaccard distance as follows:

```
jaccardDistance <- function(set1, set2){
  lengthUnion <- length(union(set1, set2))
  lengthIntersectoin <- length(intersect(set1, set2))
  d <- (lengthUnion - lengthIntersectoin) / lengthUnion
  return(d)
}
```

The implementation is in the script `indoor_auxiliary.R`. Now, we can try our function! Let's compute the distance between two instances of the same class (*'bedroomA'*).

```
# Compute jaccard distance between instances with same class:
# (bedroomA)
jaccardDistance(dataset[[1]]$accessPoints$mac,
                dataset[[4]]$accessPoints$mac)
#> [1] 0.3333333
```

Now let's try to compute the distance between instances with different classes.

```
# Jaccard distance of instances with different class:
# (bedroomA and bedroomB)
jaccardDistance(dataset[[1]]$accessPoints$mac,
                dataset[[210]]$accessPoints$mac)
#> [1] 0.6666667
```

The distance between instances of the same class was 0.33 whereas the distance between instances of the different classes was 0.66. So, our function is working as expected.

In the extreme case when the sets A and B are identical, the distance will be 0. When there are no common elements in the sets, the distance will be 1. Armed with this distance metric, we can now implement the k-NN function in R. The `knn_classifier()` implementation is in the script `indoor_auxiliary.R`. Its first argument is the dataset (the list of instances). The second argument k, is the number of nearest neighbors to use, and the last two arguments are the indices of the train and test instances, respectively. This indices are pointers to the elements in the `dataset` variable.

```
knn_classifier <- function(dataset, k, trainSetIndices, testSetIndices){

  groundTruth <- NULL
  predictions <- NULL

  for(queryInstance in testSetIndices){
    distancesToQuery <- NULL

    for(trainInstance in trainSetIndices){
      jd <- jaccardDistance(dataset[[queryInstance]]$accessPoints$mac,
                            dataset[[trainInstance]]$accessPoints$mac)
      distancesToQuery <- c(distancesToQuery, jd)
    }

    indices <- sort(distancesToQuery, index.return = TRUE)$ix
    indices <- indices[1:k]
    # Indices of the k nearest neighbors
    nnIndices <- trainSetIndices[indices]
    # Get the actual instances
    nnInstances <- dataset[nnIndices]
    # Get their respective classes
    nnClasses <- sapply(nnInstances, function(e){e[[1]]})
    prediction <- Mode(nnClasses)
    predictions <- c(predictions, prediction)
    groundTruth <- c(groundTruth,
                     dataset[[queryInstance]]$locationId)
  }

  return(list(predictions = predictions,
              groundTruth = groundTruth))
}
```

For each instance `queryInstance` in the test set, the `knn_classifier()` computes its jaccard distance to every other instance in the train set and stores those distances in `distancesToQuery`. Then, those distances are sorted in ascending order and the most common class among the first k elements is returned as the predicted class. The function `Mode()` returns the most common element. Finally, `knn_classifier()` returns a list with the predictions for every instance in the test set and their respective ground truth class for evaluation.

Now, we can try our classifier. We will use 70% of the dataset as train set and the remaining as the test set.

```
# Total number of instances
numberInstances <- length(dataset)
# Set seed for reproducibility
set.seed(12345)
# Split into train and test sets.
trainSetIndices <- sample(1:numberInstances,
                          size = round(numberInstances * 0.7),
                          replace = F)
testSetIndices <- (1:numberInstances)[-trainSetIndices]
```

The function `knn_classifier()` predicts the class for each test set instance and returns a list with their predictions and their ground truth classes. With this information, we can compute the *accuracy* on the test set which is the percentage of correctly classified instances. In this example, we set $k = 3$.

```
# Obtain predictions on the test set.
result <- knn_classifier(dataset,
                         k = 3,
                         trainSetIndices,
                         testSetIndices)
# Calculate and print accuracy.
sum(result$predictions == result$groundTruth) /
  length(result$predictions)
#> [1] 0.9454545
```

Not bad! Our simple k-NN algorithm achieved an accuracy of 94.5%. Usually, it is a good idea to visualize the predictions to have a better understanding of the classifier's behavior. **Confusion matrices** allow us to exactly do that. We can use the `confusionMatrix()` function from the `caret` package to generate a confusion matrix. Its first argument is a factor with the predictions and the second one is a factor with the corresponding true values. This function returns an object with several performance metrics (see next section) and the confusion matrix. The actual confusion matrix is stored in the `table` object.

```
library(caret)
cm <- confusionMatrix(factor(result$predictions),
                      factor(result$groundTruth))
cm$table # Access the confusion matrix.
#>             Reference
#> Prediction bedroomA bedroomB lobby tvroom
#> bedroomA         26        0     3      1
#> bedroomB          0       17     0      1
#> lobby             0        1    28      0
#> tvroom            0        0     0     33
```

The columns of the confusion matrix represent the true classes and the rows the predictions. For example, from the total 31 instances of type *'lobby'*, 28 were correctly classified as *'lobby'* while 3 were misclassified as *'bedroomA'*. Something I find useful is to plot the confusion matrix as proportions instead of counts (Figure 2.3). From this confusion matrix we see that for the class *'bedroomB'*, 94% of the instances were correctly classified while 6% were mislabeled as *'lobby'*. On the other hand, instances of type *'bedroomA'* were always classified correctly.

A confusion matrix is a good way to analyze the classification results per class and it helps to spot weaknesses which can be used to improve the model, for example, by extracting additional features.

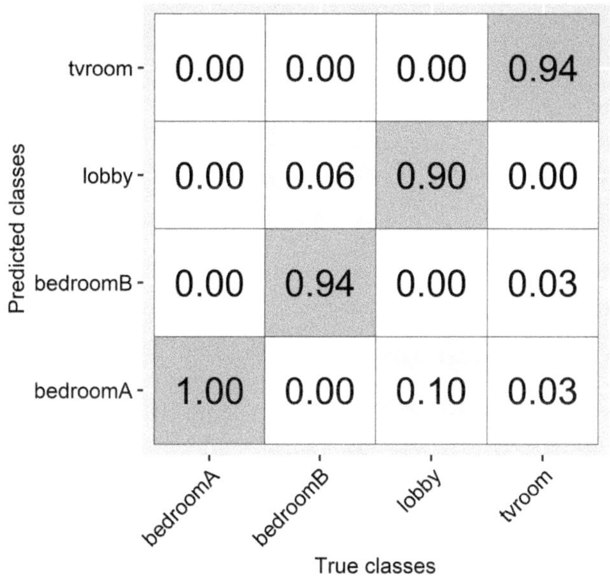

FIGURE 2.3 Confusion matrix for location predictions.

2.2 Performance Metrics

Performance metrics allow us to assess the generalization performance of a model from different angles. The most common performance metric for classification is the accuracy:

$$accuracy = \frac{\text{\# correctly classified instances}}{\text{total \# instances}} \tag{2.3}$$

In order to have a better understanding of the generalization performance of a model, it is a good practice to compute several performance metrics in addition to the accuracy. Accuracy also has some limitations, especially in highly imbalanced datasets. The following metrics provide different views of a model's performance for the binary case (when there are only two classes). These metrics can be extended to the multi-class setting using a *one vs. all* approach. That is, compare each class to the remaining classes.

Before introducing the other metrics, it is convenient to define some terms:

- True positives (TP): Positive examples classified as positives.
- True negatives (TN): Negative examples classified as negatives.
- False positives (FP): Negative examples misclassified as positives.
- False negatives (FN): Positive examples misclassified as negatives.

For the binary classification case, it is you who decide which one is the positive class. For example, if your problem is about detecting falls and you have two classes: *'fall'* and *'nofall'*, then, considering *'fall'* as the positive class makes sense since this is the one you are most interested in detecting. The following, is a list of commonly used metrics in classification:

Recall: The proportion of positives that are classified as such. Alternative names for recall are: **true positive rate**, **sensitivity**, and **hit rate**. In fact, the diagonal of the confusion matrix with proportions of the indoor location example shows the recall for each class (Figure 2.3).

$$recall = \frac{\mathrm{TP}}{\mathrm{P}} \tag{2.4}$$

Specificity: The proportion of negatives classified as such. It is also called the **true negative rate**.

$$specificity = \frac{\mathrm{TN}}{\mathrm{N}} \tag{2.5}$$

Precision: The fraction of true positives among those classified as positives. Also known as the **positive predictive value**.

$$precision = \frac{\mathrm{TP}}{\mathrm{TP} + \mathrm{FP}} \tag{2.6}$$

F1-score: This is the harmonic mean of precision and recall.

$$\mathit{F1\text{-}score} = 2 \cdot \frac{\text{precision} \cdot \text{recall}}{\text{precision} + \text{recall}} \tag{2.7}$$

The `confusionMatrix()` function from the `caret` package computes several of those metrics. From our previous confusion matrix object, we can inspect those metrics by class.

```
cm$byClass[,c("Recall", "Specificity", "Precision", "F1")]
#>                    Recall Specificity Precision        F1
#> Class: bedroomA 1.0000000   0.9523810 0.8666667 0.9285714
#> Class: bedroomB 0.9444444   0.9891304 0.9444444 0.9444444
#> Class: lobby    0.9032258   0.9873418 0.9655172 0.9333333
#> Class: tvroom   0.9428571   1.0000000 1.0000000 0.9705882
```

The mean of the metrics across all classes can be computed by taking the mean for each column of the returned object:

```
colMeans(cm$byClass[,c("Recall", "Specificity", "Precision", "F1")])
#>    Recall Specificity   Precision          F1
#> 0.9476318   0.9822133   0.9441571   0.9442344
```

2.2.1 Confusion Matrix

As briefly introduced in the previous section, a *confusion matrix* provides a nice way to understand the model's predictions and spot where it made mistakes. Figure 2.4 shows a confusion matrix for the binary case. The columns represent the true classes and the rows the predicted classes. The **P** stands for the positive cases and the **N** for the negative ones. Each entry in the matrix corresponds to the TP, TN, FP, and FN. The TP and TN are the correct classifications whereas the FN and FP are the misclassifications.

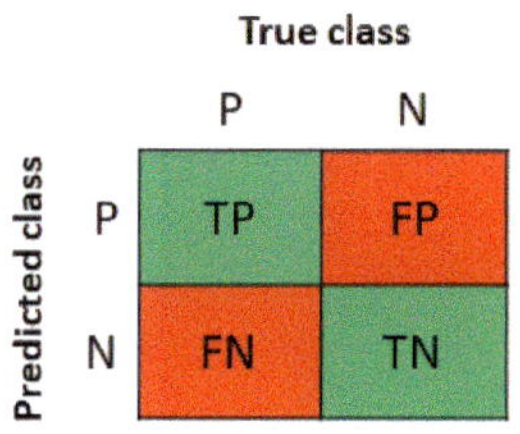

FIGURE 2.4 Confusion matrix for the binary case. P: positives, N: negatives.

Figure 2.5 shows a concrete example of a confusion matrix derived from a list of 15 instances with their predictions and their corresponding true values (ground truth). For example, the first element in the list is a **P** and it was correctly classified as a **P**. The eight element is a **P** but it was misclassified as **N**. The associated confusion matrix for these ground truth and predicted classes is shown at the bottom.

There are 7 true positives and 3 true negatives. In total, 10 instances were correctly classified (TP and TN) and 5 were misclassified (FP and FN). From this matrix we can calculate what is the total number of true positives by taking the sum of the first column, 10 in this case. The total number of true negatives is obtained by summing the second column, 5 in this case. Having this information we can compute any of the previous performance metrics: accuracy, recall, specificity, precision, and F1-score.

Ground truth:	P	P	P	P	N	P	N	P	P	P	N	N	N	P	P
Predictions:	P	P	P	P	N	P	N	N	N	N	N	P	P	P	P

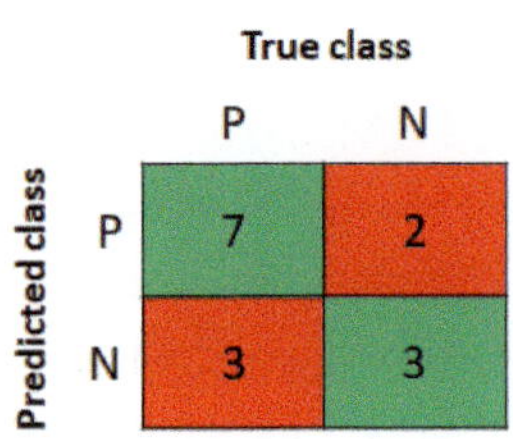

FIGURE 2.5 A concrete example of a confusion matrix for the binary case. P: positives, N: negatives.

Be aware that there is no standard that defines whether the true classes or the predicted classes go in the rows or columns, thus, you need to check for this everytime you encounter a new confusion matrix.

`shiny_metrics.R` This shiny app demonstrates how different performance metrics behave when the confusion matrix values change.

2.3 Decision Trees

Decision trees are powerful predictive models (especially when combining several of them, see chapter 3) used for classification and regression tasks. Here, the focus will be on classification. Each node in a tree represents partial or final decisions based on a single feature. If a node is a leaf, then it represents a final decision. A leaf is simply a terminal node, i.e, it has no children nodes. Given a feature vector representing an instance, the predicted class is obtained by testing the feature values and following the tree path until a leaf is reached. Figure 2.6 exemplifies a query instance with an unknown class (left) and a decision tree (right). To predict the class of an unknown instance, its features are evaluated starting at the root of the tree. In this case *number_wheels* is 4 in the query instance so we take the left path from the root. Now, we need to evaluate *weight*. This time the test is false since the weight is 2300 and we take the right path. Since this is a leaf node the final predicted class is *'truck'*. Usually, small trees are preferable (small depth) because they are easier to visualize and interpret and are less prone to overfitting. The example tree has a depth of 2. Had the number of wheels been 2 instead of 4, then testing the *weight* feature would not have been necessary.

	number_wheels	weight	Class
query instance	4	2300	?

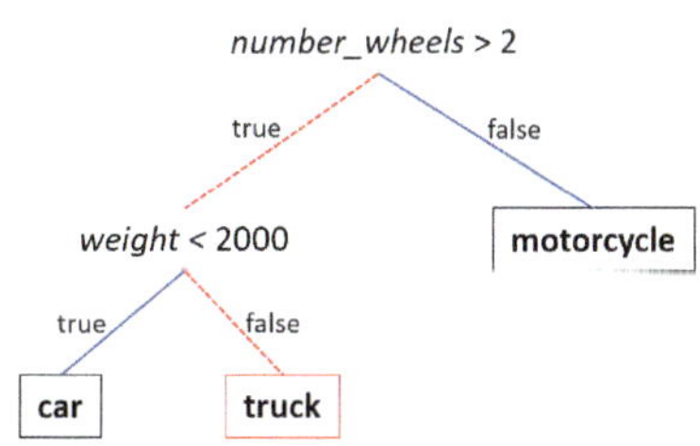

FIGURE 2.6 Example decision tree. The query instance is classified as truck by this tree.

As shown in the example, decision trees are easy to interpret and the final result can be explained by just following the path. Now let's see how these decision trees are learned from data. Consider the following artificial *concert* dataset (Figure 2.7).

The first four variables are features and the last column is the class. The class is the decision whether or not we should go to a music concert

	Tired	Rain	Metal	Price	Go
1	1	1	1	low	1
2	0	0	0	low	1
3	1	1	0	low	1
4	0	0	0	low	1
5	1	0	1	medium	1
6	0	0	1	medium	1
7	1	1	1	medium	0
8	0	1	0	medium	0
9	1	0	0	medium	0
10	0	0	0	medium	0
11	1	0	1	high	0
12	0	1	1	high	0

FIGURE 2.7 Concert dataset.

based on the other variables. In this case, all variables are binary except *Price* which has three possible values: *low*, *medium*, and *high*.

- *Tired:* Indicates whether the person is tired or not.
- *Rain:* Whether it is raining or not.
- *Metal:* Indicates whether this is a heavy metal concert or not.
- *Price:* Ticket price.
- *Go:* The decision of whether to go to the music concert or not.

The main question when building a tree is which feature should be at the root (top). Once you answer this question, you may need to grow the tree by adding another feature (node) as one of the root's children. To decide which new feature to add you need to answer the same first question: "What feature should be at the root of this subtree?". This is a recursive definition! The tree keeps growing until you reach a leaf node, there are no more features to select from, or you have reached a predefined maximum depth.

For the *concert* dataset we need to find which is the best variable to be placed at the root. Let's suppose we need to choose between *Price* and *Metal*. Figure 2.8 shows these two possibilities.

If we select *Price*, there are three possible subnodes, one for each value: *low*, *medium*, and *high*. If *Price* is *low* then four instances fall into this subtree (the first four from the table). For all of them, the value of *Go* is 1. If *Price* is *high*, two instances fall into this category and their *Go*

FIGURE 2.8 Two example trees with one variable split by Price (left) and Metal (right).

value is 0, thus if the price is high then you should not go to the concert according to this data. There are six instances for which the *Price* value is *medium*. From those, two of them have *Go=1* and the remaining four have *Go=0*. For cases when the price is *low* or *high* we can arrive at a solution. If the price is *low* then go to the concert, if the price is *high* then do not go. However, if the price is *medium* it is still not clear what to do since this subnode is not *pure*. That is, the labels of the instances are mixed: two with an output of 1 and four with an output of 0. In this case we can try to use another feature to decide and grow the tree but first, let's look at what happens if we decide to use *Metal* as the first feature at the root. In this case, we end up with two subsets with six instances each. And for each subnode, what decision should we take is still not clear because the output is 'mixed' (Go: 3, NotGo: 3). At this point we would need to continue growing the tree below each subnode.

Intuitively, it seems like *Price* is a better feature since its subnodes are more *pure*. Then we can use another feature to split the instances whose *Price* is *medium*. For example, using the *Metal* variable. Figure 2.9 shows how this would look like. Since one of the subnodes of *Metal* is still not pure we can further split it using the *Rain* variable, for example. At this point, we can not split any further. Note that the *Tired* variable was never used.

So far, we have chosen the root variable based on which one looks more pure but to automate the process, we need a way to measure this *purity* in a quantitative manner. One way to do that is by using the *entropy*. *Entropy* is a measure of uncertainty from information theory. It is 0 when there is no uncertainty and 1 when there is complete uncertainty. The entropy of a discrete variable X with values $x_1 \ldots x_n$ and probability mass function $P(X)$ is:

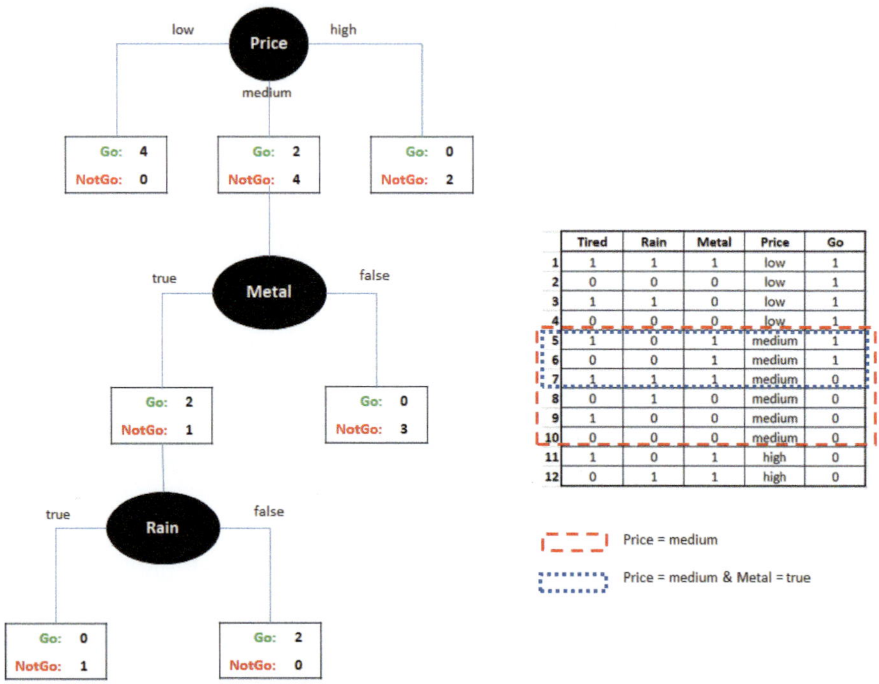

FIGURE 2.9 Tree splitting example. Left: tree splits. Right: Highlighted instances when splitting by Price and Metal.

$$H(X) = -\sum_{i=1}^{n} P(x_i)logP(x_i) \tag{2.8}$$

Take for example a fair coin with probability of heads and tails $= 0.5$ each. The entropy for that coin is:

$$H(X) = -(0.5)log(0.5) + (0.5)log(0.5) = 1$$

Since we do not know what will be the result when we drop the coin, the entropy is maximum. Now consider the extreme case when the coin is biased such that the probability of heads is 1 and the probability of tails is 0. The entropy in this case is zero:

$$H(X) = -(1)log(1) + (0)log(0) = 0$$

If we know that the result is always going to be heads, then there is no uncertainty when the coin is dropped. The entropy of p positive examples and n negative examples is:

$$H(p,n) = -(\frac{p}{p+n})log(\frac{p}{p+n}) + (\frac{n}{p+n})log(\frac{n}{p+n}) \quad (2.9)$$

Thus, we can use this to compute the entropy for the three possible values of *Price* with respect to the class. The positives are the instances where *Go=1* and the negatives are the instances where *Go=0*:

$$H_{price=low}(4,0) = -(\frac{4}{4+0})log(\frac{4}{4+0}) + (\frac{0}{4+0})log(\frac{0}{4+0}) = 0$$

$$H_{price=medium}(2,4) = -(\frac{2}{2+4})log(\frac{2}{2+4}) + (\frac{4}{2+4})log(\frac{4}{2+4}) = 0.918$$

$$H_{price=high}(0,2) = -(\frac{0}{0+2})log(\frac{0}{0+2}) + (\frac{2}{0+2})log(\frac{2}{0+2}) = 0$$

The average of those three can be calculated by taking into account the number of corresponding instances for each value and the total number of instances (12):

$$meanH(price) = (4/12)(0) + (6/12)(0.918) + (2/12)(0) = 0.459$$

Before deciding to split on *Price* the entropy of the entire dataset is 1 since there are six positive and negative examples:

$$H(6,6) = 1$$

Now we can compute the *information gain* for *Price*. Intuitively, the information gain tells you how powerful this variable is at dividing the instances based on their class, that is, how much you are learning:

$$infoGain(Price) = 1 - meanH(Price) = 1 - 0.459 = 0.541$$

Since you want to learn fast, you want your root node to be the one with the highest information gain. For the rest of the variables the information gain is:

$infoGain(Tired) = 0$

$$infoGain(Rain) = 0.020$$

$$infoGain(Metal) = 0$$

The highest information gain is produced by *Price*, thus, it is selected as the root node. Then, the process continues recursively for each branch but excluding *Price*. Since branches with values *low* and *high* are already done, we only need to further split *medium*. Sometimes it is not possible to have completely pure nodes like with *low* and *high*. This can happen for example, when there are no more attributes left or when two or more instances have the same feature values but different labels. In those situations the final prediction is the most common label (majority vote).

There exist many implementations of decision trees. Some implementations compute variable importance using the entropy (as shown here) but others use the Gini index, for example. Each implementation also treats numeric variables in different ways. Pruning the tree using different techniques is also common in order to reduce its size.

Some of the most common implementations are C4.5 trees [Quinlan, 2014] and CART [Steinberg and Colla, 2009]. The later is implemented in the `rpart` R package [Therneau and Atkinson, 2019] which will be used in the following section to build a model that predicts physical activities from smartphones sensor data.

2.3.1 Activity Recognition with Smartphones

```
smartphone_activities.R
```

As mentioned in the introduction, an example of behavior is an observable physical activity. We can infer what **physical activity** someone is doing by looking at her/his body movements. Observing physical activities can provide useful behavioral and contextual information about someone. This can also be used as a proxy to, for example, infer someone's health condition by detecting deviations in activity patterns.

Nowadays, most smartphones come with a tri-axial accelerometer sensor. This sensor measures gravitational forces from the x, y, and z axes. This information can be used to capture movement patterns from the user and automate the process of monitoring the type of physical activity being performed.

In this section, we will use decision trees to automatically classify physical activities from acceleration data. We will use the *WISDM* dataset[2] and from now on, I will refer to it as the *SMARTPHONE ACTIVITIES* dataset. It contains acceleration recordings that were collected with a smartphone and was made available by Kwapisz et al. [2010]. The dataset has 6 different activities: *'walking'*, *'jogging'*, *'walking upstairs'*, *'walking downstairs'*, *'sitting'* and *'standing'*. The data were collected by 36 volunteers with an Android phone located in their pant's pocket and with a sampling rate of 20 Hz (1 sample every 50 milliseconds).

The dataset contains two types of files. One with the raw accelerometer data and the other one after feature extraction. Figure 2.10 shows the first 10 lines of the raw accelerometer values of the first file. The first column is the id of the user that collected the data and the second column is the class. The third column is the timestamp and the remaining columns are the x, y, and z accelerometer values, respectively.

```
33,Jogging,49105962326000,-0.6946377,12.680544,0.50395286;
33,Jogging,49106062271000,5.012288,11.264028,0.95342433;
33,Jogging,49106112167000,4.903325,10.882658,-0.08172209;
33,Jogging,49106222305000,-0.61291564,18.496431,3.0237172;
33,Jogging,49106332290000,-1.1849703,12.108489,7.205164;
33,Jogging,49106442306000,1.3756552,-2.4925237,-6.510526;
33,Jogging,49106542312000,-0.61291564,10.56939,5.706926;
33,Jogging,49106652389000,-0.50395286,13.947236,7.0553403;
33,Jogging,49106762313000,-8.430995,11.413852,5.134871;
33,Jogging,49106872299000,0.95342433,1.3756552,1.6480621;
```

FIGURE 2.10 First 10 lines of raw accelerometer data.

Usually, classification models are not trained with the raw data but with *feature vectors* extracted from the raw data. Feature vectors have the advantage of being more compact, thus, making the learning phase more efficient. For activity recognition, the feature extraction process consists of defining a moving window of size w that starts at position i. At the beginning, i is the index pointing to the first accelerometer readings. Then, n statistical features are computed on the elements covered by the window such as mean, standard deviation, 0-crossings, etc. This will produce a n-dimensional feature vector and the process is repeated by moving the window s steps forward. Typical values of s are such that the overlap between the previous window position and the next one is

[2] http://www.cis.fordham.edu/wisdm/dataset.php

about 30% to 50%. An overlap of 0 is also typical, that is, $s = w$. Figure 2.11 depicts the process.

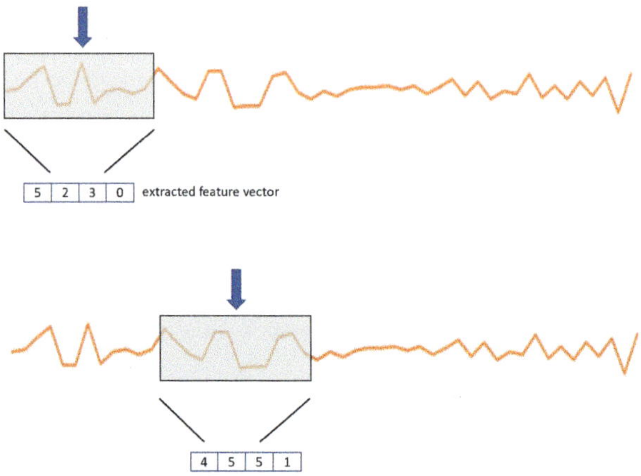

FIGURE 2.11 Moving window for feature extraction.

Once we have the set of feature vectors and their associated class labels, we can use them to train a classifier and make predictions on new data (Figure 2.12).

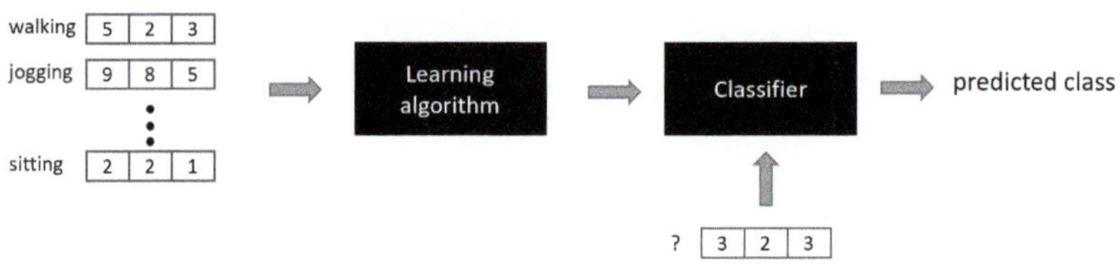

FIGURE 2.12 The extracted feature vectors are used to train a classifier.

For this example, we will use the file with features already extracted. The authors used windows of 10 seconds which is equivalent to 200 observations given the 20 Hz sampling rate and they used 0% overlap. From each window, they extracted 43 features such as the mean, standard deviation, absolute deviations, etc.

Let's read and print the first rows of the dataset. The script for this section is `smartphone_activities.R`. The data frame has several columns, but we only print the first five features and the class which is stored in the last column.

```
# Read data.
df <- read.csv(datapath,stringsAsFactors = F)

# Some code to clean the dataset.
# (cleaning code not shown here).

# Print first rows of the dataset.
head(df[,c(1:5,40)])

#>     X0   X1   X2   X3   X4    class
#> 1 0.04 0.09 0.14 0.12 0.11  Jogging
#> 2 0.12 0.12 0.06 0.07 0.11  Jogging
#> 3 0.14 0.09 0.11 0.09 0.09  Jogging
#> 4 0.06 0.10 0.09 0.09 0.11  Walking
#> 5 0.12 0.11 0.10 0.08 0.10  Walking
#> 6 0.09 0.09 0.10 0.12 0.08  Walking
#> 7 0.12 0.12 0.12 0.13 0.15 Upstairs
#> 8 0.10 0.10 0.10 0.10 0.11 Upstairs
#> 9 0.08 0.07 0.08 0.08 0.05 Upstairs
```

Our aim is to predict the class based on all the numeric features. We will use the `rpart` package [Therneau and Atkinson, 2019] which implements classification and regression trees. We will assess the performance of the decision tree with 10-fold cross-validation. We can use the `sample()` function to generate the folds. This function will sample n integers from 1 to k where n is the number of rows in the data frame.

```
# Package with implementations of decision trees.
library(rpart)

# Set seed for reproducibility.
set.seed(1234)

# Define the number of folds.
k <- 10

# Generate folds.
```

```
folds <- sample(k, size = nrow(df), replace = TRUE)

# Print first 10 values.
head(folds)
#> [1] 10  6  5  9  5  6
```

The `folds` variable stores the fold each instance belongs to. For example, the first instance belongs to fold 10, the second instance belongs to fold 6, and so on. We can now generate our test and train sets. We will iterate $k = 10$ times. For each iteration i, the test set is built using the instances that belong to fold i and the train set will be composed of the remaining instances (those that do not belong to fold i). Next, the `rpart()` function is used to train the decision tree with the train set. By default, `rpart()` performs 10-fold cross-validation internally. To avoid this, we set the parameter `xval = 0`. Then, we can use the trained model to obtain the predictions on the test set with the generic `predict()` function. The ground truth classes and the predictions are stored so the performance metrics can be computed.

```
# Variable to store ground truth classes.
groundTruth <- NULL

# Variable to store the classifier's predictions.
predictions <- NULL

for(i in 1:k){

  trainSet <- df[which(folds != i), ]
  testSet <- df[which(folds == i), ]

  # Train the decision tree
  treeClassifier <- rpart(class ~ .,
                          trainSet, xval=0)

  # Get predictions on the test set.
  foldPredictions <- predict(treeClassifier,
                             testSet, type = "class")
```

```
  predictions <- c(predictions,
                   as.character(foldPredictions))

  groundTruth <- c(groundTruth,
                   as.character(testSet$class))
}
```

The first argument of the `rpart()` function is `class ~ .` which is a formula that instructs the method to use the *class* column as the class. The `~ .` means "use all the remaining columns as features". Now, we can use the `confusionMatrix()` function to compute the performance metrics and the confusion matrix.

```
cm <- confusionMatrix(as.factor(predictions),
                      as.factor(groundTruth))

# Print accuracy
cm$overall["Accuracy"]
#> Accuracy
#> 0.7895903

# Print performance metrics per class.
cm$byClass[,c("Recall", "Specificity", "Precision", "F1")]
#>                      Recall Specificity Precision        F1
#> Class: Downstairs 0.2821970   0.9617587 0.4434524 0.3449074
#> Class: Jogging    0.9612308   0.9601898 0.9118506 0.9358898
#> Class: Sitting    0.8366013   0.9984351 0.9696970 0.8982456
#> Class: Standing   0.8983740   0.9932328 0.8632812 0.8804781
#> Class: Upstairs   0.2246835   0.9669870 0.4733333 0.3047210
#> Class: Walking    0.9360884   0.8198981 0.7642213 0.8414687

# Print overall metrics across classes.
colMeans(cm$byClass[,c("Recall", "Specificity",
                       "Precision", "F1")])
#>     Recall Specificity   Precision          F1
#>  0.6898625   0.9500836   0.7376393   0.7009518
```

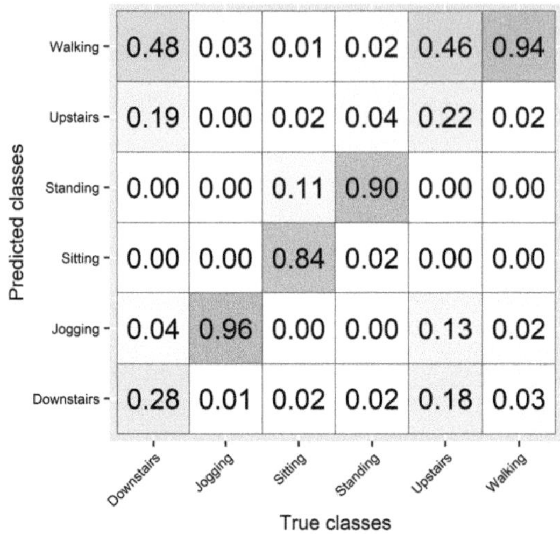

FIGURE 2.13 Confusion matrix for activities' predictions.

The overall accuracy was 78% and by looking at the individual performance metrics, some classes had low scores like *'walking downstairs'* and *'walking upstairs'*. From the confusion matrix (Figure 2.13), it can be seen that those two activities were often confused with each other but also with the *'walking'* activity. The package `rpart.plot` [Milborrow, 2019] can be used to plot the resulting tree (Figure 2.14).

```
library(rpart.plot)
# Plot the tree from the last fold.
rpart.plot(treeClassifier, fallen.leaves = F,
           shadow.col = "gray", legend.y = 1)
```

The `fallen.leaves = F` argument prevents the leaves to be plotted at the bottom. This is useful if the tree has many nodes. Each node shows the predicted class, the predicted probability of each class, and the percentage of observations in the node. The plot also shows the feature used for each split. We can see that the *YABSOLDEV* variable is at the root thus, it had the highest information gain with the initial set of instances. At the root of the tree, before looking at any of the features, the predicted class is *'Walking'*. This is because its prior probability is the highest one

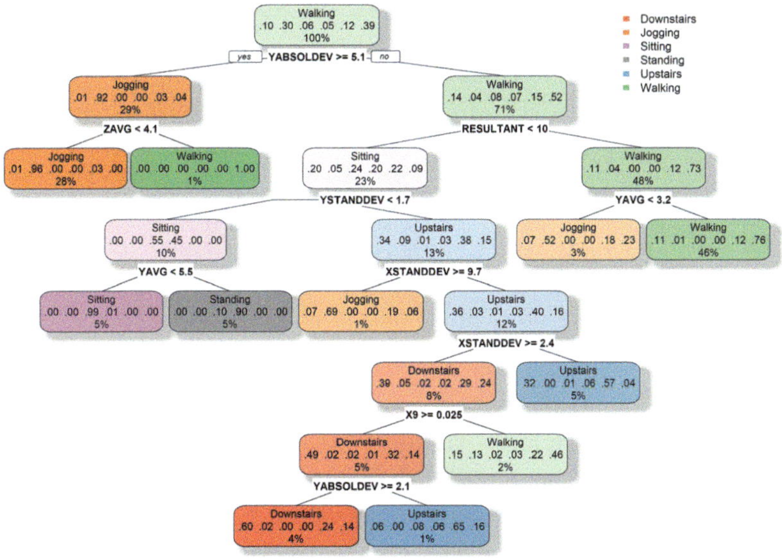

FIGURE 2.14 Resulting decision tree.

(≈ 0.39), that is, it's the most common activity present in the dataset. So, if we didn't have any other information, our best bet would be to predict the most frequent activity.

```
# Prior probabilities.
table(trainSet$class) / nrow(trainSet)
#> Downstairs    Jogging    Sitting   Standing   Upstairs    Walking
#> 0.09882885 0.29607561 0.05506472 0.04705157 0.11793713 0.38504212
```

These results look promising, but they can still be improved. In the next chapter, I will show you how to improve these results with *Ensemble Learning* which is a method that is used to aggregate many models.

2.4 Naive Bayes

Naive Bayes is yet another type of classifier. This one is based on Bayes' rule. The name *Naive* is because this method assumes that the features are independent. In the previous section we learned that decision trees are built recursively. Trees are built by first selecting a feature to be at the root and then, the root is split into subnodes and so on. How those subnodes are chosen depends on their parent node. With Naive Bayes, features don't need information about other features, thus, the parameters for each feature can be learned in parallel.

To demonstrate how Naive Bayes works I will use the *SMARTPHONE ACTIVITIES* dataset as in the previous section. For any given *query instance*, the aim is to **predict its most likely class** based on the accelerometer features. For a new *query instance*, we want to estimate its class based on the features that we have observed. Let's say we want to know what is the probability that the query instance belongs to the class *'Walking'*. This can be formulated as follows:

$$P(C = \mathit{Walking} | f_1, \ldots, f_n).$$

This reads as the conditional probability that the class is *'Walking'* **given** the observed evidence. For each instance, the evidence that we can observe are its features $f_1, \ldots, f_n$. In this dataset, each instance has 39 features. If we want to estimate the most likely class, all we need to do is to compute the conditional probability for each class and return the highest one:

$$y = \underset{k \in \{1, \ldots, K\}}{\operatorname{argmax}} \; P(C_k | f_1, \ldots, f_n) \tag{2.10}$$

where K is the total number of possible classes. The arg max notation means: Evaluate the right hand expression for every class k and return the k that resulted with the maximum probability. If instead of *arg max* we had *max* (without the *arg*) that would mean to return the actual maximum probability instead of the class k.

Now let's see how we can compute $P(C_k | f_1, \ldots, f_n)$. To compute a conditional probability we can use Bayes' rule:

$$P(H|E) = \frac{P(H)P(E|H)}{P(E)} \tag{2.11}$$

Let's dissect that formula:

1. $P(H|E)$ is called the **posterior** and it is the probability of the hypothesis H given the observed evidence E. In our example, the hypothesis can be that $C = Walking$ and the evidence consists of the measured features. This is the probability that ultimately we want to estimate for each class and pick the class with the highest probability.

2. $P(H)$ is called the **prior**. This is the probability of a hypothesis happening without having any evidence. In our example, this translates into the probability that an instance belongs to a particular class without looking at its features. In practice, this is estimated from the class counts in the training set. Suppose the training set consists of 100 instances and from those, 80 are of type *'Walking'* and 20 are of type *'Jogging'*. Then, the prior probability for *'Walking'* is $P(C = Walking) = 80/100 = 0.8$ and the prior for *'Jogging'* is $P(C = Jogging) = 20/100 = 0.2$.

3. $P(E)$ is the probability of the evidence. Since this one doesn't depend on the class we don't need to compute it. This can be thought of as a normalization factor. When choosing the final class we only need to select the one with the highest score, so there is no need to normalize them into proper probabilities between 0 and 1.

4. $P(E|H)$ is called the **likelihood**. For numerical variables we can estimate this using a *Gaussian probability density function*. This sounds intimidating! but all we need to do is to compute the *mean* and *standard deviation* for each feature-class pair and plug them in the probability density function (pdf). The formula for a Gaussian (also called normal) pdf is:

$$f(x) = \frac{1}{\sigma\sqrt{2\pi}} e^{-(x-\mu)^2/2\sigma^2} \tag{2.12}$$

where μ is the mean and σ is the standard deviation.

Suppose that for some feature $f1$ when the class is *'Walking'*, its mean is 5 and its standard deviation is 3. That is, we filter the train set and only select those instances with class *'Walking'* and compute the mean and standard deviation for feature $f1$. Figure 2.15 shows how its pdf looks like.

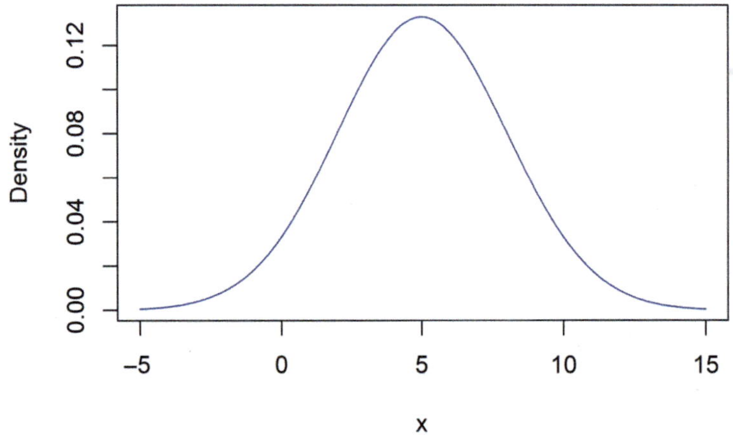

FIGURE 2.15 Gaussian probability density function with mean 5 and standard deviation 3.

If we have a query instance with a feature $f_1 = 1.7$, we can compute its likelihood given the *'Walking'* class $P(f_1 = 1.7|C = Walking)$ with equation (2.12) by plugging $x = 1.7$, $\mu = 5$, and $\sigma = 3$. In R, the function `dnorm()` implements the normal pdf.

```
dnorm(x=1.7, mean = 5, sd = 3)
#> [1] 0.07261739
```

In Figure 2.16 the solid circle shows the likelihood when $x = 1.7$.

If we have more than one feature we need to compute the likelihood for each and take their **product**: $P(f_1|C = Walking) * P(f_2|C = Walking) * \cdots * P(f_n|C = Walking)$. Each feature and class pair has its own μ and σ parameters. Thus, Naive Bayes requires to learn $K * F * 2$

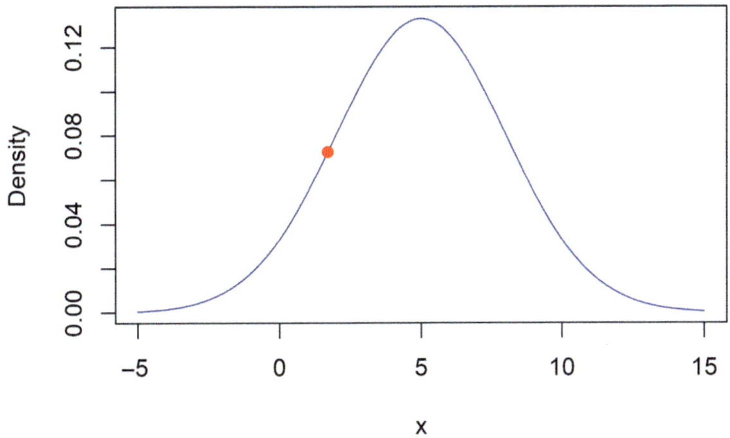

FIGURE 2.16 Likelihood (0.072) when x=1.7.

parameters for the $P(E|H)$ part plus K parameters for the priors $P(H)$. K is the number of classes, F is the number of features, and the 2 stands for the mean and standard deviation.

We have seen how we can compute $P(C_k|f_1, \dots, f_n)$ using Baye's rule by calculating the prior $P(H)$ and $P(E|H)$ which is the product of the likelihoods for each feature. If we substitute Bayes's rule (omitting the denominator) in equation (2.10) we get our Naive Bayes classifier:

$$y = \underset{k \in \{1, \dots, K\}}{\operatorname{argmax}} P(C_k) \prod_{i=1}^{F} P(f_i|C_k) \tag{2.13}$$

In the following section we will implement our own Naive Bayes algorithm in R and test it on the *SMARTPHONE ACTIVITIES* dataset. Then, we will compare our implementation with that of the well known `e1071` package [Meyer et al., 2019].

Naive Bayes works well with missing values since the features are independent. At prediction time, if an instance has one or more missing values then, those features are just ignored and the posterior probability is computed based only on the available variabels. Another advantage of the feature independence assumption is that feature selection algorithms run very fast with Naive Bayes. When building a predictive model, not all features may provide useful information and some features may even degrade the performance. Feature selection algorithms aim to find the best set of features and some of them need to try a huge number of feature combinations. With Naive Bayes, the parameters only need to be learned once and then different combinations of features can be evaluated by omitting the ones that are not used. With decision trees, for example, we would need to build entire new trees every time we want to try different input features.

Here, we have shown how we can use a Gaussian pdf to compute the likelihood $P(E|H)$ when the features are numeric. This assumes that the features have a normal distribution. However, this is not always the case. In practice, Naive Bayes can work really well even if that assumption is not met. Furthermore, nothing prevents us from using another distribution to estimate the likelihood or even defining a specific distribution for each feature. For categorical variables, $P(E|H)$ is estimated using the frequencies of the feature values.

2.4.1 Activity Recognition with Naive Bayes

`naive_bayes.R`

It's time to implement Naive Bayes. To keep it simple, first we will go through a step by step example using a single feature. Then, we will implement a function to train a Naive Bayes classifier for the case of multiple features.

Let's assume we have already split the data into train and test sets. The complete code is in the script `naive_bayes.R`. We will only use the feature *RESULTANT* which corresponds to the acceleration magnitude of the three axes of the accelerometer sensor. The following code snippet prints the first rows of the train set. The *RESULTANT* feature is in column 39 and the class is the last column (40).

```
head(trainset[,c(39:40)])
#>      RESULTANT    class
#> 1004     11.14  Walking
#> 623       1.24 Upstairs
#> 2693      9.90 Standing
#> 934      10.44 Upstairs
#> 4496     10.43  Walking
#> 2948     15.28  Jogging
```

First, we compute the prior probabilities for each class in the train set and store them in the variable `priors`. This corresponds to the $P(C_k)$ part in equation (2.13).

```
# Compute prior probabilities.
priors <- table(trainset$class) / nrow(trainset)

# Print the table of priors.
priors

#> Downstairs    Jogging    Sitting   Standing   Upstairs
#> 0.09622990 0.30266280 0.05721065 0.04640127 0.11521223
#>    Walking
#> 0.38228315
```

We can access each prior by name like this:

```
# Get the prior for "Jogging".
priors["Jogging"]
#>   Jogging
#> 0.3026628
```

This means that 30% of the instances in the train set are of type *'Jogging'*. Now we need to compute the $P(f_i|C_k)$ part from equation (2.13).

In R, we can define a method to compute the probability density function from equation (2.12) as:

```
# Probability density function of normal distribution.
f <- function(x, m, s){
  (1 / (sqrt(2*pi)*s)) * exp(-((x-m)^2) / (2 * s^2))
}
```

It's first argument `x` is the input value. The second argument `m` is the mean, and the last argument `s` is the standard deviation. For illustration purposes we are defining this function manually but remember that this pdf is already implemented with the base `dnorm()` function.

According to equation (2.13) we need to compute $P(f_i|C_k)$ for each feature i and class k. Let's assume there are only two classes, *'Walking'* and *'Jogging'*. Thus, we need to compute the mean and standard deviation for each, and for the feature $RESULTANT$ (column 39).

```
# Compute the mean and sd of
# the feature RESULTANT (column 39)
# when the class = "Standing".
mean.standing <- mean(trainset[which(trainset$class == "Standing"), 39])
sd.standing <- sd(trainset[which(trainset$class == "Standing"), 39])

# Compute mean and sd when
# the class = "Jogging".
mean.jogging <- mean(trainset[which(trainset$class == "Jogging"), 39])
sd.jogging <- sd(trainset[which(trainset$class == "Jogging"), 39])
```

Print the means:

```
mean.standing
#> [1] 9.405795
mean.jogging
#> [1] 13.70145
```

Note that the mean value for *'Jogging'* is higher for this feature. This was expected since this feature captures the overall movement across all axes. Now we have everything we need to start making predictions on new instances. We have the priors and we have the means and standard deviations for each feature-class pair.

Let's select the first instance from the test set and try to predict its class.

```
# Select a query instance from the test set.
query <- testset[1,] # Select the first one.
```

Now we compute the posterior probability for each class using the learned means and standard deviations:

```
# Compute P(Standing)P(RESULTANT|Standing)
priors["Standing"] * f(query$RESULTANT, mean.standing, sd.standing)
#> 0.003169748

# Compute P(Jogging)P(RESULTANT|Jogging)
priors["Jogging"] * f(query$RESULTANT, mean.jogging, sd.jogging)
#> 0.03884481
```

The posterior for *'Jogging'* was higher (0.038) so we classify the query instance as *'Jogging'*. If we check the true class we see that it was correctly classified!

```
# Inspect the true class of the query instance.
query$class
#> [1] "Jogging"
```

In this example we assumed that there was only one feature and we computed each step manually. However, this can easily be extended to deal with more features. So let's just do that. We can write two functions, one for training the classifier and the other for making predictions.

The following function will be used to train the classifier. It takes as input a data frame with n features. This function assumes that the class is the last column. The function returns a list with the learned priors, means, and standard deviations.

```
# Function to learn the parameters of
# a Naive Bayes classifier.
# Assumes that the last column of data is the class.
naive.bayes.train <- function(data){

  # Unique classes.
  classes <- unique(data$class)

  # Number of features.
  nfeatures <- ncol(data) - 1

  # List to store the learned means and sds.
  list.means.sds <- list()

  for(c in classes){

    # Matrix to store the mean and sd for each feature.
    # First column stores the mean and second column
    # stores the sd.
    M <- matrix(0, nrow = nfeatures, ncol = 2)

    # Populate matrix.
    for(i in 1:nfeatures){
      feature.values <- data[which(data$class == c),i]
      M[i,1] <- mean(feature.values)
      M[i,2] <- sd(feature.values)
    }

    list.means.sds[c] <- list(M)
  }

  # Compute prior probabilities.
  priors <- table(data$class) / nrow(data)

  return(list(list.means.sds=list.means.sds,
```

```
          priors=priors))
}
```

The function iterates through each class and for each, it creates a matrix `M` with F rows and 2 columns where F is the number of features. The first column stores the means and the second the standard deviations. Those matrices are saved in a list indexed by the class name so at prediction time we can retrieve each matrix individually. At the end, the prior probabilities are computed. Finally, a list is returned. The first element of the list is the list of matrices and the second element are the priors.

The next function will make predictions based on the learned parameters. Its first argument is the learned parameters and the second a data frame with the instances we want to make predictions for.

```
# Function to make predictions using
# the learned parameters.
naive.bayes.predict <- function(params, data){

  # Variable to store the prediction for each instance.
  predictions <- NULL

  n <- nrow(data)

  # Get class names.
  classes <- names(params$priors)

  # Get number of features.
  nfeatures <- nrow(params$list.means.sds[[1]])

  # Iterate instances.
  for(i in 1:n){
    query <- data[i,]
    max.probability <- -Inf
    predicted.class <- ""

    # Find the class with highest probability.
    for(c in classes){
```

```
      # Get the prior probability for class c.
      acum.prob <- params$priors[c]

      # Iterate features.
      for(j in 1:nfeatures){

        # Compute P(feature|class)
        tmp <- f(query[,j],
          params$list.means.sds[[c]][j,1],
          params$list.means.sds[[c]][j,2])

        # Accumulate result.
        acum.prob <- acum.prob * tmp
      }

      if(acum.prob > max.probability){
        max.probability <- acum.prob
        predicted.class <- c
      }
    }

    predictions <- c(predictions, predicted.class)
  }

  return(predictions)
}
```

This function iterates through each instance and computes the posterior for each class and stores the one that achieved the highest value as the prediction. Finally, it returns the list with all predictions.

Now we are ready to train our Naive Bayes classifier. All we need to do is call the function `naive.bayes.train()` and pass the train set.

```
# Learn Naive Bayes parameters.
nb.model <- naive.bayes.train(trainset)
```

The learned parameters are stored in `nb.model` and we can make predictions with the `naive.bayes.predict()` function by passing the `nb.model` and a test set.

```
# Make predictions.
predictions <- naive.bayes.predict(nb.model, testset)
```

Then, we can assess the performance of the model by computing the confusion matrix.

```
# Compute confusion matrix and other performance metrics.
groundTruth <- testset$class

cm <- confusionMatrix(as.factor(predictions),
                      as.factor(groundTruth))

# Print accuracy
cm$overall["Accuracy"]
#>  Accuracy
#> 0.7501538

# Print overall metrics across classes
colMeans(cm$byClass[,c("Recall", "Specificity",
                       "Precision", "F1")])
#>      Recall Specificity   Precision          F1
#>   0.6621381   0.9423729   0.6468372   0.6433231
```

The accuracy was 75%. In the previous section we obtained an accuracy of 78% with decision trees. However, this does not necessarily mean that decision trees are better. Moreover, in the previous section we used cross-validation and here we used hold-out validation.

Computing the posterior may cause a loss of numeric precision, specially when there are many features. This is because we are multiplying the likelihoods for each feature (see equation (2.13)) and those likelihoods are small numbers. One way to fix that is to use logarithms. In `naive.bayes.predict()` we can change `acum.prob <-`

params$priors[c] with acum.prob <- log(params$priors[c]) and acum.prob <- acum.prob * tmp with acum.prob <- acum.prob + log(tmp). If you try those changes you should get the same result as before.

There is already a popular R package (e1071) for training Naive Bayes classifiers. The following code trains a classifier using this package.

```
#### Use Naive Bayes implementation from package e1071 ####
library(e1071)

# We need to convert the class into a factor.
trainset$class <- as.factor(trainset$class)

nb.model2 <- naiveBayes(class ~., trainset)

predictions2 <- predict(nb.model2, testset)

cm2 <- confusionMatrix(as.factor(predictions2),
                       as.factor(groundTruth))

# Print accuracy
cm2$overall["Accuracy"]
#>  Accuracy
#> 0.7501538
```

As you can see, the result was the same as the one obtained with our implementation! We implemented our own for illustrative purposes but it is advisable to use already tested and proven packages. Furthermore, this one also supports categorical variables.

2.5 Dynamic Time Warping

dtw_example.R

In the previous activity recognition example, we used the extracted features represented as feature vectors to train the classifiers instead of using the raw data. In some situations this can lead to temporal-relationships information loss. In the previous example, we could classify the activities with reasonable accuracy since the extracted features were able to retain enough information from the raw data. However, in some cases, having temporal information is crucial. For example, in hand signature recognition, a query signature is checked for a match with one of the signatures in a database. The signatures need to have an almost exact match to authenticate a user. If we represent each signature as a feature vector, it can turn out that two signatures have very similar feature vectors even though they look completely different. For example, Figure 2.17 shows four datasets. They look very different but they all have the same correlation of 0.816[3].

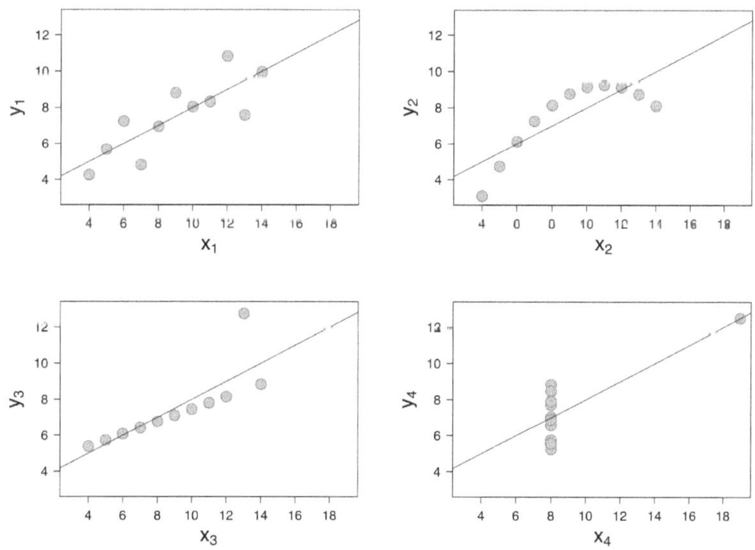

FIGURE 2.17 Four datasets with the same correlation of 0.816. (Anscombe, Francis J., 1973, Graphs in statistical analysis. American Statistician, 27, 17–21. Source: Wikipedia, User:Schutz (CC BY-SA 3.0) [https://creativecommons.org/licenses/by-sa/3.0/legalcode]).

[3] https://commons.wikimedia.org/wiki/File:Anscombe%27s_quartet_3.svg

To avoid this potential issue, we can also include time-dependent information into our models by keeping the order of the data points. Another issue is that two time series that belong to the same class will still have some differences. Every time the same person signs a document the signature will vary a bit. In the same way, when we pronounce a word, sometimes we emphasize some letters or speak at different speeds. Figure 2.18 shows two versions of the sentence "very good". In the second one (bottom) the speaker emphasizes the "e" and as a result, the two sentences are not aligned in time anymore even though they have the same meaning.

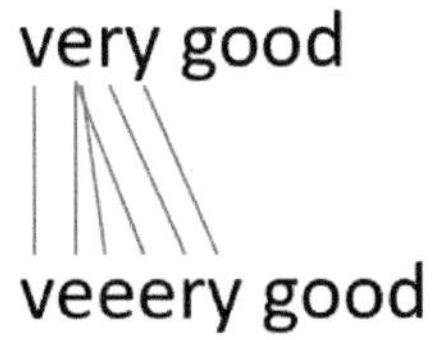

FIGURE 2.18 Time shift example between two sentences.

To compare two sequences we could use the well known Euclidean distance. However since the two sequences may not be aligned in time, the result could be misleading. Furthermore, the two sequences differ in length. To account for this "time-shift" effect in timeseries data, *Dynamic Time Warping* (DTW) [Sakoe et al., 1990] can be used instead. DTW is a method that:

- Finds an optimal match between two time-dependent sequences.
- Computes their dissimilarity.
- Finds the optimal deformation (mapping) of one of the sequences onto the other.

Another advantage of DTW is that the timeseries do not need to be of the same length. Suppose we have two timeseries, a *query*, and a *reference* we want to compare with:

$$query = (2, 2, 2, 4, 4, 3)$$
$$ref = (2, 2, 3, 3, 2)$$

The first thing to note is that the sequences differ in length. Figure 2.19 shows their plot. The *query* is the solid line and seems to be shifted to the right one position with respect to the *reference*. The plot also shows the resulting alignment after applying the DTW algorithm (dashed lines between the sequences). The resulting distance (after aligning) between the sequences is 3. In the following, we will see how the problem can be formalized and how it can be computed. Don't worry if you find the math notation a bit difficult to grasp at this pint. A step by step example will follow which should help to explain how the method works.

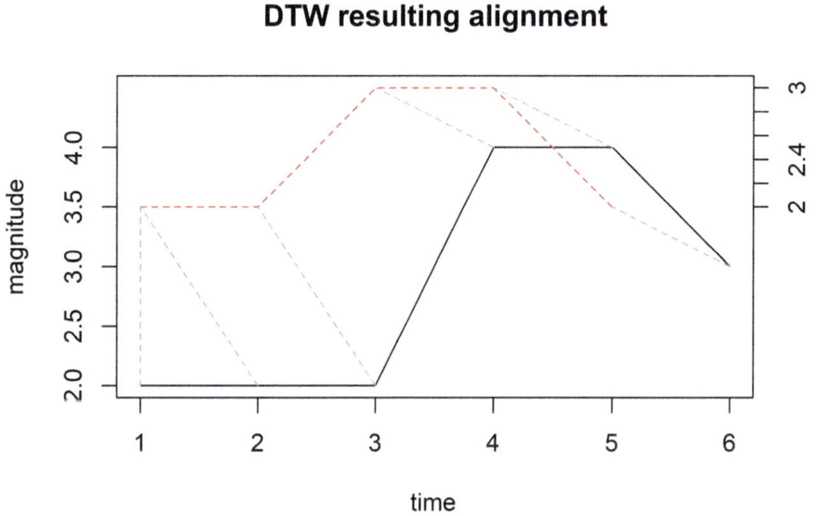

FIGURE 2.19 DTW alignment between the query and reference sequences (solid line is the query).

The problem of aligning two sequences can be formalized as follows [Rabiner and Juang, 1993]. Let X and Y be two sequences:

$$X = (x_1, x_2, \dots, x_{T_x})$$
$$Y = (y_1, y_2, \dots, y_{T_y})$$

where x_i and y_i are vectors. In the previous example, the vectors only have one element since the sequences are 1-dimensional, but DTW also works with multidimensional sequences. T_x and T_y are the sequences' lengths. Let

$$d(i_x, i_y)$$

be the *dissimilarity* (distance) between vectors x_i and y_i (e.g., Euclidean distance). Then, ϕ_x and ϕ_y are the warping functions that relate i_x and i_y to a common axis k:

$$i_x = \phi_x(k), k = 1, 2, \dots, T$$
$$i_y = \phi_y(k), k = 1, 2, \dots, T.$$

The total dissimilarity between the two sequences is:

$$d_\phi(X, Y) = \sum_{k=1}^{T} d\left(\phi_x(k), \phi_y(k)\right) \tag{2.14}$$

The aim is to find the warping function ϕ that minimizes the total dissimilarity:

$$\min_{\phi} d_\phi(X, Y) \tag{2.15}$$

The solution can be efficiently computed using dynamic programming. Usually, when solving this minimization problem, some constraints are applied:

- **Endpoint constraints.** This constraint makes sure that the first and last elements of each sequence are connected (mapped to each other).

$$\phi_x(1) = 1, \phi_y(1) = 1$$
$$\phi_x(T) = T_x, \phi_y(T) = T_y$$

- **Monotonicity.** This constraint allows 'time to flow' only from left to right. That is, we cannot go back in time.

$$\phi_x(k+1) \geq \phi_x(k)$$
$$\phi_y(k+1) \geq \phi_y(k)$$

- **Local constraints.** For example, allow jumps of at most 1 step.

$$\phi_x(k+1) - \phi_x(k) \leq 1$$
$$\phi_y(k+1) - \phi_y(k) \leq 1$$

Also, it is possible to apply global constraints, other local constraints, and apply different weights to slopes but the three described above are the most common ones. For a comprehensive list of constraints, please see [Rabiner and Juang, 1993]. Now let's get back to our example and go through the steps to compute the dissimilarity and warping functions between our query (Q) and reference (R) sequences:

$$Q = (2, 2, 2, 4, 4, 3)$$
$$R = (2, 2, 3, 3, 2)$$

The first step is to compute a *local cost matrix*. This is just a matrix that contains the distance between every pair of points between the two sequences. For this example, we will use the *Manhattan distance*. Since our sequences are 1-dimensional this distance can be computed as the absolute difference $|x_i - y_i|$. Figure 2.20 shows the resulting local cost matrix.

For example, position $(1, 1) = 0$ (*row,column*) because the first element of Q is 2 and the first element of R is also 2, thus, $|2 - 2| = 0$. The rest of the matrix is filled in the same way. In dynamic programming, partial results are computed and stored in a table. Figure 2.21 shows the final dynamic programming table computed from the local cost matrix. Initially, this table is empty. We start to fill it from bottom left at position $(1, 1)$. From the local cost matrix, the cost at position $(1, 1)$ is 0 so the cost at that position in the dynamic programming table is 0. Then we can start filling in the contiguous cells. The only direction from which we can arrive at position $(1, 2)$ is from the west (W). The cost at position $(1, 2)$ from the local cost matrix is 0 and the cost of the *minimum* of the cell from the west $(1, 1)$ is also 0. So $W : 0 + 0 = 0$. For each cell we add the current cost plus the minimum cost when coming

Local cost matrix: $|x_i - y_i|$

R						
5	0	0	0	2	2	1
4	1	1	1	1	1	0
3	1	1	1	1	1	0
2	0	0	0	2	2	1
1	0	0	0	2	2	1
	1	**2**	**3**	**4**	**5**	**6**

Q

FIGURE 2.20 Local cost matrix between Q and R.

from the contiguous cell. The minimum costs are marked with red. For some cells it is possible to arrive from three different directions: S, W, and SW, thus we need to compute the cost when coming from each of those. The final minimum cost at position $(5, 6)$ is 3. Thus, that is the global DTW distance. In the example, it is possible to get the minimum at $(5, 6)$ when arriving from the south or southwest.

Dynamic programming table

R						
5	S:2	S:2 W:2 SW:2	S:2 W:2 SW:2	S:4 W:4 SW:4	S:4 W:6 SW:4	S:3 W:5 SW:3
4	S:2	S:2 W:3 SW:2	S:2 W:3 SW:2	S:2 W:3 SW:2	S:3 W:3 SW:2	S:2 W:2 SW:2
3	S:1	S:1 W:2 SW:1	S:1 W:2 SW:1	S:3 W:2 SW:1	S:5 W:2 SW:3	S:5 W:2 SW:4
2	S:0	S:0 W:0 SW:0	S:0 W:0 SW:0	S:4 W:2 SW:2	S:6 W:4 SW:4	S:6 W:5 SW:5
1	0	W:0	W:0	W:2	W:4	W:5
	1	**2**	**3**	**4**	**5**	**6**

Q

S: south, W: west, SW: southwest

FIGURE 2.21 Dynamic programming table.

Once the table is filled in, we can backtrack starting at $(5, 6)$ to find the warping functions. Figure 2.22 shows the final warping functions. Because of the endpoint constraints, we know that $\phi_Q(1) = 1, \phi_R(1) = 1, \phi_Q(6) = 6,$ and $\phi_R(6) = 5$. Then, from $(5, 6)$ the minimum contiguous value is 2 coming from SW, thus $\phi_Q(5) = 5, \phi_R(5) = 4$, and so on. Note that we could also have chosen to arrive from the south with the same minimum value of 2 but still this would have resulted in the same overall distance. The dashed line in figure 2.21 shows the full backtracking.

ϕ_Q	1	2	3	4	5	6
ϕ_R	1	1	2	3	4	5

FIGURE 2.22 Resulting warping functions.

The runtime complexity of DTW is $O(T_x T_y)$. This is the required time to compute the local cost matrix and the dynamic programming table.

In R, the `dtw` package [Giorgino, 2009] has the function `dtw()` to compute the DTW distance between two sequences. Let's use this package to solve the previous example.

```
library("dtw")

# Sequences from the example
query <- c(2,2,2,4,4,3)
ref <- c(2,2,3,3,2)

# Find dtw distance.
alignment <- dtw(query, ref,
                 step = symmetric1, keep.internals = T)
```

The `keep.internals = T` keeps the input data so it can be accessed later, e.g., for plotting. The cost matrix and final distance can be accessed from the resulting object. The `step` argument specifies a step pattern. A step pattern describes some of the algorithm constraints such as endpoint and local constraints. In this case, we use `symmetric1` which applies the constraints explained before. We can access the cost matrix, the final distance, and the warping functions ϕ_x and ϕ_y as follows:

```
alignment$localCostMatrix
#>      [,1] [,2] [,3] [,4] [,5]
#> [1,]    0    0    1    1    0
#> [2,]    0    0    1    1    0
#> [3,]    0    0    1    1    0
#> [4,]    2    2    1    1    2
#> [5,]    2    2    1    1    2
#> [6,]    1    1    0    0    1

alignment$distance
#> [1] 3

alignment$index1
#> [1] 1 2 3 4 5 6

alignment$index2
#> [1] 1 1 2 3 4 5
```

The local cost matrix is the same one as in Figure 2.20 but in rotated form. The resulting object also has the dynamic programming table which can be plotted along with the resulting backtracking (see Figure 2.23).

```
ccm <- alignment$costMatrix
image(x = 1:nrow(ccm), y = 1:ncol(ccm),
      ccm, xlab = "Q", ylab = "R")
text(row(ccm), col(ccm), label = ccm)
lines(alignment$index1, alignment$index2)
```

And finally, the aligned sequences can be plotted. The previous Figure 2.19 shows the result of the following command.

```
plot(alignment, type="two", off=1.5,
     match.lty=2,
     match.indices=10,
     main="DTW resulting alignment",
     xlab="time", ylab="magnitude")
```

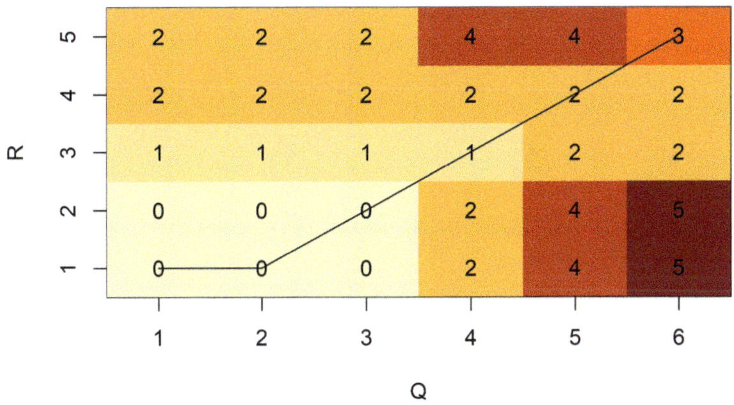

FIGURE 2.23 Dynamic programming table and backtracking.

2.5.1 Hand Gesture Recognition

`hand_gestures.R`, `hand_gestures_auxiliary.R`

Gestures are a form of communication. They are often accompanied with speech but can also be used to communicate something independently of speech (like in sign language). Gestures allow us to externalize and emphasize emotions and thoughts. They are based on body movements from arms, hands, fingers, face, head, etc. Gestures can be used as a non-verbal way to identify and study behaviors for different purposes such as for emotion [De Gelder, 2006] or for the identification of developmental disorders like autism [Anzulewicz et al., 2016].

Gestures can also be used to develop user-computer interaction applications. The following video shows an example application of gesture recognition for domotics.

Link to video: `https://youtu.be/47-35YmimN4`

The application determines the indoor location using k-NN as it was shown in this chapter. The gestures are classified using DTW (I'll show

how to do it in a moment). Based on the location and type of gesture, an specific home appliance is activated. I programmed that app some time ago using the same algorithms presented here.

To demonstrate how DTW can be used for hand gesture recognition, we will examine the *HAND GESTURES* dataset that was collected with a smartphone using its accelerometer sensor. The data was collected by 10 individuals who performed 5 repetitions of 10 different gestures (*'triangle'*, *'square'*, *'circle'*, *'a'*, *'b'*, *'c'*, *'1'*, *'2'*, *'3'*, *'4'*). The sensor is a tri-axial accelerometer that returns values for the x, y, and z axes. The participants were not instructed to hold the smartphone in any particular way. The sampling rate was set at 50 Hz. To record a gesture, the user presses the phone's screen with her/his thumb, performs the gesture in the air, and stops pressing the screen after the gesture is complete. Figure 2.24 shows the start and end positions of the 10 gestures.

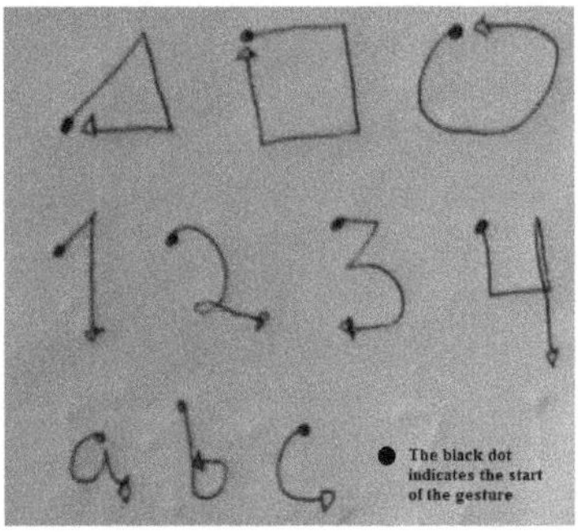

FIGURE 2.24 Paths for the 10 considered gestures.

In order to make the recognition orientation-independent, we can compute the *magnitude* of the 3 accelerometer axes. This will provide us with the overall movement patterns regardless of orientation.

$$Magnitude(t) = \sqrt{a_x(t)^2 + a_y(t)^2 + a_z(t)^2} \tag{2.16}$$

where $a_x(t)$, $a_y(t)$, and $a_z(t)$ are the accelerations at time t.

Figure 2.25 shows the raw accelerometer values (dashed lines) for a *triangle* gesture. The solid line shows the resulting magnitude. This will also simplify things since we will now work with 1-dimensional sequences (the magnitudes) instead of the other 3 axes.

The gestures are stored in text files that contain the x, y, and z recordings. The script `hand_gestures_auxiliary.R` has some auxiliary functions

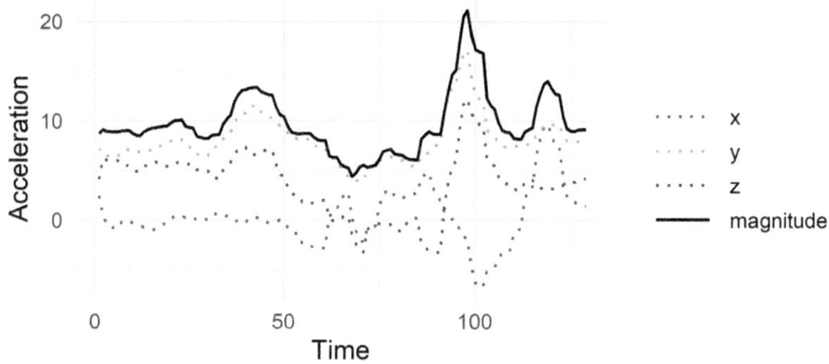

FIGURE 2.25 Triangle gesture.

to preprocess the data. Since the sequences of each gesture are of varying length, storing them as a data frame could be problematic because data frames have fixed sizes. Instead, the `gen.instances()` function processes the files and returns all hand gestures as a list. This function also computes the magnitude (equation (2.16)). The following code (from `hand_gestures.R`) calls the `gen.instances()` function and stores the results in the `instances` variable which is a list. Then, we select the first and second instances to be the query and the reference.

```
# Format instances from files.
instances <- gen.instances("../data/hand_gestures/")

# Use first instance as the query.
query <- instances[[1]]

# Use second instance as the reference.
ref <- instances[[2]]
```

Each element in `instances` is also a list that stores the *type* and *values* (magnitude) of each gesture.

```
# Print their respective classes
print(query$type)
```

```
#> [1] "1"

print(ref$type)
#> [1] "1"
```

Here, the first two instances are of type *'1'*. We can also print the magnitude values.

```
# Print values.
print(query$values)
#> [1]  9.167477  9.291464  9.729926  9.901090  ....
```

In this case, both classes are "1". We can use the `dtw()` function to compute the similarity between the *query* and the *reference* instance and plot the resulting alignment (Figure 2.26).

```
alignment <- dtw(query$values, ref$values, keep = TRUE)

# Print similarity (distance)
alignment$distance
#> [1] 68.56493

# Plot result.
plot(alignment, type="two", off=1, match.lty=2, match.indices=40,
     main="DTW resulting alignment",
     xlab="time", ylab="magnitude")
```

To perform the actual classification, we will use our well-known k-NN classifier with $k = 1$. To classify a *query instance*, we need to compute its DTW distance to every other instance in the training set and predict the label from the closest one. We will test the performance using 10-fold cross-validation. Since computing all DTW distances takes some time, we can precompute all pairs of distances and store them in a matrix. The auxiliary function `matrix.distances()` does the job. Since this can take some minutes, the results are saved so there is no need to wait next time the code is run.

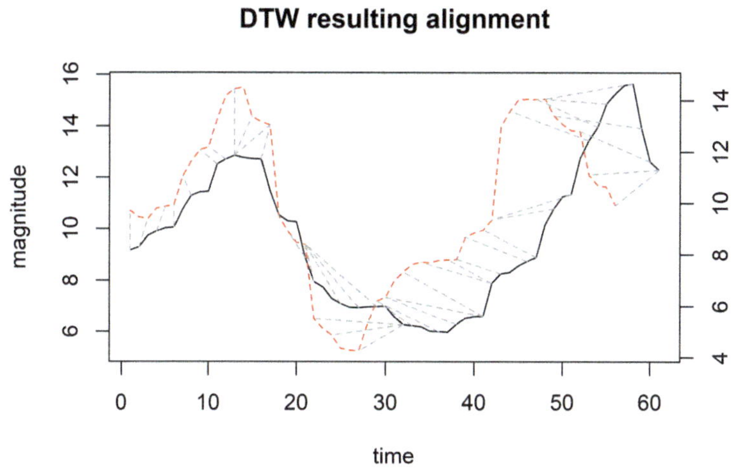

FIGURE 2.26 Resulting alignment.

```
D <- matrix.distances(instances)

# Save results.
save(D, file="D.RData")
```

The `matrix.distances()` returns a list. The first element is an array with the gestures' classes and the second element is the actual distance matrix. The elements in the diagonal are set to `Inf` to signal that we don't want to take into account the dissimilarity between a gesture and itself.

For convenience, this matrix is already stored in the file `D.RData` located this chapter's code directory. The following code performs the 10-fold cross-validation and computes the performance results.

```
# Load the DTW distances matrix.
load("D.RData")
set.seed(1234)
k <- 10 # Number of folds.
folds <- sample(k, size = length(D[[1]]), replace = T)
predictions <- NULL
```

```
groundTruth <- NULL

# Implement k-NN with k=1.
for(i in 1:k){

  trainSet <- which(folds != i)
  testSet <- which(folds == i)
  train.labels <- D[[1]][trainSet]

  for(query in testSet){

    type <- D[[1]][query]
    distances <- D[[2]][query, ][trainSet]

    # Return the closest one.
    nn <- sort(distances, index.return = T)$ix[1]
    pred <- train.labels[nn]
    predictions <- c(predictions, pred)
    groundTruth <- c(groundTruth, type)

  }
} # end of for
```

The line `distances <- D[[2]][query, ][trainSet]` retrieves the pre-computed distances between the test *query* and all gestures in the train set. Then, those distances are sorted in ascending order and the class of the closest one is used as the prediction. Finally, the performance is calculated.

```
cm <- confusionMatrix(factor(predictions),
                      factor(groundTruth))

# Compute performance metrics per class.
cm$byClass[,c("Recall", "Specificity", "Precision", "F1")]
#>                 Recall Specificity Precision        F1
#> Class: 1          0.84   0.9911111 0.9130435 0.8750000
#> Class: 2          0.84   0.9866667 0.8750000 0.8571429
```

```
#> Class: 3            0.96    0.9911111 0.9230769 0.9411765
#> Class: 4            0.98    0.9933333 0.9423077 0.9607843
#> Class: a            0.78    0.9733333 0.7647059 0.7722772
#> Class: b            0.76    0.9955556 0.9500000 0.8444444
#> Class: c            0.90    1.0000000 1.0000000 0.9473684
#> Class: circleLeft   0.78    0.9622222 0.6964286 0.7358491
#> Class: square       1.00    0.9977778 0.9803922 0.9900990
#> Class: triangle     0.92    0.9711111 0.7796610 0.8440367

# Overall performance metrics
colMeans(cm$byClass[,c("Recall", "Specificity",
                       "Precision", "F1")])
#>     Recall Specificity   Precision          F1
#>  0.8760000   0.9862222   0.8824616   0.8768178
```

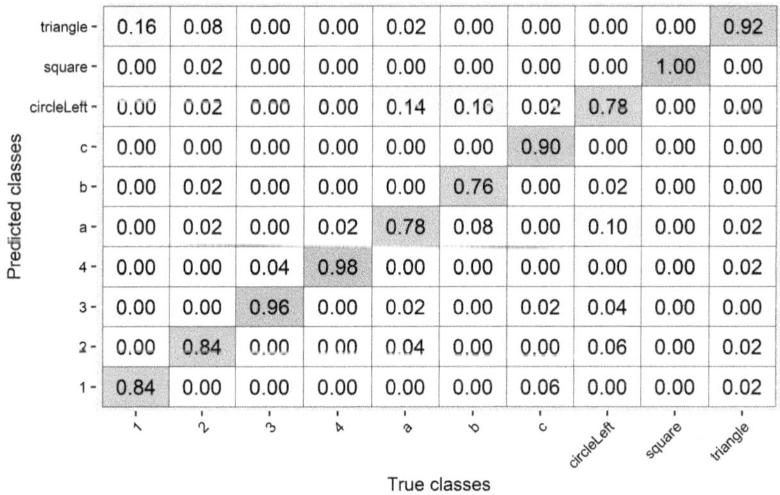

FIGURE 2.27 Confusion matrix for hand gestures' predictions.

The overall recall was 0.87 which is not bad. From the confusion matrix (Figure 2.27), we can see that the class *'a'* was often confused with *'circleLeft'* and vice versa. This makes sense since both have similar motions (see Figure 2.24). Also, *'b'* was often confused with *'circleLeft'*. The *'square'* class was always correctly classified. This example demonstrated how DTW can be used with k-NN to recognize hand gestures.

2.6 Dummy Models

```
dummy_classifiers.R
```

When faced with a new problem, you may be tempted to start trying to solve it by using a complex model. Then, you proceed to train your complex model and evaluate it. The results look reasonably good so you think you are done. However, this good performance could only be an *illusion*. Sometimes there are underlying problems with the data that can give the false impression that a model is performing well. Examples of such problems are imbalanced datasets, no correlation between the features and the classes, features not containing enough information, etc. **Dummy models** can be used to spot some of those problems. Dummy models use little or no information at all when making predictions (we'll see how in a moment).

Furthermore, for some problems (specially in regression) it is not clear what is considered to be a good performance. There are problems in which doing slightly better than random is considered a great achievement (e.g., in forecasting) but for other problems that would be unacceptable. Thus, we need some type of baseline to assess whether or not a particular model is bringing some benefit. Dummy models are not only used to spot problems but can be used as baselines as well.

Dummy models are also called *baseline models* or *dumb models*. One student I was supervising used to call them *stupid models*. When I am angry, I also call them like that, but today I'm in a good mood so I'll refer to them as *dummy*.

Now, I will present three types of dummy classifiers and how they can be implemented in R.

2.6.1 Most-frequent-class Classifier

As the name implies, the most-frequent-class classifier always predicts the most frequent label found in the train set. This means that the model does not even need to look at the features! Once it is presented with a new instance, it just outputs the most common class as the prediction.

To show how it can be implemented, I will use the *SMARTPHONES ACTIVITIES* dataset. For demonstration purposes, I will only keep two classes: *'Walking'* and *'Upstairs'*. Furthermore, I will only pick a small percent of the instances with class *'Upstairs'* to simulate an imbalanced dataset. Imbalanced means that there are classes for which only a few instances exist. More about imbalanced data and how to handle it will be covered in chapter 5. After those modifications, we can check the class counts:

```
# Print class counts.
table(dataset$class)
#> Upstairs  Walking
#>      200     2081

# In percentages.
table(dataset$class) / nrow(dataset)
#>   Upstairs    Walking
#> 0.08768084 0.91231916
```

We can see that more than 90% of the instances belong to class *'Walking'*. It's time to define the dummy classifier!

```
# Define the dummy classifier's train function.
most.frequent.class.train <- function(data){

  # Get a table with the class counts.
  counts <- table(data$class)

  # Select the label with the most counts.
  most.frequent <- names(which.max(counts))
```

```
  return(most.frequent)
}
```

The `most.frequent.class.train()` function will learn the parameters from a train set. The only thing this model needs to learn is what is the most frequent class. First, the `table()` function is used to get the class counts and then the name of the class with the max counts is returned. Now we define the predict function which takes as its first argument the learned parameters and as second argument the test set on which we want to make predictions. The parameter only consists of the name of a class.

```
# Define the dummy classifier's predict function.
most.frequent.class.predict <- function(params, data){

  # Return the same label for as many rows as there are in data.
  return(rep(params, nrow(data)))

}
```

The only thing the predict function does is to return the `params` argument that contains the class name repeated n times. Where n is the number of rows in the test data frame.

Let's try our functions. The dataset has already been split into 50% for training and 50% for testing. First we train the dummy model using the train set. Then, the learned parameter is printed.

```
# Learn the parameters.
dummy.model1 <- most.frequent.class.train(trainset)

# Print the learned parameter.
dummy.model1
#> [1] "Walking"
```

Now we can make predictions on the test set and compute the accuracy.

```
# Make predictions.
predictions <- most.frequent.class.predict(dummy.model1, testset)

# Compute confusion matrix and other performance metrics.
cm <- confusionMatrix(factor(predictions, levels),
                      factor(testset$class, levels))

# Print accuracy
cm$overall["Accuracy"]
#>  Accuracy
#>  0.9087719
```

The accuracy was 90.8%. It seems that the dummy classifier was not that dummy after all! Let's print the confusion matrix to inspect the predictions.

```
# Print confusion matrix.
cm$table

#>             Reference
#> Prediction Walking Upstairs
#>   Walking     1036      104
#>   Upstairs       0        0
```

From the confusion matrix we can see that all *'Walking'* activities were correctly classified but none of the *'Upstairs'* classes were identified. This is because the dummy model only predicts *'Walking'*. Here we can see that even though it seemed like the dummy model was doing pretty good, it was not that good after all.

We can now try with a decision tree from the `rpart` package.

```
### Let's try with a decision tree
treeClassifier <- rpart(class ~ ., trainset)

tree.predictions <- predict(treeClassifier, testset, type = "class")
```

```
cm.tree <- confusionMatrix(factor(tree.predictions, levels),
                           factor(testset$class, levels))

# Print accuracy
cm.tree$overall["Accuracy"]
#>  Accuracy
#> 0.9263158
```

Decision trees are more powerful than dummy classifiers but the accuracy was very similar!

It is a good practice to compare powerful models against dummy models. If their performances are similar, this may be an indication that there is something that needs to be checked. In this example, the problem was that the dataset was imbalanced. It is also adivisable to report not only the accuracy but other metrics. We could also have noted the imbalance problem by looking at the recall of the individual classes, for example.

2.6.2 Uniform Classifier

This is another type of dummy classifier. This one predicts classes at random with equal probability and can be implemented as follows.

```
# Define the dummy classifier's train function.
uniform.train <- function(data){

  # Get the unique classes.
  unique.classes <- unique(data$class)

  return(unique.classes)
}

# Define the dummy classifier's predict function.
```

```
uniform.predict <- function(params, data){

  # Sample classes uniformly.
  return(sample(unique.classes, size = nrow(data), replace = T))

}
```

At prediction time, it just picks a random label for each instance in the test set. This model achieved an accuracy of only 49.0% using the same dataset, but it correctly identified more classes of type *'Upstairs'*.

```
#>           Reference
#> Prediction Walking Upstairs
#>   Walking      506       54
#>   Upstairs     530       50
```

If a dataset is balanced and the accuracy of the uniform classifier is similar to the more complex model, the problem may be that the features are not providing enough information. That is, the complex classifier was not able to extract any useful patterns from the features.

2.6.3 Frequency-based Classifier

This one is similar to the uniform classifier but the probability of choosing a class is proportional to its frequency in the train set. Its implementation is similar to the uniform classifier but makes use of the `prob` parameter in the `sample()` function to specify weights for each class. The higher the weight for a class, the more probable it will be chosen at prediction time. The implementation of this one is in the script `dummy_classifiers.R`.

The frequency-based classifier achieved an accuracy of 85.5%. Much lower than the most-frequent-class model (90.8%) but it was able to detect some of the *'Upstairs'* classes.

2.6.4 Other Dummy Classifiers

Another dummy model that can be used for classification is to apply simple thresholds.

```
if(feature1 < threshold)
  return("A")
else
  return("B")
```

In fact, the previous rule can be thought of as a very simple decision tree with only one root node. Surprisingly, sometimes simple rules can be difficult to beat by more complex models. In this section I've been focusing on classification problems, but dummy models can also be constructed for **regression**. The simplest one would be to predict the mean value of y regardless of the feature values. Another dummy model could predict a random value between the min and max of y. If there is a categorical feature, one could predict the mean value based on the category. In fact, that is what we did in chapter 1 in the simple regression example.

In summary, one can construct any type of dummy model depending on the application. The takeaway is that dummy models allow us to assess how more complex models perform with respect to some baselines and help us to detect possible problems in the data and features. What I typically do when solving a problem is to start with simple models and/or rules and then, try more complex models. Of course, manual thresholds and simple rules can work remarkably well in some situations but they are not scalable. Depending on the use case, one can just implement the simple solution or go for something more complex if the system is expected to grow or be used in more general ways.

2.7 Summary

This chapter focused on **classification** models. Classifiers predict a category based on the input features. Here, it was demonstrated how classifiers can be used to detect indoor locations, classify activities, and hand gestures.

- **k-Nearest Neighbors (k-NN)** predicts the class of a test point as the majority class of the k nearest neighbors.
- Some classification performance metrics are **recall**, **specificity**, **precision**, **accuracy**, **F1-score**, etc.
- **Decision trees** are easy-to-interpret classifiers trained recursively based on feature importance (for example, purity).
- **Naive Bayes** is a type of classifier where features are assumed to be independent.
- **Dynamic Time Warping (DTW)** computes the similarity between two timeseries after aligning them in time. This can be used for classification for example, in combination with k-NN.
- **Dummy models** can help to spot possible errors in the data and can also be used as baselines.

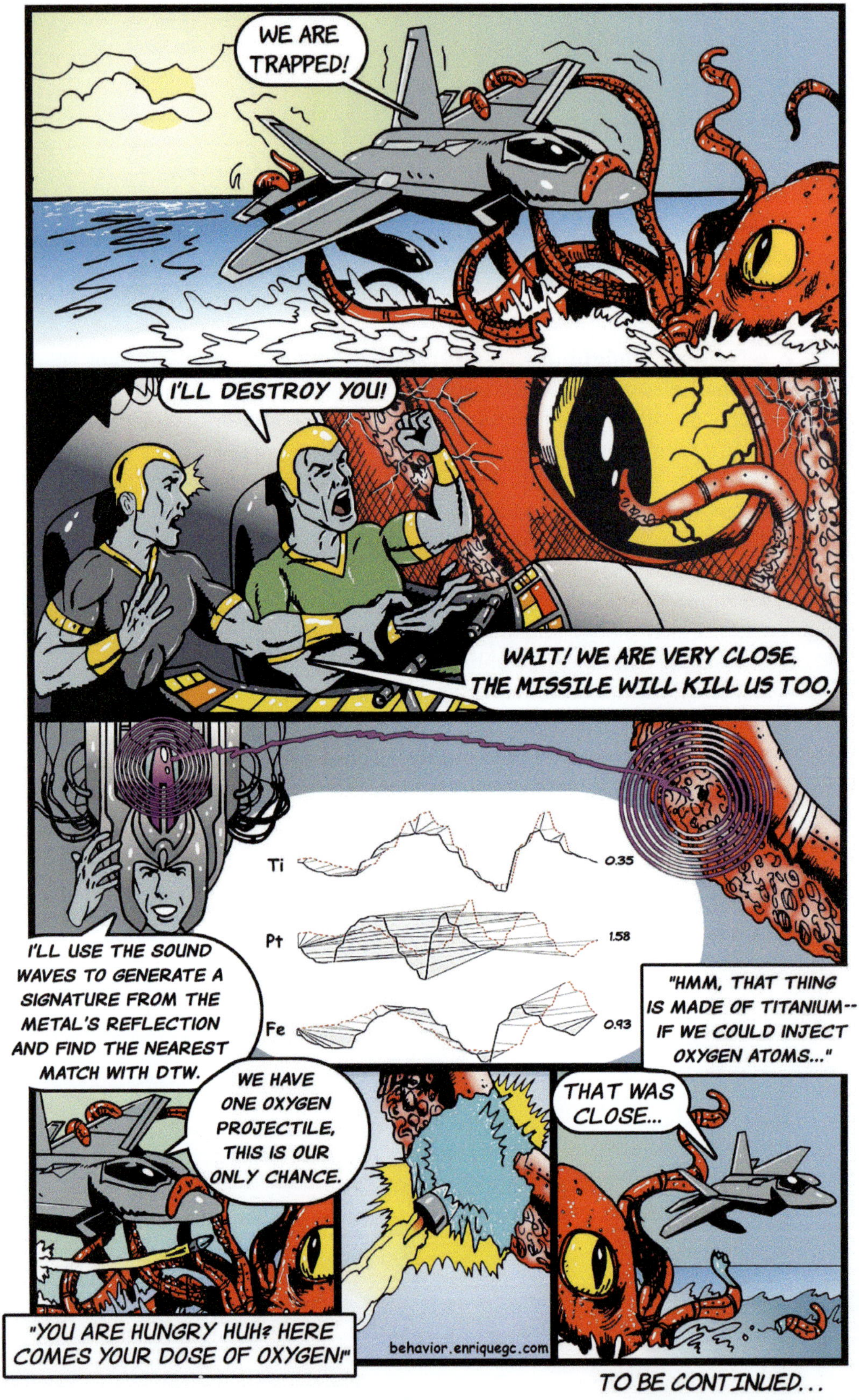
WE ARE TRAPPED!
I'LL DESTROY YOU!
WAIT! WE ARE VERY CLOSE. THE MISSILE WILL KILL US TOO.
Ti
0.35
Pt
1.58
Fe
0.93
I'LL USE THE SOUND WAVES TO GENERATE A SIGNATURE FROM THE METAL'S REFLECTION AND FIND THE NEAREST MATCH WITH DTW.
"HMM, THAT THING IS MADE OF TITANIUM-- IF WE COULD INJECT OXYGEN ATOMS..."
WE HAVE ONE OXYGEN PROJECTILE, THIS IS OUR ONLY CHANCE.
THAT WAS CLOSE...
"YOU ARE HUNGRY HUH? HERE COMES YOUR DOSE OF OXYGEN!"
behavior.enriquegc.com
TO BE CONTINUED...

3

Predicting Behavior with Ensemble Learning

In the previous chapters, we have been building single models, either for classification or regression. With **ensemble learning**, the idea is to train several models and combine their results to increase the performance. Usually, ensemble methods outperform single models. In the context of *ensemble learning*, the individual models whose results are to be combined are known as **base learners**. Base learners can be of the same type (homogeneous) or of different types (heterogeneous). Examples of ensemble methods are **Bagging**, **Random Forest**, and **Stacked Generalization**. In the following sections, the three of them will be described and example applications in behavior analysis will be presented as well.

3.1 Bagging

Bagging stands for "bootstrap aggregating" and is an ensemble learning method proposed by Breiman [1996]. Ummm..., *Bootstrap, aggregating?* Let's start with the *aggregating* part. As the name implies, this method is based on training several *base learners* (e.g., decision trees) and combining their outputs to produce a single final prediction. One way to combine the results is by taking the majority vote for classification tasks or the average for regression. In an ideal case, we would have enough data to train each *base learner* with an independent train set. However, in practice we may only have a single train set of limited size. Training several *base learners* with the same train set is equivalent to having a single learner, provided that the training procedure of the base learners is deterministic. Even if the training procedure is not deterministic, the resulting models might be very similar. What we would like to have is accurate base learners but at the same time they should be diverse. Then,

DOI: 10.1201/9781003203469-3

how can those base learners be trained? Well, this is where the *bootstrap* part comes into play.

Bootstrapping means generating new train sets by sampling instances with replacement from the original train set. If the original train set has N instances, the method selects N instances at random to produce a new train set. *With replacement* means that repeated instances are allowed. This has the effect of generating a new train set of size N by removing some instances and duplicating other instances. By using this method, n different train sets can be generated and used to train n different learners.

It has been shown that having more diverse base learners increases performance. One way to generate diverse learners is by using different train sets as just described. In his original work, Breiman [1996] used decision trees as base learners. Decision trees are considered to be very unstable. This means that small changes in the train set produce very different trees – but this is a good thing for bagging! Most of the time, the aggregated predictions will produce better results than the best individual learner from the ensemble.

Figure 3.1 shows bootstrapping in action. The train set is sampled with replacement 3 times. The numbers represent indices to arbitrary train instances. Here, we can see that in the first sample, the instance number 5 is missing but instead, instance 2 is duplicated. All samples have five elements. Then, each sample is used to train individual decision trees.

One of the disadvantages of ensemble methods is their higher computational cost both during training and inference. Another disadvantage of ensemble methods is that they are more difficult to interpret. Still, there exist model agnostic interpretability methods [Molnar, 2019] that can help to analyze the results. In the next section, I will show you how to implement your own Bagging model with decision trees in R.

3.1.1 Activity Recognition with Bagging

```
bagging_activities.R iterated_bagging_activities.R
```

In this section, we will implement Bagging with decision trees. Then, we will test our implementation on the *SMARTPHONE*

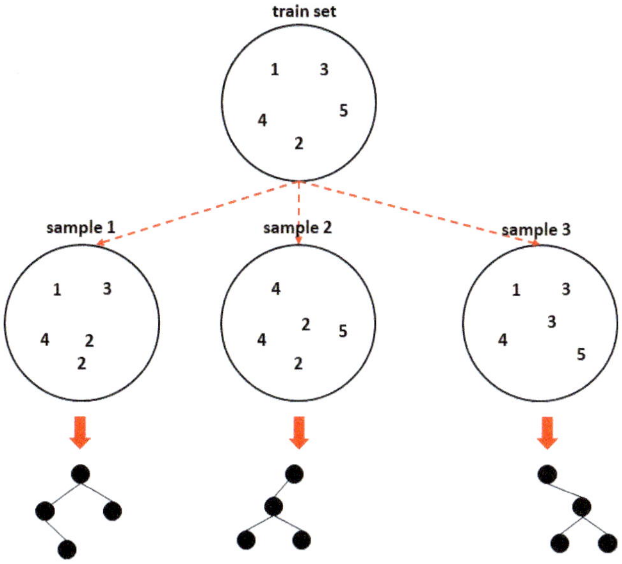

FIGURE 3.1 Bagging example.

ACTIVITIES dataset. The following code snippet shows the implementation of the `my_bagging()` function. The complete code is in the script `bagging_activities.R`. The function accepts three arguments. The first one is the formula, the second one is the train set, and the third argument is the number of base learners (10 by default). Here, we will use the `rpart` package to train the decision trees.

```
# Define our bagging classifier.
my_bagging <- function(theFormula, data, ntrees = 10){

  N <- nrow(data)

  # A list to store the individual trees
  models <- list()

  # Train individual trees and add each to 'models' list.
  for(i in 1:ntrees){

    # Bootstrap instances from data.
```

```
    idxs <- sample(1:N, size = N, replace = T)

    bootstrappedInstances <- data[idxs,]

    treeModel <- rpart(as.formula(theFormula),
                       bootstrappedInstances,
                       xval = 0,
                       cp = 0)

    models <- c(models, list(treeModel))
  }

  res <- structure(list(models = models),
                   class = "my_bagging")

  return(res)
}
```

First, a list that will store each individual learner is defined `models <- list()`. Then, the function iterates `ntrees` times. In each iteration, a bootstrapped train set is generated and used to train a `rpart` model. The `xval = 0` parameter tells rpart not to perform cross-validation internally. The `cp` parameter is also set to 0. This value controls the amount of pruning. The default is 0.01 leading to smaller trees. This makes the trees to be more similar but since we want diversity we are setting this to 0 so bigger trees are generated and as a consequence, more diverse.

Finally, an object of class `"my_bagging"` is returned. This is just a list containing the trained base learners. The `class = "my_bagging"` argument is important. It tells R that this object is of type `my_bagging`. Setting the class will allow us to use the generic `predict()` function, and R will automatically call the corresponding `predict.my_bagging()` function which we will shortly define. The class name and the function name after `predict.` need to be the same.

```
# Define the predict function for my_bagging.
predict.my_bagging <- function(object, newdata){
```

```
  ntrees <- length(object$models)
  N <- nrow(newdata)

  # Matrix to store predictions for each instance
  # in newdata and for each tree.
  M <- matrix(data = rep("",N * ntrees), nrow = N)

  # Populate matrix.
  # Each column of M contains all predictions for a given tree.
  # Each row contains the predictions for a given instance.
  for(i in 1:ntrees){
    m <- object$models[[i]]
    tmp <- as.character(predict(m, newdata, type = "class"))
    M[,i] <- tmp
  }

  # Final predictions
  predictions <- character()

  # Iterate through each row of M.
  for(i in 1:N){
    # Compute class counts
    classCounts <- table(M[i,])

    # Get the class with the most counts.
    predictions <- c(predictions,
                     names(classCounts)[which.max(classCounts)])
  }
  return(predictions)
}
```

Now let's dissect the `predict.my_bagging()` function. First, note that the function name starts with `predict.` followed by the type of object. Following this convention will allow us to call `predict()` and R will call the corresponding method based on the class of the object. The first argument `object` is an object of type "my_bagging" as returned by `my_bagging()`. The second argument `newdata` is the test set we want to generate predictions for. A matrix `M` that will store the predictions for each tree is defined. This matrix has N rows and $ntrees$ columns where N is the number of instances in `newdata` and *ntrees* is the number of trees. Thus, each column stores the predictions for each of the base learners. This function iterates through each base learner (rpart in this case), and makes a prediction for each instance in `newdata`. Then, the results are stored in matrix `M`. Finally, it iterates through each instance and computes the most common predicted class from the base learners.

Let's test our Bagging function! We will test it with the activity recognition dataset introduced in section 2.3.1 and set the number of trees to 10. The following code shows how to use our bagging functions to train the model and make predictions on a test set.

```
baggingClassifier <- my_bagging(class ~ ., trainSet, ntree = 10)
predictions <- predict(baggingClassifier, testSet)
```

The following will perform 5-fold cross-validation and print the results.

```
set.seed(1234)
k <- 5
folds <- sample(k, size = nrow(df), replace = TRUE)

# Variable to store ground truth classes.
groundTruth <- NULL

# Variable to store the classifier's predictions.
predictions <- NULL

for(i in 1:k){
  trainSet <- df[which(folds != i), ]
  testSet <- df[which(folds == i), ]
  treeClassifier <- my_bagging(class ~ ., trainSet, ntree = 10)
  foldPredictions <- predict(treeClassifier, testSet)
  predictions <- c(predictions, as.character(foldPredictions))
  groundTruth <- c(groundTruth, as.character(testSet$class))
}
cm <- confusionMatrix(as.factor(predictions), as.factor(groundTruth))

# Print accuracy
```

```
cm$overall["Accuracy"]
#> Accuracy
#> 0.861388

# Print other metrics per class.
cm$byClass[,c("Recall", "Specificity", "Precision", "F1")]
#>                      Recall Specificity Precision        F1
#> Class: Downstairs 0.5378788   0.9588957 0.5855670 0.5607108
#> Class: Jogging    0.9618462   0.9820722 0.9583078 0.9600737
#> Class: Sitting    0.9607843   0.9982394 0.9702970 0.9655172
#> Class: Standing   0.9146341   0.9988399 0.9740260 0.9433962
#> Class: Upstairs   0.5664557   0.9563310 0.6313933 0.5971643
#> Class: Walking    0.9336857   0.9226850 0.8827806 0.9075199

# Print average performance metrics across classes.
colMeans(cm$byClass[,c("Recall", "Specificity", "Precision", "F1")])
#>    Recall Specificity   Precision          F1
#> 0.8125475   0.9695105   0.8337286   0.8223970
```

The accuracy was much better now compared to 0.789 from the previous chapter without using Bagging!

The effect of adding more trees to the ensemble can also be analyzed. The script `iterated_bagging_activities.R` does 5-fold cross-validation as we just did but starts with 1 tree in the ensemble and repeats the process by adding more trees until 50.

Figure 3.2 shows the effect on the train and test accuracy with different number of trees. Here, we can see that 3 trees already produce a significant performance increase compared to 1 or 2 trees. This makes sense since having only 2 trees does not add additional information. If the two trees produce different predictions then, it becomes a random choice between the two labels. In fact, 2 trees produced worse results than 1 tree. But we cannot make strong conclusions since the experiment was run only once. One possibility to break ties when there are only two trees is to use the averaged probabilities of each label. rpart can return those probabilities by setting `type = "prob"` in the `predict()` function which is the default behavior. This is left as an exercise for the reader. In the following section, Random Forest will be described which is a way of introducing more diversity to the base learners.

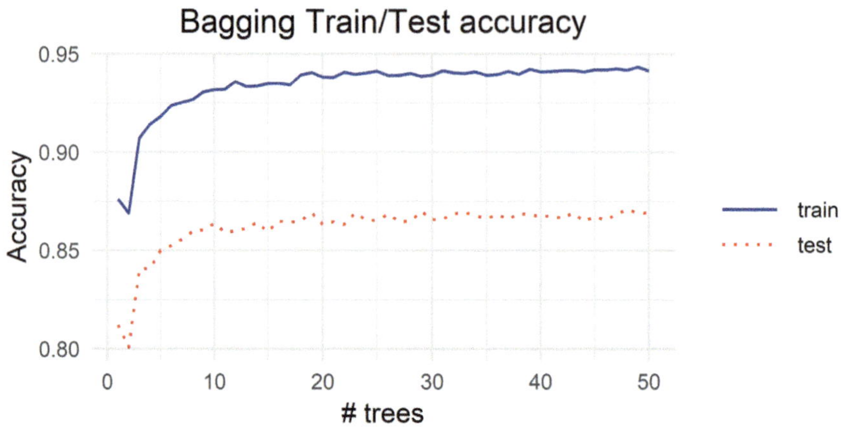

FIGURE 3.2 Bagging results for different number of trees.

3.2 Random Forest

```
rf_activities.R iterated_rf_activities.R iterated_bagging_rf.R
```

A Random Forest can be thought of as an extension of Bagging. Random Forests were proposed by Breiman [2001] and as the name implies, they introduce more randomness to the individual trees. This is with the objective of having decorrelated trees. With Bagging, most of the trees are very similar at the root because the most important variables are selected first (see chapter 2). To avoid this happening, a simple modification can be introduced. When building a tree, instead of evaluating all features at each split to find the most important one (based on some purity measure like *information gain*), a random subset of the features (usually $\sqrt{|features|}$) is sampled. This simple modification produces more decorrelated trees and in general, it results in better performance compared to Bagging.

In R, the most famous library that implements Random Forest is..., yes you guessed it: `randomForest` [Liaw and Wiener, 2002]. The following code snippet shows how to fit a Random Forest with 10 trees.

```
library(randomForest)
rf <- randomForest(class ~ ., trainSet, ntree = 10)
```

By default, `ntree = 500`. Among other things, you can control how many random features are sampled at each split with the `mtry` argument. By default, for classification `mtry = floor(sqrt(ncol(x)))` and for regression `mtry = max(floor(ncol(x)/3), 1)`.

The following code performs 5-fold cross-validation with the activities dataset already stored in `df` and prints the results. The complete code can be found in the script `randomForest_activities.R`.

```
set.seed(1234)

k <- 5

folds <- sample(k, size = nrow(df), replace = TRUE)

# Variable to store ground truth classes.
groundTruth <- NULL

# Variable to store the classifier's predictions.
predictions <- NULL

for(i in 1:k){

  trainSet <- df[which(folds != i), ]
  testSet <- df[which(folds == i), ]

  rf <- randomForest(class ~ ., trainSet, ntree = 10)

  foldPredictions <- predict(rf, testSet)

  predictions <- c(predictions, as.character(foldPredictions))

  groundTruth <- c(groundTruth, as.character(testSet$class))
}
```

```
cm <- confusionMatrix(as.factor(predictions), as.factor(groundTruth))

# Print accuracy
cm$overall["Accuracy"]
#>Accuracy
#> 0.870801

# Print other metrics per class.
cm$byClass[,c("Recall", "Specificity", "Precision", "F1")]
#>                      Recall Specificity Precision        F1
#> Class: Downstairs 0.5094697    0.9652352 0.6127563 0.5563599
#> Class: Jogging    0.9784615    0.9831268 0.9613059 0.9698079
#> Class: Sitting    0.9803922    0.9992175 0.9868421 0.9836066
#> Class: Standing   0.9512195    0.9990333 0.9790795 0.9649485
#> Class: Upstairs   0.5363924    0.9636440 0.6608187 0.5921397
#> Class: Walking    0.9543489    0.9151933 0.8752755 0.9131034

# Print other metrics overall.
colMeans(cm$byClass[,c("Recall", "Specificity", "Precision", "F1")])
#>      Recall Specificity   Precision          F1
#>  0.8183807   0.9709083   0.8460130   0.8299943
```

Those results are better than the previous ones with Bagging. Figure 3.3 shows the results when doing 5-fold cross-validation for different number of trees (the complete script is in `iterated_randomForest_activities.R`). From these results, we can see a similar behavior as Bagging. That is, the accuracy increases very quickly and then it stabilizes.

If we directly compare Bagging vs. Random Forest, Random Forest outperforms Bagging (Figure 3.4). The complete code to generate the plot is in the script `iterated_bagging_rf.R`.

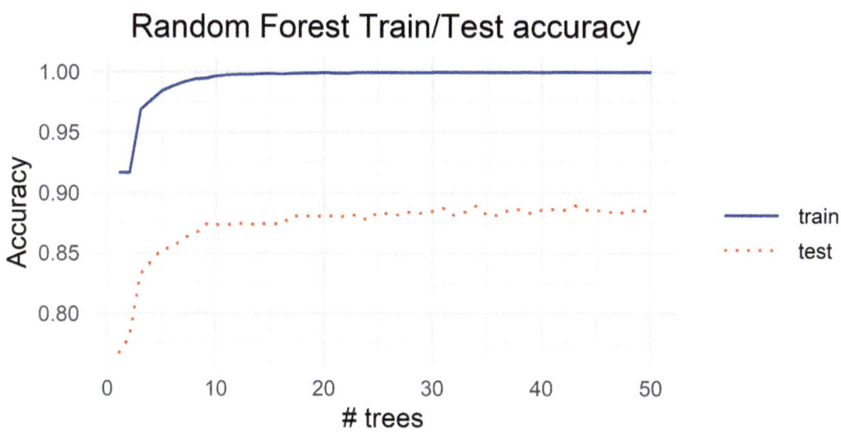

FIGURE 3.3 Random Forest results for different number of trees.

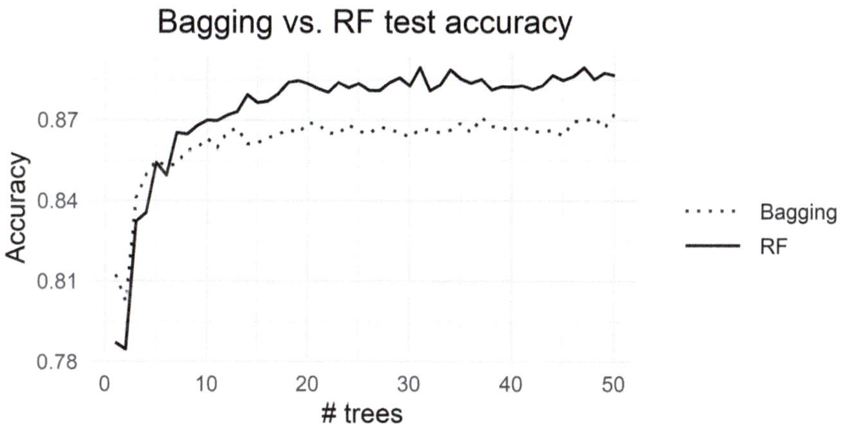

FIGURE 3.4 Bagging vs. Random Forest.

3.3 Stacked Generalization

Stacked Generalization (a.k.a *Stacking*) is a powerful ensemble learning method proposed by Wolpert [1992]. The method consists of training a set of **powerful** base learners (*first-level learners*) and combining their outputs by *stacking* them to form a new train set. The base learners' outputs are their predictions and optionally, the class probabilities of those predictions. The predictions of the base learners are known as the **meta-features**. The meta-features along with their true labels y are used to build a new train set that is used to train a **meta-learner**. The rationale behind this is that the predictions themselves contain information that can be used by the *meta-learner.*

The procedure to train a Stacking model is as follows:

1. Define a set of first level-learners $\mathscr{L}$ and a *meta-learner.*
2. Train the first-level learners $\mathscr{L}$ with training data $\mathbf{D}$.
3. Predict the classes of $\mathbf{D}$ with each learner in $\mathscr{L}$. Each learner produces a predictions vector $\mathbf{p}_i$ with $|\mathbf{D}|$ elements each.
4. Build a matrix $\mathbf{M}_{|\mathbf{D}|\times|\mathscr{L}|}$ by column binding (stacking) the prediction vectors. Then, add the true labels $\mathbf{y}$ to generate the new train set $\mathbf{D}'$.
5. Train the *meta-learner* with $\mathbf{D}'$.
6. Output the final stacking model $\mathcal{S} :< \mathscr{L}, meta\text{-}learner >$.

Figure 3.5 shows the procedure to generate the new training data $\mathbf{D}'$ used to train the *meta-learner.*

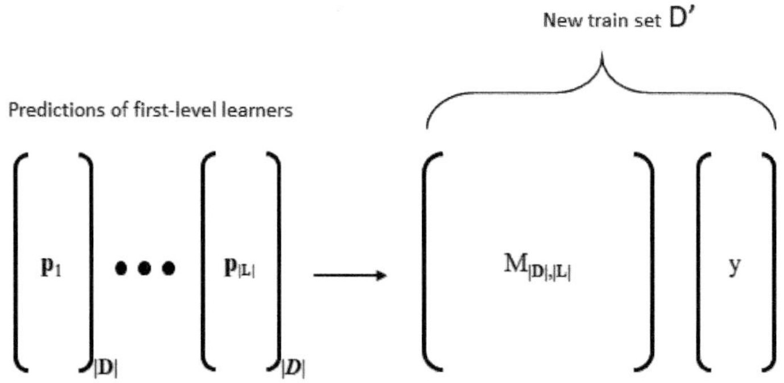

FIGURE 3.5 Process to generate the new train set D' by column-binding the predictions of the first-level learners and adding the true labels. (Reprinted from *Information Fusion* Vol. 40, Enrique Garcia-Ceja, Carlos E. Galván-Tejada, and Ramon Brena, "Multi-view stacking for activity recognition with sound and accelerometer data" pp. 45-56, Copyright 2018, with permission from Elsevier, doi: `https://doi.org/10.1016/j.inffus.2017.06.004`.)

Note that steps 2 and 3 can lead to overfitting because the predictions are made with the same data used to train the models. To avoid this, steps 2 and 3 are usually performed using k-fold cross-validation. After $\mathbf{D}'$ has been generated, the learners in $\mathscr{L}$ can be retrained using all data in $\mathbf{D}$.

Ting and Witten [1999] showed that the performance can increase by adding confidence information about the predictions. For example, the probabilities produced by the first-level learners. Most classifiers can output probabilities.

At prediction time, each first-level learner predicts the class, and optionally, the class probabilities of a given instance. These predictions are used to form a feature vector (*meta-features*) that is fed to the *meta-learner* to obtain the final prediction. Usually, first-level learners are high performing classifiers such as Random Forests, Support Vector Machines, Neural Networks, etc. The *meta-learner* should also be a powerful classifier.

In the next section, I will introduce *Multi-view Stacking* which is similar to Generalized Stacking except that each first-level learner is trained with features from a different *view*.

3.4 Multi-view Stacking for Home Tasks Recognition

`stacking_algorithms.R stacking_activities.R`

Multi-view learning refers to the case when an instance can be characterized by two or more independent 'views'. For example, one can extract features for webpage classification from a webpage's text but also from the links pointing to it. Usually, there is the assumption that the views are independent and each is sufficient to solve the problem. Then, why combine them? In many cases, each different view provides additional and complementary information, thus, allowing to train better models.

The simplest thing one can do is to extract features from each view, aggregate them, and train a single model. This approach usually works well but has some limitations. Each view may have different statistical properties, thus, different types of models may be needed for each view. When aggregating features from all views, new variable correlations may be introduced which could impact the performance. Another limitation is that features need to be in the same format (feature vectors, images, etc.), so they can be aggregated.

For video classification, we could have two views. One represented by sequences of images, and the other by the corresponding audio. For the video part, we could encode the features as the images themselves, i.e., matrices. Then, a Convolutional Neural Network (covered in chapter 8) could be trained directly from those images. For the audio part, statistical features can be extracted and stored as normal feature vectors. In this case, the two representations (views) are different. One is a matrix and the other a one-dimensional feature vector. Combining them to train a single classifier could be problematic given the nature of the views and their different encoding formats. Instead, we can train two models, one for each view and then combine the results. This is precisely the idea of *Multi-view Stacking* [Garcia-Ceja et al., 2018a]. Train a different model for each view and combine the outputs like in *Stacking*.

Here, *Multi-view Stacking* will be demonstrated using the *HOME TASKS* dataset. This dataset was collected from two sources. Acceleration and audio. The acceleration was recorded with a wrist-band watch and the audio using a cellphone. This dataset consists of 7 common home tasks: *'mop floor'*, *'sweep floor'*, *'type on computer keyboard'*, *'brush teeth'*, *'wash hands'*, *'eat chips'*, and *'watch t.v.'*. Three volunteers performed each activity for approximately 3 minutes.

The acceleration and audio signals were segmented into 3-second windows. From each window, different features were extracted. From the acceleration, 16 features were extracted from the 3 axes (x,y,z) such as mean, standard deviation, maximum values, mean magnitude, area under the curve, etc. From the audio signals, 12 features were extracted, namely, Mel Frequency Cepstral Coefficients (MFCCs). To preserve volunteers' privacy, the original audio was not released. The dataset already contains the extracted features from acceleration and audio. The first column is the label.

In order to implement *Multi-view Stacking*, two Random Forests will be trained, one for each view (acceleration and audio). The predicted outputs will be stacked to form the new training set D' and a Random Forest trained with D' will act as the *meta-learner*.

The next code snippet taken from `stacking_algorithms.R` shows the multi-view stacking function implemented in R.

```
mvstacking <- function(D, v1cols, v2cols, k = 10){

  # Generate folds for internal cross-validation.
  folds <- sample(1:k, size = nrow(D), replace = T)

  trueLabels <- NULL
  predicted.v1 <- NULL # predicted labels with view 1
  predicted.v2 <- NULL # predicted labels with view 2
  probs.v1 <- NULL # predicted probabilities with view 1
  probs.v2 <- NULL # predicted probabilities with view 2

  # Perform internal cross-validation.
  for(i in 1:k){

    train <- D[folds != i, ]
    test <- D[folds == i, ]
    trueLabels <- c(trueLabels, as.character(test$label))

    # Train learner with view 1 and make predictions.
    m.v1 <- randomForest(label ~.,
                         train[,c("label",v1cols)], nt = 100)
    raw.v1 <- predict(m.v1, newdata = test[,v1cols], type = "prob")
    probs.v1 <- rbind(probs.v1, raw.v1)
    pred.v1 <- as.character(predict(m.v1,
                                    newdata = test[,v1cols],
                                    type = "class"))
    predicted.v1 <- c(predicted.v1, pred.v1)

    # Train learner with view 2 and make predictions.
    m.v2 <- randomForest(label ~.,
                         train[,c("label",v2cols)], nt = 100)
    raw.v2 <- predict(m.v2, newdata = test[,v2cols], type = "prob")
    probs.v2 <- rbind(probs.v2, raw.v2)
    pred.v2 <- as.character(predict(m.v2,
                                    newdata = test[,v2cols],
                                    type = "class"))
```

```
    predicted.v2 <- c(predicted.v2, pred.v2)
  }

  # Build first-order learners with all data.
  learnerV1 <- randomForest(label ~.,
                            D[,c("label",v1cols)], nt = 100)
  learnerV2 <- randomForest(label ~.,
                            D[,c("label",v2cols)], nt = 100)

  # Construct meta-features.
  metaFeatures <- data.frame(label = trueLabels,
                             ((probs.v1 + probs.v2) / 2),
                             pred1 = predicted.v1,
                             pred2 = predicted.v2)

  #train meta-learner
  metalearner <- randomForest(label ~.,
                              metaFeatures, nt = 100)

  res <- structure(list(metalearner=metalearner,
                        learnerV1=learnerV1,
                        learnerV2=learnerV2,
                        v1cols = v1cols,
                        v2cols = v2cols),
                   class = "mvstacking")

  return(res)
}
```

The first argument `D` is a data frame containing the training data. `v1cols` and `v2cols` are the column names of the two views. Finally, argument `k` specifies the number of folds for the internal cross-validation to avoid overfitting (Steps 2 and 3 as described in the generalized stacking procedure).

The function iterates through each fold and trains a Random Forest with the train data for each of the two views. Within each iteration, the trained models are used to predict the labels and probabilities on the internal test set. Predicted labels and probabilities on the internal test sets are concatenated across all folds (`predicted.v1`, `predicted.v2`).

After cross-validation, the meta-features are generated by creating a data frame with the predictions of each view. Additionally, the average of class probabilities is added as a meta-feature. The true labels are also added. The purpose of cross-validation is to avoid overfitting but at the end, we do not want to waste data so both learners are re-trained with all data `D`.

Finally, the *meta-learner* which is also a Random Forest is trained with the *meta-features* data frame. A list with all the required information to make predictions is created. This includes first-level learners, the meta-learner, and the column names for each view so we know how to divide the data frame into two views at prediction time.

The following code snippet shows the implementation for making predictions using a trained stacking model.

```
predict.mvstacking <- function(object, newdata){

  # Predict probabilities with view 1.
  raw.v1 <- predict(object$learnerV1,
                    newdata = newdata[,object$v1cols],
                    type = "prob")

  # Predict classes with view 1.
  pred.v1 <- as.character(predict(object$learnerV1,
                                  newdata = newdata[,object$v1cols],
                                  type = "class"))

  # Predict probabilities with view 2.
  raw.v2 <- predict(object$learnerV2,
                    newdata = newdata[,object$v2cols],
                    type = "prob")

  # Predict classes with view 2.
  pred.v2 <- as.character(predict(object$learnerV2,
                                  newdata = newdata[,object$v2cols],
                                  type = "class"))
```

```
  # Build meta-features
  metaFeatures <- data.frame(((raw.v1 + raw.v2) / 2),
                             pred1 = pred.v1,
                             pred2 = pred.v2)

  # Set levels on factors to avoid errors in randomForest predict.
  levels(metaFeatures$pred1) <- object$metalearner$classes
  levels(metaFeatures$pred2) <- object$metalearner$classes

  predictions <- as.character(predict(object$metalearner,
                                      newdata = metaFeatures),
                              type="class")

  return(predictions)
}
```

The `object` parameter is the trained model and `newdata` is a data frame from which we want to make the predictions. First, labels and probabilities are predicted using the two views. Then, a data frame with the *meta-features* is assembled with the predicted label and the averaged probabilities. Finally, the *meta-learner* is used to predict the final classes using the *meta-features*.

The script `stacking_activities.R` shows how to use our `mvstacking()` function. With the following two lines we can train and make predictions.

```
m.stacking <- mvstacking(trainset, v1cols, v2cols, k = 10)
pred.stacking <- predict(m.stacking, newdata = testset[,-1])
```

The script performs 10-fold cross-validation and for the sake of comparison, it builds three models. One with only audio features, one with only acceleration features, and the Multi-view Stacking one combining both types of features.

Table 3.1 shows the results for each view and with Multi-view Stacking. Clearly, combining both views with Multi-view Stacking achieved the best results compared to using a single view.

TABLE 3.1 Stacking results.

	Accuracy	Recall	Specificity	Precision	F1
Audio	0.8463	0.8414	0.9741	0.8488	0.8439
Accelerometer	0.8586	0.8494	0.9765	0.8548	0.8512
Multi-view Stacking	0.9394	0.9349	0.9899	0.9372	0.9358

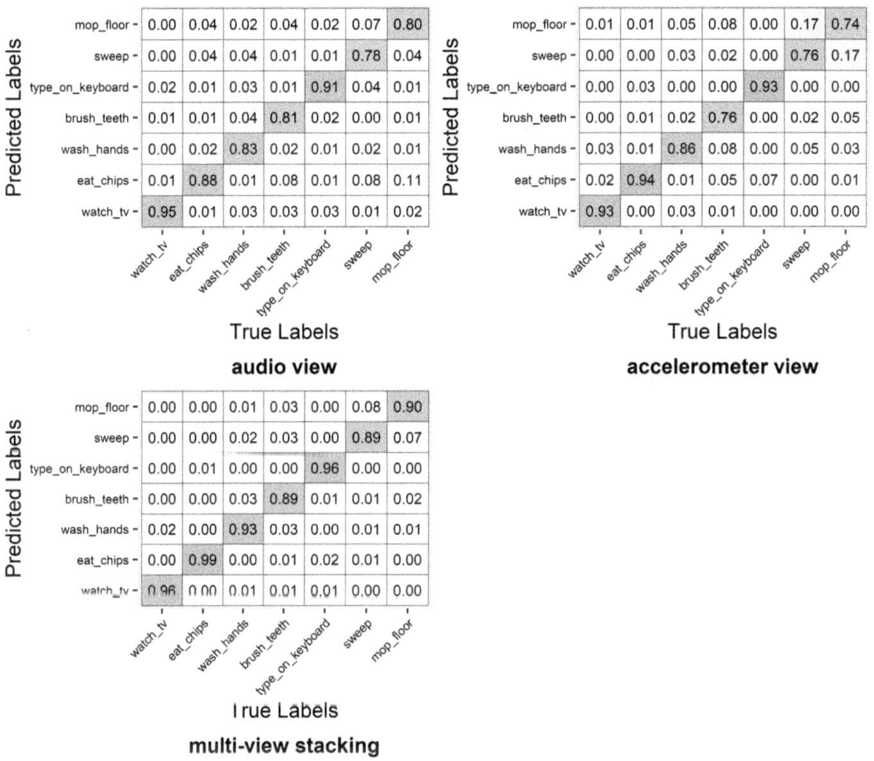

FIGURE 3.6 Confusion matrices.

Figure 3.6 shows the resulting confusion matrices for the three cases. By looking at the recall (anti-diagonal) of the individual classes, it seems that audio features are better at recognizing some activities like *'sweep'* and *'mop floor'* whereas the accelerometer features are better for classifying *'eat chips'*, *'wash hands'*, *'type on keyboard'*, etc. thus, those two views are somehow complementary. All recall values when using Multi-view Stacking are higher than for any of the other views.

3.5 Summary

In this chapter, several ensemble learning methods were introduced. In general, ensemble models perform better than single models.

- The main idea of ensemble learning is to train several models and combine their results.
- **Bagging** is an ensemble method consisting of n *base-learners*, each, trained with bootstrapped training samples.
- **Random Forest** is an ensemble of trees. It introduces randomness to the trees by selecting random features in each split.
- Another ensemble method is called **stacked generalization**. It consists of a set of *base-learners* and a *meta-learner*. The later is trained using the outputs of the *base-learners*.
- **Multi-view learning** can be used when an instance can be represented by two or more *views* (for example, different sensors).

behavior.enriquegc.com

4

Exploring and Visualizing Behavioral Data

EDA.R

Exploratory data analysis (EDA) refers to the process of understanding your data. There are several available methods and tools for doing so, including summary statistics and visualizations. In this chapter, I will cover some of them. As mentioned in section 1.5, data exploration is one of the first steps of the data analysis pipeline. It provides valuable input to the decision process during the next data analysis phases, for example, the selection of preprocessing tasks and predictive methods. Even though there already exist several EDA techniques, you are not constrained by them. You can always apply any means that you think will allow you to better understand your data and gain new insights.

4.1 Talking with Field Experts

Sometimes you will be involved in the whole data analysis process starting with the idea, defining the research questions, hypotheses, conducting the data collection, and so on. In those cases, it is easier to understand the initial structure of the data since you might had been the one responsible for designing the data collection protocol.

Unfortunately (or fortunately for some), it is often the case that you are already given a dataset. It may have some documentation or not. In those cases, it becomes important to talk with the field experts that designed the study and the data collection protocol to understand what was the purpose and motivation of each piece of data. Again, it is often not easy to directly have access to those who conducted the initial study.

DOI: 10.1201/9781003203469-4

One of the reasons may be that you found the dataset online and maybe the project is already over. In those cases, you can try to contact the authors. I have done that several times and they were very responsive. It is also a good idea to try to find experts in the field even if they were not involved in the project. This will allow you to understand things from their perspective and possibly to explain patterns/values that you may find later in the process.

4.2 Summary Statistics

After having a better understanding of how the data was collected and the meaning of each variable, the next step is to find out how the actual data looks like. It is always a good idea to start looking at some summary statistics. This provides general insights about the data and will help you in selecting the next preprocessing steps. In R, an easy way to do this is with the `summary()` function. The following code reads the *SMARTPHONE ACTIVITIES* dataset and due to limited space, only prints a summary of the first 5 columns, column 33, 35, and the last one (the class).

```
# Read activities dataset.
dataset <- read.csv(file.path(datasets_path,
                              "smartphone_activities",
                              "WISDM_ar_v1.1_raw.txt"),
                              stringsAsFactors = T)
# Print first 5 columns,
# column 33, 35 and the last one (the class).
summary(dataset[,c(1:5,33,35,ncol(dataset))])

#> UNIQUE_ID          user               X0                  X1
#> Min.   :  1.0   Min.   : 1.00   Min.   :0.00000   Min.   :0.00000
#> 1st Qu.:136.0   1st Qu.:10.00   1st Qu.:0.06000   1st Qu.:0.07000
#> Median :271.0   Median :19.00   Median :0.09000   Median :0.10000
#> Mean   :284.4   Mean   :18.87   Mean   :0.09414   Mean   :0.09895
#> 3rd Qu.:412.0   3rd Qu.:28.00   3rd Qu.:0.12000   3rd Qu.:0.12000
#> Max.   :728.0   Max.   :36.00   Max.   :1.00000   Max.   :0.81000
#>
```

```
#> X2                XAVG          ZAVG              class
#> Min.    :0.00000  Min.    :0    ?0.22   :  29   Downstairs: 528
#> 1st Qu.:0.08000   1st Qu.:0    ?0.21   :  27   Jogging   :1625
#> Median :0.10000   Median :0    ?0.11   :  26   Sitting   : 306
#> Mean   :0.09837   Mean   :0    ?0.13   :  26   Standing  : 246
#> 3rd Qu.:0.12000   3rd Qu.:0    ?0.16   :  26   Upstairs  : 632
#> Max.    :0.95000  Max.    :0    ?0.23   :  26   Walking   :2081
#> (Other):5258
```

For numerical variables, the output includes some summary statistics like the *min*, *max*, *mean*, etc. For factor variables, the output is different. It displays the unique values with their respective counts. If there are more than six unique values, the rest is omitted. For example, the **class** variable (the last one) has 528 instances with the value *'Downstairs'*. By looking at the *min* and *max* values of the numerical variables, we see that those are not the same for all variables. For some variables, their maximum value is 1, for others, it is less than 1 and for some others, it is greater than 1. It seems that the variables are not in the same scale. This is important because some algorithms are sensitive to different scales. In chapters 2 and 3, we mainly used decision-tree-based algorithms which are not sensitive to different scales, but some others like neural networks are. In chapter 5, a method to transform variables into the same scale will be introduced.

It is good practice to check the *min* and *max* values of all variables to see if they have different ranges since some algorithms are sensitive to different scales.

The output of the `summary()` function also shows some strange values. The statistics of the variable *XAVG* are all 0*s*. Some other variables like *ZAVG* were encoded as characters and it seems that the *'?'* symbol is appended to the numbers. In summary, the `summary()` function (I know, too many summaries in this sentence), allowed us to spot some errors in the dataset. What we do with that information will depend on the domain and application.

4.3 Class Distributions

When it comes to behavior sensing, many of the problems can be modeled as classification tasks. This means that there are different possible categories to choose from. It is often a good idea to plot the class counts (class distribution). The following code shows how to do that for the *SMARTPHONE ACTIVITIES* dataset. First, the `table()` method is used to get the actual class counts. Then, the plot is generated with `ggplot` (see Figure 4.1).

```
t <- table(dataset$class)
t <- as.data.frame(t)
colnames(t) <- c("class","count")

p <- ggplot(t, aes(x=class, y=count, fill=class)) +
  geom_bar(stat="identity", color="black") +
  theme_minimal() +
  geom_text(aes(label=count), vjust=-0.3, size=3.5) +
  scale_fill_brewer(palette="Set1")

print(p)
```

The most common activity turned out to be *'Walking'* with 2081 instances. It seems that the volunteers were a bit sporty since *'Jogging'* is the second most frequent activity. One thing to note is that there are some big differences here. For example, *'Walking'* vs. *'Standing'*. Those differences in class counts can have an impact when training classification models. This is because classifiers try to minimize the overall error regardless of the performance of individual classes, thus, they tend to prioritize the majority classes. This is called the **class imbalance problem**. This occurs when there are many instances of some classes but fewer of some other classes. For some applications this can be a problem. For example, in fraud detection, datasets have many legitimate transactions but just a few of illegal ones. This will bias a classifier to be good at detecting legitimate transactions but what we are really interested in is in detecting the illegal transactions. This is something

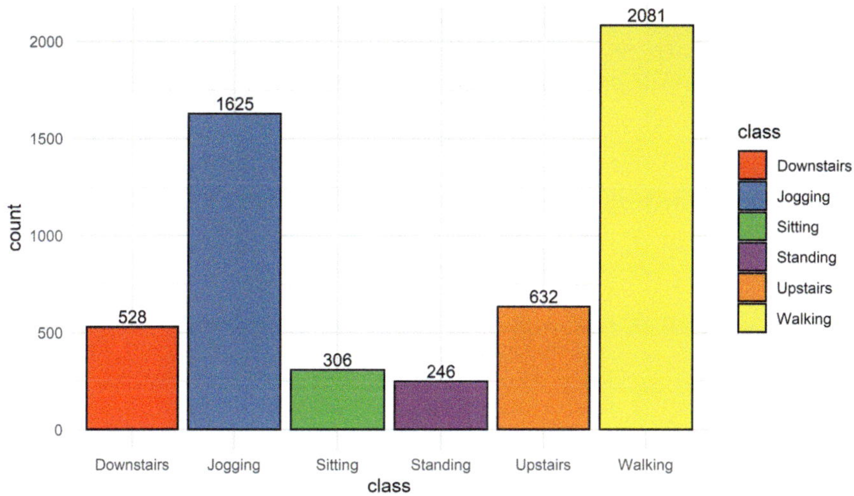

FIGURE 4.1 Distribution of classes.

very common to find in behavior sensing datasets. For example in the medical domain, it is much easier to collect data from healthy controls than from patients with a given condition. In chapter 5, some of the oversampling techniques that can be used to deal with the class imbalance problem will be presented.

When the classes are imbalanced, it is also recommended to validate the generalization performance using *stratified subsets*. This means that when dividing the dataset into train and test sets, the distribution of classes should be preserved. For example, if the dataset has class *'A'* and *'B'* and 80% of the instances are of type *'A'* then both, the train set and the test set should have 80% of their instances of type *'A'*. In cross-validation, this is known as **stratified cross-validation**.

4.4 User-class Sparsity Matrix

In behavior sensing, usually two things are involved: *individuals* and *behaviors*. Individuals will express different behaviors to different extents.

For the activity recognition example, some persons may go jogging frequently while others may never go jogging at all. Some behaviors will be present or absent depending on each individual. We can plot this information with what I call a **user-class sparsity matrix**. Figure 4.2 shows this matrix for the activities dataset. The code to generate this plot is included in the script `EDA.R`.

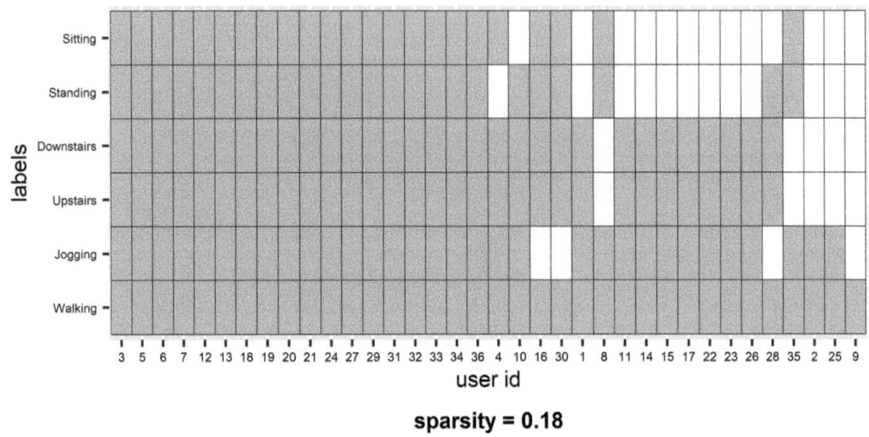

FIGURE 4.2 User-class sparsity matrix.

The x-axis shows the user ids and the y-axis the classes. A colored entry (gray in this case) means that the corresponding user has at least one associated instance of the corresponding class. For example, user 3 performed all activities and thus, the dataset contains at least one instance for each of the six activities. On the other hand, user 25 only has instances for two activities. Users are sorted in descending order (users that have more classes are at the left). At the bottom of the plot, the sparsity is shown (0.18). This is just the percentage of empty cells in the matrix. When all users have at least one instance of every class the sparsity is 0. When the sparsity is different from 0, one needs to decide what to do depending on the application. The following cases are possible:

- Some users did not perform all activities. If the classifier was trained with, for example, 6 classes and a user never goes *'jogging'*, the classifier may still sometimes predict *'jogging'* even if a particular user never does that. This can degrade the predictions' performance for that particular user and can be worse if that user never performs other activities. A possible solution is to train different classifiers with different class subsets. If you know that some users never go *'jogging'* then you train a classifier that excludes *'jogging'* and use that one for that set of users. The disadvantage of this is that there are many possible combinations so you need to train many models. Since several classifiers can generate prediction scores and/or probabilities per class, another solution would be to train a single model with all classes and predict the most probable class excluding those that are not part of a particular user.

- Some users can have unique classes. For example, suppose there is a new user that has an activity labeled as *'Eating'* which no one else has, and thus, it was not included during training. In this situation, the classifier will never predict *'Eating'* since it was not trained for that activity. One solution could be to add the new user's data with the new labels and retrain the model. But if not too many users have the activity *'Eating'* then, in the worst case, they will die from starvation. In a less severe case, the overall system performance can degrade because as the number of classes increases, it becomes more difficult to find separation boundaries between categories, thus, the models become less accurate. Another possible solution is to build **user-dependent** models for each user. These, and other types of models in **multi-user settings** will be covered in chapter 9.

4.5 Boxplots

Boxplots are a good way to visualize the relationship between variables and classes. R already has the `boxplot()` function. In the *SMARTPHONE ACTIVITIES* dataset, the *RESULTANT* variable represents the 'total amount of movement' considering the three axes [Kwapisz et al., 2010]. The following code displays a set of boxplots (one for each class) with respect to the *RESULTANT* variable (Figure 4.3).

```
boxplot(RESULTANT ~ class, dataset)
```

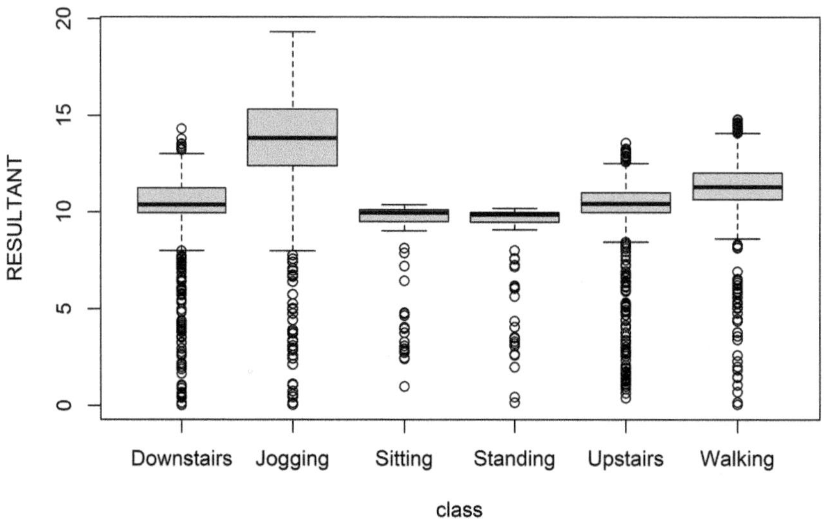

FIGURE 4.3 Boxplot of RESULTANT variable across classes.

The solid black line in the middle of each box marks the *median*[1]. Overall, we can see that this variable can be good at separating high-intensity activities like jogging, walking, etc. from low-intensity ones like sitting or standing. With boxplots we can inspect one feature at a time. If you want to visualize the relationship between predictors, correlation plots can be used instead. Correlation plots will be presented in the next subsection.

4.6 Correlation Plots

Correlation plots are useful for visualizing the relationships between pairs of variables. The most common type of relationship is the **Pearson correlation**. The Pearson correlation measures the degree of **linear** association between two variables. It takes values between −1 and 1. A

[1]For a more complete explanation about boxplots please see: `https://towardsdatascience.com/understanding-boxplots-5e2df7bcbd51`

correlation of 1 means that as one of the variables increases, the other one does too. A value of -1 means that as one of the variables increases, the other decreases. A value of 0 means that there is no association between the variables. Figure 4.4 shows several examples of correlation values. Note that the correlations of the examples at the bottom are all 0s. Even though there are some noticeable patterns in some of the examples, their correlation is 0 because those relationships are not linear.

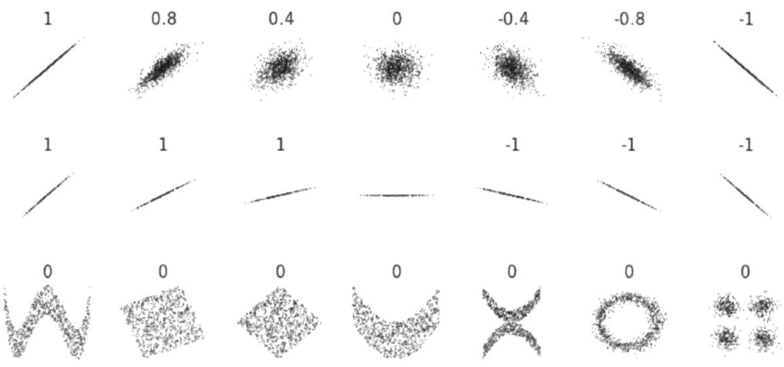

FIGURE 4.4 Pearson correlation examples. (Author: Denis Boigelot. Source: Wikipedia (CC0 1.0)).

The Pearson correlation (denoted by r) between two variables x and y can be calculated as follows:

$$r = \frac{\sum_{i=1}^{n}(x_i - \bar{x})(y_i - \bar{y})}{\sqrt{\sum_{i=1}^{n}(x_i - \bar{x})^2}\sqrt{\sum_{i=1}^{n}(y_i - \bar{y})^2}} \tag{4.1}$$

The following code snippet uses the `corrplot` library to generate a correlation plot (Figure 4.5) for the *HOME TASKS* dataset. Remember that this dataset contains two sets of features. One set extracted from audio and the other one extracted from the accelerometer sensor. First, the Pearson correlation between each pair of variables is computed with the `cor()` function and then the `corrplot()` function is used to generate the actual plot. Here, we specify that we only want to display the upper diagonal with `type = "upper"`. The `tl.pos` argument controls where to print the labels. In this example, at the top and in the diagonal. Setting `diag = FALSE` instructs the function not to print the principal diagonal which is all ones since it is the correlation between each variable and itself.

```
library(corrplot)

# Load home activities dataset.
dataset <- read.csv(file.path(datasets_path,
                              "home_tasks",
                              "sound_acc.csv"))

CORRS <- cor(dataset[,-1])
corrplot(CORRS, diag = FALSE, tl.pos = "td", tl.cex = 0.5,
         method = "color", type = "upper")
```

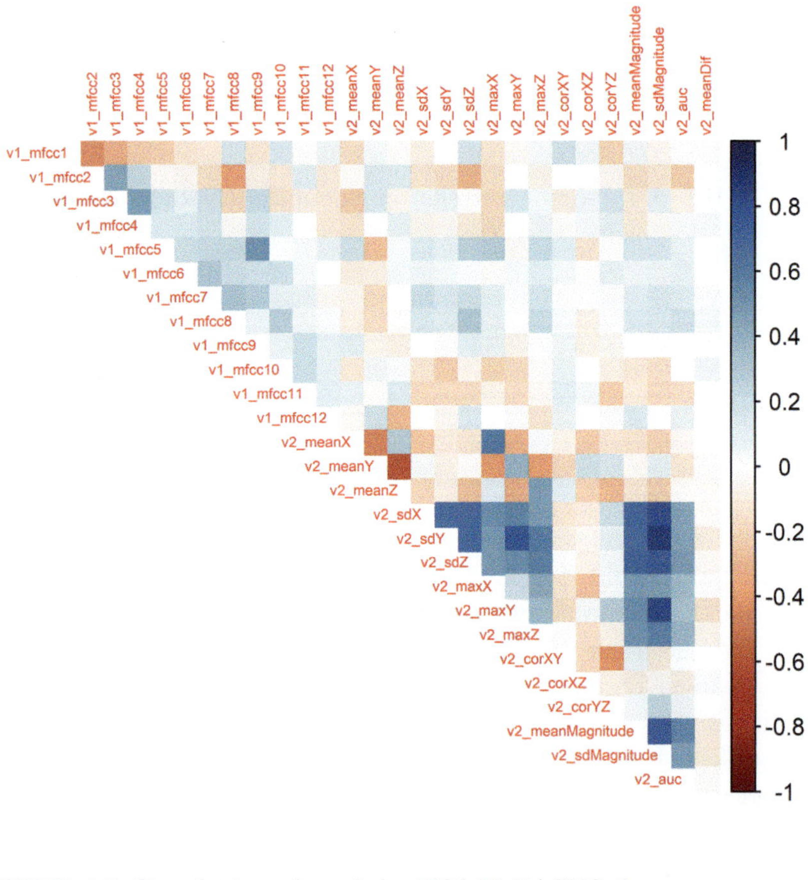

FIGURE 4.5 Correlation plot of the HOME TASKS dataset.

It looks like the correlations between sound features (v1_) and acceleration features (v2_) are not too high. In this case, this is good since we want both sources of information to be as independent as possible so that they capture different characteristics and complement each other as explained in section 3.4. On the other hand, there are high correlations between some acceleration features. For example *v2_maxY* with *v2_sdMagnitude*.

Please, be aware that the Pearson correlation only captures linear relationships.

4.6.1 Interactive Correlation Plots

When plotting correlation plots, it is useful to also visualize the actual correlation values. When there are many variables, it becomes difficult to do that. One way to overcome this limitation is by using interactive plots. The following code snippet uses the function `iplotCorr()` from the `qtlcharts` package to generate an interactive correlation plot. The nice thing about it, is that you can actually inspect the cell values by hovering the mouse. If you click on a cell, the corresponding scatter plot is also rendered. This makes these types of plots very convenient tools to explore variable relationships.

```
library(qtlcharts) # Library for interactive plots.

# Load home activities dataset.
dataset <- read.csv(file.path(datasets_path,
                              "home_tasks",
                              "sound_acc.csv"))

iplotCorr(dataset[,-1], reorder=F,
          chartOpts=list(cortitle="Correlation matrix",
                         scattitle="Scatterplot"))
```

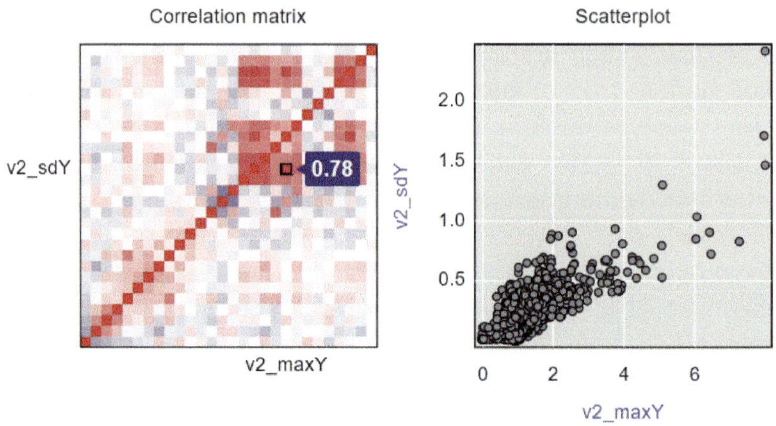

Please note that at the time this book was written, printed paper does not support interactive plots. Check the online html version instead to see the actual result or run the code on a computer.

4.7 Timeseries

Behavior is something that usually depends on time. Thus, being able to visualize timeseries data is essential. To illustrate how timeseries data can be plotted, I will use the `ggplot` package and the *HAND GESTURES* dataset. Recall that the data was collected with a tri-axial accelerometer, thus, for each hand gesture we have 3-dimensional timeseries. Each dimension represents one of the x, y, and z axes. First, we read one of the text files that stores a hand gesture from user 1. Each column represents an axis. Then, we need to do some formatting. We will create a data frame with three columns. The first one is a timestep represented as integers from 1 to the number of points per axis. The second column is a factor that represents the axis x, y, or z. The last column contains the actual values.

```
dataset <- read.csv(file.path(datasets_path,
                              "hand_gestures/1/1_20130703-120056.txt"),
                    header = F)
# Do some preprocessing.
type <- c(rep("x", nrow(dataset)),
          rep("y", nrow(dataset)),
          rep("z", nrow(dataset)))
type <- as.factor(type)
values <- c(dataset$V1, dataset$V2, dataset$V3)
t <- rep(1:nrow(dataset), 3)
df <- data.frame(timestep = t, type = type, values = values)

# Print first rows.
head(df)
#>   timestep type    values
#> 1        1    x 0.6864655
#> 2        2    x 0.9512450
#> 3        3    x 1.3140911
#> 4        4    x 1.4317709
#> 5        5    x 1.5102241
#> 6        6    x 1.5298374
```

Note that the last column (*values*) contains the values of all axes instead of having one column per axis. Now we can use the `ggplot()` function. The lines are colored by type of axis and this is specified with `colour = type`. The `type` column should be a factor. The line type is also dependent on the type of axis and is specified with `linetype = type`. The resulting plot is shown in Figure 4.6.

```
tsPlot <- ggplot(data = df,
                 aes(x = timestep,
                     y = values,
                     colour = type,
                     linetype = type)) +
  ggtitle("Hand gesture '1', user 1") +
  xlab("Timestep") +
  ylab("Acceleration") +
  geom_line(aes(color=type)) +
  theme_minimal() +
```

```
  theme(plot.title = element_text(hjust = 0.5),
        legend.position="right",
        legend.key.width = unit(1.0,"cm"),
        legend.key.size = unit(0.5,"cm"))
print(tsPlot)
```

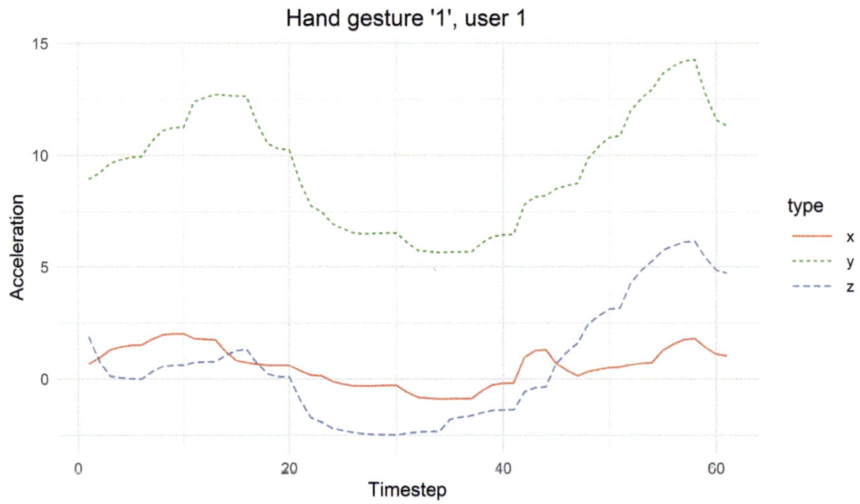

FIGURE 4.6 Timeseries plot for hand gesture ‘1’ user 1.

4.7.1 Interactive Timeseries

Sometimes it is useful to interactively zoom, highlight, select, etc. parts of the plot. In R, there is a package called `dygraphs` [Vanderkam et al., 2018] that generates fancy interactive plots for timeseries data[2]. The following code snippet reads a hand gesture file and adds a column at the beginning called `timestep`.

```
library(dygraphs)
```

[2]For a comprehensive list of available features of the `dygraph` package, the reader is advised to check its demos website: `https://rstudio.github.io/dygraphs/index.html`

```
# Read the hand gesture '1' for user 1.
dataset <- read.csv(file.path(datasets_path,
                              "hand_gestures/1/1_20130703-120056.txt"),
                    header = F,
                    col.names = c("x","y","z"))

dataset <- cbind(timestep = 1:nrow(dataset), dataset)
```

Then we can generate a minimal plot with one line of code with:

```
dygraph(dataset)
```

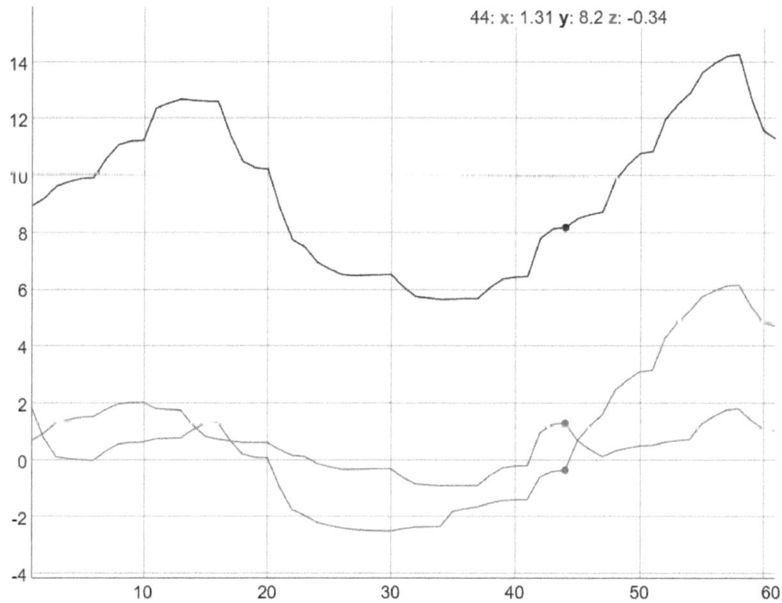

If you run the code, you will be able to zoom in by clicking and dragging over a region. A double click will restore the zoom. It is possible to add a lot of customization to the plots. For example, the following code adds a text title, fills the area under the lines, adds a point of interest line, and shades the region between 30 and 40.

```
dygraph(dataset, main = "Hand Gesture '1'") %>%
  dyOptions(fillGraph = TRUE, fillAlpha = 0.25) %>%
  dyEvent("10", "Point of interest", labelLoc = "top") %>%
  dyShading(from = "30", to = "40", color = "#CCCCCC")
```

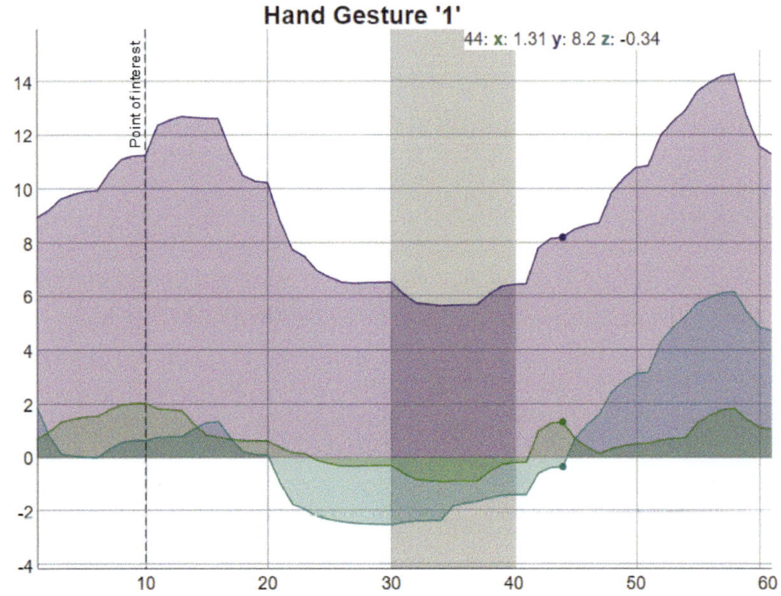

4.8 Multidimensional Scaling (MDS)

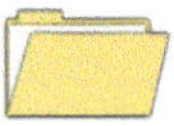

```
iterative_mds.R
```

In many situations, our data is comprised of several variables. If the number of variables is more than 3 (3-dimensional data), it becomes difficult to plot the relationships between data points. Take, for example, the *HOME TASKS* dataset which has 27 predictor variables from accelerometer and sound. One thing that we may want to do is to visually inspect the data points and check whether or not points from the same class are closer compared to points from different classes. This can give you an idea of the difficulty of the problem at hand. If points of the same class are very close and grouped together then, it is likely that a classification model will not have trouble separating the data points. But how do we plot such relationships with high dimensional data? One method is by using multidimensional scaling (MDS) which consists of a set of techniques aimed at reducing the dimensionality of data so it can be visualized in 2D or 3D. The objective is to plot the data such that the original distances between pairs of points are preserved in a given lower dimension d.

There exist several MDS methods but most of them take a distance matrix as input (for example, Euclidean distance). In R, generating a distance matrix from a set of points is easy. As an example, let's generate some sample data points.

```
# Generate 3 2D random points.
x <- runif(3)
y <- runif(3)
df <- data.frame(x,y)
labels <- c("a","b","c")
print(df)
#>           x         y
#> 1 0.4457900 0.5978606
#> 2 0.4740106 0.5019398
#> 3 0.8890085 0.4109234
```

The `dist()` function can be used to compute the distance matrix. By default, this function computes the Euclidean distance between rows:

```
dist(df)
#>            1          2
#> 2 0.09998603
#> 3 0.48102824 0.42486143
```

The output is the Euclidean distance between the pairs of rows $(1, 2)$, $(1, 3)$ and $(2, 3)$.

One way to obtain cartesian coordinates in a d dimensional space for n points from their distance matrix D is to use an iterative algorithm [Borg et al., 2012]. Such an algorithm consists of the following general steps:

1. Initialize n data points with random coordinates C of dimension d.
2. Compute a distance matrix D' from C.
3. Move the coordinates C such that the distances of D' get closer to the original ones in D.
4. Repeat from step 2 until the error between D' and D cannot be reduced any further or until some predefined max number of iterations.

The script `iterative_mds.R` implements this algorithm (`iterativeMDS()` function) which is based on the implementation from [Segaran, 2007]. Its first argument `D` is a distance matrix, the second argument `maxit` is the total number of iterations and the last argument `lr` controls how fast the points are moved in each iteration. The script also shows how to apply the method to the *eurodist* dataset which consists of distances between several European cities. Figure 4.7 shows the initial random coordinates of the cities. Then, Figure 4.8 shows the result after 30 iterations. Finally, Figure 4.9 shows the final result. By only knowing the distance matrix, the algorithm was able to find a visual mapping that closely resembles the real positions.

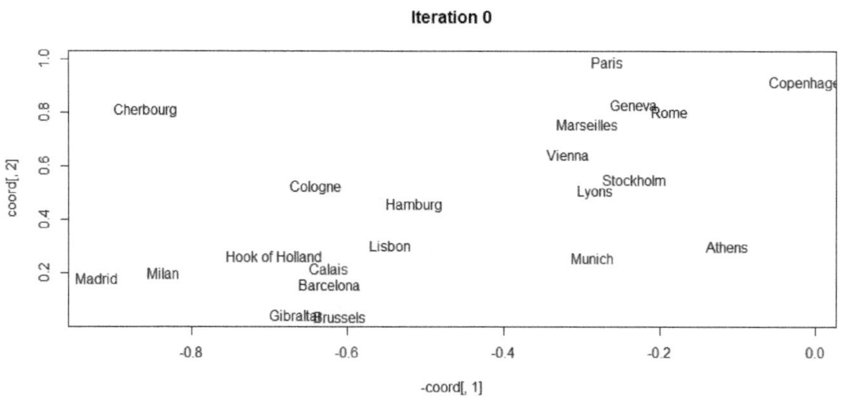

FIGURE 4.7 MDS initial coordinates.

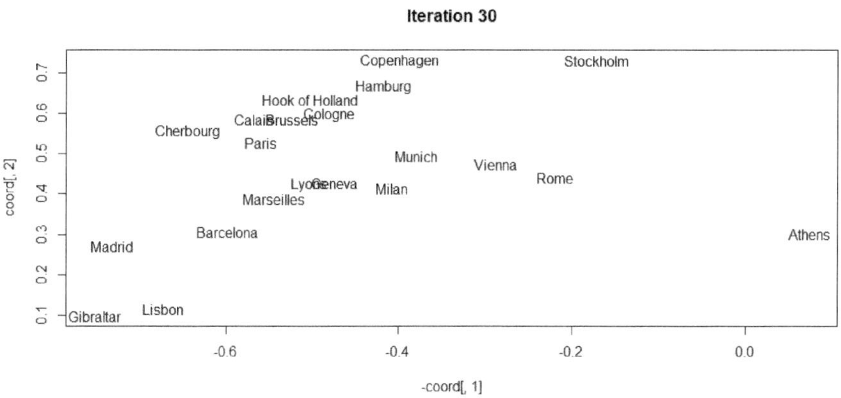

FIGURE 4.8 MDS coordinates after iteration 30.

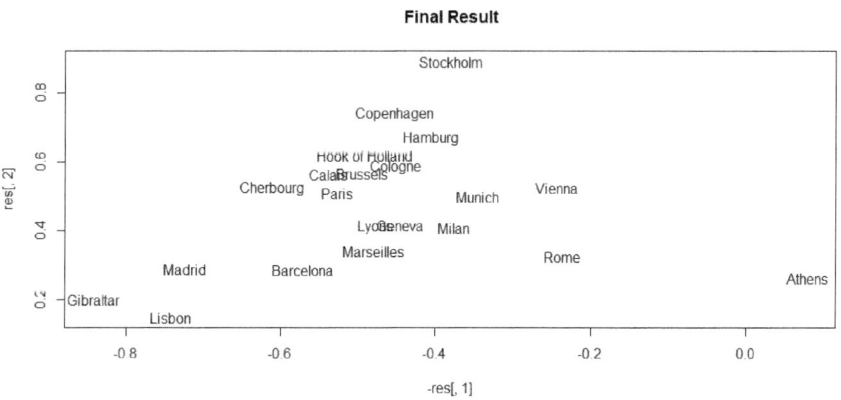

FIGURE 4.9 MDS final coordinates.

R already has efficient implementations to perform MDS and one of them is via the function `cmdscale()`. Its first argument is a distance matrix and the second argument k is the target dimension. It also has some other additional parameters that can be tuned. This function implements classical MDS based on Gower [1966]. The following code snippet uses the *HOME TASKS* dataset. It selects the accelerometer-based features (v2_*), uses the `cmdscale()` function to reduce them into 2, dimensions and plots the result.

```
dataset <- read.csv(file.path(datasets_path, "home_tasks/sound_acc.csv"))
colNames <- names(dataset)
v2cols <- colNames[grep(colNames, pattern = "v2_")]
cols <- as.integer(dataset$label)
labels <- unique(dataset$label)
d <- dist(dataset[,v2cols])
fit <- cmdscale(d, k = 2) # k is the number of dim
x <- fit[,1]; y <- fit[,2]

plot(x, y, xlab="Coordinate 1",
     ylab="Coordinate 2",
     main="Accelerometer features in 2D",
     pch=19,
     col=cols,
     cex=0.7)
legend("topleft",
       legend = labels,
       pch=19,
       col=unique(cols),
       cex=0.7,
       horiz = F)
```

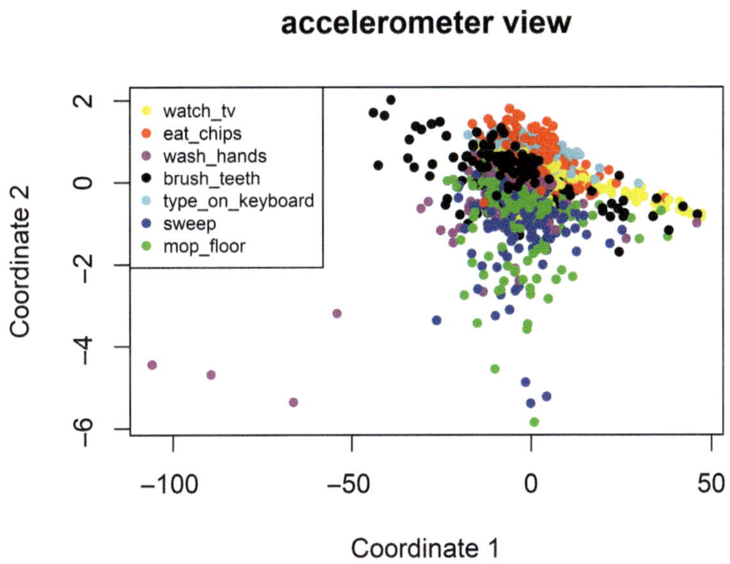

We can also reduce the data into 3 dimensions and use the `scatterplot3d` package to generate a 3D scatter plot:

```
library(scatterplot3d)
fit <- cmdscale(d,k = 3)
x <- fit[,1]; y <- fit[,2]; z <- fit[,3]
scatterplot3d(x, y, z,
              xlab = "",
              ylab = "",
              zlab = "",
              main="Accelerometer features in 3D",
              pch=19,
              color=cols,
              tick.marks = F,
              cex.symbols = 0.5,
              cex.lab = 0.7,
              mar = c(1,0,1,0))

legend("topleft",legend = labels,
```

```
       pch=19,
       col=unique(cols),
       cex=0.7,
       horiz = F)
```

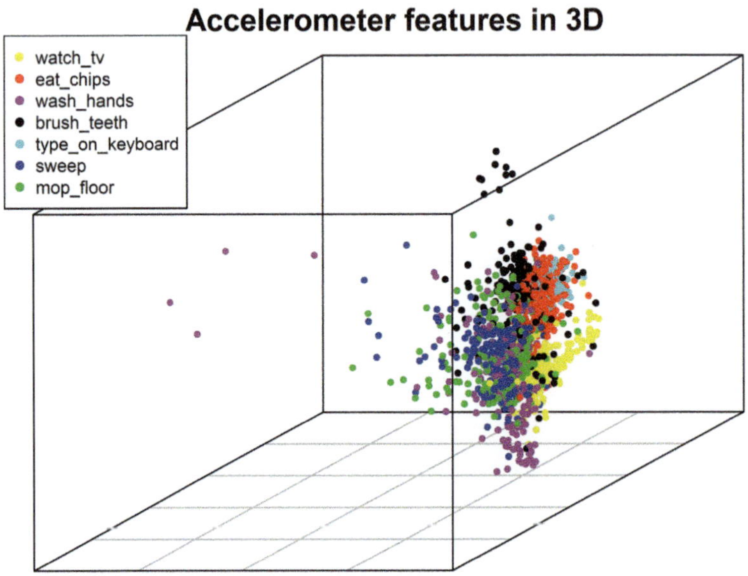

From those plots, it can be seen that the different points are more or less grouped together based on the type of activity. Still, there are several points with no clear grouping which would make them difficult to classify. In section 3.4 of chapter 3, we achieved a classification accuracy of 85% when using only the accelerometer data.

4.9 Heatmaps

Heatmaps are a good way to visualize the 'intensity' of events. For example, a heatmap can be used to depict website interactions by overlapping colored pixels relative to the number of clicks. This visualization eases the process of identifying the most relevant sections of the given website, for example. In this section, we will generate a heatmap of weekly motor activity behaviors of individuals with and without diagnosed depression. The *DEPRESJON* dataset will be used for this task. It contains motor activity recordings captured with an actigraphy device which is like a watch but has several sensors including accelerometers. The device registers the amount of movement every minute. The data contains recordings of 23 patients and 32 controls (those without depression). The participants wore the device for 13 days on average.

The accompanying script `auxiliary_eda.R` has the function `computeActivityHour()` that returns a matrix with the average activity level of the depressed patients or the controls (those without depression). The matrix dimension is 24×7 and it stores the average activity level at each day and hour. The `type` argument is used to specify if we want to compute this matrix for the depressed or control participants.

```
source("auxiliary_eda.R")

# Generate matrix with mean activity levels
# per hour for the control and condition group.
map.control <- computeActivityHour(datapath, type = "control")
map.condition <- computeActivityHour(datapath, type = "condition")
```

Since we want to compare the heatmaps of both groups we will normalize the matrices such that the values are between 0 and 1 in both cases. The script also contains a method `normalizeMatrices()` to do the normalization.

```
# Normalize matrices.
res <- normalizeMatrices(map.control, map.condition)
```

Then, the `pheatmap` package [Kolde, 2019] can be used to create the actual heatmap from the matrices.

```
library(pheatmap)
library(gridExtra)

# Generate heatmap of the control group.
a <- pheatmap(res$M1, main="control group",
              cluster_row = FALSE,
              cluster_col = FALSE,
              show_rownames = T,
              show_colnames = T,
              legend = T,
              color = colorRampPalette(c("white",
                                         "blue"))(50))

# Generate heatmap of the condition group.
b <- pheatmap(res$M2, main="condition group",
              cluster_row = FALSE,
              cluster_col = FALSE,
              show_rownames = T,
              show_colnames = T,
              legend = T, color = colorRampPalette(c("white",
                                                     "blue"))(50))

# Plot both heatmaps together.
grid.arrange(a$gtable, b$gtable, nrow=2)
```

Figure 4.10 shows the two heatmaps. Here, we can see that overall, the condition group has lower activity levels. It can also be observed that people in the control group wakes up at around $6:00$ but in the condition group, the activity starts to increase until $7:00$ in the morning. Activity levels around midnight look higher during weekends compared to weekdays.

All in all, heatmaps provide a good way to look at the overall patterns of a dataset and can provide some insights to further explore some aspects of the data.

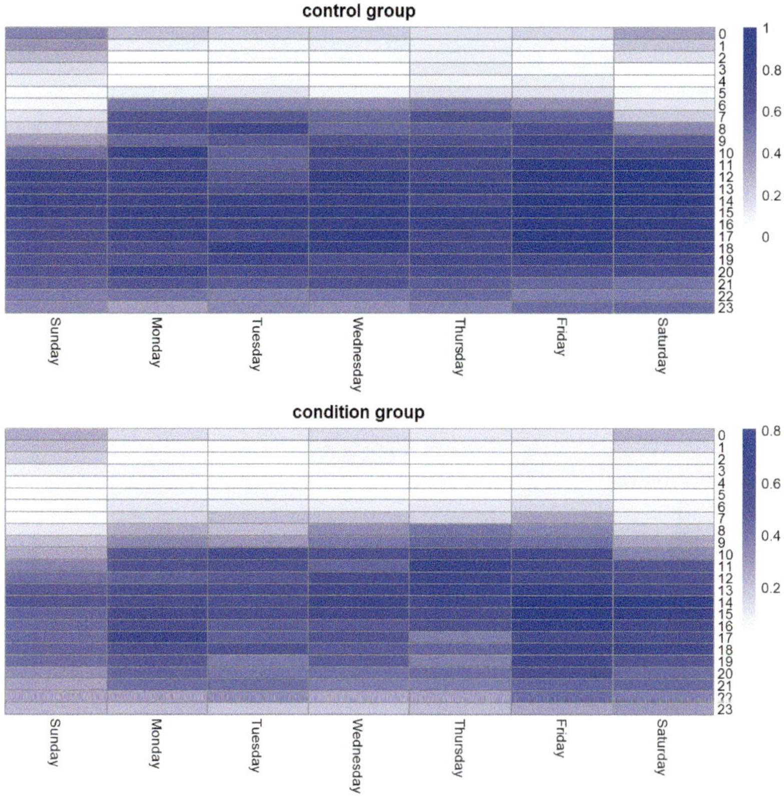

FIGURE 4.10 Activity level heatmaps for the control and condition group.

4.10 Automated EDA

Most of the time, doing an EDA involves more or less the same steps: print summary statistics, generate boxplots, visualize variable distributions, look for missing values, etc. If your data is stored as a data frame, all those tasks require almost the same code. To speed up this process, some packages have been developed. They provide convenient functions to explore the data and generate automatic reports.

The `DataExplorer` package [Cui, 2020] has several interesting functions to explore a dataset. The following code uses the `plot_str()` function to plot the structure of `dataset` which is a data frame read from the *HOME*

TASKS dataset. The complete code is available in script `EDA.R`. The output is shown in Figure 4.11. This plot shows the number of observations, the number of variables, the variable names, and their types.

```
library(DataExplorer)
dataset <- read.csv(file.path(datasets_path, "home_tasks/sound_acc.csv"))
plot_str(dataset)
```

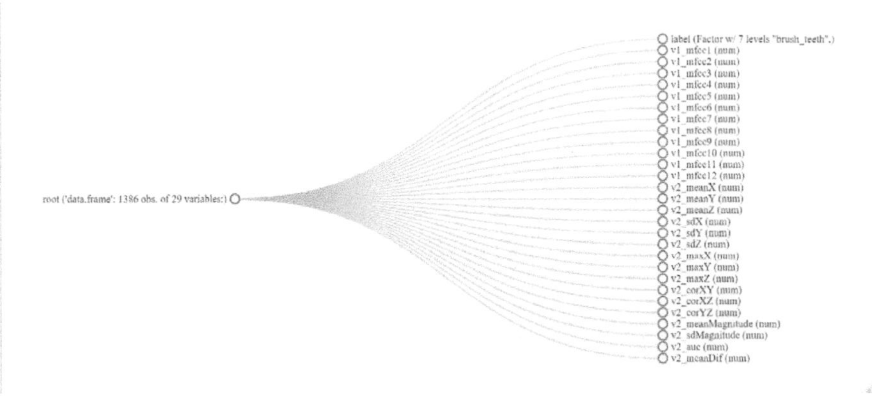

FIGURE 4.11 Output of function plotstr().

Another useful function is `introduce()`. This one prints some statistics like the number of rows, columns, missing values, etc. Table 4.1 shows the output result.

```
introduce(dataset)
```

The package provides more functions to explore your data. The `create_report()` function can be used to automatically call several of those functions and generate a report in html. The package also offers functions to do feature engineering such as replacing missing values, create dummy variables (covered in chapter 5), etc. For a more detailed presentation of the package's capabilities please check its vignette[3].

[3] `https://cran.r-project.org/web/packages/DataExplorer/vignettes/dataexplorer-intro.html`

TABLE 4.1 Output of the introduce() function.

rows	1386
columns	29
discrete_columns	1
continuous_columns	28
all_missing_columns	0
total_missing_values	0
complete_rows	1386
total_observations	40194
memory_usage	328680

There is another similar package called `inspectdf` [Rushworth, 2019] which has similar functionality. It also offers some functions to check if the categorical variables are imbalanced. This is handy if one of the categorical variables is the response variable (the one we want to predict) since having imbalanced classes may pose some problems (more on this in chapter 5). The following code generates a plot (Figure 4.12) that represents the counts of categorical variables. This dataset only has one categorical variable: *label*.

```
library(inspectdf)
show_plot(inspect_cat(dataset))
```

Here, we can see that the most frequent class is *'eat_chips'* and the less frequent one is *'sweep'*. We can confirm this by printing the actual counts:

```
table(dataset$label)
#>     brush_teeth      eat_chips  mop_floor      sweep type_on_keyboard
#>             180            282        181        178              179
#>      wash_hands       watch_tv
#>             180            206
```

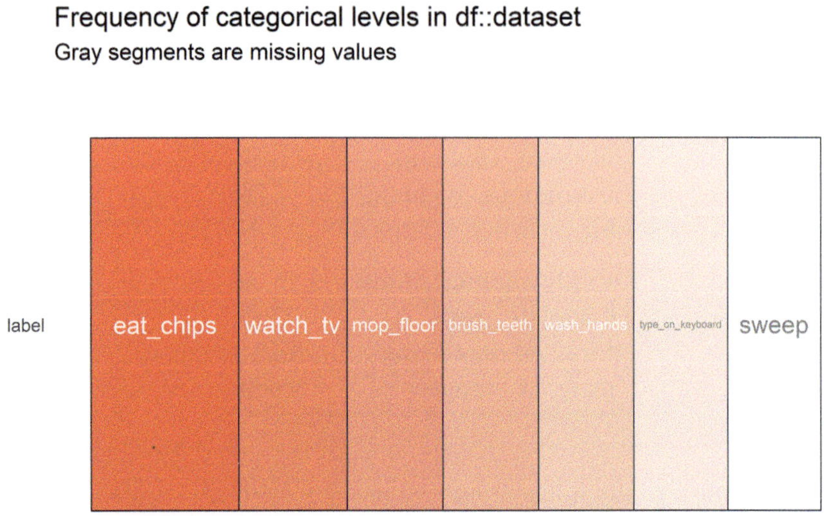

FIGURE 4.12 Heatmap of counts of categorical variables.

This chapter provided a brief introduction to some exploratory data analysis tools and methods however, this is only a tiny subset of what is available. There is already an entire book about EDA with R which I recommend you to check [Peng, 2016].

4.11 Summary

One of the first tasks in a data analysis pipeline is to familiarize yourself with the data. There are several techniques and tools that can provide support during this process.

- Talking with field experts can help you to better understand the data.
- Generating summary statistics is a good way to gain general insights of a dataset. In R, the `summary()` function will compute such statistics.

- For classification problems, one of the first steps is to check the distribution of classes.
- In multi-user settings, generating a **user-class sparsity matrix** can be useful to detect missing classes per user.
- **Boxplots** and **correlation plots** are used to understand the behavior of the variables.
- R, has several packages for creating interactive plots such as `dygraphs` for timeseries and `qtlcharts` for correlation plots.
- **Multidimensional scaling (MDS)** can be used to project high-dimensional data into 2 or 3 dimensions so they can be plotted.
- R has some packages like `DataExplorer` that provide some degree of automation for exploring a dataset.

5

Preprocessing Behavioral Data

preprocessing.R

Behavioral data comes in many flavors and forms, but when training predictive models, the data needs to be in a particular format. Some sources of variation when collecting data are:

- **Sensors' format.** Each type of sensor and manufacturer stores data in a different format. For example, .csv files, binary files, images, proprietary formats, etc.
- **Sampling rate.** The sampling rate is how many measurements are taken per unit of time. For example, a heart rate sensor may return a single value every second, thus, the sampling rate is 1 Hz. An accelerometer that captures 50 values per second has a sampling rate of 50 Hz.
- **Scales and ranges.** Some sensors may return values in *degrees* (e.g., a temperature sensor) while others may return values in some other scale, for example, in *centimeters* for a proximity sensor. Furthermore, ranges can also vary. That is, a sensor may capture values in the range of 0–1000, for example.

During the data exploration step (chapter 4) we may also find that values are missing, inconsistent, noisy, and so on, thus, we also need to take care of that.

This chapter provides an overview of some common methods used to clean and preprocess the data before one can start training reliable models.

Several of the methods presented here can lead to *information injection*

DOI: 10.1201/9781003203469-5

if not implemented correctly, and this can cause overfitting. That is, inadvertently transferring information from the train set to the test set. This is something undesirable because both sets need to be independent so the generalization performance can be estimated accurately. You can find more details about information injection and how to avoid it in section 5.5 of this chapter.

5.1 Missing Values

Many datasets will have missing values and we need ways to identify and deal with that. Missing data could be due to faulty sensors, processing errors, unavailable information, and so on. In this section, I present some tools that ease the identification of missing values. Later, some imputation methods used to fill in the missing values are presented.

To demonstrate some of these concepts, the *SHEEP GOATS* dataset [Kamminga et al., 2017] will be used. Due to its big size, the files of this dataset are not included with the accompanying book files but they can be downloaded from `https://easy.dans.knaw.nl/ui/datasets/id/easy-dataset:76131`. The data were released as part of a study about animal behaviors. The researchers placed inertial sensors on sheep and goats and tracked their behavior during one day. They also video-recorded the session and annotated the data with different types of behaviors such as *grazing*, *fighting*, *scratch-biting*, etc. The device was placed on the neck with a random orientation and it collected acceleration, orientation, magnetic field, temperature, and barometric pressure. Figure 5.1 shows a schematic view of the setting.

We will start by loading a .csv file that corresponds to one of the sheep and check if there are missing values. The `naniar` package [Tierney et al., 2019] offers a set of different functions to explore and deal with missing values. The `gg_miss_var()` function allows you to quickly check which variables have missing values and how many. The following code loads the data and then plots the number of missing values in each variable.

FIGURE 5.1 Device placed on the neck of the sheep. (Author: Lady-ofHats. Source: Wikipedia (CC0 1.0)).

```
library(naniar)

# Path to S1.csv file.
datapath <- file.path(datasets_path,
                      "sheep_goats","S1.csv")

# Can take some seconds to load since the file is big.
df <- read.csv(datapath, stringsAsFactors = TRUE)

# Plot missing values.
gg_miss_var(df)
```

Figure 5.2 shows the resulting output. The plot shows that there are missing values in four variables: *pressure*, *cz*, *cy*, and *cx*. The last three correspond to the compass (magnetometer). For *pressure*, the number of missing values is more than 2 million! For the rest, it is a bit less (more than 1 million).

To further explore this issue, we can plot each observation in a row with the function `vis_miss()`.

```
# Select first 1000 rows.
# It can take some time to plot bigger data frames.
vis_miss(df[1:1000,])
```

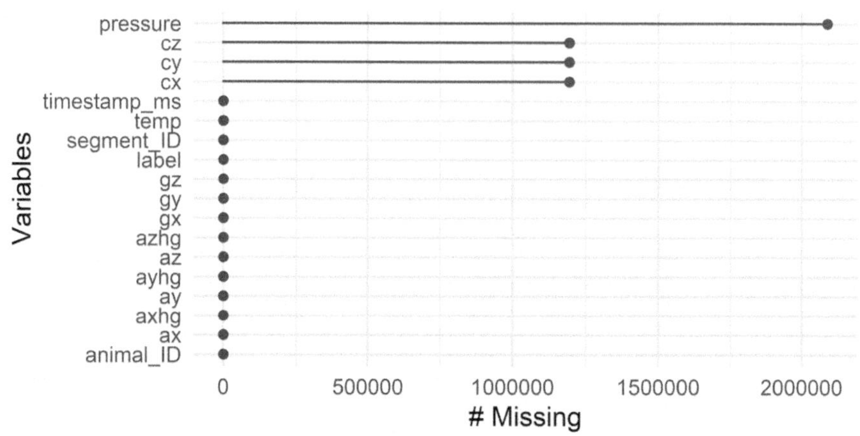

FIGURE 5.2 Missing values counts.

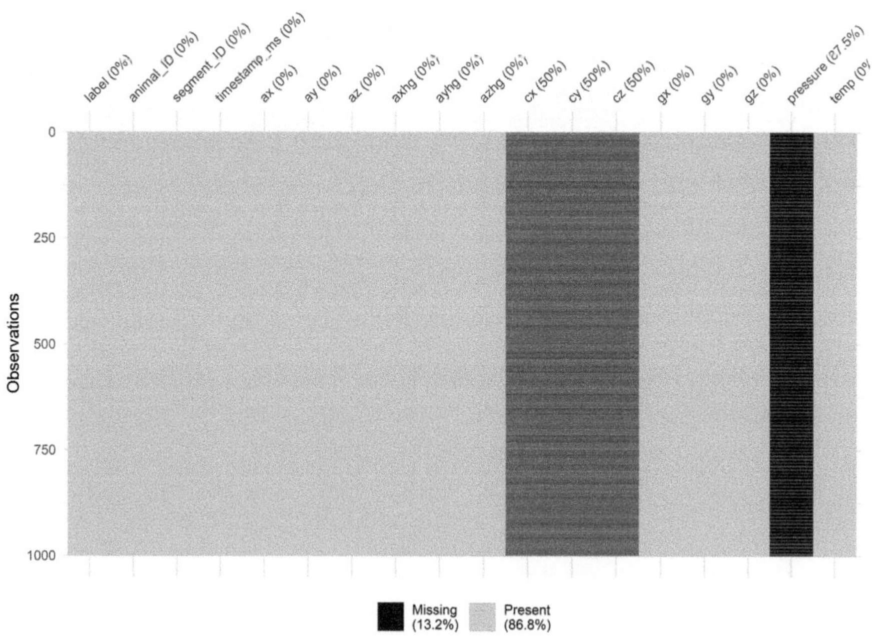

FIGURE 5.3 Rows with missing values.

Figure 5.3 shows every observation per row and missing values are black colored (if any). From this image, it seems that missing values are systematic. It looks like there is a clear stripes pattern, especially for the compass variables. Based on these observations, it doesn't look like random sensor failures or random noise.

If we explore the data frame's values, for example with the RStudio viewer (Figure 5.4), two things can be noted. First, for the compass values, there is a missing value for each present value. Thus, it looks like 50% of compass values are missing. For *pressure*, it seems that there are 7 missing values for each available value.

timestamp_ms	ax	ay	az	axhg	ayhg	azhg	cx	cy	cz	gx	gy	gz	pressure
1	-2.73178000	-6.68701	-6.57208	2.132330	-5.3758800	17.86960	1.5525	-0.4755	0.5415	2.0122000	-51.341500	-32.6220000	NaN
6	-2.78206000	-6.82347	-6.62954	1.711870	-3.2735800	17.32900	NaN	NaN	NaN	-0.1219510	-47.317100	-33.5366000	NaN
11	-2.82755000	-6.96713	-6.54814	3.093390	-3.6339800	17.02860	1.5405	-0.4785	0.5655	-1.8902400	-42.561000	-35.0000000	NaN
16	-2.85149000	-7.14669	-6.47871	1.651810	-4.4148300	18.22990	NaN	NaN	NaN	-3.1097600	-37.743900	-36.6463000	1008.22
21	-2.89220000	-7.30710	-6.37815	1.171280	-3.4537800	16.54810	1.5405	-0.4785	0.5655	-2.9878000	-33.048800	-38.3537000	NaN
26	-2.90656000	-7.45315	-6.20577	0.630690	-4.8953600	18.29000	NaN	NaN	NaN	-2.0122000	-28.841500	-39.6951000	NaN
31	-2.89459000	-7.53455	-6.09324	3.153450	-6.1567400	18.77050	1.5240	-0.4950	0.5700	-0.0609756	-25.426800	-40.7317000	NaN
36	-2.88501000	-7.52258	-5.99748	1.711870	-6.5171300	16.78840	NaN	NaN	NaN	2.0122000	-22.865900	-41.5244000	NaN
41	-2.86347000	-7.44118	-6.00226	2.913190	-5.9765400	17.50920	1.5450	-0.4770	0.5670	3.4756100	-21.158500	-42.3171000	NaN
46	-2.82995000	-7.33344	-6.14352	0.991085	-6.0366100	18.16990	NaN	NaN	NaN	3.9024400	-20.426800	-43.1098000	NaN
51	-2.79403000	-7.16824	-6.40928	2.312530	-4.0544400	16.90850	1.5270	-0.4830	0.5580	2.8048800	-20.304900	-43.3537000	NaN
56	-2.77249000	-7.01980	-6.77320	-0.480526	-4.2346300	18.83060	NaN	NaN	NaN	0.3658540	-20.731700	-43.1098000	1008.22
61	-2.76291000	-6.88812	-7.22091	2.973250	-3.8141700	16.72830	1.5540	-0.4860	0.5460	-3.1097600	-21.524400	-42.3780000	NaN
66	-2.73178000	-6.79235	-7.66384	2.702960	-2.1023000	16.51810	NaN	NaN	NaN	-7.1951200	-22.256100	-41.9512000	NaN
71	-2.65756000	-6.74686	-8.01339	-0.180197	-5.1055900	16.51810	1.5240	-0.4920	0.5640	-12.0732000	-22.743900	-41.8902000	NaN
76	-2.54743000	-6.76601	-8.26000	1.321450	-3.7240800	15.49700	NaN	NaN	NaN	-16.9512000	-22.743900	-42.1341000	NaN
81	-2.36308000	-6.83066	-8.39407	2.702960	-4.9253900	15.13660	1.5570	-0.4860	0.5610	-21.6463000	-22.439000	-42.8659000	NaN
86	-2.12126000	-6.91206	-8.29112	2.883160	-2.5227600	17.89960	NaN	NaN	NaN	-25.8537000	-21.768300	-43.5366000	NaN
91	-1.85311000	-7.06289	-8.15705	3.904270	-4.2046000	16.69830	1.5315	-0.4965	0.5775	-30.0000000	-21.219500	-43.3537000	NaN
96	-1.57299000	-7.25683	-7.93199	3.243550	-3.4838100	16.15770	NaN	NaN	NaN	-33.5366000	-20.975600	-41.7683000	1008.22

FIGURE 5.4 Displaying the data frame in RStudio. Source: Data from Kamminga, MSc J.W. (University of Twente) (2017): Generic online animal activity recognition on collar tags. DANS. `https://doi.org/10.17026/dans-zp6-fmna`

So, what could be the root cause of those missing values? Remember that at the beginning of this chapter it was mentioned that **one of the sources of variation is sampling rate**. If we look at the data set documentation, all sensors have a sampling rate of 200 Hz except for the compass and the pressure sensor. The compass has a sampling rate of 100 Hz. That is half compared to the other sensors! This explains why 50% of the rows are missing. Similarly, the pressure sensor has a sampling rate of 25 Hz. By visualizing and then inspecting the missing data, we have just found out that the missing values are not caused by random noise or sensor failures but because some sensors are not as fast as others!

Now that we know there are missing values we need to decide what to do with them. The following subsection lists some ways to deal with missing values.

5.1.1 Imputation

Imputation is the process of filling in missing values. One of the reasons for imputing missing values is that some predictive models cannot deal with missing data. Another reason is that it may help in increasing the predictions' performance, for example, if we are trying to predict the sheep behavior from a discrete set of categories based on the inertial data. There are different ways to handle missing values:

- **Discard rows.** If the rows with missing values are not too many, they can simply be discarded.
- **Mean value.** Fill the missing values with the mean value of the corresponding variable. This method is simple and can be effective. One of the problems with this method is that it is sensitive to outliers (as it is the arithmetic mean).
- **Median value.** The median is robust against outliers, thus, it can be used instead of the arithmetic mean to fill the gaps.
- **Replace with the closest value.** For timeseries data, as is the case of the sheep readings, one could also replace missing values with the closest known value.
- **Predict the missing values.** Use the other variables to predict the missing one. This can be done by training a predictive model. A regressor if the variable is numeric or a classifier if the variable is categorical.

Another problem with the mean and median values is that they can be correlated with other variables, for example, with the class that we want to predict. One way to avoid this, is to compute the mean (or median) for each class, but still, some hidden correlations may bias the estimates.

In R, the `simputation` package [van der Loo, 2019] has implemented various imputation techniques including: group-wise median imputation, model-based with linear regression, random forests, etc. The following code snippet (complete code is in `preprocessing.R`) uses the `impute_lm()` method to impute the missing values in the sheep data using linear regression.

```
library(simputation)

# Replace NaN with NAs.
# Since missing values are represented as NaN,
# first we need to replace them with NAs.

# Code to replace NaN with NA was taken from Hong Ooi:
# https://stackoverflow.com/questions/18142117/#
# how-to-replace-nan-value-with-zero-in-a-huge-data-frame/18143097
is.nan.data.frame <- function(x)do.call(cbind, lapply(x, is.nan))
df[is.nan(df)] <- NA

# Use simputation package to impute values.
# The first 4 columns are removed since we
# do not want to use them as predictor variables.
imp_df <- impute_lm(df[,-c(1:4)],
                    cx + cy + cz + pressure ~ . - cx - cy - cz - pressure)
# Print summary.
summary(imp_df)
```

Originally, the missing values are encoded as `NaN` but in order to use the `simputation` package functions, we need them as `NA`. First, `NaN`s are replaced with `NA`. The first argument of `impute_lm()` is a data frame and the second argument is a formula. We discard the first 4 variables of the data frame since we do not want to use them as predictors. The left-hand side of the formula (everything before the ~ symbol) specifies the variables we want to impute. The right-hand side specifies the variables used to build the linear models. The '.' indicates that we want to use all variables while the '-' is used to specify variables that we do not want to include. The vignettes[1] of the package contain more detailed examples.

[1] https://cran.r-project.org/web/packages/simputation/vignettes/intro.html

The mean, median, etc. and the predictive models to infer missing values should be trained using data only from the train set to avoid information injection.

5.2 Smoothing

Smoothing comprises a set of algorithms with the aim of highlighting patterns in the data or as a preprocessing step to clean the data and remove noise. These methods are widely used on timeseries data but also with spatio-temporal data such as images. With timeseries data, they are often used to emphasize long-term patterns and reduce short-term signal artifacts. For example, in Figure 5.5[2] a stock chart was smoothed using two methods: moving average and exponential moving average. The smoothed versions make it easier to spot the overall trend rather than focusing on short-term variations.

The most common smoothing method for timeseries is the **simple moving average**. With this method, the first element of the resulting smoothed series is computed by taking the average of the elements within a window of predefined size. The window's position starts at the first element of the original series. The second element is computed in the same way but after moving the window one position to the right. Figure 5.6 shows this procedure on a series with 5 elements and a window size of size 3. After the third iteration, it is not possible to move the window one more step to the right while covering 3 elements since the end of the timeseries has been reached. Because of this, the smoothed series will have some missing values at the end. Specifically, it will have $w-1$ fewer elements where w is the window size. A simple solution is to compute the average of the elements covered by the window even if they are less than the window size.

In the previous example the average is taken from the elements to the right of the pointer. There is a variation called *centered moving average* in which the center point of the window has the same elements to the

[2]https://commons.wikimedia.org/wiki/File:Moving_Average_Types_comparison_-_Simple_and_Exponential.png

FIGURE 5.5 Stock chart with two smoothed versions. One with moving average and the other one with an exponential moving average. (Author: Alex Kofman. Source: Wikipedia (CC BY-SA 3.0) [https://creativecommons.org/licenses/by-sa/3.0/legalcode]).

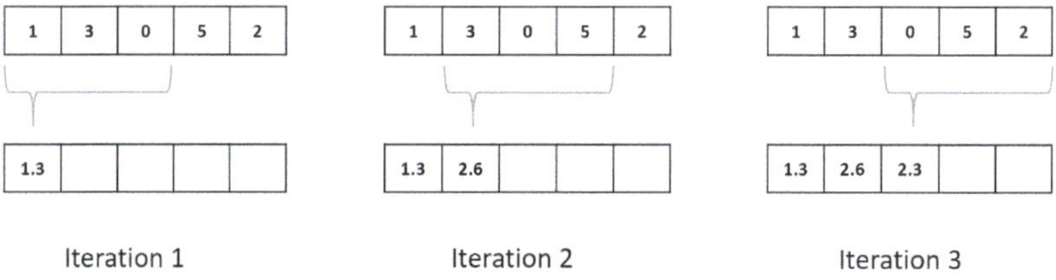

FIGURE 5.6 Simple moving average step by step with window size = 3. Top: original array; bottom: smoothed array.

left and right (Figure 5.7). Note that with this version of moving average some values at the beginning and at the end will be empty. Also note that the window size should be odd. In practice, both versions produce very similar results.

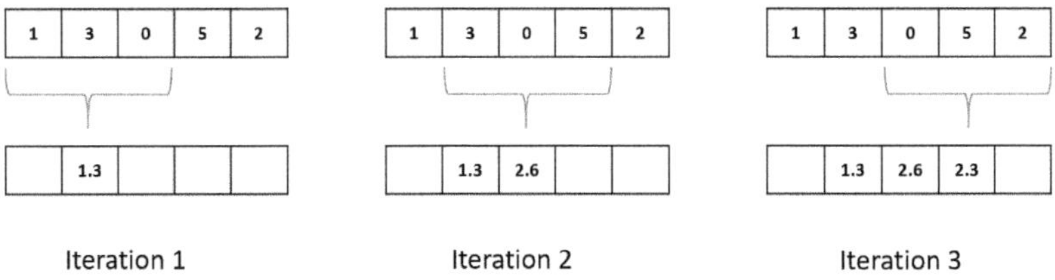

FIGURE 5.7 Centered moving average step by step with window size = 3.

In the `preprocessing.R` script, the function `movingAvg()` implements the simple moving average procedure. In the following code, note that the output vector will have the same size as the original one, but the last elements will contain `NA` values when the window cannot be moved any longer to the right.

```
movingAvg <- function(x, w = 5){
  # Applies moving average to x with a window of size w.
  n <- length(x) # Total number of points.
  smoothedX <- rep(NA, n)

  for(i in 1:(n-w+1)){
    smoothedX[i] <- mean(x[i:(i-1+w)])
  }

  return(smoothedX)
}
```

We can apply this function to a segment of accelerometer data from the *SHEEP AND GOATS* data set.

```
datapath <- "../Sheep/S1.csv"
df <- read.csv(datapath)
```

```
# Only select a subset of the whole series.
dfsegment <- df[df$timestamp_ms < 6000,]
x <- dfsegment$ax

# Compute simple moving average with a window of size 21.
smoothed <- movingAvg(x, w = 21)
```

Figure 5.8 shows the result after plotting both the original vector and the smoothed one. It can be observed that many of the small peaks are no longer present in the smoothed version. The window size is a parameter that needs to be defined by the user. If it is set too large some important information may be lost from the signal.

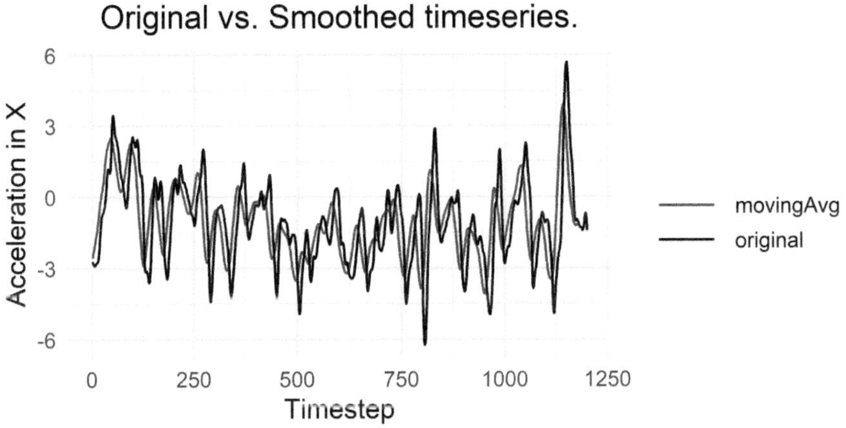

FIGURE 5.8 Original time series and smoothed version using a moving average window of size 21.

One of the disadvantages of this method is that the arithmetic mean is sensitive to noise. Instead of computing the mean, one can use the median which is more robust against outlier values. There also exist other derived methods (not covered here) such as weighted moving average and exponential moving average[3] which assign more importance to data points closer to the central point in the window. Smoothing a signal before feature extraction is a common practice and is used to remove some of the unwanted noise.

[3] `https://en.wikiversity.org/wiki/Moving_Average`

5.3 Normalization

Having variables on different scales can have an impact during learning and at inference time. Consider a study where the data was collected using a wristband that has a light sensor and an accelerometer. The measurement unit of the light sensor is *lux* whereas the accelerometer's is m/s^2. After inspecting the dataset, you realize that the *min* and *max* values of the light sensor are 0 and 155, respectively. The *min* and *max* values for the accelerometer are −0.4 and 7.45, respectively. Why is this a problem? Well, several learning methods are based on distances such as k-NN and Nearest centroid thus, distances will be more heavily affected by bigger scales. Furthermore, other methods like neural networks (covered in chapter 8) are also affected by different scales. They have a harder time learning their parameters (weights) when data is not normalized. On the other hand, some methods are not affected, for example, tree-based learners such as decision trees and random forests. Since most of the time you may want to try different methods, it is a good idea to normalize your predictor variables.

A common normalization technique is to scale all the variables between 0 and 1. Suppose there is a numeric vector x that you want to normalize between 0 and 1. Let $max(x)$ and $min(x)$ be the maximum and minimum values of x. The following can be used to normalize the ith value of x:

$$z_i = \frac{x_i - min(x)}{max(x) - min(x)} \tag{5.1}$$

where z_i is the new normalized i^{th} value. Thus, the formula is applied to every value in x. The $max(x)$ and $min(x)$ values are parameters learned from the data. Notice that if you will split your data into training and test sets the *max* and *min* values (the parameters) are learned only from the train set and then used to normalize both the train and test set. This is to avoid information injection (section 5.5). Be also aware that after the parameters are learned from the train set, and once the model is deployed in production, it is likely that some input values will be 'out of range'. If the train set is not very representative of what you will find in real life, some values will probably be smaller than the learned $min(x)$ and some will be greater than the learned $max(x)$. Even if the train set is representative of the real-life phenomenon, there is nothing that will prevent some values to be out of range. A simple way to handle this is to truncate the values. In some cases, we do know what are the possible minimum and maximum values. For example in image processing, images are usually represented as color intensities between 0 and 255. Here, we know that the *min* value cannot be less than 0 and the *max* value cannot be greater than 255.

Let's see an example using the *HOME TASKS* dataset. The following code first loads the dataset and prints a summary of the first 4 variables.

```
# Load home activities dataset.
dataset <- read.csv(file.path(datasets_path,
                              "home_tasks",
                              "sound_acc.csv"),
                    stringsAsFactors = T)

# Check first 4 variables' min and max values.
summary(dataset[,1:4])

#>               label       v1_mfcc1        v1_mfcc2          v1_mfcc3
#> brush_teeth    :180   Min.   :103   Min.   :-17.20   Min.   :-20.90
#> eat_chips      :282   1st Qu.:115   1st Qu.: -8.14   1st Qu.: -7.95
#> mop_floor      :181   Median :120   Median : -3.97   Median : -4.83
#> sweep          :178   Mean   :121   Mean   : -4.50   Mean   : -5.79
#> type_on_keyboard:179  3rd Qu.:126   3rd Qu.: -1.30   3rd Qu.: -3.09
#> wash_hands     :180   Max.   :141   Max.   :  8.98   Max.   :  3.27
#> watch_tv       :206
```

Since *label* is a categorical variable, the class counts are printed. For the three remaining variables, we get some statistics including their *min* and *max* values. As we can see, the min value of *v1_mfcc1* is very different from the *min* value of *v1_mfcc2* and the same is true for the maximum values. Thus, we want all variables to be between 0 and 1 in order to use classification methods sensitive to different scales. Let's assume we want to train a classifier with this data so we divide it into train and test sets:

```
# Divide into 50/50% train and test set.
set.seed(1234)
folds <- sample(2, nrow(dataset), replace = T)
trainset <- dataset[folds == 1,]
testset <- dataset[folds == 2,]
```

Now we can define a function that normalizes every numeric or integer variable. If the variable is not numeric or integer it will skip them. The function will take as input a train set and a test set. The parameters (*max* and *min*) are learned from the train set and used to normalize both, the train and test sets.

```
# Define a function to normalize the train and test set
# based on the parameters learned from the train set.
normalize <- function(trainset, testset){

  # Iterate columns
  for(i in 1:ncol(trainset)){

    c <- trainset[,i] # trainset column
    c2 <- testset[,i] # testset column

    # Skip if the variable is not numeric or integer.
    if(class(c) != "numeric" && class(c) != "integer")next;

    # Learn the max value from the trainset's column.
    max <- max(c, na.rm = T)
    # Learn the min value from the trainset's column.
    min <- min(c, na.rm = T)

    # If all values are the same set it to max.
    if(max==min){
      trainset[,i] <- max
      testset[,i] <- max
    }
    else{
```

```
      # Normalize trainset's column.
      trainset[,i] <- (c - min) / (max - min)

      # Truncate max values in testset.
      idxs <- which(c2 > max)
      if(length(idxs) > 0){
        c2[idxs] <- max
      }

      # Truncate min values in testset.
      idxs <- which(c2 < min)
      if(length(idxs) > 0){
        c2[idxs] <- min
      }

      # Normalize testset's column.
      testset[,i] <- (c2 - min) / (max - min)
    }
  }

  return(list(train=trainset, test=testset))
}
```

Now we can use the previous function to normalize the train and test sets. The function returns a list of two elements: a normalized train and test sets.

```
# Call our function to normalize each set.
normalizedData <- normalize(trainset, testset)

# Inspect the normalized train set.
summary(normalizedData$train[,1:4])

#>           label          v1_mfcc1         v1_mfcc2         v1_mfcc3
#> brush_teeth   : 88   Min.   :0.000   Min.   :0.000   Min.   :0.000
#> eat_chips     :139   1st Qu.:0.350   1st Qu.:0.403   1st Qu.:0.527
#> mop_floor     : 91   Median :0.464   Median :0.590   Median :0.661
```

```
#> sweep           : 84   Mean   :0.474   Mean   :0.568   Mean   :0.616
#> type_on_keyboard: 94   3rd Qu.:0.613   3rd Qu.:0.721   3rd Qu.:0.730
#> wash_hands      :102   Max.   :1.000   Max.   :1.000   Max.   :1.000
#> watch_tv        : 99

# Inspect the normalized test set.
summary(normalizedData$test[,1:4])
#>                label        v1_mfcc1          v1_mfcc2         v1_mfcc3
#> brush_teeth     : 92   Min.   :0.0046   Min.   :0.000   Min.   :0.000
#> eat_chips       :143   1st Qu.:0.3160   1st Qu.:0.421   1st Qu.:0.500
#> mop_floor       : 90   Median :0.4421   Median :0.606   Median :0.644
#> sweep           : 94   Mean   :0.4569   Mean   :0.582   Mean   :0.603
#> type_on_keyboard: 85   3rd Qu.:0.5967   3rd Qu.:0.728   3rd Qu.:0.724
#> wash_hands      : 78   Max.   :0.9801   Max.   :1.000   Max.   :1.000
#> watch_tv        :107
```

Now, the variables on the train set are exactly between 0 and 1 for all numeric variables. For the test set, not all *min* values will be exactly 0 but a bit higher. Conversely, some *max* values will be lower than 1. This is because the test set may have a *min* value that is greater than the *min* value of the train set and a *max* value that is smaller than the *max* value of the train set. However, after normalization, all values are guaranteed to be within 0 and 1.

5.4 Imbalanced Classes

Ideally, classes will be uniformly distributed, that is, there is approximately the same number of instances per class. In real-life (as always), this is not the case. And in many situations (more often than you may think), **class counts are heavily skewed**. When this happens the dataset is said to be imbalanced. Take as an example, bank transactions. Most of them will be normal, whereas a small percent will be fraudulent. In the medical field this is very common. It is easier to collect samples from healthy individuals compared to samples from individuals with some rare conditions. For example, a database may have thousands of images from healthy tissue but just a dozen with signs of cancer. Of course, having just a few cases with diseases is a good thing for the world! but not for machine learning methods. This is because predictive models will try to learn their parameters such that the error is reduced, and most of the time this error is based on accuracy. Thus, the models will be biased towards making correct predictions for the majority classes (the ones with higher counts) while paying little attention to minority classes. This is a problem because for some applications we are more interested in detecting the minority classes (illegal transactions, cancer cases, etc.).

Suppose a given database has 998 instances with class *'no cancer'* and only 2 instances with class *'cancer'*. A trivial classifier that always predicts *'no cancer'* will have an accuracy of 98.8% but will not be able to detect any of the *'cancer'* cases! So, what can we do?

- **Collect more data from the minority class.** In practice, this can be difficult, expensive, etc. or just impossible because the study was conducted a long time ago and it is no longer possible to replicate the context.
- **Delete data from the majority class.** Randomly discard instances from the majority class. In the previous example, we could discard 996 instances of type *'no cancer'*. The problem with this is that we end up with insufficient data to learn good predictive models. If you have a huge dataset this can be an option, but in practice, this is rarely the case and you have the risk of having underrepresented samples.
- **Create synthetic data.** One of the most common solutions is to create synthetic data from the minority classes. In the following sections two methods that do that will be discussed: *random oversampling* and *Synthetic Minority Oversampling Technique (SMOTE)*.
- **Adapt your learning algorithm.** Another option is to use an algorithm that takes into account class counts and weights them accordingly. This is called *cost-sensitive classification*. For example, the `rpart()` method to train decision trees has a `weight` parameter which can be used to assign more weight to minority classes. When training neural networks it is also possible to assign different weights to different classes.

The following two subsections cover two techniques to create synthetic data.

5.4.1 Random Oversampling

```
shiny_random-oversampling.Rmd
```

This method consists of duplicating data points from the minority class. The following code will create an imbalanced dataset with 200 instances of class *'class1'* and only 15 instances of class *'class2'*.

```
set.seed(1234)

# Create random data
n1 <- 200 # Number of points of majority class.
n2 <- 15 # Number of points of minority class.

# Generate random values for class1.
x <- rnorm(mean = 0, sd = 0.5, n = n1)
y <- rnorm(mean = 0, sd = 1, n = n1)
df1 <- data.frame(label=rep("class1", n1),
                  x=x, y=y, stringsAsFactors = T)

# Generate random values for class2.
x2 <- rnorm(mean = 1.5, sd = 0.5, n = n2)
y2 <- rnorm(mean = 1.5, sd = 1, n = n2)
df2 <- data.frame(label=rep("class2", n2),
                  x=x2, y=y2, stringsAsFactors = T)

# This is our imbalanced dataset.
imbalancedDf <- rbind(df1, df2)

# Print class counts.
summary(imbalancedDf$label)
#> class1 class2
#<    200     15
```

If we want to exactly balance the class counts, we will need 185 additional instances of type *'class2'*. We can use our well known `sample()` function to pick 185 points from data frame `df2` (which contains only instances of class *'class2'*) and store them in `new.points`. Notice the `replace = T` parameter. This allows the function to pick repeated elements. Then, the new data points are appended to the imbalanced data set which now becomes balanced.

```
# Generate new points from the minority class.
new.points <- df2[sample(nrow(df2), size = 185, replace = T),]

# Add new points to the imbalanced dataset and save the
# result in balancedDf.
balancedDf <- rbind(imbalancedDf, new.points)

# Print class counts.
summary(balancedDf$label)
#> class1 class2
#>    200    200
```

The code associated with this chapter includes a shiny app[4] `shiny_random-oversampling.Rmd`. Shiny apps are interactive web applications. This shiny app graphically demonstrates how random oversampling works. Figure 5.9 depicts the shiny app. The user can move the slider to generate new data points. Please note that the boundaries do not change as the number of instances increases (or decreases). This is because the new points are just duplicates so they overlap with existing ones.

It is a common mistake to generate synthetic data on the entire dataset before splitting into train and test sets. This will cause your model to be highly overfitted since several duplicate data points can end up in both sets. Create synthetic data *only* from the *train set*.

[4]`https://shiny.rstudio.com/`

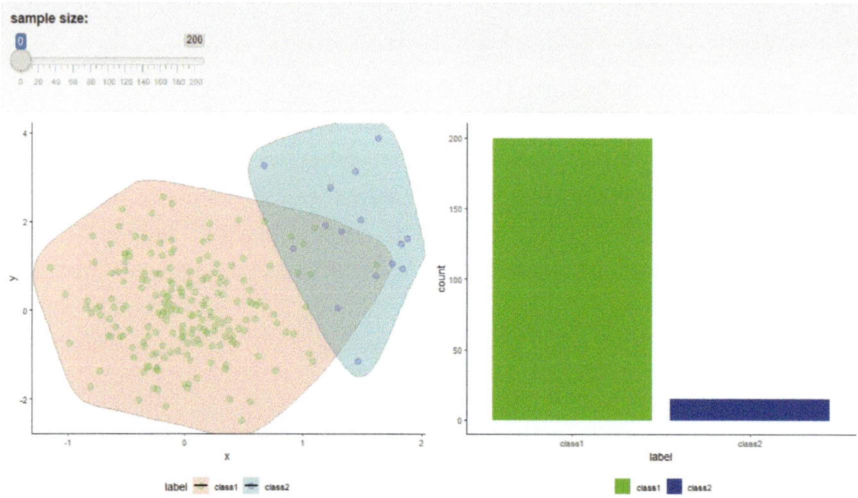

FIGURE 5.9 Shiny app with random oversampling example.

Random oversampling is simple and effective in many cases. A potential problem is that the models can overfit since there are many duplicate data points. To overcome this, the SMOTE method creates entirely new instances instead of duplicating them.

5.4.2 SMOTE

```
shiny_smote-oversampling.Rmd
```

SMOTE is another method that can be used to augment the data points from the minority class [Chawla et al., 2002]. One of the limitations of random oversampling is that it creates duplicates. This has the effect of having fixed boundaries and the classifiers can overspecialize. To avoid this, SMOTE creates entirely new data points.

SMOTE operates on the feature space (on the predictor variables). To generate a new point, take the difference between a given point a (taken from the minority class) and one of its randomly selected nearest neighbors b. The difference is multiplied by a random number between 0 and 1 and added to a. This has the effect of selecting a point along the line between a and b. Figure 5.10 illustrates the procedure of generating a new point in two dimensions.

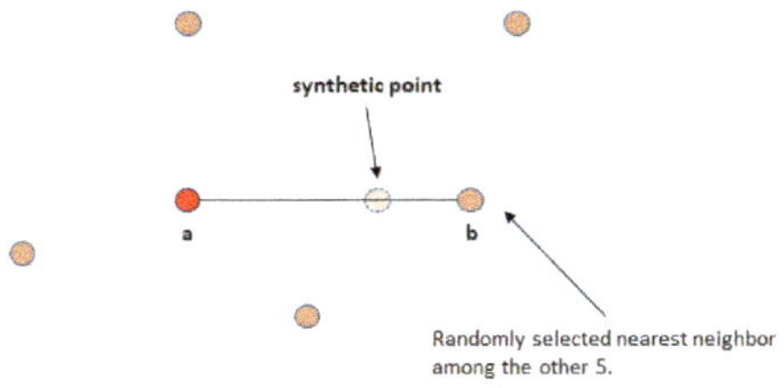

FIGURE 5.10 Synthetic point generation.

The number of nearest neighbors k is a parameter defined by the user. In their original work [Chawla et al., 2002], the authors set $k = 5$. Depending on how many new samples need to be generated, k' neighbors are randomly selected from the original k nearest neighbors. For example, if 200% oversampling is needed, $k' = 2$ neighbors are selected at random out of the $k = 5$ and one data point is generated with each of them. This is performed for each data point in the minority class.

An implementation of SMOTE is also provided in `auxiliary_functions/functions.R`. An example of its application can be found in `preprocessing.R` in the corresponding directory of this chapter's code. The `smote.class(completeDf, targetClass, N, k)` function has several arguments. The first one is the data frame that contains the minority and majority class, that is, the complete dataset. The second argument is the minority class label. The third argument `N` is the percent of smote and the last one (`k`) is the number of nearest neighbors to consider.

The following code shows how the function `smote.class()` can be used to generate new points from the imbalanced dataset that was introduced in the previous section 'Random Oversampling'. Recall that it has 200 points of class *'class1'* and 15 points of class *'class2'*.

```
# To balance the dataset, we need to oversample 1200%.
# This means that the method will create 12 * 15 new points.
ceiling(180 / 15) * 100
#> [1] 1200
```

```
# Percent to oversample.
N <- 1200

# Generate new data points.
synthetic.points <- smote.class(imbalancedDf,
                                targetClass = "class2",
                                N = N,
                                k = 5)$synthetic

# Append the new points to the original dataset.
smote.balancedDf <- rbind(imbalancedDf,
                          synthetic.points)

# Print class counts.
summary(smote.balancedDf$label)
#> class1 class2
#>    200    195
```

The parameter `N` is set to 1200. This will create 12 new data points for every minority class instance (15). Thus, the method will return 180 instances. In this case, k is set to 5. Finally, the new points are appended to the imbalanced dataset having a total of 195 samples of class 'class2'.

Again, a shiny app is included with this chapter's code. Figure 5.11 shows the distribution of the original points and after applying SMOTE. Note how the boundary of *'class2'* changes after applying SMOTE. It slightly spans in all directions. This is particularly visible in the lower right corner. This boundary expansion is what allows the classifiers to generalize better as compared to training them using random oversampled data.

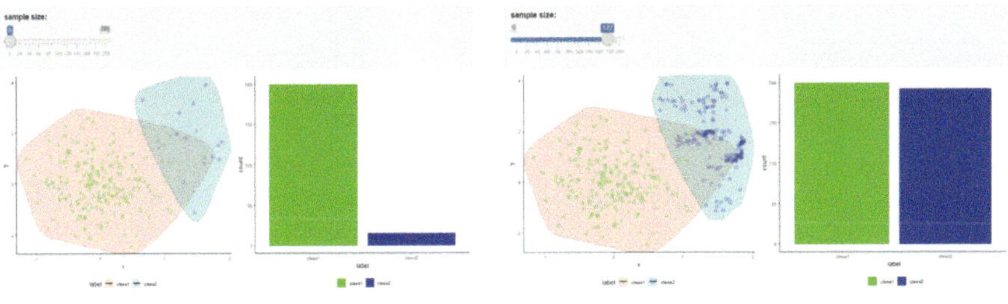

a) Before SMOTE b) After SMOTE

FIGURE 5.11 Shiny app with SMOTE example. a) Before applying SMOTE. b) After applying SMOTE.

5.5 Information Injection

The purpose of dividing the data into train/validation/test sets is to accurately estimate the generalization performance of a predictive model when it is presented with previously unseen data points. So, it is advisable to construct such set splits in a way that they are as independent as possible. Often, before training a model and generating predictions, the data needs to be preprocessed. Preprocessing operations may include imputing missing values, normalizing, and so on. During those operations, some information can be inadvertently transferred from the train to the test set thus, violating the assumption that they are independent.

Information injection occurs when information from the train set is transferred to the test set. When having train/validation/test sets, information injection occurs when information from the train set leaks into the validation and/or test set. It also happens when information from the validation set is transferred to the test set.

Suppose that as one of the preprocessing steps, you need to subtract the mean value of a feature for each instance. For now, suppose a dataset has a single feature x of numeric type and a categorical response variable y. The dataset has n rows. As a preprocessing step, you decide that you need to subtract the mean of x from each data point. Since you want to predict y given x, you train a classifier by splitting your data into train

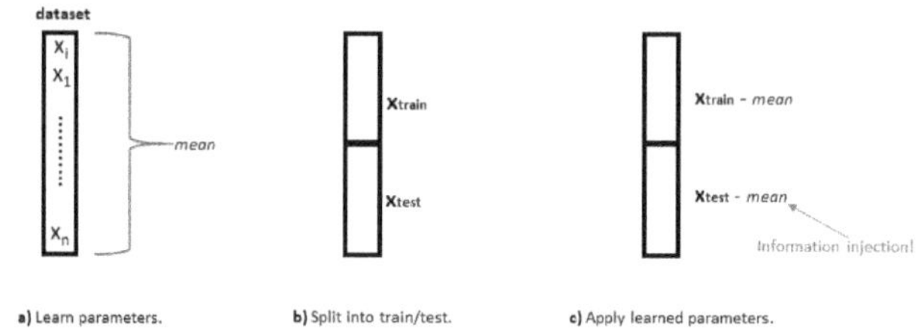

FIGURE 5.12 Information injection example. a) Parameters are learned from the entire dataset. b) The dataset is split intro train/test sets. c) The learned parameters are applied to both sets and information injection occurs.

and test sets as usual. So you proceed with the steps depicted in Figure 5.12.

First, (a) you compute the *mean* value of the of variable x from the entire dataset. This *mean* is known as the parameter. In this case, there is only one parameter but there could be several. For example, we could additionally need to compute the standard deviation. Once we know the mean value, the dataset is divided into train and test sets (b). Finally, the *mean* is subtracted from each element in both train and test sets (c). Without realizing, we have transferred information from the train set to the test set! But, how did this happen? Well, the *mean* parameter was computed using information from the *entire* dataset. Then, that *mean* parameter was used on the test set, but it was calculated using data points that also belong to that same test set!

Figure 5.13 shows how to correctly do the preprocessing to avoid information injection. The dataset is first split (a). Then, the *mean* parameter is calculated only with data points from the train set. Finally, the *mean*

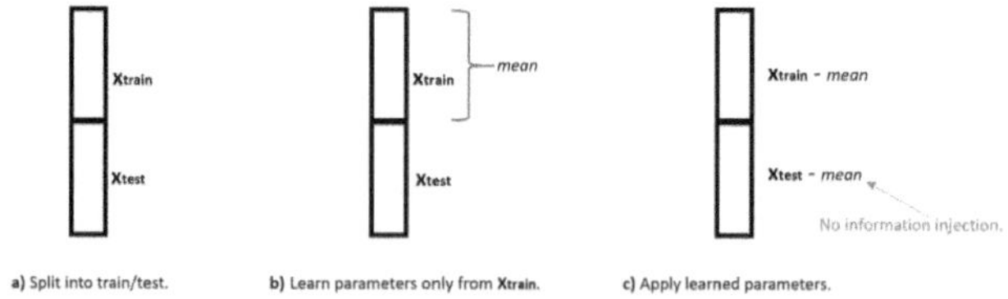

FIGURE 5.13 No information injection example. a) The dataset is first split into train/test sets. b) Parameters are learned only from the train set. c) The learned parameters are applied to the test set.

parameter is subtracted from both sets. Here, the mean contains information only from the train set.

In the previous example, we assumed that the dataset was split into train and test sets only once. The same idea applies when performing k-fold cross-validation. In each of the k iterations, the preprocessing parameters need to be learned only from the train split.

5.6 One-hot Encoding

Several algorithms need some or all of their input variables to be in numeric format, either the response and/or predictor variables. In R, for most classification algorithms, the class is usually encoded as a factor but some implementations may require it to be numeric. Sometimes there may be categorical variables as predictors such as gender (*'male'*, *'female'*). Some algorithms need those to be in numeric format because they, for example, are based on distance computations such as k-NN. Other models need to perform arithmetic operations on the predictor variables like neural networks.

One way to convert categorical variables into numeric ones is called **one-hot encoding**. The method works by creating new variables, sometimes called **dummy variables** which are boolean, one for each possible category. Suppose a dataset has a categorical variable *Job* (Figure 5.14) with three possible values: *programmer*, *teacher*, and *dentist*. This variable can be one-hot encoded by creating 3 new boolean dummy variables and setting them to 1 for the corresponding category and 0 for the rest.

Name	Age	Job
Jane	50	programmer
Karl	45	teacher
Thomas	30	dentist

→

Name	Age	programmer	teacher	dentist
Jane	50	1	0	0
Karl	45	0	1	0
Thomas	30	0	0	1

FIGURE 5.14 One-hot encoding example

You should be aware of the dummy variable trap which means that one variable can be predicted from the others. For example, if the possible values are just *male* and *female*, then if the dummy variable for *male* is 1, we know that the dummy variable for *female* must be 0. The solution to this is to drop one of the newly created variables. Which one? It does not matter which one. This trap only applies when the variable is a predictor. If it is a response variable, nothing should be dropped.

Figure 5.15 presents a guideline for how to convert non-numeric variables into numeric ones for classification tasks. This is only a guideline and the actual process will depend on each application.

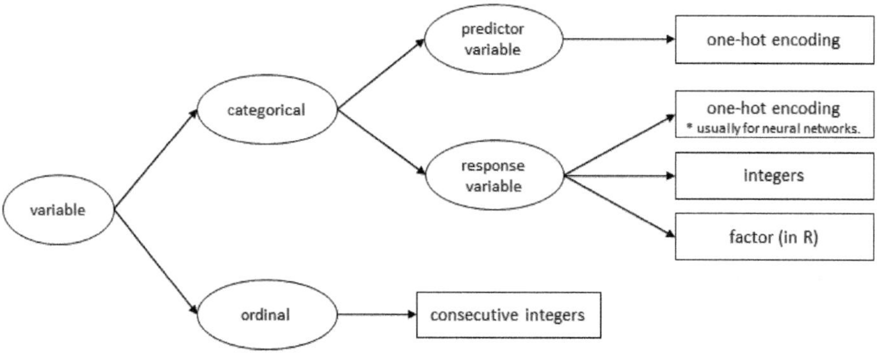

FIGURE 5.15 Variable conversion guidelines.

The `caret` package has a function `dummyVars()` that can be used to one-hot encode the categorical variables of a data frame. Since the *STUDENTS' MENTAL HEALTH* dataset [Nguyen et al., 2019] has several categorical variables, it can be used to demonstrate how to apply `dummyVars()`. This dataset collected at a University in Japan contains survey responses from students about their mental health and help-seeking behaviors. We begin by loading the data.

```
# Load students mental health behavior dataset.
# stringsAsFactors is set to F since the function
# that we will use to one-hot encode expects characters.
dataset <- read.csv(file.path(datasets_path,
                              "students_mental_health",
                              "data.csv"),
                              stringsAsFactors = F)
```

Note that the `stringsAsFactors` parameter is set to `FALSE`. This is necessary because `dummyVars()` needs characters to work properly. Before one-hot encoding the variables, we need to do some preprocessing to clean the dataset. This dataset contains several fields with empty characters ‘“”’. Thus, we will replace them with `NA` using the `replace_with_na_all()` function from the `naniar` package. This package was first described in the missing values section of this chapter, but that function was not mentioned. The function takes as its first argument the dataset and the second one is a formula that includes a condition.

```
# The dataset contains several empty strings.
# Replace those empty strings with NAs so the following
# methods will work properly.
# We can use the replace_with_na_all() function
# from naniar package to do the replacement.
library(naniar)
dataset <- replace_with_na_all(dataset,
                               ~.x %in% common_na_strings)
```

In this case, the condition is `~.x %in% common_na_strings` which means: replace all fields that contain one of the characters in `common_na_strings`. The variable `common_na_strings` contains a set of common strings that can be regarded as missing values, for example ‘NA’, ‘na’, ‘NULL’, empty strings, and so on. Now, we can use the `vis_miss()` function described in the missing values section to get a visual idea of the missing values.

```
# Visualize missing values.
vis_miss(dataset, warn_large_data = F)
```

Figure 5.16 shows the output plot. We can see that the last rows contain many missing values so we will discard them and only keep the first rows (1–268).

```
# Since the last rows starting at 269
# are full of missing values we will discard them.
dataset <- dataset[1:268,]
```

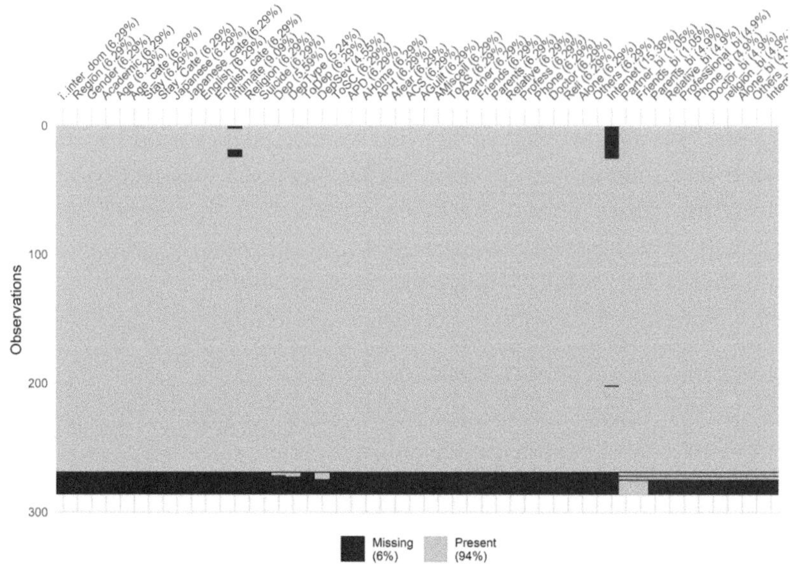

FIGURE 5.16 Missing values in the students mental health dataset.

As an example, we will one-hot encode the *Stay_Cate* variable which represents how long a student has been at the university: 1 year (Short), 2–3 years (Medium), or at least 4 years (Long). The `dummyVars()` function takes a formula as its first argument. Here, we specify that we only want to convert `Stay_Cate`. This function does not do the actual encoding but returns an object that is used with `predict()` to obtain the encoded variable(s) as a new data frame.

```
# One-hot encode the Stay_Cate variable.
# This variable Stay_Cate has three possible
# values: Long, Short and Medium.
# First, create a dummyVars object with the dummyVars()
#function from caret package.
library(caret)

dummyObj <- dummyVars( ~ Stay_Cate, data = dataset)

# Perform the actual encoding using predict()
```

```
encodedVars <- data.frame(predict(dummyObj,
                                  newdata = dataset))
```

Stay_CateLong	Stay_CateMedium	Stay_CateShort
1	0	0
0	0	1
1	0	0
0	0	1
0	0	1
1	0	0
0	0	1
0	1	0
1	0	0
0	1	0

FIGURE 5.17 One-hot encoded `Stay_Cate`.

If we inspect the resulting data frame (Figure 5.17) we see that it has 3 variables, one for each possible value: Long, Medium, and Short. If this variable is used as a predictor variable, we should delete one of its columns to avoid the dummy variable trap. We can do this by setting the parameter `fullRank = TRUE`.

```
dummyObj <- dummyVars( ~ Stay_Cate, data = dataset, fullRank = TRUE)
encodedVars <- data.frame(predict(dummyObj, newdata = dataset))
```

In this situation, the column with 'Long' was discarded (Figure 5.18). If you want to one-hot encode all variables at once you can use `~ .` as the formula. But be aware that the dataset may have some categories encoded as numeric and thus will not be transformed. For example, the *Age_cate* encodes age categories but the categories are represented as integers from 1 to 5. In this case, it may be ok not to encode this variable since lower integer numbers also imply smaller ages and bigger integer numbers represent older ages. If you still want to encode this variable you could first convert it to character by appending a letter at the beginning. Sometimes you should encode a variable, for example, if it represents colors. In that situation, it does not make sense to leave it as numeric since there is not semantic order between colors.

Stay_CateMedium	Stay_CateShort
0	0
0	1
0	0
0	1
0	1
0	0
0	1
1	0
0	0
1	0

FIGURE 5.18 One-hot encoded `Stay_Cate` dropping one of the columns.

Actually, in some very rare situations, it would make sense to leave color categories as integers. For example, if they represent a gradient like white, light blue, blue, dark blue, and black in which case this could be treated as an ordinal variable.

5.7 Summary

Programming functions that train predictive models expect the data to be in a particular format. Furthermore, some methods make assumptions about the data like having no missing values, having all variables in the same scale, and so on. This chapter presented several commonly used methods to preprocess datasets before using them to train models.

- When collecting data from different sensors, we can face several sources of variation like **sensors' format**, **different sampling rates**, **different scales**, and so on.
- Some preprocessing methods can lead to **information injection**. This happens when information from the train set is leaked to the test set.
- **Missing values** is a common problem in many data analysis tasks. In R, the `naniar` package can be used to spot missing values.

- **Imputation** is the process of inferring missing values. The `simputation` package can be used to impute missing values in datasets.
- **Normalization** is the process of transforming a set of variables to a common scale. For example from 0 to 1.
- An **imbalanced dataset** has a disproportionate number of classes of a certain type with respect to the others. Some methods like **random over/under sampling** and **SMOTE** can be used to balance a dataset.
- **One-hot-encoding** is a method that converts categorical variables into numeric ones.

6

Discovering Behaviors with Unsupervised Learning

So far, we have been working with supervised learning methods, that is, models for which the training instances have two elements: (1) a set of input values (features) and (2) the expected output (label). As mentioned in chapter 1, there are other types of machine learning methods and one of those is **unsupervised learning** which is the topic of this chapter. In unsupervised learning, the training instances do not have a response variable (e.g., a label). Thus, the objective is to extract knowledge from the available data without any type of guidance (supervision). For example, given a set of variables that characterize a person, we would like to find groups of people with similar behaviors. For physical activity behaviors, this could be done by finding groups of very active people versus finding groups of people with low physical activity. Those groups can be useful for delivering targeted suggestions or services thus, enhancing and personalizing the user experience.

This chapter starts with one of the most popular unsupervised learning algorithms: *k*-**means clustering**. Next, an example of how this technique can be applied to find groups of students with similar characteristics is presented. Then, **association rules mining** is presented, which is another type of unsupervised learning method. Finally, association rules are used to find criminal patterns from a homicide database.

6.1 *k*-means Clustering

kmeans_steps.R

DOI: 10.1201/9781003203469-6

This is one of the most commonly used unsupervised methods due to its simplicity and efficacy. Its objective is to find groups of points such that points in the same group are similar and points from different groups are as dissimilar as possible. The number of groups k needs to be defined a priori. The method is based on computing distances to **centroids**. The centroid of a set of points is computed by taking the mean of each of their features. The k-means algorithm is as follows:

```
Generate k centroids at random.
  Repeat until no change or max iterations:
      Assign each data point to the closest centroid.
      Update centroids.
```

To measure the distance between a data point and a centroid, the Euclidean distance is typically used, but other distances can be used as well depending on the application. As an example, let's cluster user responses from the *STUDENTS' MENTAL HEALTH* dataset. This database contains questionnaire responses about depression, acculturative stress, social connectedness, and help-seeking behaviors from students at a University in Japan. To demonstrate how k-means work, we will only choose two variables so we can plot the results. The variables are *ToAS* (Total Acculturative Stress) and *ToSC* (Total Social Connectedness). The *ToAS* measures the emotional challenges when adapting to a new culture while *ToSC* measures emotional distance with oneself and other people. For the clustering, the parameter k will be set to 3, that is, we want to group the points into 3 disjoint groups. The code that implements the k-means algorithm can be found in the script `kmeans_steps.R`. The algorithm begins by selecting 3 centroids at random. Figure 6.1 shows a scatterplot of the variables *ToAS* and *ToSC* along with the random centroids.

Next, at the first iteration, each point is assigned to the closest centroid. This is depicted in Figure 6.2 (top left). Then, the centroids are updated (moved) based on the new assignments. In the next iteration, the points are reassigned to the closest centroids and so on. Figure 6.2 shows the first 4 iterations of the algorithm.

From iteration 1 to 2 the centroids moved considerably. After that, they began to stabilize. Formally, the algorithm tries to minimize the total within cluster variation of all clusters. The cluster variation of a single cluster C_k is defined as:

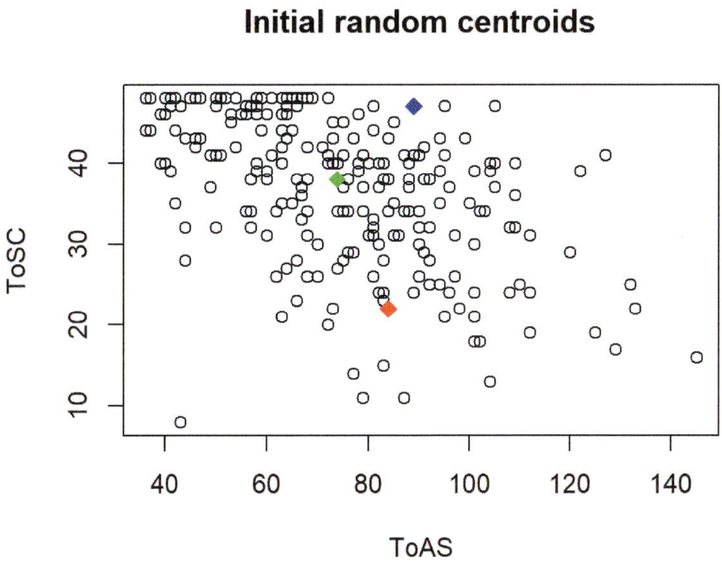

FIGURE 6.1 Three centroids chosen randomly.

$$W(C_k) = \sum_{x_i \in C_k} (x_i - \mu_k)^2 \tag{6.1}$$

where x_i is a data point and μ_k is the centroid of cluster C_k. Thus, the total within cluster variation $TWCV$ is:

$$TWCV = \sum_{i=1}^{k} W(C_i) \tag{6.2}$$

that is, the sum of all within-cluster variations across all clusters. The objective is to find the μ_k centroids that make $TWCV$ minimal. Finding the global optimum is a difficult problem. However, the iterative algorithm described above often produces good approximations.

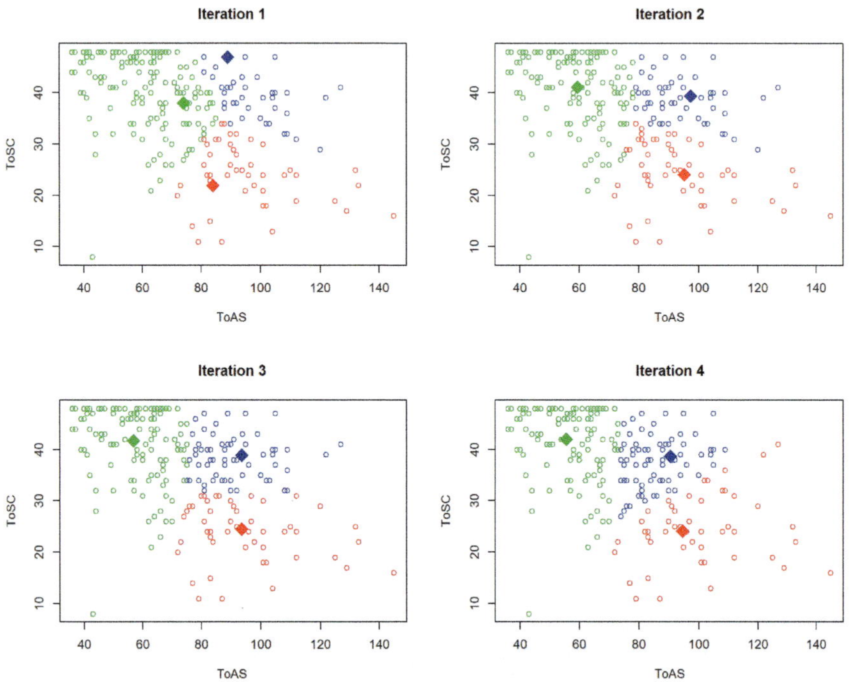

FIGURE 6.2 First 4 iterations of *k*-means.

6.1.1 Grouping Student Responses

```
group_students.R
```

In the previous example, we only used two variables to perform the clustering. Let's now use more variables from the *STUDENTS' MENTAL HEALTH* dataset to find groups. The full code can be found in `group_students.R`. After removing missing values, one-hot encoding categorical variables, and some additional cleaning, the following 10 variables were selected:

```
# Select which variables are going to be used for clustering.
selvars <- c("Stay","English_cate","Intimate"
```

```
,"APD","AHome","APH","Afear",
"ACS","AGuilt","ToAS")
```

Additionally, it is advisable to normalize the data between 0 and 1 since we are dealing with distance computations and we want to put the same weight on each variable. To plot the 10 variables, we can use **MDS** (described in chapter 4) to project the data into 2 dimensions (Figure 6.3).

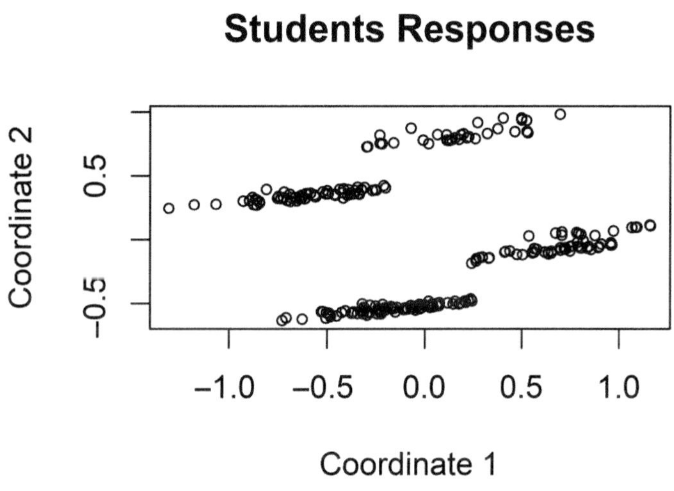

FIGURE 6.3 Students responses projected into 2D with MDS.

Visually, it seems that there are 4 distinct groups of points. Based on this initial guess, we can set $k = 4$ and use the `kmeans()` function included in base R to find the groups automatically.

```
clusters <- kmeans(normdf, 4)
```

The first argument of `kmeans()` is a data frame or a matrix and the second argument the number of clusters. Figure 6.4 shows the resulting clustering. The `kmeans()` method returns an object that contains several components including `cluster` that stores the assigned cluster for each data point and `centers` that stores the centroids.

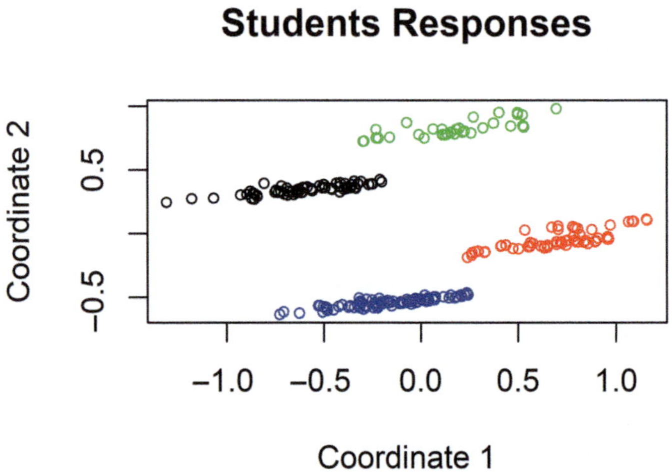

FIGURE 6.4 Students responses groups when k=4.

The k-means algorithm found the same clusters as we would intuitively expect. We can check how different the groups are by inspecting some of the variables. For example, by plotting a boxplot of the *Intimate* variable (Figure 6.5). This variable is 1 if the student has an intimate partner or 0 otherwise. Since there are only two possible values the boxplot looks flat. This shows that *cluster_1* and *cluster_3* are different from *cluster_2* and *cluster_4*.

Additionally, let's plot the *ACS* variable which represents the total score of culture shock (see Figure 6.6). This one has a minimum value of 3 and a max value of 13.

cluster_2 and *cluster_4* were similar based on the *Intimate* variable, but if we take a look at the difference in medians based on *ACS*, *cluster_2* and *cluster_4* are the most dissimilar clusters which gives an intuitive idea of why those two clusters were split into two different ones by the algorithm.

So far, the number of groups k has been chosen arbitrarily or by visual inspection. But, *is there an automatic way to select the best k?* As

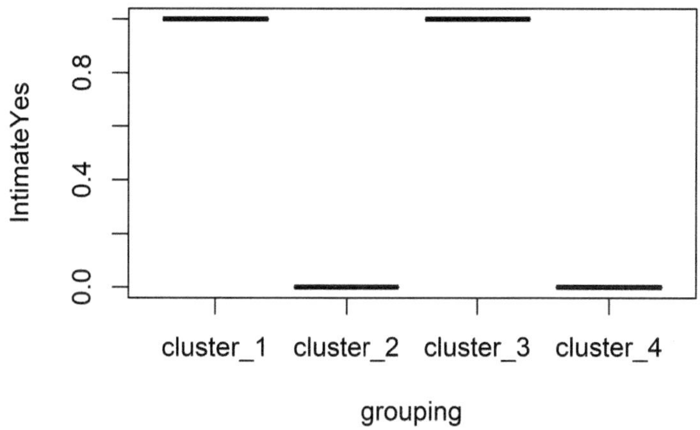

FIGURE 6.5 Boxplot of Intimate variable.

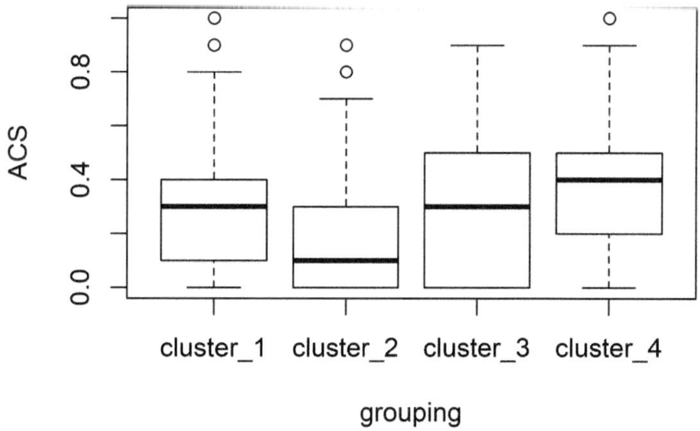

FIGURE 6.6 Boxplot of ACS variable.

always... this depends on the task at hand but there is a method called **Silhouette index** that can be used to select the optimal k based on an optimality criterion. This index is presented in the next section.

6.2 The Silhouette Index

As opposed to supervised learning, in unsupervised learning there is **no ground truth** to validate the results. In clustering, one way to validate the resulting groups is to plot them and manually explore the clusters' data points and look for similarities and/or differences. But sometimes we may also want to automate the process and have a quantitative way to measure how well the clustering algorithm grouped the points with the given set of parameters. If we had such a method we could do parameter optimization, for example, to find the best k. Well, there is something called *the silhouette index* [Rousseeuw, 1987] and it can be used to measure the correctness of the clusters.

This index is computed for each data point and tells us how well they are clustered. The total silhouette index is the mean of all points' indices and gives us an idea of how well the points were clustered overall. This index goes from -1 to 1 and I'll explain in a moment how to interpret it, but first let's see how it is computed.

To compute the silhouette index two things are needed: the already created groups and the distances between points. Let:

$a(i)$ = average dissimilarity (distance) of point i to all other points in A, where A is the cluster to which i has been assigned to (Figure 6.7).

$d(i, C)$ = average dissimilarity between i and all points in some cluster C.

$b(i) = \min_{C \neq A} d(i, C)$. The cluster B for which the minimum is obtained is the neighbor of point i. (The second best choice for i).

Thus, $s(i)$ (the silhouette index of point i) is obtained with the formula:

$$s(i) = \frac{b(i) - a(i)}{\max\{a(i), b(i)\}} \tag{6.3}$$

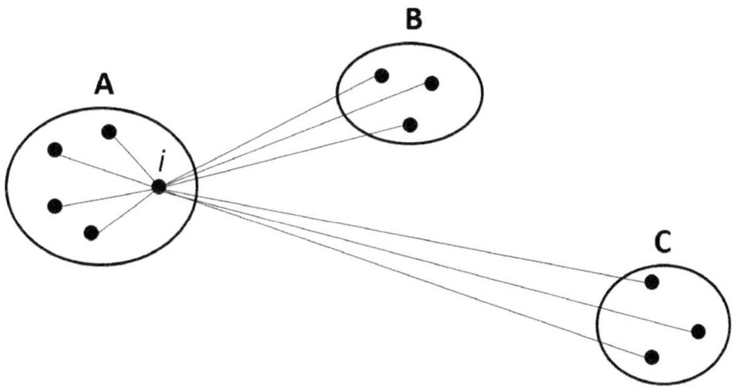

FIGURE 6.7 Three resulting clusters: A, B, and C. (Reprinted from *Journal of computational and applied mathematics* Vol. 20, Rousseeuw, P. J., "Silhouettes: a graphical aid to the interpretation and validation of cluster analysis" pp. 53-65, Copyright 1987, with permission from Elsevier. `doi:https://doi.org/10.1016/0377-0427(87)90125-7`).

When $s(i)$ is close to 1, it means that the *within* dissimilarity $a(i)$ is much smaller than the smallest *between* dissimilarity $b(i)$ thus, i can be considered to be well clustered. When $s(i)$ is close to 0 it is not clear whether i belongs to A or B. When $s(i)$ is close to -1, $a(i)$ is larger than $b(i)$ meaning that i may have been misgrouped. The total silhouette index S is the average of all indices $s(i)$ of all points.

In R, the `cluster` package has the function `silhouette()` that computes the silhouette index. The following code snippet clusters the student responses into 4 groups and computes the index of each point with the `silhouette()` function. Its first argument is the cluster assignments as returned by `kmeans()`, and the second argument is a `dist` object that contains the distances between each pair of points. We can compute this information from our data frame with the `dist()` function. The `silhouette()` function returns an object with the silhouette index of each data point. We can compute the total index by taking the average which in this case was 0.346.

```
library(cluster) # Load the required package.
set.seed(1234)
clusters <- kmeans(normdf, 4) # Try with k=4
```

```
# Compute silhouette indices for all points.
si <- silhouette(clusters$cluster, dist(normdf))

# Print first rows.
head(si)
#>      cluster neighbor sil_width
#> [1,]       1        4 0.3482364
#> [2,]       2        4 0.3718735
#> [3,]       3        1 0.3322198
#> [4,]       1        4 0.3998996
#> [5,]       1        4 0.3662811
#> [6,]       3        1 0.1463607

# Compute total Silhouette index by averaging the individual indices.
mean(si[,3])
# [1] 0.3466427
```

One nice thing about this index is that it can be presented visually. To generate a silhouette plot, use the generic `plot()` function and pass the object returned by `silhouette()`.

```
plot(si, cex.names=0.6, col = 1:4,
     main = "Silhouette plot, k=4",
     border=NA)
```

Figure 6.8 shows the silhouette plot when $k = 4$. The horizontal lines represent the individual silhouette indices. In this plot, all of them are positive. The height of each cluster gives a visual idea of the number of data points contained in it with respect to other clusters. We can see for example that cluster 2 is the smallest one. On the right side, is the number of points in each cluster and their average silhouette index. At the bottom, the total silhouette index is printed (0.35). We can try to cluster the points into 7 groups instead of 4 and see what happens.

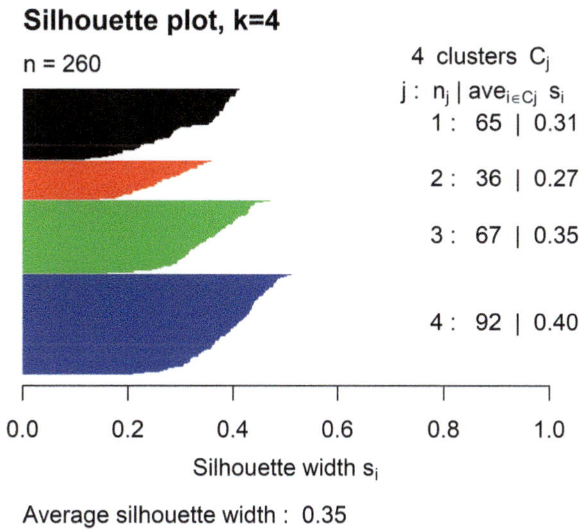

FIGURE 6.8 Silhouette plot when k=4.

```
set.seed(1234)
clusters <- kmeans(normdf, 7)
si <- silhouette(clusters$cluster, dist(normdf))
plot(si, cex.names=0.6, col = 1:7,
     main = "Silhouette plot, k=7",
     border=NA)
```

Here, cluster 2 and 4 have data points with negative indices and the overall score is 0.26. This suggests that $k = 4$ produces more coherent clusters as compared to $k = 7$.

In this section, we used the Silhouette index to validate the clustering results. Over the years, several other clustering validation methods have been developed. In their paper, Halkidi et al. [2001] present an overview of other clustering validation methods.

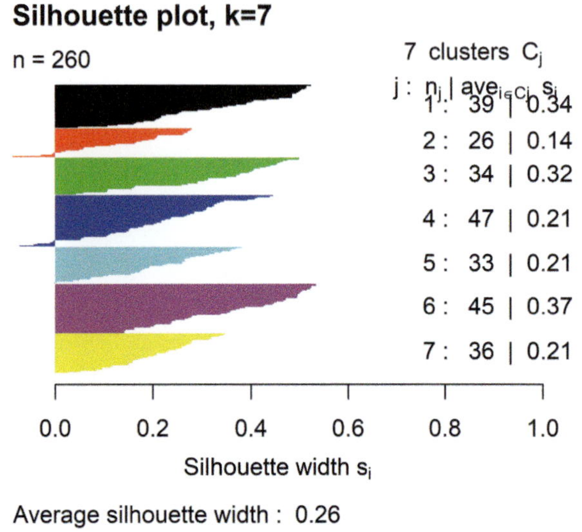

FIGURE 6.9 Silhouette plot when k=7.

6.3 Mining Association Rules

Association rule mining consists of a set of methods to extract patterns (rules) from transactional data. For example, shopping behavior can be analyzed by finding rules from customers' shopping transactions. A **transaction** is an event that involves a set of items. For example, when someone buys a soda, a bag of chips, and a chocolate bar the purchase is registered as *one* transaction containing 3 items. I apologize for using this example for those of you with healthy diets. Based on a database that contains many transactions, it is possible to uncover item relationships. Those relationships are usually expressed as implication rules of the form $X \implies Y$ where X and Y are sets of items. Both sets are disjoint, this means that items in X are not in Y and vice-versa which can be formally represented as $X \cap Y = \emptyset$. That is, the intersection of the two sets is the empty set. $X \implies Y$ is read as: if X then Y. The left-hand-side (lhs) X is called the **antecedent** and the right-hand-side (rhs) Y is called the **consequent**.

In the unhealthy supermarket example, a rule like $\{chips, chocolate\} \implies \{soda\}$ can be interpreted as *if someone buys chips and chocolate then, it is likely that this same person will also buy soda.* These types of rules can be used for targeted advertisements, product placement decisions, etc.

The possible number of rules that can be generated grows exponentially as the number of items increases. Furthermore, not all rules may be interesting. The most well-known algorithm to find interesting association rules is called **Apriori** [Agrawal and Srikant, 1994]. To quantify if a rule is interesting or not, this algorithm uses two importance measures: **support** and **confidence**.

- **Support.** The support $\text{supp}(X)$ of an itemset X is the proportion of transactions that contain all the items in X. This quantifies how frequent the itemset is.
- **Confidence.** The confidence of a rule $\text{conf}(X \implies Y) = \text{supp}(X \cup Y)/\text{supp}(X)$ and can be interpreted as the conditional probability that Y occurs given that X is present. This can also be thought of as the probability that a transaction that contains X also contains Y. The $\cup$ operator is the union of two sets. This means taking all elements from both sets and removing repeated elements.

Now that there is a way to measure the importance of the rules, the Apriori algorithm first finds itemsets that satisfy a minimum support and generates rules from those itemsets that satisfy a minimum confidence. Those minimum thresholds are set by the user. The lower the thresholds, the more rules returned by the algorithm. One thing to note is that Apriori only generates rules with itemsets of size 1 on the right-hand side. Another common metric to measure the importance of a rule is the **lift**. Lift is typically used after Apriori has generated the rules to further filter and/or rank the results.

- **Lift.** The lift of a rule $\text{lift}(X \implies Y) = \text{supp}(X \cup Y)/(\text{supp}(X)\text{supp}(Y))$ is similar to the confidence but it also takes into consideration the frequency of Y. A lift of 1 means that there is no association between X and Y. A lift greater than 1 means that Y is likely to occur if X occurs and a lift less than 1 means that Y is unlikely to occur when X occurs.

Let's compute all those metrics using an example. The following table shows a synthetic example database of transactions from shoppers with unhealthy behaviors.

Transaction ID	Items
1	{chocolate}
2	{chocolate, chips, soda}
3	{chocolate, soda}
4	{soda}
5	{soda}
6	{candies, ice cream}
7	{soda, ice cream}
8	{chips, soda}
9	{candies, chocolate, chips}
10	{ice cream, chocolate, soda chips}

FIGURE 6.10 Example database with 10 transactions.

The support of the itemset consisting of a single item *'chocolate'* is $\text{supp}(\{chocolate\}) = 5/10 = 0.5$ because *'chocolate'* appears in 5 out of the 10 transactions. The support of $\{chips, soda\}$ is $3/10 = 0.3$.

The confidence of the rule $\{chocolate, chips\} \implies \{soda\}$ is:

$$\begin{aligned}\text{conf}(\{chocolate, chips\} \implies \{soda\}) &= \frac{\text{supp}(\{chocolate, chips, soda\})}{\text{supp}(\{chocolate, chips\})} \\ &= (2/10)/(3/10) \\ &= 0.66\end{aligned}$$

The lift of $\{soda\} \implies \{icecream\}$ is:

$$\begin{aligned}\text{lift}(\{soda\} \implies \{icecream\}) &= \frac{\text{supp}(\{soda, icecream\})}{\text{supp}(\{soda\})\text{supp}(\{icecream\})} \\ &= (2/10)/((7/10)(3/10)) \\ &= 0.95.\end{aligned}$$

Association rules mining is unsupervised in the sense that there are no labels or ground truth. Many applications of association rules are targeted to market basket analysis to gain insights into shoppers' behavior and take actions to increase sales. To find such rules it is necessary to have 'transactions' (sets of items), for example, supermarket products.

However, this is not the only application of association rules. There are other problems that can be structured as transactions of items. For example in medicine, *diseases* can be seen as transactions and *symptoms* as items. Thus, one can apply association rules algorithms to find symptoms and disease relationships. Another application is in recommender systems. Take, for example, movies. Transactions can be the set of movies watched by every user. If you watched a movie m then, the recommender system can suggest another movie that co-occurred frequently with m and that you have not watched yet. Furthermore, other types of relational data can be transformed into transaction-like structures to find patterns and this is precisely what we are going to do in the next section to mine criminal patterns.

6.3.1 Finding Rules for Criminal Behavior

```
crimes_process.R crimes_rules.R
```

In this section, we will use association rules mining to find patterns in the *HOMICIDE REPORTS*[1] dataset. This database contains homicide reports from 1980 to 2014 in the United States. The database is structured as a table with 24 columns and 638454 rows. Each row corresponds to a homicide report that includes city, state, year, month, sex of victim, sex of perpetrator, if the crime was solved or not, weapon used, age of the victim and perpetrator, the relationship type between the victim and the perpetrator, and some other information.

Before trying to find rules, the data needs to be preprocessed and converted into transactions. Each homicide report will be a transaction and the items are the possible values of 3 of the columns: **Relationship**, **Weapon**, and **Perpetrator.Age**. The **Relationship** variable can take values like *Stranger*, *Neighbor*, *Friend*, etc. In total, there are 28 possible relationship values including *Unknown*. For the purpose of our analysis, we will remove rows with unknown values in **Relationship** and **Weapon**. Since **Perpetrator.Age** is an integer, we need to convert it into categories. The following age groups are created: child ($<$ 13 years), teen (13 to 17 years), adult (18 to 45 years), and lateAdulthood ($>$ 45

[1] https://www.kaggle.com/murderaccountability/homicide-reports

years). After these cleaning and preprocessing steps, the dataset has 3 columns and 328238 rows (see Figure 6.11). The script used to perform the preprocessing is `crimes_process.R`.

Relationship	Weapon	Perpetrator.CatAge
R.Acquaintance	Blunt Object	teen
R.Acquaintance	Strangulation	adult
R.Acquaintance	Strangulation	adult
R.Acquaintance	Rifle	adult
R.Wife	Knife	adult
R.Wife	Knife	adult
R.Stranger	Shotgun	lateAdulthood
R.Girlfriend	Blunt Object	adult
R.Ex-Husband	Handgun	adult
R.Acquaintance	Knife	adult
R.Brother	Blunt Object	adult
R.Acquaintance	Handgun	adult
R.Brother	Handgun	adult
R.Stepdaughter	Rifle	adult
R.Stepdaughter	Rifle	adult

FIGURE 6.11 First rows of preprocessed crimes data frame. Source: Data from the Murder Accountability Project, founded by Thomas Hargrove (CC BY-SA 4.0) [`https://creativecommons.org/licenses/by-sa/4.0/legalcode`].

Now, we have a data frame that contains only the relevant information. Each row will be used to generate one transaction. An example transaction may be *{R.Wife, Knife, Adult}*. This one represents the case where the perpetrator is an *adult* who used a *knife* to kill his *wife*. Note the 'R.' at the beginning of 'Wife'. This 'R.' was added for clarity in order to identify that this item is a relationship. One thing to note is that every transaction will consist of exactly 3 items. This is a bit different than the market basket case in which every transaction can include a varying number of products. Although this item-size constraint was a design decision based on the structure of the original data, this will not prevent us from performing the analysis to find interesting rules.

To find the association rules, the `arules` package [Hahsler et al., 2019] will be used. This package has an interface to an efficient implementation in C of the Apriori algorithm. This package needs the transactions to be stored as an object of type 'transactions'. One way to create this object is to use a **logical matrix** and cast it into a transactions object. The rows of the logical matrix represent transactions and columns represent items. The number of columns equals the total number of possible items. A `TRUE` value indicates that the item is present in the transaction and `FALSE` otherwise. In our case, the matrix has 46 columns. The `crimes_process.R` script has code to generate this matrix `M`. The 46 items (columns of `M`) are:

```
as.character(colnames(M))
#> [1] "R.Acquaintance"            "R.Wife"                   "R.Stranger"
#> [4] "R.Girlfriend"              "R.Ex-Husband"             "R.Brother"
#> [7] "R.Stepdaughter"            "R.Husband"                "R.Friend"
#> [10] "R.Family"                 "R.Neighbor"               "R.Father"
#> [13] "R.In-Law"                 "R.Son"                    "R.Ex-Wife"
#> [16] "R.Boyfriend"              "R.Mother"                 "R.Sister"
#> [19] "R.Common-Law Husband"     "R.Common-Law Wife"        "R.Stepfather"
#> [22] "R.Stepson"                "R.Stepmother"             "R.Daughter"
#> [25] "R.Boyfriend/Girlfriend"   "R.Employer"               "R.Employee"
#> [28] "Blunt Object"             "Strangulation"            "Rifle"
#> [31] "Knife"                    "Shotgun"                  "Handgun"
#> [34] "Drowning"                 "Firearm"                  "Suffocation"
#> [37] "Fire"                     "Drugs"                    "Explosives"
#> [40] "Fall"                     "Gun"                      "Poison"
#> [43] "teen"                     "adult"                    "lateAdulthood"
#> [46] "child"
```

The following snippet shows how to convert the matrix into an `arules` transactions object. Before the conversion, the package `arules` needs to be loaded. For convenience, the transactions are saved in a file `transactions.RData`.

```
library(arules)

# Convert into a transactions object.
transactions <- as(M, "transactions")
```

```
# Save transactions file.
save(transactions, file="transactions.RData")
```

Now that the database is in the required format we can start the analysis. The `crimes_rules.R` script has the code to perform the analysis. First, the transactions file that we generated before is loaded:

```
library(arules)
library(arulesViz)

# Load preprocessed data.
load("transactions.RData")
```

Note that additionally to the `arules` package, we also loaded the `arulesViz` package [Hahsler, 2019]. This package has several functions to generate cool plots of the learned rules! A summary of the transactions can be printed with the `summary()` function:

```
# Print summary.
summary(transactions)

#> transactions as itemMatrix in sparse format with
#> 328238 rows (elements/itemsets/transactions) and
#> 46 columns (items) and a density of 0.06521739
#>
#> most frequent items:
#>    adult          Handgun R.Acquaintance      R.Stranger
#> 257026            160586          117305           77725
#> Knife          (Other)
#> 61936           310136
#>
#> element (itemset/transaction) length distribution:
#>    sizes
#> 3
#> 328238
#>
```

```
#> Min. 1st Qu.  Median    Mean 3rd Qu.     Max.
#> 3       3       3       3       3       3
#>
#> includes extended item information - examples:
#>    labels
#> Relationship1 R.Acquaintance
#> Relationship2         R.Wife
#> Relationship3     R.Stranger
```

The summary shows the total number of rows (transactions) and the number of columns. It also prints the most frequent items, in this case, *adult* with 257026 occurrences, *Handgun* with 160586, and so on. The itemset sizes are also displayed. Here, all itemsets have a size of 3 (by design). Some other summary statistics are also printed.

We can use the `itemFrequencyPlot()` function from the `arulesViz` package to plot the frequency of items.

```
itemFrequencyPlot(transactions,
                  type = "relative",
                  topN = 15,
                  main = 'Item frequecies')
```

The `type` argument specifies that we want to plot the relative frequencies. Use `"absolute"` instead to plot the total counts. `topN` is used to select how many items are plotted. Figure 6.12 shows the output.

Now it is time to find some interesting rules! This can be done with the `apriori()` function as follows:

```
# Run apriori algorithm.
resrules <- apriori(transactions,
                    parameter = list(support = 0.001,
                                     confidence = 0.5,
                                     # Find rules with at least 2 items.
                                     minlen = 2,
                                     target = 'rules'))
```

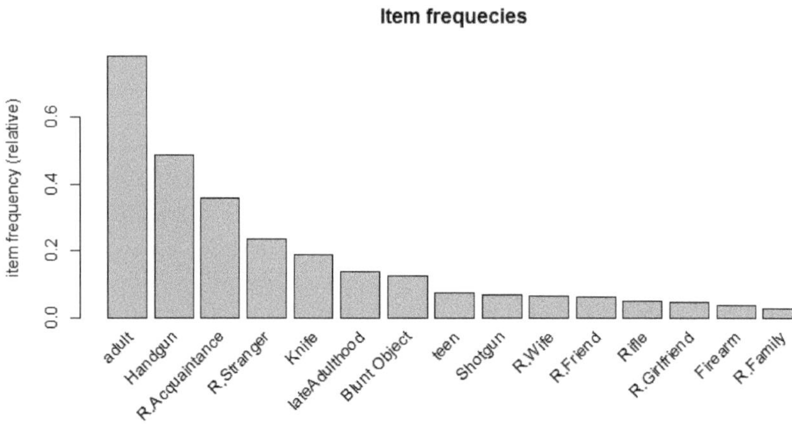

FIGURE 6.12 Frequences of the top 15 items.

The first argument is the transactions object. The second argument `parameter` specifies a list of algorithm parameters. In this case we want rules with a minimum support of 0.001 and a confidence of at least 0.5. The `minlen` argument specifies the minimum number of allowed items in a rule (antecedent + consequent). We set it to 2 since we want rules with at least one element in the antecedent and one element in the consequent, for example, *{item1 => item2}*. This Apriori algorithm creates rules with only one item in the consequent. Finally, the `target` parameter is used to specify that we want to find rules because the function can also return item sets of different types (see the documentation for more details). The returned rules are saved in the `resrules` variable that can be used later to explore the results. We can also print a summary of the returned results.

```
# Print a summary of the results.
summary(resrules)

#> set of 141 rules
#>
#> rule length distribution (lhs + rhs):sizes
#> 2  3
#> 45 96
#>
```

```
#> Min. 1st Qu.  Median    Mean 3rd Qu.    Max.
#> 2.000   2.000   3.000   2.681   3.000   3.000
#>
#> summary of quality measures:
#>    support            confidence             lift              count
#> Min.    :0.001030   Min.    :0.5045   Min.    :0.6535   Min.    :    338
#> 1st Qu.:0.001767   1st Qu.:0.6478   1st Qu.:0.9158   1st Qu.:    580
#> Median :0.004424   Median :0.7577   Median :1.0139   Median :   1452
#> Mean    :0.021271   Mean    :0.7269   Mean    :1.0906   Mean    :   6982
#> 3rd Qu.:0.012960   3rd Qu.:0.8131   3rd Qu.:1.0933   3rd Qu.:   4254
#> Max.    :0.376836   Max.    :0.9539   Max.    :4.2777   Max.    :123692
#>
#> mining info:
#>     data ntransactions support confidence
#> transactions        328238   0.001        0.5
```

By looking at the summary, we see that the algorithm found 141 rules that satisfy the support and confidence thresholds. The rule length distribution is also printed. Here, 45 rules are of size 2 and 96 rules are of size 3. Then, some standard statistics are shown for support, confidence, and lift. The `inspect()` function can be used to print the actual rules. Rules can be sorted by one of the importance measures. The following code sorts by lift and prints the first 20 rules. Figure 6.13 shows the output.

```
# Print the first n (20) rules with highest lift in decreasing order.
inspect(sort(resrules, by='lift', decreasing = T)[1:20])
```

The first rule with a lift of 4.27 says that if a homicide was committed by an *adult* and the victim was the *stepson*, then is it likely that a *blunt object* was used for the crime. By looking at the rules, one can also note that whenever *blunt object* appears either in the lhs or rhs, the victim was most likely an infant. Another thing to note is that when the victim was *boyfriend*, the crime was likely committed with a *knife*. This is also mentioned in the reports 'Homicide trends in the United States' [Cooper et al., 2012]:

```
> inspect(sort(resrules, by='lift', decreasing = T)[1:20])
     lhs                                 rhs            support     confidence coverage    lift     count
[1]  {R.Stepson,adult}                => {Blunt Object} 0.001197302 0.5361528  0.002233136 4.277728   393
[2]  {R.Son,adult}                    => {Blunt Object} 0.010172497 0.5148805  0.019757006 4.108005  3339
[3]  {R.Daughter,adult}               => {Blunt Object} 0.008280577 0.5047354  0.016405779 4.027062  2718
[4]  {R.Boyfriend,adult}              => {Knife}        0.009508345 0.5210351  0.018248954 2.761294  3121
[5]  {R.Boyfriend}                    => {Knife}        0.010800090 0.5068630  0.021307710 2.686187  3545
[6]  {R.Ex-Husband}                   => {Handgun}      0.001185116 0.6451078  0.001837082 1.318601   389
[7]  {R.Stranger,lateAdulthood}       => {Handgun}      0.010921953 0.6399500  0.017066884 1.308059  3585
[8]  {R.Husband,lateAdulthood}        => {Handgun}      0.004423619 0.6210436  0.007122880 1.269414  1452
[9]  {R.Stranger,teen}                => {Handgun}      0.014693606 0.6186506  0.023751059 1.264523  4823
[10] {R.Stranger}                     => {Handgun}      0.146485172 0.6186169  0.236794643 1.264454 48082
[11] {R.Stranger,adult}               => {Handgun}      0.120787356 0.6169683  0.195775626 1.261084 39647
[12] {R.Stepson,Blunt Object}         => {adult}        0.001197302 0.9538835  0.001255187 1.218168   393
[13] {R.Daughter,Blunt Object}        => {adult}        0.008280577 0.9398340  0.008810680 1.200226  2718
[14] {R.Son,Blunt Object}             => {adult}        0.010172497 0.9350322  0.010879301 1.194094  3339
[15] {R.Ex-Wife,lateAdulthood}        => {Handgun}      0.001029741 0.5787671  0.001779197 1.183001   338
[16] {R.In-Law,lateAdulthood}         => {Handgun}      0.001675613 0.5771249  0.002903381 1.179644   550
[17] {R.Acquaintance,teen}            => {Handgun}      0.016445384 0.5768327  0.028509801 1.179047  5398
[18] {R.Stranger,Strangulation}       => {adult}        0.001617729 0.9139415  0.001770057 1.167159   531
[19] {R.Boyfriend/Girlfriend,Knife}   => {adult}        0.001401422 0.8949416  0.001565937 1.142895   460
[20] {R.Girlfriend,Strangulation}     => {adult}        0.001398376 0.8929961  0.001565937 1.140411   459
```

FIGURE 6.13 Output of the inspect() function.

From 1980 through 2008 'Boyfriends were more likely to be killed by knives than any other group of intimates'.

According to rule 20, crimes involving *girlfriend* have a strong relationship with *strangulation*. This can also be confirmed in [Cooper et al., 2012]:

From 1980 through 2008 'Girlfriends were more likely to be killed by force...'.

The resulting rules can be plotted with the `plot()` function (see Figure 6.14). By default, it generates a scatterplot with the *support* in the x axis and *confidence* in the y axis colored by *lift*.

```
# Plot a default scatterplot of support vs. confidence colored by lift.
plot(resrules)
```

The plot shows that rules with a high *lift* also have a low *support* and *confidence*. Hahsler [2017] mentioned that rules with high *lift* typically

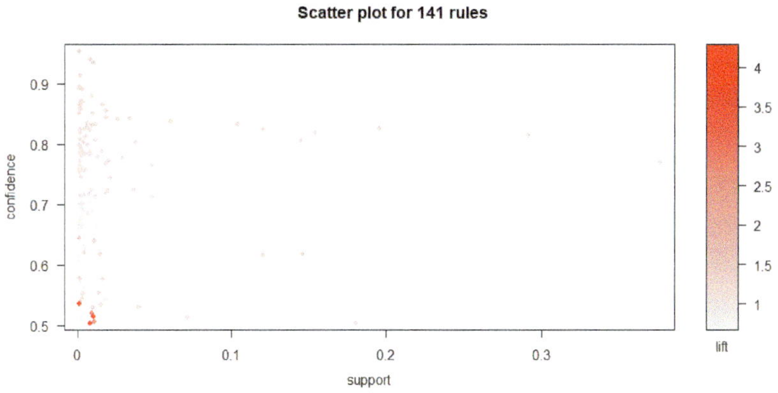

FIGURE 6.14 Scatterplot of rules support vs. confidence colored by lift.

have low *support*. The plot can be customized for example to show the *support* and *lift* in the axes and color them by confidence. The axes can be set with the `measure` parameter and the coloring with the `shading` parameter. The function also supports different plotting engines including static and interactive. The following code generates a customized interactive plot by setting `engine = "htmlwidget"`. This is very handy if you want to know which points correspond to which rules. By hovering the mouse on the desired point the corresponding rule is shown as a tooltip box (Figure 6.15). The interactive plots also allow to zoom in regions by clicking and dragging.

```
# Customize scatterplot to make it interactive
# and plot support vs. lift colored by confidence.
plot(resrules, engine = "htmlwidget",
     measure = c("support", "lift"), shading = "confidence")
```

The `arulesViz` package has a nice option to plot rules as a graph. This is done by setting `method = "graph"`. We can also make the graph interactive for easier exploration by setting `engine="htmlwidget"`. For clarity, the font size is reduced with `cex=0.9`. Here we plot the first 25 rules.

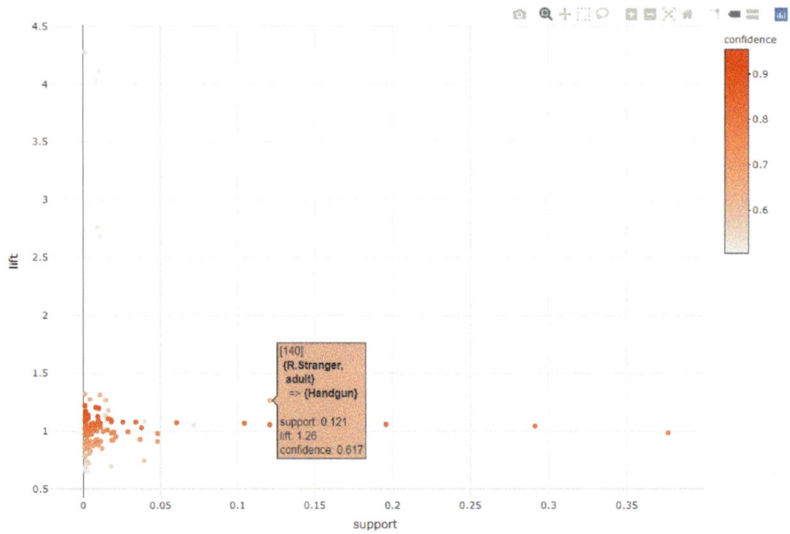

FIGURE 6.15 Interactive scatterplot of rules.

```
# Plot rules as a graph.
plot(head(sort(resrules, by = "lift"), n=25),
     method = "graph",
     control=list(cex=.9),
     engine="htmlwidget")
```

Figure 6.16 shows a zoomed-in portion of the entire graph. Circles represent rules and rounded squares items. The size of the circle is relative to the *support* and color relative to the *lift*. Incoming arrows represent the items in the antecedent and the outgoing arrow of a circle points to the item in the consequent part of the rule. From this graph, some interesting patterns can be seen. First, when the age category of the perpetrator is *lateAdulthood*, the victims were the *husband* or *ex-wife*. When the perpetrator is a *teen*, the victim was likely a *friend* or *stranger*.

The `arulesViz` package has a cool function `ruleExplorer()` that generates a shiny app with interactive controls and several plot types. When running the following code (output not shown) you may be asked to install additional shiny related packages.

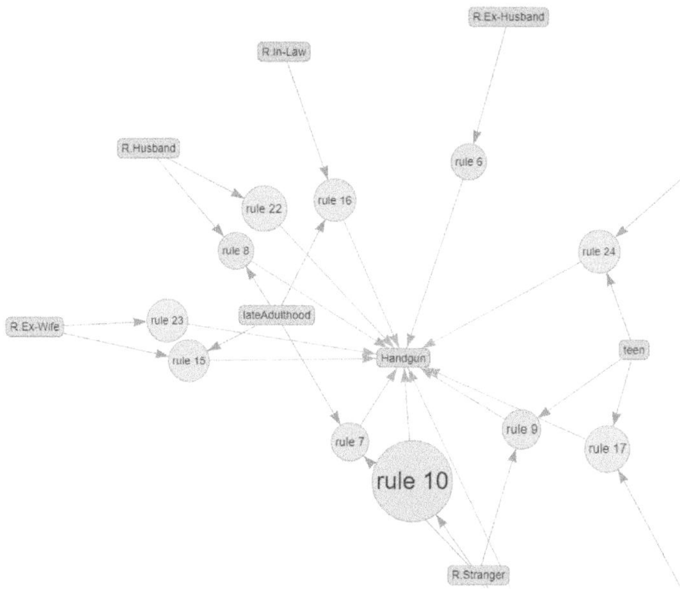

FIGURE 6.16 Interactive graph of rules.

```
# Opens a shiny app with several interactive plots.
ruleExplorer(resrules)
```

Sometimes Apriori returns thousands of rules. There is a convenient `subset()` function to extract rules of interest. For example, we can select only the rules that contain *R.Girlfriend* in the antecedent (lhs) and print the top three with highest lift (Figure 6.17 shows the result):

```
# Subset transactions.
rulesGirlfriend <- subset(resrules, subset = lhs %in% "R.Girlfriend")

# Print rules with highest lift.
inspect(head(rulesGirlfriend, n = 3, by = "lift"))
```

In this section, we showed how interesting rules can be extracted from a crimes database. Several preprocessing steps were required to transform the tabular data into transactional data. This example already demonstrated how the same data can be represented in different ways (tabular and transactional). The next chapter will cover more details about how

```
> inspect(head(rulesGirlfriend, n = 3, by = "lift"))
    lhs                               rhs     support   confidence coverage  lift   count
[1] {R.Girlfriend,Strangulation} => {adult} 0.0013984 0.89300    0.0015659 1.1404  459
[2] {R.Girlfriend,Blunt Object}  => {adult} 0.0062333 0.82734    0.0075342 1.0566 2046
[3] {R.Girlfriend,Knife}         => {adult} 0.0083872 0.82277    0.0101938 1.0507 2753
```

FIGURE 6.17 Output of the inspect() function.

data can be transformed into **different representations** suitable for different types of learning algorithms.

6.4 Summary

One of the types of machine learning is **unsupervised learning** in which there are no labels. This chapter introduced some unsupervised methods such as clustering and association rules.

- The objective of k-**means clustering** is to find groups of points such that points in the same group are similar and points from different groups are as dissimilar as possible.
- The **centroid** of a group is calculated by taking the mean value of each feature.
- In k-**means**, one needs to specify the number of groups k before running the algorithm.
- The **Silhouette Index** is a measure that tells us how well a set of points were clustered. This measure can be used to find the optimal number of groups k.
- **Association rules** can find patterns in an unsupervised manner.
- The **Apriori algorithm** is the most well-known method for finding association rules.
- Before using the *Apriori algorithm*, one needs to format the data as **transactions**.
- A **transaction** is an event that involves a set of items.

WHAT HAPPENED?
A WOMAN IN NIGHTGOWN WITH GREEN HAIR AND MOTORCYCLE BOOTS TOOK MY LITTLE DOLL.
YOU'VE HEARD IT DARLING. RUN A-PRIORI ON THE ENTIRE DATABASE AND SEND ME THE TOP RULES SORTED BY LIFT.
I AM MISS KARLENE BUT YOU CAN CALL ME K-MISS. I COMMAND YOU TO RELEASE THE DOLLS!
NEVER! THESE ARE MY BELOVED DAUGHTERS.
I CAN'T MOVE.
GRAVITATIONAL FORCES WILL PULL YOUR ATOMS TOWARDS THEIR CENTROIDS. BYE.
EL NEVADO NEWS
K-MISS RESCUES HUNDREDS OF KIDNAPPED DOLLS
behavior.enriquegc.com

7

Encoding Behavioral Data

Behavioral data comes in many different flavors and shapes. Data stored in databases also have different structures (relational, graph, plain text, etc.). As mentioned in chapter 1, before training a predictive model, data goes through a series of steps, from data collection to preprocessing (Figure 1.7). During those steps, data is transformed and shaped with the aim of easing the operations in the subsequent tasks. Finally, the data needs to be encoded in a very specific format as expected by the predictive model. For example, decision trees and many other classifier methods expect their input data to be formatted as **feature vectors** while Dynamic Time Warping expects the data to be represented as **timeseries**. Images are usually encoded as n-dimensional matrices. When it comes to social network analysis, a **graph** is the preferred representation.

So far, I have been mentioning two key terms: **encode** and **representation**. The Cambridge Dictionary[1] defines the verb *encode* as:

> *"To put information into a form in which it can be stored, and which can only be read using special technology or knowledge...".*

while TechTerms.com[2] defines it as:

> *"Encoding is the process of converting data from one form to another".*

[1] https://dictionary.cambridge.org/dictionary/english/encode

[2] https://techterms.com/definition/encoding

DOI: 10.1201/9781003203469-7

Both definitions are similar, but in this chapter's context, the second one makes more sense. The Cambridge Dictionary[3] defines *representation* as:

"The way that someone or something is shown or described".

TechTerms.com returned no results for that word. From now on, I will use the term *encode* to refer to the process of transforming the data and *representation* as the way data is 'conceptually' described. Note the 'conceptually' part which means the way we humans think about it. This means that data can have a conceptual representation but that does not necessarily mean it is digitally stored in that way. For example, a physical activity like *walking* captured with a motion sensor can be *conceptually* represented by humans as a feature vector but its actual digital format inside a computer is binary (see Figure 7.1).

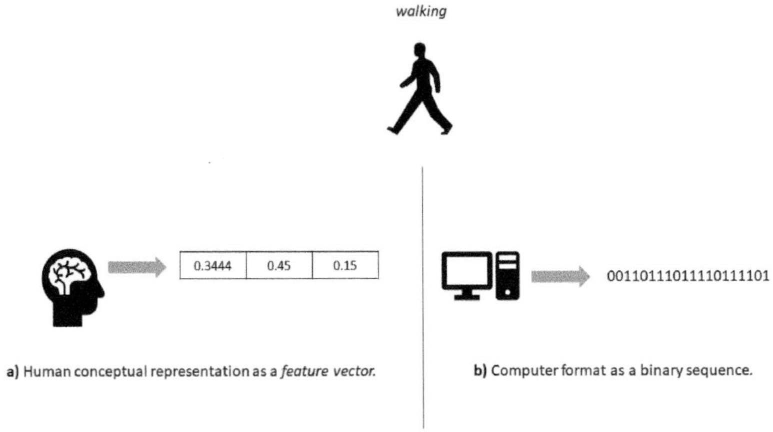

FIGURE 7.1 The real world walking activity as a) human conceptual representation and b) computer format.

It is also possible to encode the same data into different representations (see Figure 7.2 for an example) depending on the application or the predictive model to be used. Each representation has its own advantages and limitations (discussed in the following subsections) and they capture

[3] `https://dictionary.cambridge.org/dictionary/english/representation`

different aspects of the real-world phenomenon. Sometimes it is useful to encode the same data into different representations so more information can be extracted and complemented as discussed in section 3.4. In the next sections, several types of representations will be presented along with some ideas of how the same raw data can be encoded into different ones.

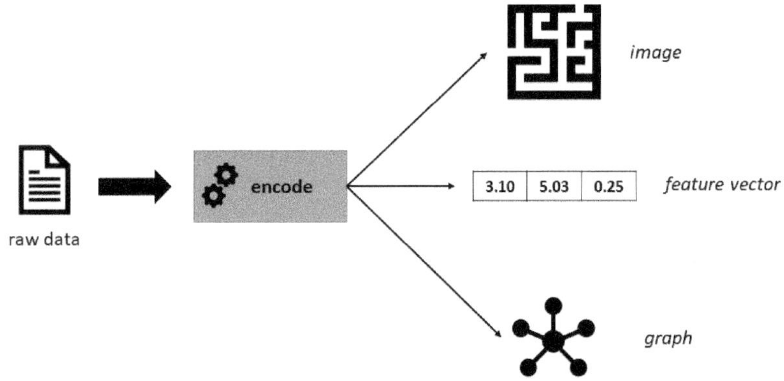

FIGURE 7.2 Example of some raw data encoded into different representations.

7.1 Feature Vectors

From previous chapters, we have already seen how data can be represented as feature vectors. For example, when classifying physical activities (section 2.3.1) or clustering questionnaire answers (section 6.1.1). Feature vectors are compact representations of real-world phenomena or objects and usually, they are modeled in a computer as numeric arrays. Most machine learning algorithms work with feature vectors. Generating feature vectors requires knowledge of the application domain. Ideally, the feature vectors should represent the real-world situation as accurately as possible. We could achieve a good mapping by having feature vectors of infinite size, unfortunately, that is infeasible. In practice, small feature vectors are desired because that reduces storage requirements and computational time.

The process of designing and extracting feature vectors from raw data is known as **feature engineering**. This also involves the process of deciding which features to extract. This requires domain knowledge as the features should capture the information needed to solve the problem. Suppose we want to classify if a person is *'tired'* or *'not tired'*. We have access to some details about the person like age, height, the activities performed during the last 30 minutes, and so on. For simplicity, let's assume we can generate feature vectors of size 2 and we have two options:

- **Option 1.** Feature vectors where the first element is *age* and the second element is *height*.
- **Option 2.** Feature vectors where the first element is the *number of squats* done by the user during the last 30 minutes and the second element is *heart rate*.

Clearly, for this specific classification problem the second option is more likely to produce better results. The first option may not even contain enough information and will lead the predictive model to produce random predictions. With the second option, the boundaries between classes are more clear (see Figure 7.3) and classifiers will have an easier time finding them.

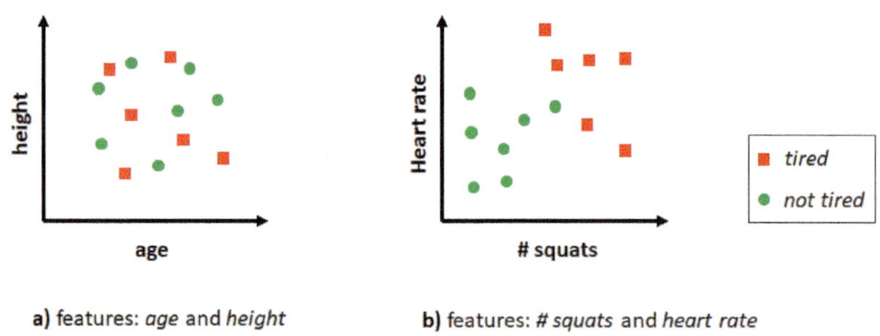

FIGURE 7.3 Two different feature vectors for classifying tired and not tired.

In R, feature vectors are stored as data frames where rows are individual instances and columns are features. Some of the advantages and limitations of feature vectors are listed below.

Advantages:

- Efficient in terms of memory.

- Most machine learning algorithms support them.
- Efficient in terms of computations compared to other representations.

Limitations:

- Are static in the sense that they cannot capture temporal relationships.
- A lot of information and/or temporal relationships may be lost.
- Some features may be redundant leading to decreased performance.
- It requires effort and domain knowledge to extract them.
- They are difficult to plot if the dimension is > 2 unless some dimensionality reduction method is applied such as Multidimensional Scaling (chapter 4).

7.2 Timeseries

A timeseries is a sequence of data points ordered in time. We have already worked with timeseries data in previous chapters when classifying physical activities and hand gestures (chapter 2). Timeseries can be multi-dimensional. For example, typical inertial sensors capture motion forces in three axes. Timeseries analysis methods can be used to find underlying time-dependent patterns while timeseries forecasting methods aim to predict future data points based on historical data. Timeseries analysis is a very extensive topic and there are a number of books on the topic. For example, the book "Forecasting: Principles and Practice" by Hyndman and Athanasopoulos [2018] focuses on timeseries forecasting with R.

In this book we mainly use timeseries data collected from sensors in the context of behavior predictions using machine learning. We have already seen how classification models (like decision trees) can be trained with timeseries converted into feature vectors (section 2.3.1) or by using the raw timeseries data with Dynamic Time Warping (section 2.5.1).

Advantages:

- Many problems have this form and can be naturally modeled as timeseries.

- Temporal information is preserved.
- Easy to plot and visualize.

Limitations:

- Not all algorithms support timeseries of varying lengths so, one needs to truncate and/or do some type of padding.
- Many timeseries algorithms are slower than the ones that work with feature vectors.
- Timeseries can be very long, thus, making computations very slow.

7.3 Transactions

Sometimes we may want to represent data as transactions, as we did in section 6.3. Data represented as transactions are usually intended to be used by association rule mining algorithms (see section 6.3). As a minimum, a transaction has a unique identifier and a set of items. Items can be types of products, symptoms, ingredients, etc. A set of transactions is called a database. Figure 7.4 taken from chapter 6 shows an example database with 10 transactions. In this example, items are sets of products from a supermarket.

Transaction ID	Items
1	{chocolate}
2	{chocolate, chips, soda}
3	{chocolate, soda}
4	{soda}
5	{soda}
6	{candies, ice cream}
7	{soda, ice cream}
8	{chips, soda}
9	{candies, chocolate, chips}
10	{ice cream, chocolate, soda chips}

FIGURE 7.4 Example database with 10 transactions.

Transactions can include additional information like customer id, date, total cost, etc. Transactions can be coded as logical matrices where rows represent transactions and columns represent items. A `TRUE` value indicates that the particular item is present and `FALSE` indicates that the particular item is not part of that set. When the number of possible items is huge and item sets contain a small number of items, this type of matrix can be memory-inefficient. This is called a *sparse matrix*, that is, a matrix where many of its entries are `FALSE` (or empty, in general). Transactions can also be stored as lists or in a relational database such as MySQL. Below are some advantages of representing data as transactions.

Advantages:

- Association rule mining algorithms such as Apriori can be used to extract interesting behavior relationships.
- Recommendation systems can be built based on transactional data.

Limitations:

- Can be inefficient to store them as a logical matrices.
- There is no order associated with the items or temporal information.

7.4 Images

`timeseries_to_images.R plot_activity_images.R`

Images are rich visual representations that capture a lot of information –including spatial relationships. Pictures taken from a camera, drawings, scanned documents, etc., already are examples of images. However, other types of non-image data can be converted into images. One of the main advantages of analyzing images is that they retain spatial information (distance between pixels). This information is useful when using predictive models that take advantage of those properties such as Convolutional Neural Networks (CNNs) which will be presented in chapter 8. CNNs have proven to produce state of the art results in many vision-based tasks and are very flexible models in the sense that they can be adapted for a variety of applications with little effort.

Before CNNs were introduced by Lecun [LeCun et al., 1998], image classification used to be feature-based. One first needed to extract hand-crafted features from images and then use a classifier to make predictions. Also, images can be *flattened* into one-dimensional arrays where each element represents a pixel (Figure 7.5). Then, those 1D arrays can be used as feature vectors to perform training and inference.

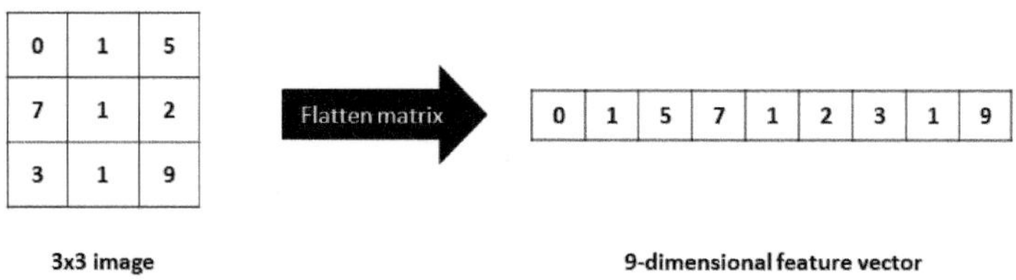

FIGURE 7.5 Flattening a matrix into a 1D array.

Flattening an image can lead to information loss and the dimension of the resulting vector can be very high, sometimes limiting its applicability and/or performance. Feature extraction from images can also be a complicated task and is very application dependent. CNNs have changed that. They take as input raw images, that is, matrices and automatically extract features and perform classification or regression.

What if the data are not represented as images but we still want to take advantage of featureless models like CNNs? Depending on the type of data, it may be possible to encode it as an image. For example, timeseries data can be encoded as an image. In fact, a timeseries can already be considered an image with a height of 1 but they can also be reshaped into square matrices.

Take for example the *SMARTPHONE ACTIVITIES* dataset which contains accelerometer data for each of the x, y, and z axes. The script `timeseries_to_images.R` shows how the acceleration timeseries can be converted to images. A window size of 100 is defined. Since the sampling rate was 20 Hz, each window corresponds to $100/20 = 5$ seconds. For each window, we have 3 timeseries (x,y,z). We can reshape each of them into 10×10 matrices by arranging the elements into columns. Then, the three matrices can be stacked to form a 3D image similar to an RGB image. Figure 7.6 shows the process of reshaping 3 timeseries of size 9 into 3×3 matrices to generate an RGB-like image.

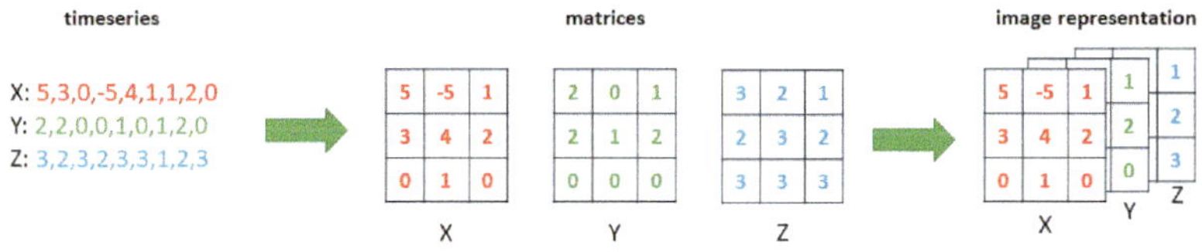

FIGURE 7.6 Encoding 3 accelerometer timeseries as an image.

The script then moves to the next window with no overlap and repeats the process. Actually, the script saves each image as one line of text. The first 100 elements correspond to the x axis, the next 100 to y, and the remaining to z. Thus each line has 300 values. Finally, the user id and the corresponding activity label are added at the end. This format will make it easy to read the file and reconstruct the images later on. The resulting file is called `images.txt` and is already included in the `smartphone_activities` dataset folder.

The script `plot_activity_images.R` shows how to read the `images.txt` file and reconstruct the images so we can plot them. Figure 7.7 shows three different activities plotted as colored images of 10×10 pixels. Before generating the plots, the images were normalized between 0 and 1.

FIGURE 7.7 Three activities captured with an accelerometer represented as images.

We can see that the patterns for *'jogging'* look more "chaotic" compared to the others while the *'sitting'* activity looks like a plain solid square. Then, we can use those images to train a CNN and perform inference. CNNs will be covered in chapter 8 and used to build adaptive models using these activity images.

Advantages:

- Spatial relationships can be captured.
- Can be multi-dimensional. For example 3D RGB images.
- Can be efficiently processed with CNNs.

Limitations:

- Computational time can be higher than when processing feature vectors. Still, modern hardware and methods allow us to perform operations very efficiently.
- It can take some extra processing to convert non-image data into images.

7.5 Recurrence Plots

Recurrence plots (RPs) are visual representations similar to images but typically they only have one dimension (depth). They are encoded as $n \times n$ matrices, that is, the same number of rows and columns (a square matrix). Even though these are like a special case of images, I thought it would be worth having them in their own subsection! Just as with images, timeseries can be converted into RPs and then used to train a CNN.

A RP is a visual representation of time patterns of dynamical systems (for example, timeseries). RPs were introduced by Eckmann et al. [1987] and they depict all the times when a trajectory is roughly in the same state. They are visual representations of the dynamics of a system. Biological systems possess behavioral patterns and activity dynamics that can be captured with RPs, for example, the dynamics of ant colonies [Neves et al., 2017].

At this point, you may be curious about how a RP looks like. So let me begin by showing a picture[4] of four time series with their respective RP (Figure 7.8).

[4] https://commons.wikimedia.org/wiki/File:Rp_examples740.gif

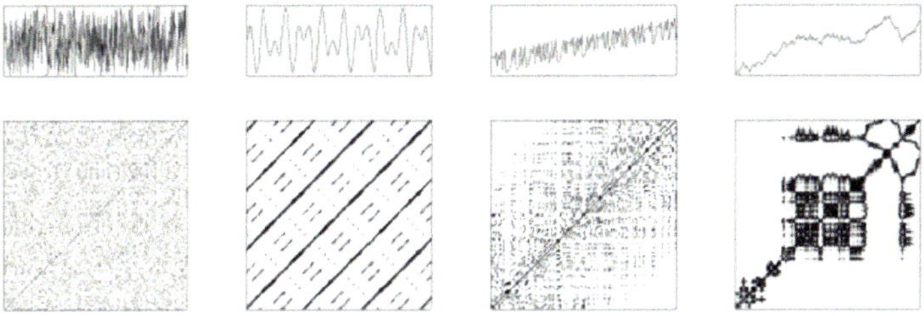

FIGURE 7.8 Four timeseries (top) with their respective RPs (bottom). (Author: Norbert Marwan/Pucicu at German Wikipedia. Source: Wikipedia (CC BY-SA 3.0) [https://creativecommons.org/licenses/by-sa/3.0/legalcode]).

The first RP (leftmost) does not seem to have a clear pattern (white noise) whereas the other three show some patterns like diagonals of different sizes, some square and circular shapes, and so on. RPs can be characterized by small-scale and large-scale patterns. Examples of small-scale patterns are diagonals, horizontal/vertical lines, dots, etc. Large-scale patterns are called *typology* and they depict the global characteristics of the dynamic system [5].

The visual interpretation of RPs requires some experience and is out of the scope of this book. However, they can be used as a visual pattern extraction tool to represent the data and then, in conjunction with machine learning methods like CNNs, used to solve classification problems.

There is an objective way to analyze RPs known as **recurrence quantification analysis (RQA)** [Zbilut and Webber, 1992]. It introduces several measures like percentage of recurrence points (recurrence rate), percentage of points that form vertical lines (laminarity), average length of diagonal lines, length of the longest diagonal line, etc. Those measures can then be used as features to train classification models.

[5] http://www.recurrence-plot.tk/glance.php

But how are RPs computed? Well, that is the topic of the next section.

7.5.1 Computing Recurrence Plots

It's time to delve into the details about how these mysterious plots are computed. Suppose there is a timeseries with n elements (points). To compute its RP we need to compute the distance between each pair of points. We can store this information in a $n \times n$ matrix. Let's call this a *distance matrix* D. Then, we need to define a threshold ϵ. For each entry in D, if the distance is less or equal than the threshold ϵ, it is set to 1 and 0 otherwise.

Formally, a recurrence of a state at time i at a different time j is marked within a two-dimensional squared matrix with ones and zeros where both axes represent time:

$$R_{i,j}(x) = \begin{cases} 1 & \textbf{if } ||\vec{x}_i - \vec{x}_j|| \leq \epsilon \\ 0 & \textbf{otherwise}, \end{cases} \tag{7.1}$$

where $\vec{x}$ are the states and $||\cdot||$ is a norm (for example Euclidean distance). $R_{i,j}$ is the square matrix and will be 1 if $\vec{x}_i \approx \vec{x}_j$ up to an error ϵ. The ϵ is important since systems often do not recur exactly to a previously visited state.

The threshold ϵ needs to be set manually which can be difficult in some situations. If not set properly, the RP can end up having excessive ones or zeros. If you plan to use RPs as part of an automated process and fed them to a classifier, you can use the distance matrix instead. The advantage is that you don't need to specify any parameter except for the distance function. The distance matrix can be defined as:

$$D_{i,j}(x) = ||\vec{x}_i - \vec{x}_j|| \tag{7.2}$$

which is similar to equation (7.1) but without the extra step of applying a threshold.

Advantages:

- RPs capture dynamic patterns of a system.
- They can be used to extract small and large scale patterns.
- Timeseries can be easily encoded as RPs.
- Can be used as input to CNNs for supervised learning tasks.

Limitations:

- Computationally intensive since all pairs of distances need to be calculated.
- Their visual interpretation requires experience.
- A threshold needs to be defined and it is not always easy to find the correct value. However, the distance matrix can be used instead.

7.5.2 Recurrence Plots of Hand Gestures

`recurrence_plots.R`

In this section, I am going to show you how to compute recurrence plots in R using the *HAND GESTURES* dataset. The code can be found in the script `recurrence_plots.R`. First, we need a norm (distance function), for example the Euclidean distance:

```
# Computes Euclidean distance between x and y.
norm2 <- function(x, y){
  return(sqrt((x - y)^2))
}
```

The following function computes a distance matrix and a recurrence plot and returns both of them. The first argument `x` is a vector representing a timeseries, `e` is the threshold and `f` is a distance function.

```
rp <- function(x, e, f=norm2){
  #x: vector
  #e: threshold
  #f: norm (distance function)
  N <- length(x)

  # This will store the recurrence plot.
  M <- matrix(nrow=N, ncol=N)

  # This will store the distance matrix.
```

```
  D <- matrix(nrow=N, ncol=N)

  for(i in 1:N){
    for(j in 1:N){

      # Compute the distance between a pair of points.
      d <- f(x[i], x[j])

      # Store result in D.
      # Start filling values from bottom left.
      D[N - (i-1), j] <- d

      if(d <= e){
        M[N - (i-1), j] <- 1
      }
      else{
        M[N - (i-1), j] <- 0
      }
    }
  }
  return(list(D=D, RP=M))
}
```

This function first defines two square matrices `M` and `D` to store the recurrence plot and the distance matrix, respectively. Then, it iterates the matrices from bottom left to top right and fills the corresponding values for `M` and `D`. The distance between elements `i` and `j` from the vector is computed. That distance is directly stored in `D`. To generate the RP we check if the distance is less or equal to the threshold. If that is the case the corresponding entry in `M` is set to 1. Finally, both matrices are returned by the function.

Now, we can try our `rp()` function on the *HAND GESTURES* dataset to convert one of the timeseries into a RP. First, we read one of the gesture files. For example, the first gesture *'1'* from user 1. We only extract the acceleration from the x axis and store it in variable `x`.

```
df <- read.csv(file.path(datasets_path,
                        "hand_gestures/1/1_20130703-120056.txt"),
               header = F)
x <- df$V1
```

If we plot vector `x` we get something like in Figure 7.9.

```
# Plot vector x.
plot(x, type="l", main="Hand gesture 1", xlab = "time", ylab = "")
```

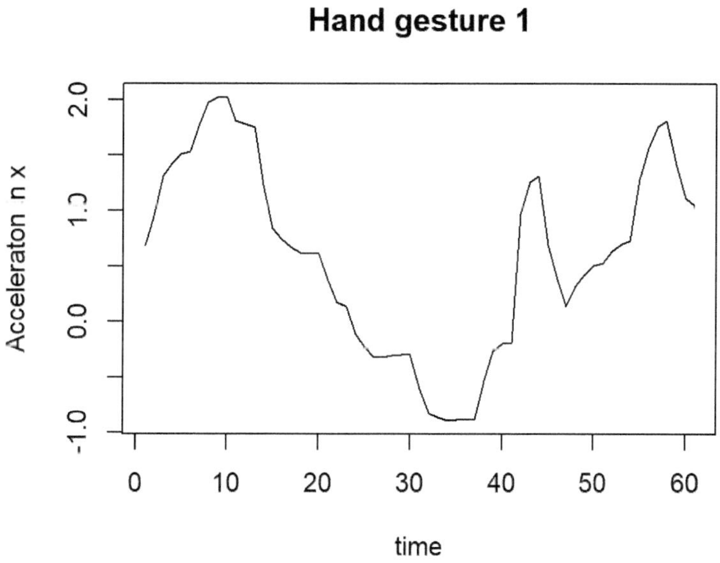

FIGURE 7.9 Acceleration of x of gesture 1.

Now the `rp()` function that we just defined is used to calculate the RP and distance matrix of vector `x`. We set a threshold of 0.5 and store the result in `res`.

```
# Compute RP and distance matrix.
res <- rp(x, 0.5, norm2)
```

Let's first plot the distance matrix stored in `res$D`. The `pheatmap()` function can be used to generate the plot.

```
library(pheatmap)
pheatmap(res$D, main="Distance matrix of gesture 1", cluster_row = FALSE,
         cluster_col = FALSE,
         legend = F,
         color = colorRampPalette(c("white", "black"))(50))
```

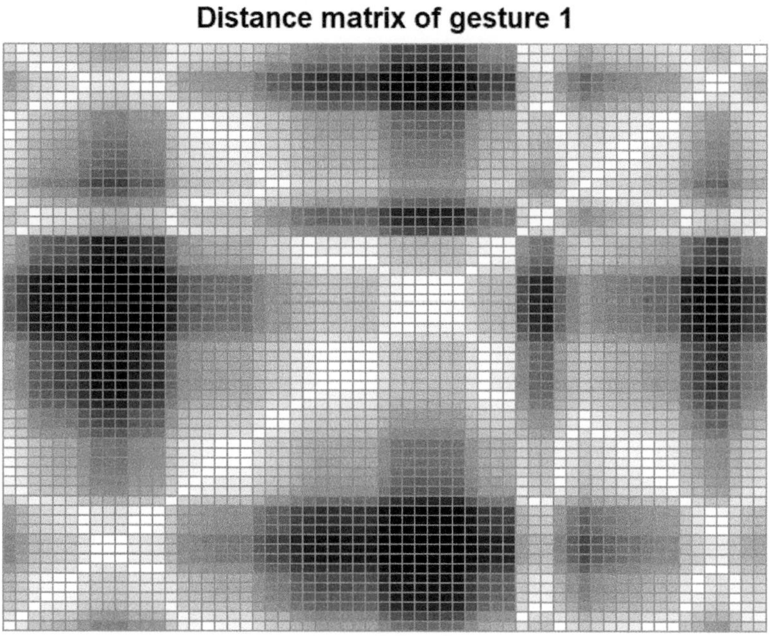

FIGURE 7.10 Distance matrix of gesture 1.

From figure 7.10 we can see that the diagonal cells are all white. Those represent values of 0, the distance between a point and itself. Apart from that, there are no other human intuitive patterns to look for. Now, let's see how the recurrence plot stored in `res$RP` looks like (Figure 7.11).

```
pheatmap(res$RP, main="RP with threshold = 0.5", cluster_row = FALSE,
         cluster_col = FALSE,
```

```
legend = F,
color = colorRampPalette(c("white", "black"))(50))
```

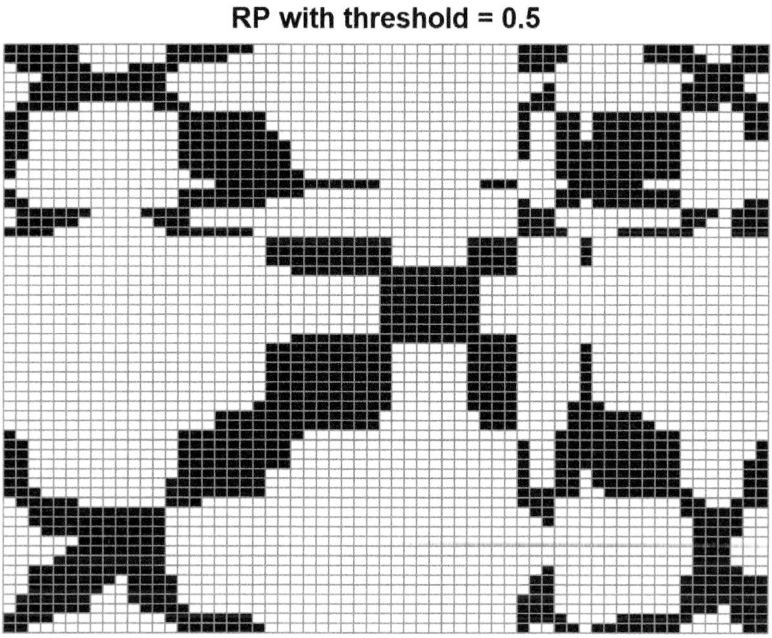

FIGURE 7.11 RP of gesture 1 with a threshold of 0.5.

Here, we see that this is kind of an inverted version of the distance matrix. Now, the diagonal is black because small distances are encoded as ones. There are also some clusters of points and vertical and horizontal line patterns. If we wanted to build a classifier, we would not need to interpret those extraterrestrial images. We could just treat each distance matrix or RP as an image and feed them directly to a CNN (CNNs will be covered in chapter 8).

Finally, we can try to see what happens if we change the threshold. Figure 7.12 shows two RPs. In the left one, a small threshold of 0.01 was used. Here, many details were lost and only very small distances show up. In the plot to the right, a threshold of 1.5 was used. Here, the plot is cluttered with black pixels which makes it difficult to see any patterns. On the other hand, a distance matrix will remain the same regardless of the threshold selection.

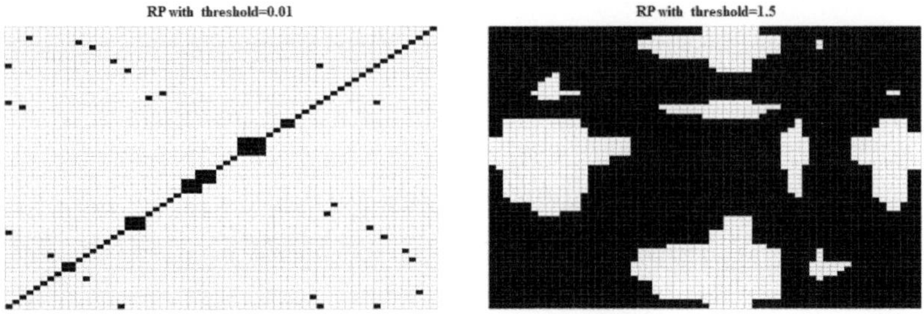

FIGURE 7.12 RP of gesture 1 with two different thresholds.

`shiny_rp.R` This shiny app allows you to select hand gestures, plot their corresponding distance matrix and recurrence plot, and see how the threshold affects the final result.

7.6 Bag-of-Words

The main idea of the Bag-of-Words (BoW) encoding is to represent a complex entity as a set of its constituent parts. It is called Bag-of-Words because one of the first applications was in natural language processing. Say there is a set of documents about different topics such as medicine, arts, engineering, etc., and you would like to classify them automatically based on their words. In BoW, each document is represented as a table that contains the unique words across all documents and their respective counts for each document. With this representation, one may see that documents about medicine will contain higher counts of words like *treatment*, *diagnosis*, *health*, etc., compared to documents about art or engineering. Figures 7.13 and 7.14 show the conceptual view and the table view, respectively.

From these representations, it is now easy to build a document classifier. The word-counts table can be used as an input feature vector. That is, each position in the feature vector represents a word and its value is an integer representing the total count for that word.

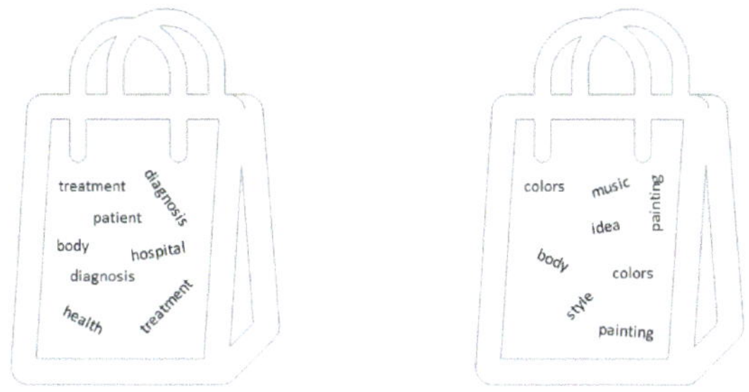

a) BoW of medical document b) BoW of art document

FIGURE 7.13 Conceptual view of two documents as BoW.

Word	Count
body	1
colors	0
diagnosis	2
health	1
hospital	1
idea	0
music	0
painting	0
patient	1
style	0
treatment	2

a) BoW of medical document

Word	Count
body	1
colors	2
diagnosis	0
health	0
hospital	0
idea	1
music	1
painting	2
patient	0
style	1
treatment	0

b) BoW of art document

FIGURE 7.14 Table view of two documents as BoW.

Note that in practice documents will differ in length, thus, it is a good idea to use percentages instead of total counts. This can be achieved by dividing each word count by the total number of counts. Also note that some frequent words like 'the', 'is', 'it' can cause problems, so some extra preprocessing is needed. This was a simple example but if you are interested in more advanced text processing techniques I refer you to the book "Text Mining with R: A Tidy Approach" by Silge and Robinson [2017].

BoW can also be used for image classification in complex scenarios. For example when dealing with composed scenes like classrooms, parks, shops, and streets. First, the scene (document) can be decomposed into smaller elements (words) by identifying objects like trees, chairs, cars, cashiers, etc. In this case, instead of bags of words we have bags of objects but the idea is the same. The object identification part can be done in a *supervised* manner where there is already a classifier that assigns labels to objects.

Using a supervised approach can work in some simple cases but is not scalable for more complex ones. *Why?* Because the classifier would need to be trained for each type of object. Furthermore, those types of objects need to be manually defined beforehand. If we want to apply this method on scenes where most of their elements do not have a corresponding label in the object classifier we will be missing a lot of information and will end up having incomplete word count tables.

A possible solution is to instead, use an *unsupervised* approach. The image scene can be divided into squared (but not necessarily) patches. Conceptually, each patch may represent an independent object (a tree, a chair, etc.). Then, feature extraction can be performed on each patch so ultimately patches are encoded as feature vectors. Again, each feature vector represents an individual possible object inside the complex scene. At this point, those feature vectors do not have a label so we can't build the BoW (table counts) for the whole scene. Then, how are those *unlabeled* feature vectors useful? We could use a pre-trained classifier to assign them labels –but we would be relying into the supervised approach along with its aforementioned limitations. Instead, we can use an *unsupervised* method, for example, *k-means*! which was presented in chapter 6.

We can cluster all the *unlabeled* feature vectors into k groups where k is the number of possible unique labels. After the clustering, we can compute the centroid of each group. To assign a label to an *unlabeled feature vector*, we can compute the closest centroid and use its id as the label. The id of each centroid can be an integer. Intuitively, similar feature vectors will end up in the same group. For example, there could be a group of objects that look like *chairs*, another for objects that look like *cars*, and so on. Usually, it may happen that elements in the same groups will not look similar for the human eye, but they are similar in the feature space. Also, the objects' shape inside the groups may not make sense at all for the human eye. If the objective is to classify the complex scene, then we do not necessarily need to understand the individual objects nor do they need to have a corresponding mapping into a real-world object.

Once the feature vectors are labeled, we can build the word-count table but instead of having 'meaningful' words, the entries will be ids with their corresponding counts. As you might have guessed, one limitation is that we do not know how many clusters (labels) there should be for a given problem. One approach is to try out for different values of k and use the one that optimizes your performance metric of interest.

But, what this BoW thing has to do with behavior? Well, we can use this method to decompose complex behaviors into simpler ones and encode them as BoW as we will see in the next subsection for complex activities analysis.

Advantages

- Able to represent complex situations/objects/etc., by decomposing them into simpler elements.
- The resulting BoW can be very efficient and effective for classification tasks.
- Can be used in several domains including text, computer vision, sensor data, and so on.
- The BoW can be constructed in an unsupervised manner.

Limitations

- Temporal and spatial information is not preserved.
- It may require some effort to define how to generate the words.
- There are cases where one needs to find the optimal number of words.

7.6.1 BoW for Complex Activities.

`bagwords/bow_functions.R bagwords/bow_run.R`

So far, I have been talking about BoW applications for text and images. In this section, I will show you how to decompose **complex activities** from accelerometer data into simpler activities and encode them as BoW. In chapters 2 and 3, we trained supervised models for *simple* activity recognition. Those activities were like: *walking*, *jogging*, *standing*, etc. For those, it is sufficient to divide them into windows of size equivalent to a couple of seconds in order to infer their labels. On the other hand, the duration of *complex* activities are longer and they are composed of many simple activities. One example is the activity **shopping**. When we are shopping we perform many different activities including *walking*, *taking groceries*, *paying*, *standing while looking at the stands*, and so on. Another example is **commuting**. When we commute, we need to walk but also take the train, or drive, or cycle.

Using the same approach for simple activity classification on complex ones may not work. Representing a complex activity using fixed-size windows can cause some conflicts. For example, a window may be covering the time span when the user was *walking*, but *walking* can be present in different types of complex activities. If a window happens to be part of a segment when the person was walking, there is not enough information to know which was the complex activity at that time. This is where BoW comes into play. If we represent a complex activity as a bag of *simple activities* then, a classifier will have an easier time differentiating between classes. For instance, when **exercising**, the frequencies (counts) of high-intensity activities (like running or jogging) will be higher compared to when someone is shopping.

In practice, it would be very tedious to manually label all possible simple activities to form the BoW. Instead, we will use the unsupervised approach discussed in the previous section to automatically label the simple activities so we only need to manually label the complex ones.

Here, I will use the *COMPLEX ACTIVITIES* dataset which consists of five complex activities: *'commuting'*, *'working'*, *'being at home'*, *'shopping'* and *'exercising'*. The duration of the activities varies from some minutes to a couple of hours. Accelerometer data at 50 Hz. was collected with a cellphone placed in the user's belt. The dataset has 80 accelerometer files, each representing a complex activity.

The task is to go from the raw accelerometer data of the complex activity to a BoW representation where each word will represent a simple activity. The overall steps are as follows:

1. Divide the raw data into small fixed-length windows and generate feature vectors from them. Intuitively, these are the simple activities.

2. Cluster the feature vectors.
3. Label the vectors by assigning them to the closest centroid.
4. Build the word-count table.

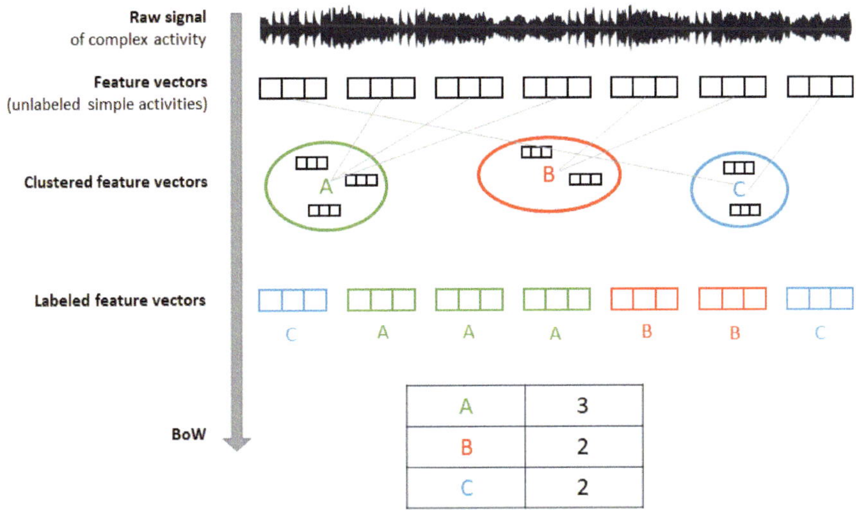

FIGURE 7.15 BoW steps. From raw signal to BoW table.

Figure 7.15 shows the overall steps graphically. All the functions to perform the above steps are implemented in `bow_functions.R`. The functions are called in the appropriate order in `bow_run.R`.

First of all, and to avoid overfitting, we need to hold out an independent set of instances. These instances will be used to generate the clusters and their respective centroids. The dataset is already divided into a train and test set. The train set contains 13 instances out of the 80. The remaining 67 are assigned to the test set.

In the first step, we need to extract the feature vectors from the raw data. This is implemented in the function `extractSimpleActivities()`. This function divides the raw data of each file into fixed-length windows of size 150 which corresponds to 3 seconds. Each window can be thought of as a simple activity. For each window, it extracts 14 features like mean, standard deviation, correlation between axes, etc. The output is stored in the folder `simple_activities/`. Each file corresponds to one of the complex activities and each row in a file is a feature vector (simple activity). **At this time the feature vectors (simple activities) are unlabeled.** Notice that in the script `bow_run.R` the function is called twice:

```
# Extract simple activities for train set.
extractSimpleActivities(train = TRUE)
# Extract simple activities for test set (may take some minutes).
extractSimpleActivities(train = FALSE)
```

This is because we divided the data into train and test sets. So we need to extract the features from both sets by setting the `train` parameter accordingly.

The second step consists of clustering the extracted feature vectors. To avoid overfitting, this step is only performed on the train set. The function `clusterSimpleActivities()` implements this step. The feature vectors are grouped into 15 groups. This can be changed by setting `constants$wordsize <- 15` to some other value. The function stores all feature vectors from all files in a single data frame and runs k-means. Finally, the resulting centroids are saved in the text file `clustering/centroids.txt` inside the train set directory.

The next step is to label each feature vector (simple activity) by assigning it to its closest centroid. The function `assignSimpleActivitiesToCluster()` reads the centroids from the text file, and for each simple activity in the test set it finds the closest centroid using the Euclidean distance. The label (an integer from 1 to 15) of the closest centroid is assigned and the resulting files are saved in the `labeled_activities/` directory. Each file contains the assigned labels (integers) for the corresponding feature vectors file in the `simple_activities/` directory. Thus, if a file inside `simple_activities/` has 100 feature vectors then, its corresponding file in `labeled_activities/` should have 100 labels.

In the last step, the function `convertToHistogram()` will generate the bag of words from the labeled activities. The BoW are stored as histograms (encoded as vectors) with each element representing a label and its corresponding counts. In this case, the labels are $w1..w15$. The w stands for word and was only appended for clarity to show that this is a label. This function will convert the counts into percentages (normalization) in case we want to perform classification, that is, the percentage of time that each word (simple activity) occurred during the entire complex activity. The resulting `histograms/histograms.csv` file contains the BoW as one histogram per row. One per each complex activity. The first column is the complex activity's label in text format.

Figures 7.16 and 7.17 show the histogram for one instance of *'working'* and *'exercising'*. The x-axis shows the labels of the simple activities and the y-axis their relative frequencies.

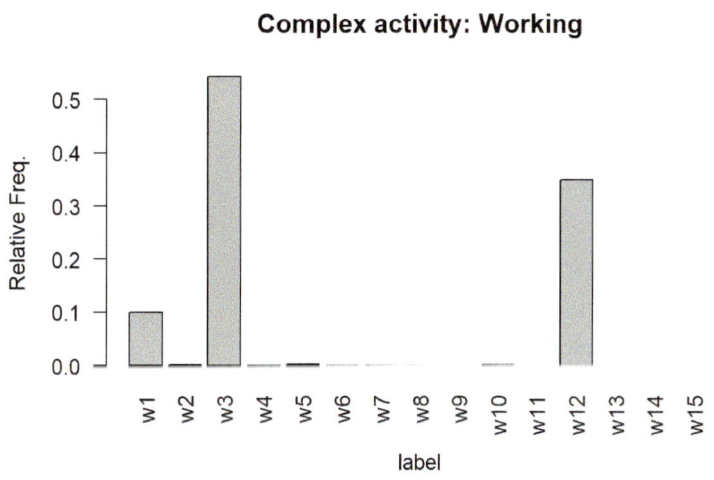

FIGURE 7.16 Histogram of working activity.

Here, we can see that the *'working'* activity is composed mainly by the simple activities *w1*, *w3*, and *w12*. The *exercising* activity is mainly composed of *w15* and *w14* which perhaps are high-intensity movements like jogging or running.

Once the complex activities are encoded as BoW (histograms), one could train a classifier using the histogram frequencies as features.

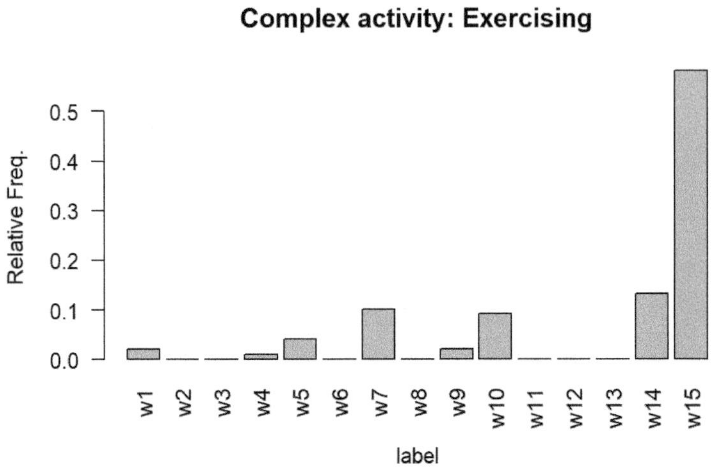

FIGURE 7.17 Histogram of exercising activity.

7.7 Graphs

Graphs are one of the most general data structures (and my favorite one). The two basic components of a graph are its **vertices** and **edges**. Vertices are also called **nodes** and edges are also called **arcs**. Vertices are connected by edges. Figure 7.18 shows three different types of graphs. Graph (a) is an undirected graph that consists of 3 vertices and 3 edges. Graph (b) is a directed graph, that is, its edges have a direction. Graph (c) is a weighted directed graph because its edges have a direction and they also have an associated weight.

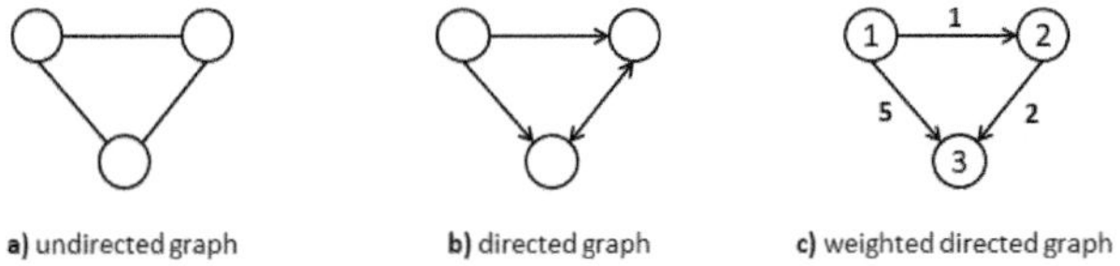

FIGURE 7.18 Three different types of graphs.

Weights can represent anything, for example, distances between cities or number of messages sent between devices. In the previous graph, the vertices also have a label (integer numbers but could be strings). In general, vertices and edges can have any number of attributes, not just weight and/or labels. Many data structures like binary trees and lists are graphs *with constraints*. For example, a list is also a graph in which all vertices are connected as a sequence: a->b->c. Trees are also graphs with the constraint that there is only one root node and nodes can only have edges to their children. Graphs are very useful to represent many types of real-world things like interactions, social relationships, geographical locations, the world wide web, and so on.

There are two main ways to encode a graph. The first one is as an **adjacency list**. An adjacency list consists of a list of tuples per node. The tuples represent edges. The first element of a tuple indicates the target node and the second element the weight of the edge. Figure 7.19-b shows the adjacency list representation of the corresponding weighted directed graph in the same figure.

The second main way to encode a graph is as an **adjacency matrix**. This is a square $n \times n$ matrix where n is the number of nodes. Edges are represented as entries in the matrix. If there is an edge between node a and node b, the corresponding cell contains the edge's weight where rows represent the source nodes and columns the destination nodes. Otherwise, it contains a 0 or just an empty value. Figure 7.19-c shows the corresponding adjacency matrix. The disadvantage of the adjacency matrix is that for sparse graphs (many nodes and few edges), a lot of space is wasted. In practice, this can be overcome by using a sparse matrix implementation.

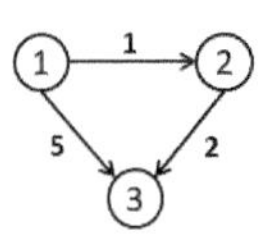

a) graphic representation

Node id	Adjacent nodes
1	(2,w:1), (3,w:5)
2	(3,w:2)
3	

b) adjacency list

	1	2	3
1	0	1	5
2	0	0	2
3	0	0	0

c) adjacency matrix

FIGURE 7.19 Different ways to store a graph.

Advantages:

- Many real-world situations can be naturally represented as graphs.
- Some partial order is preserved.

- Specialized graph analytics can be performed to gain insights and understand the data. See for example the book by Samatova et al. [2013].
- Can be plotted and different visual properties can be tuned to convey information such as edge width and colors, vertex size and color, distance between nodes, etc.

Limitations:

- Some graph analytic algorithms are computationally demanding.
- It can be difficult to use graphs to solve classification problems.
- It is not always clear if the data can be represented as a graph.

7.7.1 Complex Activities as Graphs

```
plot_graphs.R
```

In the previous section, it was shown how complex activities can be represented as Bag-of-Words. This was done by decomposing the complex activities into simpler ones. The BoW is composed of the simple activities counts (frequencies). In the process of building the BoW in the previous section, some intermediate text files stored in `labeled_activities/` were generated. These files contain the sequence of simple activities (their ids as integers) that constitute the complex activity. From these sequences, histograms were generated and in doing so, the order was lost.

One thing we can do is build a graph where vertices represent simple activities and edges represent the interactions between them. For instance, if we have a sequence of simple activities ids like: $3, 2, 2, 4$ we can represent this as a graph with 3 vertices and 3 edges. One vertex per activity. The first edge would go from vertex 3 to vertex 2, the next one from vertex 2 to vertex 2, and so on. In this way we can use a graph to capture the interactions between simple activities.

The script `plot_graphs.R` implements a function named `ids.to.graph()` that reads the sequence files from `labeled_activities/` and converts them into weighted directed graphs. The weight of the edge (a, b) is equal to the total number of transitions from vertex a to vertex b. The script uses the `igraph` package [Csardi and Nepusz, 2006] to store and plot the resulting graphs. The `ids.to.graph()` function receives as its first argument the sequence of ids. Its second argument indicates whether the edge weights should be normalized or not. If normalized, the sum of all weights will be 1.

The following code snippet reads one of the sequence files, converts it into a graph, and plots the graph.

```
datapath <- "../labeled_activitires/"

# Select one of the 'work' complex activities.
filename <- "2_20120606-111732.txt"

# Read it as a data frame.
df <- read.csv(paste0(datapath, filename), header = F)

# Convert the sequence of ids into an igraph graph.
g <- ids.to.graph(df$V1, relative.weights = T)

# Plot the result.
set.seed(12345)
plot(g, vertex.label.cex = 0.7,
     edge.arrow.size = 0.2,
     edge.arrow.width = 1,
     edge.curved = 0.1,
     edge.width = E(g)$weight * 8,
     edge.label = round(E(g)$weight, digits = 3),
     edge.label.cex = 0.4,
     edge.color = "orange",
     edge.label.color = "black",
     vertex.color = "skyblue"
     )
```

Figure 7.20 shows the resulting plot. The plot can be customized to change the vertex and edge color, size, curvature, etc. For more details please read the `igraph` package documentation.

The width of the edges is proportional to its weight. For instance, transitions from simple activity 3 to itself are very frequent (53.2% of the time) for the *'work'* complex activity, but transitions from 8 to 4 are

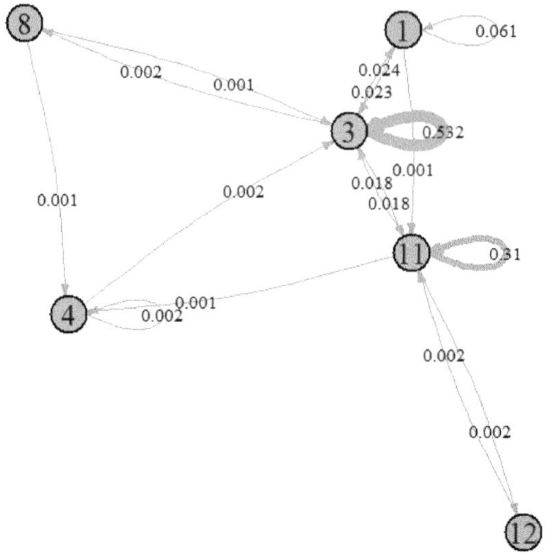

FIGURE 7.20 Complex activity 'working' plotted as a graph. Nodes are simple activities and edges transitions between them.

very infrequent. Note that with this graph representation, some temporal dependencies are preserved but the complete sequence order is lost. Still this captures more information compared to BoW. The relationships between consecutive simple activities are preserved.

It is also possible to get the adjacency matrix with the method `as_adjacency_matrix()`.

```
as_adjacency_matrix(g)

#> 6 x 6 sparse Matrix of class "dgCMatrix"
#>    1 11 12 3 4 8
#> 1  1  1  . 1 . .
#> 11 .  1  1 1 1 .
#> 12 .  1  . . . .
#> 3  1  1  . 1 . 1
#> 4  .  .  . 1 1 .
#> 8  .  .  . 1 1 .
```

In this matrix, there is a 1 if the edge is present and a '.' if there is no edge. However, this adjacency matrix does not contain information about the weights. We can print the adjacency matrix with weights by specifying `attr = "weight"`.

```
as_adjacency_matrix(g, attr = "weight")

#> 6 x 6 sparse Matrix of class "dgCMatrix"
#>              1           11         12           3           4          8
#> 1  0.06066946 0.001046025 .          0.023012552 .           .
#> 11 .          0.309623431 0.00209205 0.017782427 0.001046025 .
#> 12 .          0.002092050 .          .           .           .
#> 3  0.02405858 0.017782427 .          0.532426778 .           0.00209205
#> 4  .          .           .          0.002092050 0.002092050 .
#> 8  .          .           .          0.001046025 0.001046025 .
```

The adjacency matrices can then be used to train a classifier. Since many classifiers expect one-dimensional vectors and not matrices, we can flatten the matrix. This is left as an exercise for the reader to try. Which representation produces better classification results (adjacency matrix or BoW)?

The book "Practical graph mining with R" [Samatova et al., 2013] is a good source to learn more about graph analytics with R.

7.8 Summary

Depending on the problem at hand, the data can be encoded in different forms. Representing data in a particular way, can simplify the problem solving process and the application of specialized algorithms. This chapter presented different ways in which data can be encoded along with some of their advantages/disadvantages.

- **Feature vectors** are fixed-size arrays that capture the properties of an instance. This is the most common form of data representation in machine learning.

- Most machine learning algorithms expect their inputs to be encoded as feature vectors.
- **Transactions** is another way in which data can be encoded. This representation is appropriate for association rule mining algorithms.
- Data can also be represented as **images**. Algorithms like CNNs (covered in chapter 8) can work directly on images.
- The **Bag-of-Words** representation is useful when we want to model a complex behavior as a composition of simpler ones.
- A **graph** is a general data structure composed of *vertices* and *edges* and is used to model relationships between entities.
- Sometimes it is possible to convert data into multiple representations. For example, timeseries can be converted into images, recurrence plots, etc.

8

Predicting Behavior with Deep Learning

Deep learning (DL) consists of a set of model architectures and algorithms with applications in supervised, semi-supervised, unsupervised and reinforcement learning. Deep learning is mainly based on artificial neural networks (ANNs). One of the main characteristics of DL is that the models are composed of several levels. Each level transforms its input into more abstract representations. For example, for an image recognition task, the first level corresponds to raw pixels, the next level transforms pixels into simple shapes like horizontal/vertical lines, diagonals, etc. The next level may abstract more complex shapes like wheels, windows, and so on; and the final level could detect if the image contains a car or a human, or maybe both.

Examples of DL architectures include deep neural networks (DNNs), Convolutional Neural Networks (CNNs), recurrent neural networks (RNNs), and autoencoders, to name a few. One of the reasons of the success of DL is due to its flexibility to deal with different types of data and problems. For example, CNNs can be used for image classification, RNNs can be used for timeseries data, and autoencoders can be used to generate new data and perform anomaly detection. Another advantage of DL is that it is not always required to do feature engineering. That is, extract different features depending on the problem domain. Depending on the problem and the DL architecture, it is possible to feed the raw data (with some preprocessing) to the model. The model will then, automatically extract features at each level with an increasing level of abstraction. DL has achieved state-of-the-art results in many different tasks including speech recognition, image recognition, and translation. It has also been successfully applied to different types of behavior prediction.

In this chapter, an introduction to artificial neural networks will be presented. Next, I will explain how to train deep models in R using Keras and TensorFlow. The models will be applied to behavior prediction tasks.

DOI: 10.1201/9781003203469-8

This chapter also includes a section on Convolutional Neural Networks and their application to behavior prediction.

8.1 Introduction to Artificial Neural Networks

Artificial neural networks (ANNs) are mathematical models *inspired* by the brain. Here, I would like to emphasize the word *inspired* because ANNs do not model how a biological brain actually works. In fact, there is little knowledge about how a biological brain works. ANNs are composed of **units** (also called **neurons** or **nodes**) and connections between units. Each unit can receive inputs from other units. Those inputs are processed inside the unit and produce an output. Typically, units are arranged into layers (as we will see later) and connections between units have an associated weight. Those weights are learned during training and they are the core elements that make a network behave in a certain way.

For the rest of the chapter I will mostly use the term **units** to refer to neurons/nodes. I will also use the term **network** to refer to artificial neural networks.

Before going into details of how multi-layer ANNs work, let's start with a very simple neural network consisting of a **single unit**. See Figure 8.1. Even though this network only has one node, it is already composed of several interesting elements which are the basis of more complex networks. First, it has n input variables $x_1 \ldots x_n$ which are real numbers. Second, the unit has a set of n weights $w_1 \ldots w_n$ associated with each input. These weights can take real numbers as values. Finally, there is an output y' which is binary (it can take two values: 1 or 0).

This simple network consisting of one unit with a binary output is called a **perceptron** and was proposed by Rosenblatt [1958].

This single unit also known as *perceptron* is capable of making binary decisions based on the input and the weights. To get the final decision y'

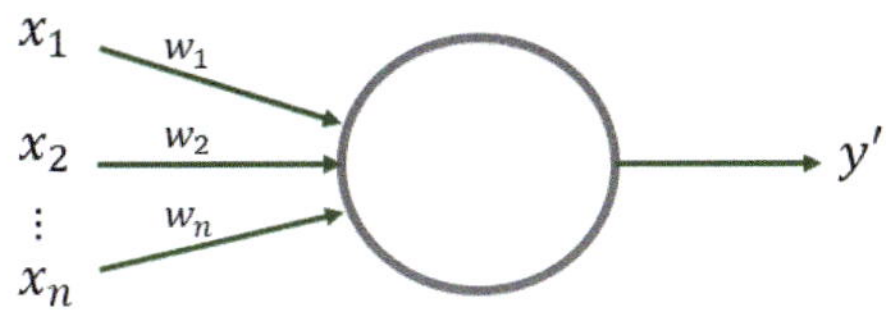

FIGURE 8.1 A neural network composed of a single unit (perceptron).

the inputs are multiplied by their corresponding weights and the results are summed. If the sum is greater than a given threshold, then the output is 1 and 0 otherwise. Formally:

$$y' = \begin{cases} 1 & \textit{if } \sum_i w_i x_i > t, \\ 0 & \textit{if } \sum_i w_i x_i \leq t \end{cases} \tag{8.1}$$

where t is a threshold. We can use a perceptron to make important decisions in life. For example, suppose you need to decide whether or not to go to the movies. Assume this decision is based on two pieces of information:

1. You have money to pay the entrance (or not) and,
2. it is a horror movie (or not).

There are two additional assumptions as well:

1. The movie theater only projects 1 film.
2. You don't like horror movies.

This decision-making process can be modeled with the perceptron of Figure 8.2. This perceptron has two binary input variables: *money* and *horror*. Each variable has an associated weight. Suppose there is a decision threshold of $t = 3$. Finally, there is a binary output: 1 means you should go to the movies and 0 indicates that you should not go.

In this example, the weights (5 and -3) and the threshold $t = 3$ were already provided. The weights and the threshold are called the *parameters* of the network. Later, we will see how the parameters can be learned automatically from data.

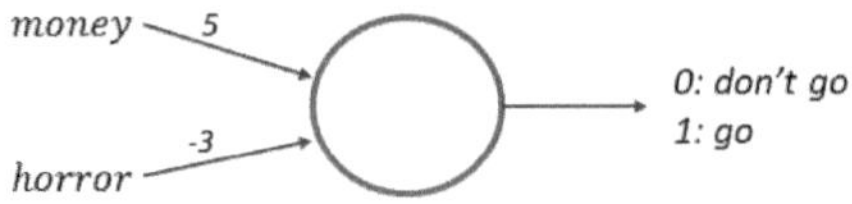

FIGURE 8.2 Perceptron to decide whether or not to go to the movies based on two input variables.

Suppose that today was payday and the theater is projecting an action movie. Then, we can set the input variables $money = 1$ and $horror = 0$. Now we want to decide if we should go to the movie theater or not. To get the final answer we can use Equation (8.1). This formula tells us that we need to multiply each input variable with their corresponding weights and add them:

$$(money)(5) + (horror)(-3)$$

Substituting *money* and *horror* with their corresponding values:

$$(1)(5) + (0)(-3) = 5$$

Since $5 > t$ (remember the threshold $t = 3$), the final output will be 1, thus, the advice is to go to the movies. Let's try the scenario when you have money but they are projecting a horror movie: $money = 1$, $horror = 1$.

$$(1)(5) + (1)(-3) = 2$$

In this case, $2 < t$ and the final output is 0. Even if you have money, you should not waste it on a movie that you know you most likely will not like. This process of applying operations to the inputs and obtaining the final result is called **forward propagation** because the inputs are 'pushed' all the way through the network (a single perceptron in this case). For bigger networks, the outputs of the current layer become the inputs of the next layer, and so on.

For convenience, a simplified version of Equation (8.1) can be used. This alternative representation is useful because it provides flexibility to change the internals of the units (neurons) as we will see. The first simplification consists of representing the inputs and weights as vectors:

$$\sum_i w_i x_i = w \cdot x \tag{8.2}$$

The summation becomes a dot product between w and x. Next, the threshold t can be moved to the left and renamed to b which stands for **bias**. This is only for notation but you can still think of the *bias* as a threshold.

$$y' = f(x) = \begin{cases} 1 & \textit{if } w \cdot x + b > 0, \\ 0 & \textit{otherwise} \end{cases} \tag{8.3}$$

The output y' is a function of x with w and b as fixed parameters. One thing to note is that first, we are performing the operation $w \cdot x + b$ and then, another operation is applied to the result. In this case, it is a comparison. If the result is greater than 0 the final output is 1. You can think of this second operation as another function. Call it $g(x)$.

$$f(x) = g(w \cdot x + b) \tag{8.4}$$

In neural networks terminology, this $g(x)$ is known as the **activation function**. Its result indicates how much active this unit is based on its inputs. If the result is 1, it means that this unit is active. If the result is 0, it means the unit is inactive.

This new notation allows us to use different activation functions by substituting $g(x)$ with some other function in Equation (8.4). In the case of the perceptron, the activation function $g(x)$ is the threshold function, which is known as the *step function*:

$$g(x) = step(x) = \begin{cases} 1 & \textit{if } x > 0 \\ 0 & \textit{if } x \leq 0 \end{cases} \tag{8.5}$$

Figure 8.3 shows the plot of the step function.

It is worth noting that perceptrons have two major limitations:

1. The output is binary.
2. Perceptrons are linear functions.

The first limitation imposes some restrictions on its applicability. For example, a perceptron cannot be used to predict real-valued outputs which

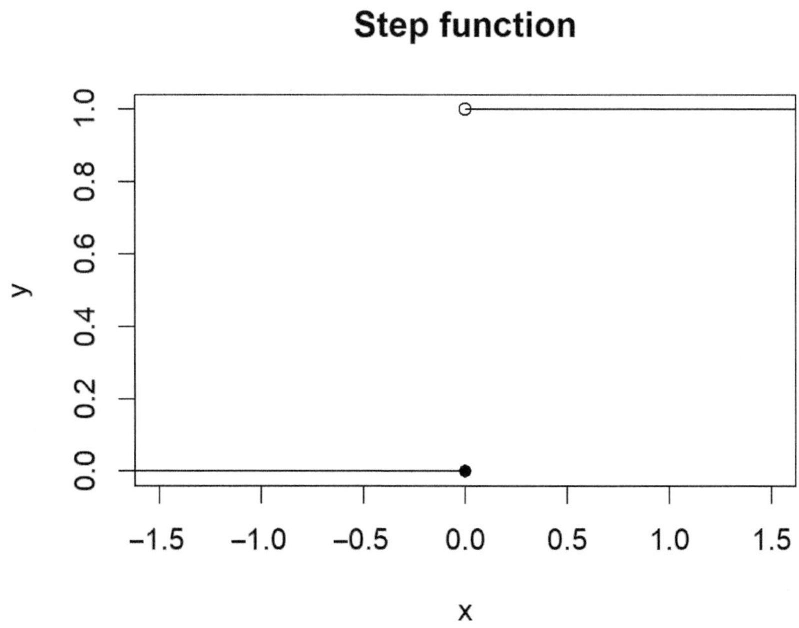

FIGURE 8.3 The step function.

is a fundamental aspect for regression problems. The second limitation makes the perceptron only capable of solving linear problems. Figure 8.4 graphically shows this limitation. In the first case, the outputs of the OR logical operator can be classified (separated) using a line. On the other hand, it is not possible to classify the output of the XOR function using a single line.

To overcome those limitations, several modifications to the perceptron were introduced. This allows us to build models capable of solving more complex non-linear problems. One such modification is to change the activation function. Another improvement is to add the ability to have several layers of interconnected units. In the next section, two new types of units will be presented. Then, the following section will introduce neural networks also known as multilayer perceptrons which are more complex models built by connecting many units and arranging them into layers.

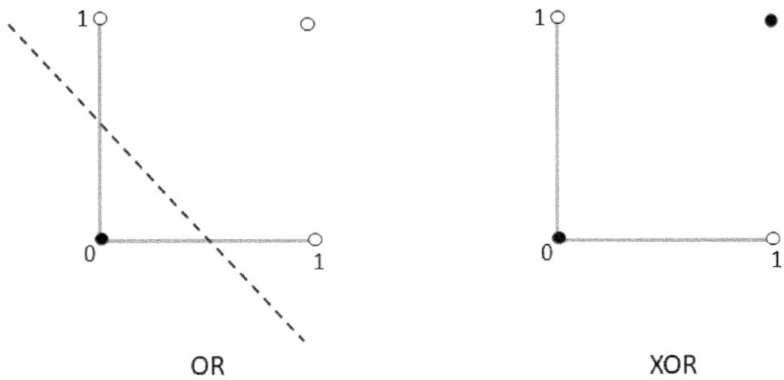

FIGURE 8.4 The OR and the XOR logical operators.

8.1.1 Sigmoid and ReLU Units

As previously mentioned, perceptrons have some limitations that restrict their applicability including the fact that they are linear models. In practice, problems are complex and most of them are non-linear. One way to overcome this limitation is to introduce non-linearities and this can be done by using a different type of activation function. Remember that a unit can be modeled as $f(x) = g(wx + b)$ where $g(x)$ is some activation function. For the perceptron, $g(x)$ is the *step function*. However, another practical limitation not mentioned before is that the step function can change abruptly from 0 to 1 and vice versa. Small changes in x, w, or b can completely change the output. This is a problem during learning and inference time. Instead, we would prefer a smooth version of the step function, for example, the **sigmoid function** which is also known as the **logistic function**:

$$s(x) = \frac{1}{1 + e^{-x}} \tag{8.6}$$

This function has an 'S' shape (Figure 8.5) and as opposed to a step function, this one is smooth. The range of this function is from 0 to 1.

If we substitute the activation function in Equation (8.4) with the sigmoid function we get our **sigmoid unit**:

$$f(x) = \frac{1}{1 + e^{-(w \cdot x + b)}} \tag{8.7}$$

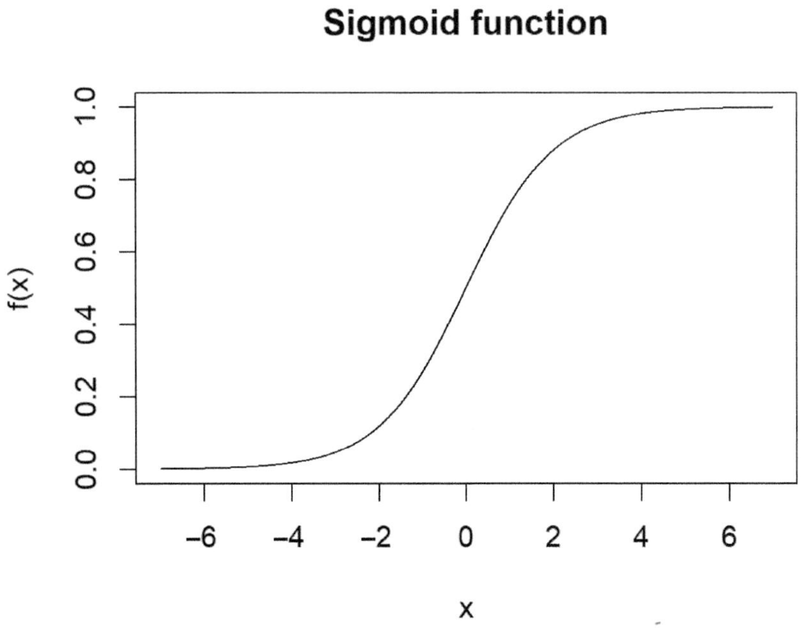

FIGURE 8.5 Sigmoid function.

Sigmoid units have been one of the most commonly used types of units when building bigger neural networks. Another advantage is that the outputs are real values that can be interpreted as probabilities. For instance, if we want to make binary decisions we can set a threshold. For example, if the output of the sigmoid unit is > 0.5 then return a 1. Of course, that threshold would depend on the application. If we need more confidence about the result we can set a higher threshold.

In the last years, another type of unit has been successfully applied to train neural networks, the **rectified linear unit** or **ReLU** for short (Figure 8.6).

The activation function of this unit is the rectifier function:

$$rectifier(x) = \begin{cases} 0 & if\ x < 0, \\ x & if\ x \geq 0 \end{cases} \tag{8.8}$$

This one is also called the *ramp function* and is one of the simplest non-linear functions and probably the most common one used in modern big

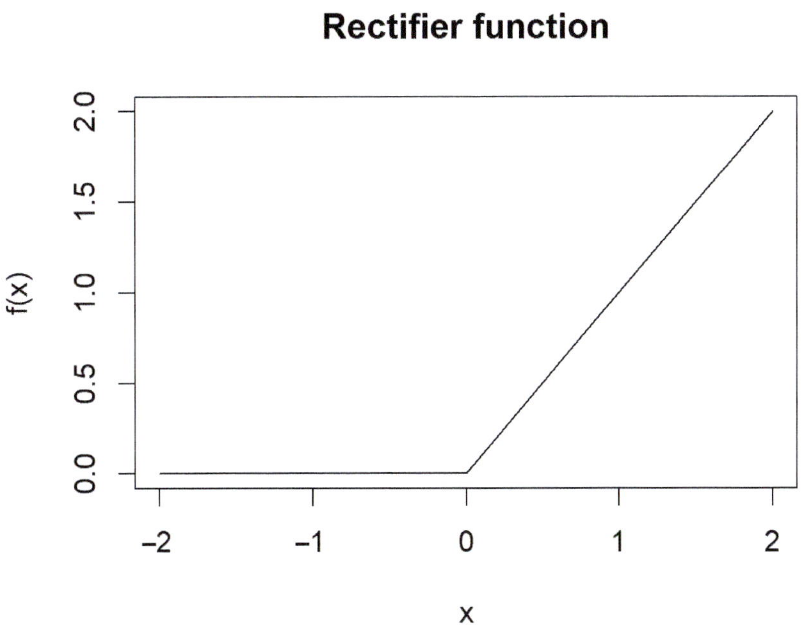

FIGURE 8.6 Rectifier function.

neural networks. These units present several advantages, being among them, efficiency during training and inference time.

In practice, many other activation functions are used but the most common ones are sigmoid and ReLU units. In the following link, you can find an extensive list of activation functions: `https://en.wikipedia.org/wiki/Activation_function`

So far, we have been talking about **single units**. In the next section, we will see how these single units can be assembled to build bigger artificial neural networks.

8.1.2 Assembling Units into Layers

Perceptrons, sigmoid, and ReLU units can be thought of as very simple neural networks. By connecting several units, one can build more complex neural networks. For historical reasons, neural networks are also called **multilayer perceptrons** regardless whether the units are perceptrons or not. Typically, units are grouped into layers. Figure 8.7 shows an example neural network with 3 layers. An **input layer** with 3 nodes, a **hidden layer** with 2 nodes, and an **output layer** with 1 node.

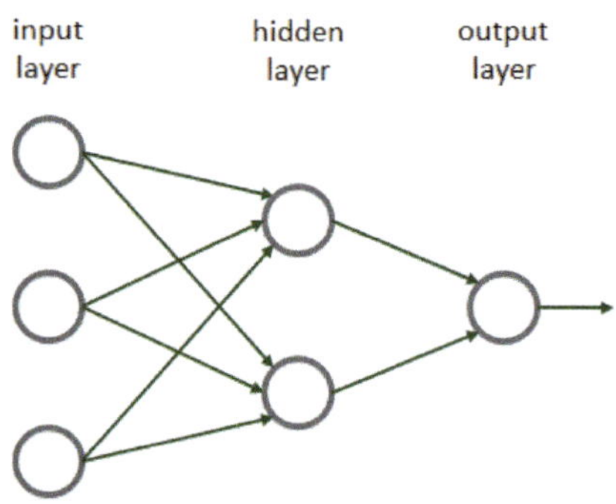

FIGURE 8.7 Example neural network.

In this type of diagram, the nodes represent units (perceptrons, sigmoids, ReLUs, etc.) except for the input layer. In the input layer, nodes represent input variables (input features). In the above example, the 3 nodes in the input layer simply indicate that the network takes as input 3 variables. In this layer, no operations are performed but the input values are passed to the next layer after multipliying them by their corresponding edge weights.

This network only has one hidden layer. Hidden layers are called like that because they do not have direct contact with the external world. Finally, there is an output layer with a single unit. We could also have an output layer with more than one unit. Most of the time, we will have **fully connected** neural networks. That is, all units have incoming connections from all nodes in the previous layer (as in the previous example).

For each specific problem, we need to define several building blocks for the network. For example, the number of layers, the number of units in each layer, the type of units (sigmoid, ReLU, etc.), and so on. This is known as the **architecture** of the network. Choosing a good architecture for a given problem is not a trivial task. It is advised to start with an architecture that was used to solve a similar problem and then fine-tune it for your specific problem. There exist some automatic ways to optimize the network architecture but those methods are out of the scope of this book.

We already saw how a unit can produce a result based on the inputs by using *forward propagation*. For more complex networks the process is the same! Consider the network shown in Figure 8.8. It consists of two inputs and one output. It also has one hidden layer with 2 units.

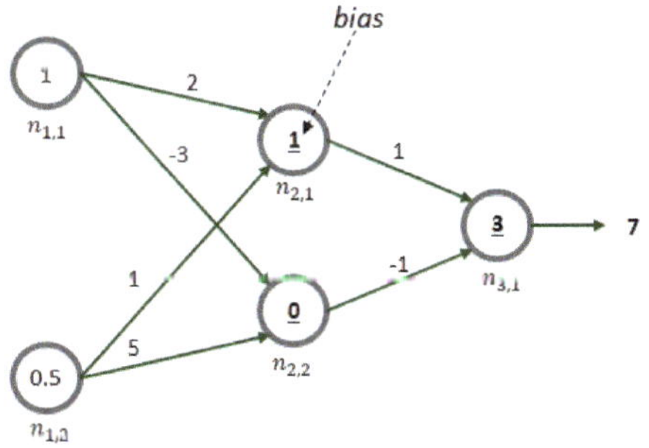

FIGURE 8.8 Example of forward propagation.

Each node is labeled as $n_{l,n}$ where l is the layer and n is the unit number. The two input values are 1 and 0.5. They could be temperature measurements, for example. Each edge has an associated weight. For simplicity, let's assume that the activation function of the units is the identity function $g(x) = x$. The bold underlined number inside the nodes of the hidden and output layers are the biases. Here we assume that the network is already trained (later we will see how those weights and biases are learned). To get the final result, for each node, its inputs are multiplied by their corresponding weights and added. Then, the bias is added. Next, the activation function is applied. In this case, it is just the identify function (returns the same value). The outputs of the nodes in the hidden layer become the inputs of the next layer and so on.

In this example, first we need to compute the outputs of nodes $n_{2,1}$ and $n_{2,2}$:

output of $n_{2,1} = (1)(2) + (0.5)(1) + 1 = 3.5$

output of $n_{2,2} = (1)(-3) + (0.5)(5) + 0 = -0.5$

Finally, we can compute the output of the last node using the outputs of the previous nodes:

output of $n_{3,1} = (3.5)(1) + (-0.5)(-1) + 3 = 7.$

8.1.3 Deep Neural Networks

By increasing the number of layers and the number of units in each layer, one can build more complex networks. But what is a deep neural network (DNN)? There is not a strict rule but some people say that a network with more than 2 hidden layers is a deep network. Yes, that's all it takes to build a DNN! Figure 8.9 shows an example of a deep neural network.

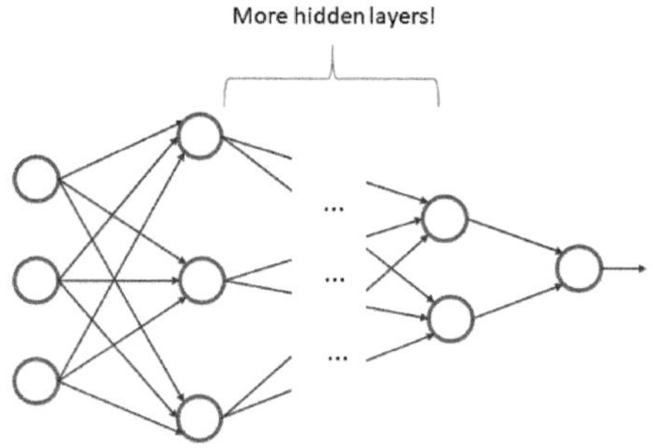

FIGURE 8.9 Example of a deep neural network.

A DNN has nothing special compared to a traditional neural network except that it has many layers. One of the reasons why they became so popular until recent years is because before, it was not possible to efficiently train them. With the advent of specialized hardware like graphics processing units (GPUs), it is now possible to efficiently train big DNNs. The introduction of ReLU units was also a key factor that allowed the training of even bigger networks. The availability of big quantities of data was another key factor that allowed the development of deep learning technologies. Note that deep learning is not limited to DNNs but it also encompasses other types of architectures like convolutional networks and recurrent neural networks, to name a few. Convolutional layers will be covered later in this chapter.

8.1.4 Learning the Parameters

We have seen how *forward propagation* can be used at inference time to compute the output of the network based on the input values. In the previous examples, we assumed that the network's parameters (weights and biases) were already learned. In practice, you most likely will use libraries and frameworks to build and train neural networks. Later in this chapter, I will show you how to use TensorFlow and Keras within R. But, before that, I will explain how the networks' parameters are learned and how to code and train a very simple network from scratch.

Back to the problem, the objective is to find the parameters' values based on training data such that the predicted result for any input data point is as close as possible as the true value. Put in other words, we want to find the parameters' values that reduce the network's prediction error.

One way to estimate the network's error is by computing the squared difference between the prediction y' and the real value y, that is, $error = (y' - y)^2$. This is how the error can be computed for a single training data point. The error function is typically called the **loss function** and denoted by $L(\theta)$ where θ represents the parameters of the network (weights and biases). In this example the loss function is $L(\theta) = (y' - y)^2$.

If there is more than one training data point (which is often the case), the loss function is just the average of the individual squared differences which is known as the **mean squared error (MSE)**:

$$L(\theta) = \frac{1}{N}\sum_{n=1}^{N}(y'_n - y_n)^2 \tag{8.9}$$

The mean squared error (MSE) loss function is commonly used for regression problems. For classification problems, the average cross-entropy loss function is usually preferred (covered later in this chapter).

The problem of finding the best parameters can be formulated as an optimization problem, that is, find the optimal parameters such that the loss function is minimized. This is the learning/training phase of a neural network. Formally, this can be stated as:

$$\underset{\theta}{\operatorname{argmin}}\, L(\theta) \tag{8.10}$$

This notation means: find and return the weights and biases that make the loss function be as small as possible.

The most common method to train neural networks is called **gradient descent**. The algorithm updates the parameters in an iterative fashion based on the loss. This algorithm is suitable for complex functions with millions of parameters.

Suppose there is a network with only 1 weight and no bias with MSE as loss function (Equation (8.9)). Figure 8.10 shows a plot of the loss function. This is a quadratic function that only depends on the value of w. The task is to find the w where the function is at its minimum.

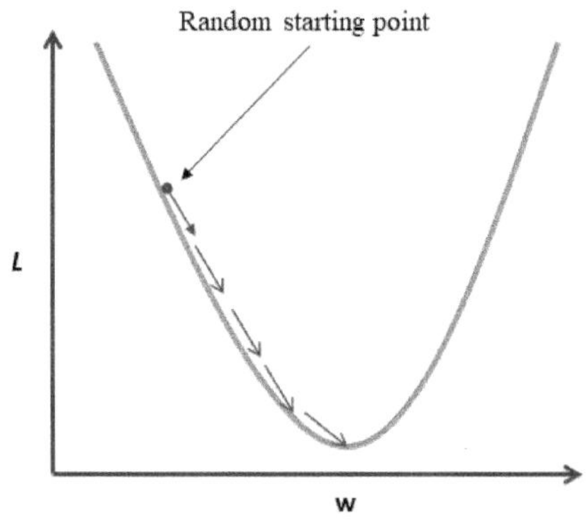

FIGURE 8.10 Gradient descent in action.

Gradient descent starts by assigning w a random value. Then, at each step and based on the error, w is updated in the direction that minimizes the loss function. In the previous figure, the **global minimum** is found after 5 iterations. In practice, loss functions are more complex and have many **local minima** (Figure 8.11). For complex functions, it is difficult to find a global minimum but gradient descent can find a local minimum that is good enough to solve the problem at hand.

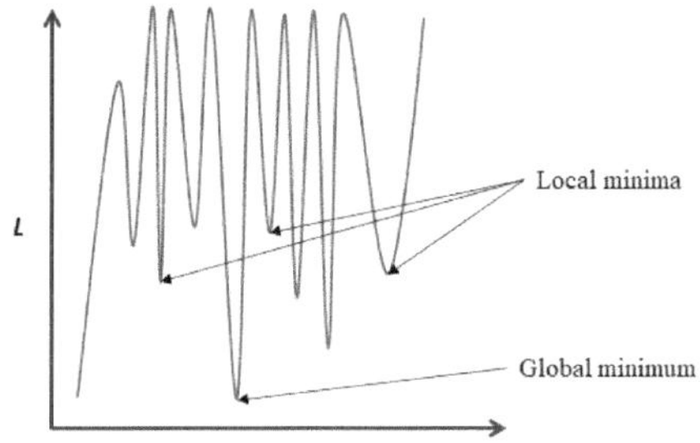

FIGURE 8.11 Function with 1 global minimum and several local minima.

But in what direction and how much is w moved in each iteration? The direction and magnitude are estimated by computing the derivative of the loss function with respect to the weight $\frac{\partial L}{\partial w}$. The derivative is also called the gradient and denoted by ∇L. The iterative gradient descent procedure is listed below:

loop until convergence or max iterations (*epochs*)
  for each w_i in W **do:**
    $w_i = w_i - \alpha \frac{\partial L(W)}{\partial w_i}$

The outer loop is run until the algorithm converges or until a predefined number of iterations is reached. Each iteration is also called an **epoch**. Each weight is updated with the rule: $w_i = w_i - \alpha \frac{\partial L(W)}{\partial w_i}$. The derivative part will give us the direction and magnitude. The α is called the **learning rate** and it controls how 'fast' we move. The learning rate is a constant defined by the user, thus, it is a **hyperparameter**. A high learning rate can cause the algorithm to miss the local minima and the loss can start to increase. A small learning rate will cause the algorithm to take more time to converge. Figure 8.12 illustrates both scenarios.

Selecting an appropriate learning rate will depend on the application but common values are between 0.0001 and 0.05.

Let's see how gradient descent works with a step by step example. Consider a very simple neural network consisting of an input layer with only one input feature and an output layer with one unit and no bias. To make it even simpler, the activation function of the output unit is the identity function $f(x) = x$. Assume that as training data we have a single data point. Figure 8.13 shows the simple network and the training data. The

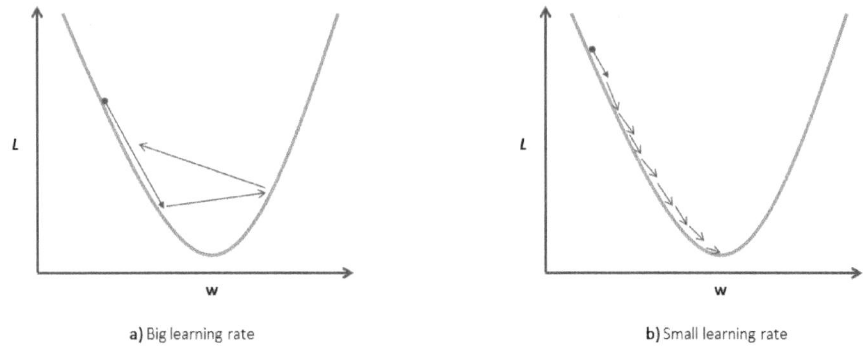

FIGURE 8.12 Comparison between high and low learning rates. a) Big learning rate. b) Small learning rate.

training data point only has one input variable (x) and an output (y). We want to train this network such that it can make predictions on new data points. The training point has an input feature of $x = 3$ and the expected output is $y = 1.5$. For this particular training point, it seems that the output is equal to the input divided by 2. Thus, based on this single training data point the network should learn how to divide any other input by 2.

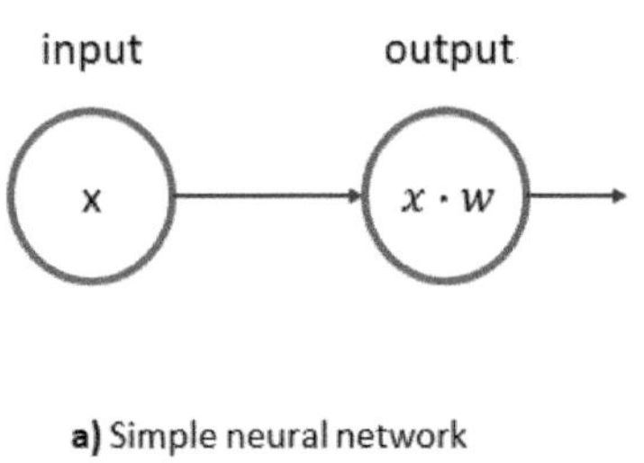

x	y
3	1.5

b) Training data with only a single point

FIGURE 8.13 a) A simple neural network consisting of one unit. b) The training data with only one row.

Before we start the training we need to define 3 things:

1. The loss function. This is a regression problem so we can use the MSE. Since there is a single data point our loss function becomes $L(w) = (y' - y)^2$. Here, y is the ground truth output value and y' is the predicted value. We know how to make predictions using forward propagation. In this case, it is the

product between the input value and the single weight, and the activation function has no effect (it returns the same value as its input). We can rewrite the loss function as $L(w) = (xw - y)^2$.

2. We need to define a learning rate. For now, we can set it to $\alpha = 0.05$.

3. The weights need to be initialized at random. Let's assume the single weight is 'randomly' initialized with $w = 2$.

Now we can use gradient descent to iteratively update the weight. Remember that the updating rule is:

$$w = w - \alpha \frac{\partial L(w)}{\partial w} \tag{8.11}$$

The partial derivative of the loss function with respect to w is:

$$\frac{\partial L(w)}{\partial w} = 2x(xw - y) \tag{8.12}$$

If we substitute the derivative in the updating rule we get:

$$w = w - \alpha 2x(xw - y) \tag{8.13}$$

We already know that $\alpha = 0.05$, the input value is $x = 3$, the output is $y = 1.5$ and the initial weight is $w = 2$. So we can start updating w. Figure 8.14 shows the initial state (iteration 0) and 3 additional iterations. In the initial state, $w = 2$ and with that weight the loss is 20.25. In iteration 1, the weight is updated and now its value is 0.65. With this new weight, the loss is 0.2025. That was a substantial reduction in the error! After three iterations we see that the final weight is $w = 0.501$ and the loss is very close to zero.

It	$w = w - \propto 2x(xw - y)$	loss $(xw - y)^2$
0	Initial weight = **2**	$(3 * 2 - 1.5)^2 = 20.25$
1	$2 - (0.05) * (2 * 3)(3 * 2 - 1.5) = \mathbf{0.65}$	$(3 * 0.65 - 1.5)^2 = 0.2025$
2	$0.65 - (0.05) * (2 * 3)(3 * 0.65 - 1.5) = \mathbf{0.51}$	$(3 * 0.51 - 1.5)^2 = 0.0009$
3	$0.51 - (0.05) * (2 * 3)(3 * 0.51 - 1.5) = \mathbf{0.501}$	$(3 * 0.501 - 1.5)^2 = 0.000009$

FIGURE 8.14 First 3 gradient descent iterations (epochs).

Now, we can start doing predictions with our very simple neural network! To do so, we use forward propagation on the new input data using the learned weight $w = 0.501$. Figure 8.15 shows the predictions on new training data points that were never seen before by the network.

input	prediction
10	$10 * 0.501 = 5.01$
780	$780 * 0.501 = 390.78$
-2400	$-2400 * 0.501 = -1202.4$

FIGURE 8.15 Example predictions on new data points.

Even though the predictions are not perfect, they are very close to the expected value (division by 2) considering that the network is very simple and was only trained with a single data point and for only 3 epochs!

If the training set has more than one data point, then we need to compute the derivative of each point and accumulate them (the derivative of a sum is equal to the sum of the derivatives). In the previous example, the update rule becomes:

$$w = w - \alpha \sum_{i-1}^{N} 2x_i(x_i w - y) \tag{8.14}$$

This means that before updating a weight, first, we need to compute the derivative for each point and add them. This needs to be done for every parameter in the network. Thus, one **epoch** is a pass through all training points and all parameters.

8.1.5 Parameter Learning Example in R

```
gradient_descent.R
```

In the previous section, we went step by step to train a neural network with a single unit and with a single training data point. Here, we will see how we can implement that simple network in R but when we have more training data. The code can be found in the script `gradient_descent.R`.

This code implements the same network as the previous example. That is, one neuron, one input, no bias, and activation function $f(x) = x$. We start by creating a sample training set with 3 points. Again, the output is the input divided by 2.

```
train_set <- data.frame(x = c(3.0,4.0,1.0), y = c(1.5, 2.0, 0.5))
# Print the train set.
print(train_set)
#>   x   y
#> 1 3 1.5
#> 2 4 2.0
#> 3 1 0.5
```

Then we need to implement three functions: forward propagation, the loss function, and the derivative of the loss function.

```
# Forward propagation w*x
fp <- function(w, x){
    return(w * x)
}

# Loss function (y - y')^2
loss <- function(w, x, y){
  predicted <- fp(w, x) # This is y'
  return((y - predicted)^2)
}

# Derivative of the loss function. 2x(xw - y)
derivative <- function(w, x, y){
  return(2.0 * x * ((x * w) - y))
}
```

Now we are all set to implement the `gradient.descent()` function. The first parameter is the train set, the second parameter is the learning rate α, and the last parameter is the number of epochs. The initial weight is initialized to some 'random' number (selected manually here for the sake of the example). The function returns the final learned weight.

```
# Gradient descent.
gradient.descent <- function(train_set, lr = 0.01, epochs = 5){

  w = -2.5 # Initialize weight at 'random'

  for(i in 1:epochs){
    derivative.sum <- 0.0
    loss.sum <- 0.0

    # Iterate each data point in train_set.
    for(j in 1:nrow(train_set)){
      point <- train_set[j, ]

      derivative.sum <- derivative.sum + derivative(w, point$x, point$y)

      loss.sum <- loss.sum + loss(w, point$x, point$y)
    }

    # Update weight.
    w <-  w - lr * derivative.sum

    # mean squared error (MSE)
    mse <- loss.sum / nrow(train_set)

    print(paste0("epoch: ", i, " loss: ",
                 formatC(mse, digits = 8, format = "f"),
                 " w = ", formatC(w, digits = 5, format = "f")))
  }

  return(w)
}
```

Now, let's train the network with a learning rate of 0.01 and for 10 epochs. This function will print for each epoch, the loss and the current weight.

```
#### Train the 1 unit network with gradient descent ####
lr <- 0.01 # set learning rate.
```

```
set.seed(123)

# Run gradient decent to find the optimal weight.
learned_w = gradient.descent(train_set, lr, epochs = 10)

#> [1] "epoch: 1 loss: 78.00000000 w = -0.94000"
#> [1] "epoch: 2 loss: 17.97120000 w = -0.19120"
#> [1] "epoch: 3 loss: 4.14056448 w = 0.16822"
#> [1] "epoch: 4 loss: 0.95398606 w = 0.34075"
#> [1] "epoch: 5 loss: 0.21979839 w = 0.42356"
#> [1] "epoch: 6 loss: 0.05064155 w = 0.46331"
#> [1] "epoch: 7 loss: 0.01166781 w = 0.48239"
#> [1] "epoch: 8 loss: 0.00268826 w = 0.49155"
#> [1] "epoch: 9 loss: 0.00061938 w = 0.49594"
#> [1] "epoch: 10 loss: 0.00014270 w = 0.49805"
```

From the output, we can see that the loss decreases as the weight is updated. The final value of the weight at iteration 10 is 0.49805. We can now make predictions on new data.

```
# Make predictions on new data using the learned weight.
fp(learned_w, 7)
#> [1] 3.486366

fp(learned_w, -88)
#> [1] -43.8286
```

Now, you can try to change the training set to make the network learn a different arithmetic operation!

In the previous example, we considered a very simple neural network consisting of a single unit. In this case, the partial derivative with respect to the single weight was calculated directly. For bigger networks with more layers and activations, the final output becomes a composition of functions. That is, the activation values of a layer l depend on its weights which are also affected by the previous layer's $l-1$ weights and so on. So, the derivatives (gradients) can be computed using the chain rule $f(g(x))' = f'(g(x)) \cdot g'(x)$. This can be performed efficiently by an algorithm known as **backpropagation**.

> "What backpropagation actually lets us do is compute the partial derivatives $\partial C_x / \partial w$ and $\partial C_x / \partial b$ for a single training example". (Michael Nielsen, 2019)[1].

Here, C refers to the loss function which is also called the cost function. In modern deep learning libraries like TensorFlow, this procedure is efficiently implemented with a computational graph. If you want to learn the details about backpropagation I recommend you to check this post by DEEPLIZARD (`https://deeplizard.com/learn/video/XE3krf3CQls`) which consists of 5 parts including videos.

8.1.6 Stochastic Gradient Descent

We have seen how gradient descent iterates over all training points before updating each parameter. To recall, an epoch is one pass through all parameters and for each parameter, the derivative with each training point needs to be computed. If the training set consists of thousands or millions of points, this method becomes very time-consuming. Furthermore, in practice neural networks do not have one or two parameters but thousands or millions. In those cases, the training can be done more efficiently by using **stochastic gradient descent (SGD)**. This method adds two main modifications to the classic gradient descent:

1. At the beginning, the training set is shuffled (this is the stochastic part). This is necessary for the method to work.
2. The training set is divided into b batches with m data points each. This m is known as the **batch size** and is a hyperparameter that we need to define.

Then, at each epoch all batches are iterated and the parameters are updated based on each batch and not the entire training set, for example:

[1] `http://neuralnetworksanddeeplearning.com/chap2.html`

$$w = w - \alpha \sum_{i=1}^{m} 2x_i(x_i w - y) \quad (8.15)$$

Again, an epoch is one pass through all parameters and all batches. Now you may be wondering why this method is more efficient if an epoch still involves the same number of operations but they are split into chunks. Part of this is because since the parameter updates are more frequent, the loss also improves quicker. Another reason is that the operations within each batch can be optimized and performed in parallel, for example, by using a GPU. One thing to note is that each update is based on less information by only using m points instead of the entire data set. This can introduce some noise in the learning but at the same time this can help to get out of local minima. In practice, SGD needs more epochs to converge compared to gradient descent but overall, it will take less time. From now on, this is the method we will use to train our networks.

Typical batch sizes are: 4,8,16,32,64,128, etc. There is a divided opinion in this respect. Some say it's better to choose small batch sizes but others say the bigger the better. For any particular problem, it is difficult to say what batch size is the optimal. Usually, one needs to choose the batch size empirically by trying different ones.

Be aware that when using GPUs, a big batch size can cause out of memory errors since the GPU may not have enough memory to allocate the batch.

8.2 Keras and TensorFlow with R

TensorFlow[2] is an open-source computational library used mainly for machine learning and more specifically, for deep learning. It has many available tools and extensions to perform a wide variety of tasks such as

[2] https://www.tensorflow.org

data pre-processing, model optimization, reinforcement learning, probabilistic reasoning, to name a few. TensorFlow is very flexible and is used for research, development, and in production environments. It provides an API that contains the necessary building blocks to build different types of neural networks including CNNs, autoencoders, Recurrent Neural Networks, etc. It has two main versions. A CPU version and a GPU version. The latter allows the execution of programs by taking advantage of the computational power of graphic processing units. This makes training models much faster. Despite all this flexibility and power, it can take some time to learn the basics. Sometimes you need a way to build and test machine learning models in a simple way, for example, when trying new ideas or prototyping. Fortunately, there exists an interface to TensorFlow called Keras[3].

Keras offers an API that abstracts many of the TensorFlow's details making it easier to build and train machine learning models. Keras is what I will use when building deep learning models in this book. Keras does not only provide an interface to TensorFlow but also to other deep learning engines such as Theano[4], Microsoft Cognitive Toolkit[5], etc. Keras was developed by François Chollet and later, it was integrated with TensorFlow.

Most of the time its API should be enough to do common tasks and it provides ways to add extensions in case that is not enough. In this book, we will only use a subset of the available Keras functions but that will be enough for our purposes of building models to predict behaviors. If you want to learn more about Keras, I recommend the book *"Deep Learning with R"* by Chollet and Allaire [2018].

Examples in this book will use Keras with TensorFlow as the backend. In R, we can access Keras through the `keras` package [Allaire and Chollet, 2019].

Instructions on how to install Keras and TensorFlow can be found in Appendix A. At this point, I would recommend you to install them since the next section will make use of Keras.

[3]`https://keras.io/`

[4]`https://en.wikipedia.org/wiki/Theano_(software)`

[5]`https://en.wikipedia.org/wiki/Microsoft_Cognitive_Toolkit`

In the next section, we will start with a simple model built with Keras and the following examples will introduce more functions. By the end of this chapter you will be able to build and train efficient deep neural networks including Convolutional Neural Networks.

8.2.1 Keras Example

`keras_simple_network.R`

If you haven't already installed Keras and TensorFlow, I would recommend you to do so at this point. Instructions on how to install the required software can be found in Appendix A.

In the previous section, I showed how to implement gradient descent in R (see `gradient_descent.R`). Now, I will show how to implement the same simple network using Keras. Recall that our network has one unit, one input, one output, and no bias. The code can be found in the script `keras_simple_network.R`. First, the `keras` library is loaded and a sample training set is created. Then, the function `keras_model_sequential()` is used to instantiate a new empty model. It is called sequential because it consists of a sequence of layers. At this point it does not have any layers yet.

```
library(keras)

# Generate a train set.
# First element is the input x and
# the second element is the output y.
train_set <- data.frame(x = c(3.0,4.0,1.0),
                        y = c(1.5, 2.0, 0.5))

# Instantiate a sequential model.
model <- keras_model_sequential()
```

We can now start adding layers (only one in this example). To do so, the `layer_dense()` method can be used. The *dense* name means that this will be a densely (fully) connected layer. This layer will be the output layer with a single unit.

```
model %>%
  layer_dense(units = 1,
              use_bias = FALSE,
              activation = 'linear',
              input_shape = 1)
```

The first argument `units = 1` specifies the number of units in this layer. By default, a bias is added in each layer. To make it the same as in the previous example, we will not use a bias so `use_bias` is set to `FALSE`. The `activation` specifies the activation function. Here it is set to `'linear'` which means that no activation function is applied $f(x) = x$. Finally, we need to specify the number of inputs with `input_shape`. In this case, there is only one feature.

Before training the network we need to compile the model and specify the learning algorithm. In this case, stochastic gradient descent with a learning rate of $\alpha = 0.01$. We also need to specify which loss function to use (we'll use mean squared error). At every epoch, some performance metrics can be computed. Here, we specify that we want the mean squared error and mean absolute error. These metrics are computed on the train data. After compiling the model, the `summary()` method can be used to print a textual description of it. Figure 8.16 shows the output of the `summary()` function.

```
model %>% compile(
  optimizer = optimizer_sgd(lr = 0.01),
  loss = 'mse',
  metrics = list('mse','mae')
)
summary(model)
```

From this output, we see that the network consists of a single dense layer with 1 unit. To start the actual training procedure we need to call the `fit()` function. Its first argument is the input training data (features) as a matrix. The second argument specifies the corresponding true outputs.

```
> summary(model)
Model: "sequential"
________________________________________________________________________________
Layer (type)                    Output Shape                     Param #
================================================================================
dense (Dense)                   (None, 1)                        1
================================================================================
Total params: 1
Trainable params: 1
Non-trainable params: 0
________________________________________________________________________________
```

FIGURE 8.16 Summary of the simple neural network.

We let the algorithm run for 30 epochs. The batch size is set to 3 which is also the total number of data points in our data. In this example the dataset is very small so we set the batch size equal to the total number of instances. In practice, datasets can contain thousands of instances but the batch size will be relatively small (e.g., 8, 16, 32, etc.).

Additionally, there is a `validation_split` parameter that specifies the fraction of the train data to be used for validation. This is set to 0 (the default) since the dataset is very small. If the validation split is greater than 0, its performance metrics will also be computed. The `verbose` parameter sets the amount of information to be printed during training. A 0 will not print anything. A 2 will print one line of information per epoch. The last parameter `view_metrics` specifies if you want the progress of the loss and performance metrics to be plotted. The `fit()` function returns an object with summary statistics collected during training and is saved in the variable `history`.

```
history <- model %>% fit(
  as.matrix(train_set$x), as.matrix(train_set$y),
  epochs = 30,
  batch_size = 3,
  validation_split = 0,
  verbose = 2,
  view_metrics = TRUE
)
```

Figure 8.17 presents the output of the `fit()` function in RStudio. In the console, the training loss, mean squared error, and mean absolute error are printed during each epoch. In the viewer pane, plots of the same metrics are shown. Here, we can see that the loss is nicely decreasing over time. The loss at epoch 30 should be close to 0.

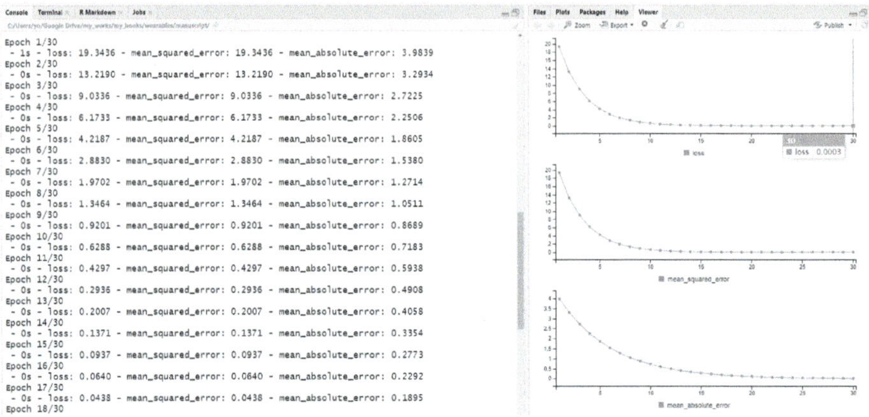

FIGURE 8.17 fit() function output.

The information saved in the `history` variable can be plotted with `plot(history)`. This will generate plots for the *loss*, *MSE*, and *MAE*.

> The results can slightly differ every time the training is run due to random weight initializations performed by the back end.

Once the model is trained, we can perform inference on new data points with the `predict_on_batch()` function. Here we are passing three data points.

```
model %>% predict_on_batch(c(7, 50, -220))
#>        [,1]
#> [1,]    3.465378
#> [2,]   24.752701
#> [3,] -108.911880
```

Now, try setting a higher learning rate, for example, 0.05. With this learning rate, the algorithm will converge much faster. In my computer, at epoch 11 the loss was already 0.

One practical thing to note is that if you make any changes in the `compile()` or `fit()` functions, you will have to rerun the code that instantiates and defines the network. This is because the model object saves the current state including the learned weights. If you rerun the `fit()` function on a previously trained model, it will start with the previously learned weights.

8.3 Classification with Neural Networks

Neural networks are trained iteratively by modifying their weights while aiming to minimize the loss function. When the network predicts real numbers, the MSE loss function is normally used. For classification problems, the network should predict the most likely class out of k possible categories. To make a neural network work for classification problems, we need to introduce new elements to its architecture:

1. Add more units to the output layer.
2. Use a **softmax** activation function in the output layer.
3. Use **average cross-entropy** as the loss function.

Let's start with point number 1 (add more units to the output layer). This means that if the number of classes is k, then the last layer needs to have k units, one for each class. That's it! Figure 8.18 shows an example of a neural network with an output layer having 3 units. Each unit predicts a score for each of the 3 classes. Let's call the vector of predicted scores y'.

Point number 2 says that a **softmax** activation function should be used in the output layer. When training the network, just as with regression, we need a way to compute the error between the predicted values y' and the true values y. In this case, y is a one-hot encoded vector with a 1 at the position of the true class and 0s elsewhere. If you are not familiar with one-hot encoding, you can check the topic in chapter 5. As opposed to other classifiers like decision trees, k-NN, etc., neural networks need the classes to be one-hot encoded.

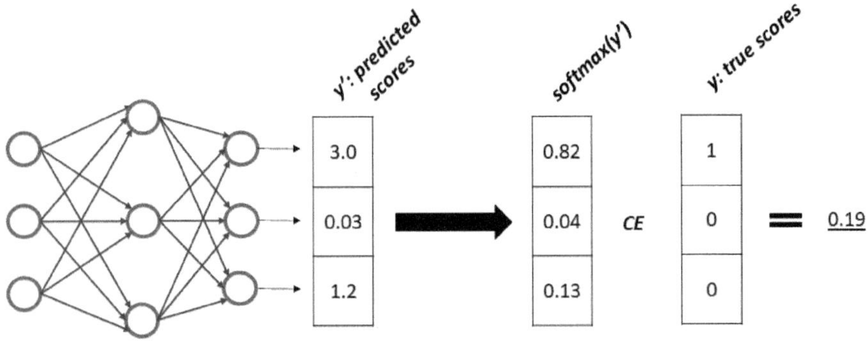

FIGURE 8.18 Neural network with 3 output scores. Softmax is applied to the scores and the cross-entropy with the true scores is calculated. This gives us an estimate of the similarity between the network's predictions and the true values.

With regression problems, one way to compare the prediction with the true value is by using the squared difference: $(y'-y)^2$. With classification, y and y' are vectors so we need another way to compare them. The true values y are represented as a vector of probabilities with a 1 at the position of the true class. The output scores y' do not necessarily sum up to 1 thus, they are not proper probabilities. Before comparing y and y' we need both to be probabilities. The **softmax** activation function is used to convert y' into a vector of probabilities. The softmax function is applied individually to each element of a vector:

$$softmax(x,i) = \frac{e^{x_i}}{\sum_j e^{x_j}} \tag{8.16}$$

where x is a vector and i is an index pointing to a particular element in the vector. Thus, to convert y' into a vector of probabilities we need to apply softmax to each of its elements. One thing to note is that this activation function depends on all the values in the vector (the output values of all units). Figure 8.18 shows the resulting vector of probabilities after applying softmax to each element of y'. In R this can be implemented like the following:

```
# Scores from the figure.
scores <- c(3.0, 0.03, 1.2)
```

```
# Softmax function.
softmax <- function(scores){
  exp(scores) / sum(exp(scores))
}
probabilities <- softmax(scores)
print(probabilities)
#> [1] 0.82196 0.04217 0.13587
print(sum(probabilities)) # Should sum up to 1.
#> [1] 1
```

We used R's vectorization capabilities to compute the final vector of probabilities within the same function without having to iterate through each element. When using Keras, these operations are efficiently computed by the backend (for example, TensorFlow).

Finally, point 3 states that we need to use **average cross-entropy** as the **loss function**. Now that we have converted y' into probabilities, we can compute its dissimilarity with y. The distance (dissimilarity) between two vectors (A,B) of probabilities can be computed using **cross-entropy**:

$$CE(A,B) = -\sum_i B_i log(A_i) \tag{8.17}$$

Thus, to get the dissimilarity between y' and y first we apply softmax to y' (to transform it into proper probabilities) and then, we compute the cross entropy between the resulting vector of probabilities and y:

$$CE(softmax(y'), y). \tag{8.18}$$

In R this can be implemented with the following:

```
# Cross-entropy
CE <- function(A,B){
 - sum(B * log(A))
}

y <- c(1, 0, 0)
```

```
print(CE(softmax(scores), y))
#> [1] 0.1961
```

Be aware that when computing the cross-entropy with equation (8.17) **order matters**. The first element should be the predicted scores y' and the second element should be the true one-hot encoded vector y. We don't want to apply a log function to a vector with values of 0. Most of the time, the predicted scores y' will be different from 0. That's why we prefer to apply the log function to them. In the very rare case when the predicted scores have zeros, we can add a very small number. In practice, this is taken care of by the backend (e.g., Tensorflow).

Now we know how to compute the cross-entropy for each training instance. The total loss function is then, the **average cross-entropy across the training points**. The next section shows how to build a neural network for classification using Keras.

8.3.1 Classification of Electromyography Signals

`keras_electromyography.R`

In this example, we will train a neural network with Keras to classify hand gestures based on muscle electrical activity. The *ELECTROYMYOGRAPHY* dataset will be used here. The electrical activity was recorded with an electromyography (EMG) sensor worn as an armband. The data were collected and made available by Yashuk [2019]. The armband device has 8 sensors which are placed on the skin surface and measure electrical activity from the right forearm at a sampling rate of 200 Hz. A video of the device can be found here: `https://youtu.be/OuwDHfY2Awg`

The data contains 4 different gestures: 0-rock, 1-scissors, 2-paper, 3-OK, and has 65 columns. The last column is the class label from 0 to 3. The first 64 columns are electrical measurements. 8 consecutive readings for each of the 8 sensors. The objective is to use the first 64 variables to predict the class.

The script `keras_electromyography.R` has the full code. We start by splitting the `dataset` into train (60%), validation (10%) and test (30%) sets. We will use the validation set to monitor the performance during each epoch. We also need to normalize the three sets but only learn the normalization parameters from the train set. The `normalize()` function included in the script will do the job.

One last thing we need to do is to format the data as matrices and one-hot encode the class. The following code defines a function that takes as input a data frame and the expected number of classes. It assumes that the first columns are the features and the last column contains the class. First, it converts the features into a matrix and stores them in `x`. Then, it converts the class into an array and one-hot encodes it using the `to_categorical()` function from Keras. The classes are stored in `y` and the function returns a list with the features and one-hot encoded classes. Then, we can call the function with the train, validation, and test sets.

```
# Define a function to format features and one-hot encode the class.
format.to.array <- function(data, numclasses = 4){
  x <- as.matrix(data[, 1:(ncol(data)-1)])
  y <- as.array(data[, ncol(data)])
  y <- to_categorical(y, num_classes = numclasses)
  l <- list(x=x, y=y)
  return(l)
}

# Format data
trainset <- format.to.array(trainset, numclasses = 4)
valset <- format.to.array(valset, numclasses = 4)
testset <- format.to.array(testset, numclasses = 4)
```

Let's print the first one-hot encoded classes from the train set:

```
head(trainset$y)

#>      [,1] [,2] [,3] [,4]
#> [1,]    0    0    1    0
#> [2,]    0    0    1    0
#> [3,]    0    0    1    0
#> [4,]    0    0    0    1
#> [5,]    1    0    0    0
#> [6,]    0    0    0    1
```

The first three instances belong to the class *'paper'* because the 1*s* are in the third position. The corresponding integers are 0-rock, 1-scissors, 2-paper, 3-OK. So *'paper'* comes in the third position. The fourth instance belongs to the class *'OK'*, the fifth to *'rock'*, and so on.

Now it's time to define the neural network architecture! We will do so inside a function:

```
# Define the network's architecture.
get.nn <- function(ninputs = 64, nclasses = 4, lr = 0.01){

  model <- keras_model_sequential()

  model %>%
    layer_dense(units = 32, activation = 'relu',
                input_shape = ninputs) %>%
    layer_dense(units = 16, activation = 'relu') %>%
    layer_dense(units = nclasses, activation = 'softmax')

  model %>% compile(
    loss = 'categorical_crossentropy',
    optimizer = optimizer_sgd(lr = lr),
    metrics = c('accuracy')
  )

  return(model)
}
```

The first argument takes the number of inputs (features), the second argument specifies the number of classes and the last argument is the learning rate α. The first line instantiates an empty keras sequential model. Then we add three layers. The first two are hidden layers and the last one will be the output layer. The input layer is implicitly defined when setting the `input_shape` parameter in the first layer. The first hidden layer has 32 units with a ReLU activation function. Since this is the first hidden layer, we also need to specify what is the expected input by setting the `input_shape`. In this case, the number of input features is 64. The next hidden layer has 16 ReLU units. For the output layer, the number of units needs to be equal to the number of classes (4, in this case). Since this is a classification problem we also set the activation function to `softmax`.

Then, the model is compiled and the loss function is set to `categorical_crossentropy` because this is a classification problem. Stochastic gradient descent is used with a learning rate passed as a parameter. During training, we want to monitor the *accuracy*. Finally, the function returns the compiled model.

Now we can call our function to create the model. This one will have 64 inputs and 4 outputs and the learning rate is set to 0.01. It is always useful to print a summary of the model with the `summary()` function.

```
model <- get.nn(64, 4, lr = 0.01)
summary(model)
```

```
> summary(model)
________________________________________________________________________________
Layer (type)                        Output Shape                        Param #
================================================================================
dense (Dense)                       (None, 32)                          2080
________________________________________________________________________________
dense_1 (Dense)                     (None, 16)                          528
________________________________________________________________________________
dense_2 (Dense)                     (None, 4)                           68
================================================================================
Total params: 2,676
Trainable params: 2,676
Non-trainable params: 0
________________________________________________________________________________
```

FIGURE 8.19 Summary of the network.

From the summary, we can see that the network has 3 layers. The second column shows the output shape which in this case corresponds to the number of units in each layer. The last column shows the number of parameters of each layer. For example, the first layer has 2080 parameters! Those come from the weights and biases. There are 64 (inputs) * 32 (units) = 2048 weights plus the 32 biases (one for each unit). The biases are included by default on each layer unless otherwise specified.

The second layer receives 32 inputs on each of its 16 units. Thus 32 * 16 + 16 (biases) = 528. The last layer has 16 inputs from the previous layer on each of its 4 units plus 4 biases giving a total of 68 parameters. In total, the network has 2676 parameters. Here, we see how fast the number of parameters grows when adding more layers and units. Now, we use the `fit()` function to train the model.

```
history <- model %>% fit(
  trainset$x, trainset$y,
  epochs = 300,
  batch_size = 8,
  validation_data = list(valset$x, valset$y),
  verbose = 1,
  view_metrics = TRUE
)
```

The model is trained for 300 epochs with a batch size of 8. We used the `validation_data` parameter to specify the validation set to compute the performance on unseen data. The training will take some minutes to complete. Bigger models can take hours or even several days. Thus, it is a good idea to save a model once it is trained. You can do so with the `save_model_hdf5()` or `save_model_tf()` methods. The former saves the model in `hdf5` format while the later saves it in TensorFlow's `SavedModel` format. The `SavedModel` is stored as a directory containing the necessary serialized files to restore the model's state.

```
# Save model as hdf5.
save_model_hdf5(model, "electromyography.hdf5")

# Alternatively, save model as SavedModel.
save_model_tf(model, "electromyography_tf")
```

We can load a previously saved model with:

```
# Load model.
model <- load_model_hdf5("electromyography.hdf5")

# Or alternatively if the model is in SavedModel format.
model <- load_model_tf("electromyography")
```

The source code files include the trained models used in this book in case you want to reproduce the results. Both, the `hdf5` and `SavedModel` versions are included.

Due to some version incompatibilities with the h5py underlying library, you may get the following error when trying to load the `hdf5` files. `AttributeError: 'str' object has no attribute 'decode'`. If you encounter this error, load the models in `SavedModel` format using the `load_model_tf()` method instead.

Figure 8.20 shows the train and validation loss and accuracy as produced by `plot(history)`. We see that both the training and validation loss are decreasing over time. The accuracy increases over time

Now, we evaluate the performance of the trained model with the test set using the `evaluate()` function.

```
# Evaluate model.
model %>% evaluate(testset$x, testset$y)

#>      loss  accuracy
#> 0.4045424 0.8474576
```

The accuracy was pretty decent ($\approx 84\%$). To get the actual class predictions you can use the `predict_classes()` function.

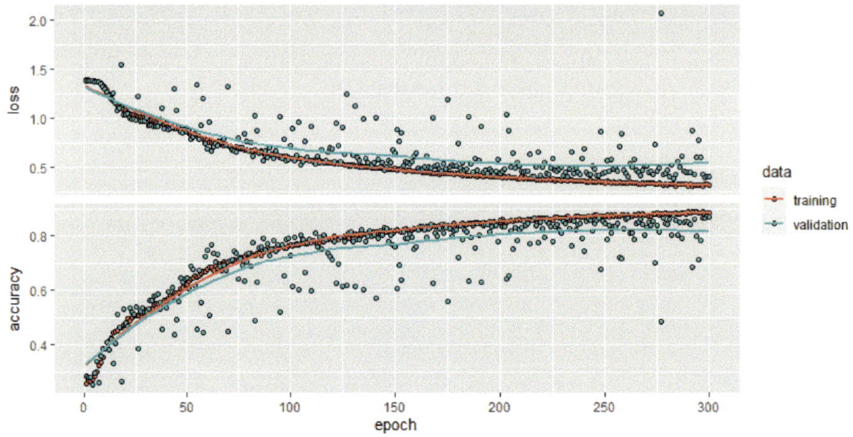

FIGURE 8.20 Loss and accuracy of the electromyography model.

```
# Predict classes.
classes <- model %>% predict_classes(testset$x)
head(classes)
#> [1] 2 2 1 3 0 1
```

Note that this function returns the classes with numbers starting with 0 just as in the original dataset.

Sometimes it is useful to access the actual predicted scores for each class. This can be done with the `predict_on_batch()` function.

```
# Make predictions on the test set.
predictions <- model %>% predict_on_batch(testset$x)
head(predictions)
#>              [,1]         [,2]         [,3]         [,4]
#> [1,] 1.957638e-05 8.726048e-02 7.708290e-01 1.418910e-01
#> [2,] 3.937355e-05 2.571992e-04 9.965665e-01 3.136863e-03
#> [3,] 4.261451e-03 7.343097e-01 7.226156e-02 1.891673e-01
#> [4,] 8.669784e-06 2.088269e-04 1.339851e-01 8.657974e-01
#> [5,] 9.999956e-01 7.354113e-26 1.299388e-08 4.451362e-06
#> [6,] 2.513005e-05 9.914154e-01 7.252949e-03 1.306421e-03
```

To obtain the actual classes from the scores, we can compute the index of the maximum column. Then we subtract -1 so the classes start at 0.

```
classes <- max.col(predictions) - 1
head(classes)
#> [1] 2 2 1 3 0 1
```

Since the true classes are also one-hot encoded we need to do the same to get the ground truth.

```
groundTruth <- max.col(testset$y) - 1

# Compute accuracy.
sum(classes == groundTruth) / length(classes)
#> [1] 0.8474576
```

The integers are mapped to class strings. Then, a confusion matrix is generated.

```
# Convert classes to strings.
# Class mapping by index: rock 0, scissors 1, paper 2, ok 3.
mapping <- c("rock", "scissors", "paper", "ok")
# Need to add 1 because indices in R start at 1.
str.predictions <- mapping[classes+1]
str.groundTruth <- mapping[groundTruth+1]

library(caret)
cm <- confusionMatrix(as.factor(str.predictions),
                      as.factor(str.groundTruth))
cm$table
#>           Reference
#> Prediction  ok paper rock scissors
#>   ok       681   118   24       27
#>   paper     54   681   47       12
#>   rock      29    18  771        1
#>   scissors 134    68    8      867
```

Now, try to modify the network by making it deeper (adding more layers) and fine-tune the hyperparameters like the learning rate, batch size, etc., to increase the performance.

8.4 Overfitting

One important thing to look at when training a network is **overfitting**. That is, when the model memorizes instead of learning (see chapter 1). Overfitting means that the model becomes very specialized at mapping inputs to outputs from the *train set* but fails to do so with new *test samples*. One reason is that a model can become too complex and with so many parameters that it will perfectly adapt to its training data but will miss more general patterns preventing it to perform well on unseen instances. To diagnose this, one can plot loss/accuracy curves during training epochs.

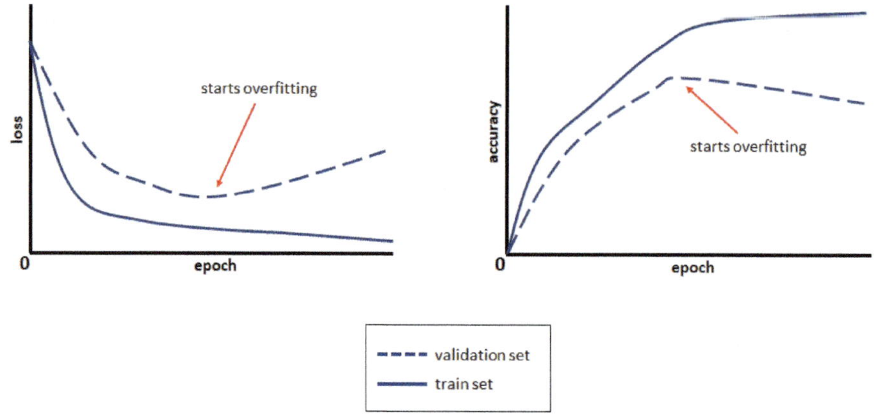

FIGURE 8.21 Loss and accuracy curves.

In Figure 8.21 we can see that after some epochs the *validation loss* starts to increase even though the *train loss* is still decreasing. This is because the model is getting better on reducing the error on the train set but its performance starts to decrease when presented with new instances. Conversely, one can observe a similar effect with the accuracy. The model keeps improving its performance on the train set but at some point, the accuracy on the validation set starts to decrease. Usually, one stops the training before overfitting starts to occur. In the following, I will introduce you to two common techniques to combat overfitting in neural networks.

8.4.1 Early Stopping

keras_electromyography_earlystopping.R

Neural networks are trained for several epochs using gradient descent. But the question is: *For how many epochs?*. As can be seen in Figure 8.21, too many epochs can lead to overfitting and too few can cause underfitting. *Early stopping* is a simple but effective method to reduce the risk of overfitting. The method consists of setting a large number of epochs and stop updating the network's parameters when a condition is met. For example, one condition can be to stop when there is no performance improvement on the validation set after n epochs or when there is a decrease of some percent in accuracy.

Keras provides some mechanisms to implement early stopping and this is accomplished via **callbacks**. A callback is a function that is run at different stages during training such as at the beginning or end of an epoch or at the beginning or end of a batch operation. Callbacks are passed as a list to the `fit()` function. You can define custom callbacks or use some of the built-in ones including `callback_early_stopping()`. This callback will cause the training to stop when a metric stops improving. The metric can be *accuracy*, *loss*, etc. The following callback will stop the training if after 10 epochs (`patience`) there is no improvement of at least 1% (`min_delta`) in accuracy on the validation set.

```
callback_early_stopping(monitor = "val_acc",
                        min_delta = 0.01,
                        patience = 10,
                        verbose = 1,
                        mode = "max")
```

The `min_delta` parameter specifies the minimum change in the monitored metric to qualify as an improvement. The `mode` specifies if training should be stopped when the metric has stopped decreasing, if it is set to `"min"`.

If it is set to `"max"`, training will stop when the monitored metric has stopped increasing.

It may be the case that the best validation performance was achieved not in the last epoch but at some previous point. By setting the `restore_best_weights` parameter to `TRUE` the model weights from the epoch with the best value of the monitored metric will be restored.

The script `keras_electromyography_earlystopping.R` shows how to use the early stopping callback in Keras with the electromyography dataset. The following code is an extract that shows how to define the callback and pass it to the `fit()` function.

```
# Define early stopping callback.
my_callback <- callback_early_stopping(monitor = "val_acc",
                                       min_delta = 0.01,
                                       patience = 50,
                                       verbose = 1,
                                       mode = "max",
                                       restore_best_weights = TRUE)


history <- model %>% fit(
  trainset$x, trainset$y,
  epochs = 500,
  batch_size = 8,
  validation_data = list(valset$x, valset$y),
  verbose = 1,
  view_metrics = TRUE,
  callbacks = list(my_callback)
)
```

This code will cause the training to stop if after 50 epochs there is no improvement in accuracy of at least 1% and will restore the model's weights to the ones during the epoch with the highest accuracy. Figure 8.22 shows how the training stopped at epoch 241.

If we evaluate the final model on the test set, we see that the accuracy is 86.4%, a noticeable increase compared to the 84.7% that we got when training for 300 epochs without early stopping.

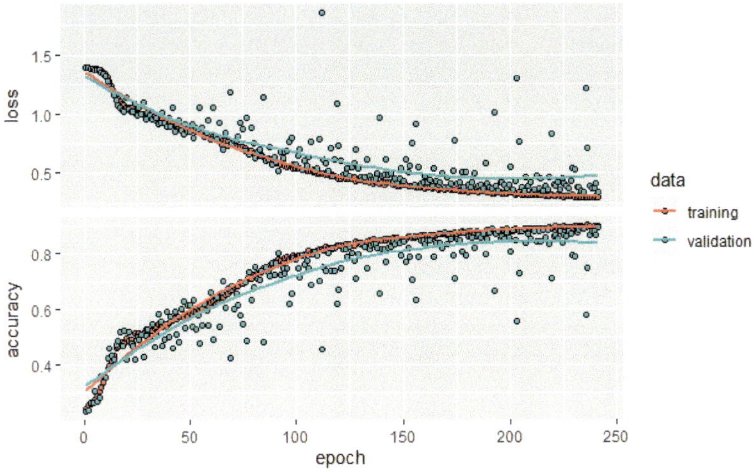

FIGURE 8.22 Early stopping example.

```
# Evaluate model.
model %>% evaluate(testset$x, testset$y)

#> $loss
#> [1] 0.3777530

#> $acc
#> [1] 0.8641243
```

8.4.2 Dropout

Dropout is another technique to reduce overfitting proposed by Srivastava et al. [2014]. It consists of 'dropping' some of the units from a hidden layer for each sample during training. In theory, it can also be applied to input and output layers but that is not very common. The incoming and outgoing connections of a dropped unit are discarded. Figure 8.23 shows an example of applying dropout to a network. In Figure 8.23 (b), the middle unit was removed from the network whereas in Figure 8.23 (c), the top and bottom units were removed.

Each unit has an associated probability p (independent of other units) of being dropped. This probability is another hyperparameter but typically

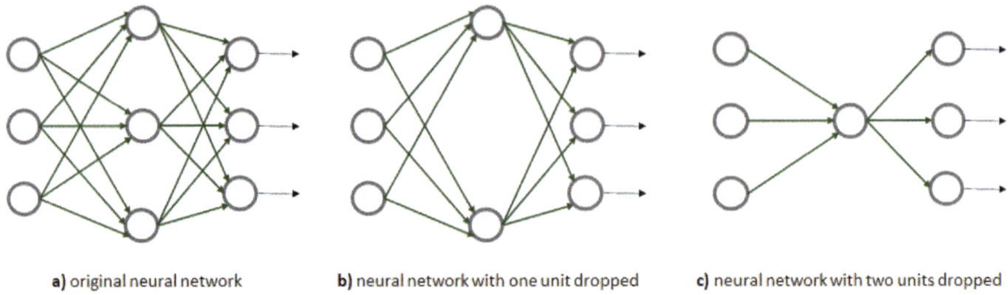

FIGURE 8.23 Dropout example.

it is set to 0.5. Thus, during each iteration and for each sample, half of the units are discarded. The effect of this, is having more simple networks (see Figure 8.23) and thus, less prone to overfitting. Intuitively, you can also think of dropout as training an **ensemble of neural networks**, each having a slightly different structure.

From the perspective of one unit that receives inputs from the previous hidden layer with dropout, approximately half of its incoming connections will be gone (if $p = 0.5$). See Figure 8.24.

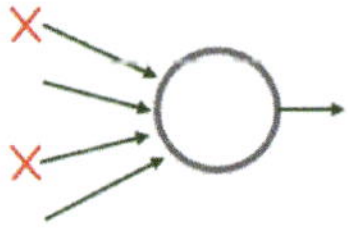

FIGURE 8.24 Incoming connections to one unit when the previous layer has dropout.

Dropout has the effect of making units not to rely on any single incoming connection. This makes the whole network able to compensate for the lack of connections by learning alternative paths. In practice and for many applications, this results in a more robust model. A side effect of applying dropout is that the expected value of the activation function of a unit will be diminished because some of the previous activations will be 0. Recall that the output of a neuron is computed as:

$$f(x) = g(w \cdot x + b) \tag{8.19}$$

where x contains the input values from the previous layer, w the corresponding weights and $g()$ is the activation function. With dropout, approximately half of the values of x will be 0 (if $p = 0.5$). To compensate for that, the input values need to be scaled, in this case, by a factor of 2.

$$f(x) = g(w \cdot 2x + b) \tag{8.20}$$

In modern implementations, this scaling is done during training so at inference time there is no need to apply dropout. The predictions are done as usual. In Keras, the `layer_dropout()` can be used to add dropout to any layer. Its parameter `rate` is a float between 0 and 1 that specifies the fraction of units to drop. The following code snippet builds a neural network with 2 hidden layers. Then, dropout with a rate of 0.5 is applied to both of them.

```
model <- keras_model_sequential()

  model %>%
    layer_dense(units = 256, activation = 'relu', input_shape = 1000) %>%
    layer_dropout(0.5) %>%
    layer_dense(units = 128, activation = 'relu') %>%
    layer_dropout(0.5) %>%
    layer_dense(units = 2, activation = 'softmax')
```

It is very common to apply dropout to networks in computer vision because the inputs are images or videos containing a lot of input values (pixels) but the number of samples is often very limited causing overfitting. In section 8.6 Convolutional Neural Networks (CNNs) will be introduced. They are suitable for computer vision problems. In the corresponding smile detection example (section 8.8), we will use dropout. When building CNNs, dropout is almost always added to the different layers.

8.5 Fine-tuning a Neural Network

When deciding for a neural network's architecture, no formula will tell you how many hidden layers or number of units each layer should have.

There is also no formula for determining the batch size, the learning rate, type of activation function, for how many epochs should we train the network, and so on. All those are called the **hyperparameters** of the network. Hyperparameter tuning is a complex optimization problem and there is a lot of research going on that tackles the issue from different angles. My suggestion is to start with a simple architecture that has been used before to solve a similar problem and then fine-tune it for your specific task. If you are not aware of such a network, there are some guidelines (described below) to get you started. Always keep in mind that those are only recommendations, so you do not need to abide by them and you should feel free to try configurations that deviate from those guidelines depending on your problem at hand.

Training neural networks is a time-consuming process, especially in deep networks. Training a network can take from several minutes to weeks. In many cases, performing cross-validation is not feasible. A common practice is to divide the data into train/validation/test sets. The training data is used to train a network with a given architecture and a set of hyperparameters. The validation set is used to evaluate the generalization performance of the network. Then, you can try different architectures and hyperparameters and evaluate the performance again and again with the validation set. Typically, the network's performance is monitored during training epochs by plotting the loss and accuracy of the train and validation sets. Once you are happy with your model, you test its performance on the test set **only once** and that is the result that is reported.

Here are some starting point guidelines, however, also take into consideration that those hyperparameters can be dependent on each other. So, if you modify a hyperparameter it may impact other(s).

Number of hidden layers. Most of the time one or two hidden layers are enough to solve not too complex problems. One advice is to start with one hidden layer and if that one is not enough to capture the complexity of the problem, add another layer and so on.

Number of units. If a network has too few units it can underfit, that is, the model will be too simple to capture the underlying data patterns. If the network has too many units this can result in overfitting. Also, it will take more time to learn the parameters. Some guidelines mention that the number of units should be somewhere between the number of input features and the number of units in the output layer[6]. Huang [2003] has even proposed a formula for the two-hidden layer case to calculate the number of units that are enough to learn N samples: $2\sqrt{(m+2)N}$ where m is the number of output units.

My suggestion is to first gain some practice and intuition with simple problems. A good way to do so is with the TensorFlow playground (`https://playground.tensorflow.org/`) created by Daniel Smilkov and Shan Carter. This is a web-based implementation of a neural network that you can fine-tune to solve a predefined set of classification and regression problems. For example, Figure 8.25 shows how I tried to solve the XOR problem with a neural network with 1 hidden layer and 1 unit with a sigmoid activation function. After more than $1,000$ epochs the loss is still quite high (0.38). Try to add more neurons and/or hidden layers and see if you can solve the XOR problem with fewer epochs.

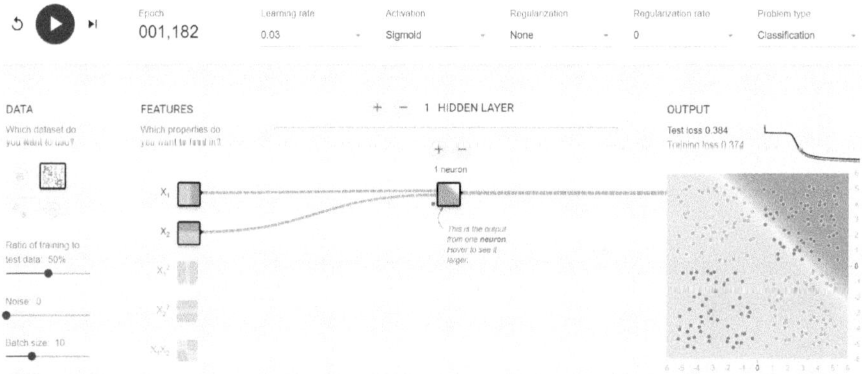

FIGURE 8.25 Screenshot of the TensorFlow playground. (Daniel Smilkov and Shan Carter, `https://github.com/tensorflow/playground` (Apache License 2.0)).

Batch size. Batch sizes typically range between 4 and 512. Big batch sizes provide a better estimate of the gradient but are more computationally expensive. On the other hand, small batch sizes are faster to compute but will incur in more noise in the gradient estimation requiring more epochs to converge. When using a GPU or other specialized hardware, the computations can be performed in parallel thus, allowing bigger batch sizes to be computed in a reasonable time. Some people argue that the noise introduced with small batch sizes is good to escape

[6]`https://www.heatonresearch.com/2017/06/01/hidden-layers.html`

from local minima. Keskar et al. [2016] showed that in practice, big batch sizes can result in degraded models. A good starting point is 32 which is the default in Keras.

Learning rate. This is one of the most important hyperparameters. The learning rate specifies how fast gradient descent 'moves' when trying to find an optimal minimum. However, this doesn't mean that the algorithm will *learn* faster if the learning rate is set to a high value. If it is too high, the loss can start oscillating. If it is too low, the learning will take a lot of time. One way to fine-tune it, is to start with the default one. In Keras, the default learning rate for stochastic gradient descent is 0.01. Then, based on the loss plot across epochs, you can decrease/increase it. If learning is taking long, try to increase it. If the loss seems to be oscillating or stuck, try reducing it. Typical values are 0.1, 0.01, 0.001, 0.0001, 0.00001. Additionally to stochastic gradient descent, Keras provides implementations of other optimizers[7] like Adam[8] which have adaptive learning rates, but still, one needs to specify an initial one.

Before training a network it is a good practice to shuffle the rows of the train set if the data points are independent. Neural networks tend to 'forget' patterns learned from previous points during training as the wights are updated. For example, if the train set happens to be oredered by class labels, the network may 'forget' how to identify the first classes and will put more emphasis on the last ones.

It is also a good practice to normalize the input features before training a network. This will make the training process more efficient.

8.6 Convolutional Neural Networks

Convolutional Neural Networks or CNNs for short, have become extremely popular due to their capacity to solve computer vision problems.

[7] https://keras.io/api/optimizers/

[8] https://keras.io/api/optimizers/adam/

Most of the time they are used for image classification tasks but can also be used for regression and for time series data. If we wanted to perform image classification with a traditional neural network, first we would need to either build a feature vector by:

1. extracting features from the image or,
2. flattening the image pixels into a 1D array.

The first solution requires a lot of image processing expertise and domain knowledge. Extracting features from images is not a trivial task and requires a lot of preprocessing to reduce noise, artifacts, segment the objects of interest, remove background, etc. Additionally, considerable effort is spent on feature engineering. The drawback of the second solution is that spatial information is lost, that is, the relationship between neighboring pixels. CNNs solve the two previous problems by automatically extracting features while preserving spatial information. As opposed to traditional networks, CNNs can take as input n-dimensional images and process them efficiently. The main building blocks of a CNN are:

1. **Convolution layers**
2. **Pooling operations**
3. **Traditional fully connected layers**

Figure 8.26 shows a simple CNN and its basic components. First, the input image goes through a convolution layer with 4 kernels (details about the convolution operation are described in the next subsection). This layer is in charge of extracting features by applying the kernels on top of the image. The result of this operation is a convolved image, also known as **feature maps**. The number of feature maps is equal to the number of kernels, in this case, 4. Then, a **pooling operation** is applied on top of the feature maps. This operation reduces the size of the feature maps by downsampling them (details on this in a following subsection). The output of the pooling operation is a set of feature maps with reduced size. Here, the outputs are 4 reduced feature maps since the pooling operation is applied to each feature map independently of the others. Then, the feature maps are flattened into a one-dimensional array. Conceptually, this array represents all the features extracted from the previous steps. These features are then used as inputs to a neural network with its respective input, hidden, and output layers. An '*' and underlined text means that parameter learning occurs in that layer. For example, in the convolution layer, the parameters of the kernels need to be learned. On the other hand, the pooling operation does not require parameter learning since it is a fixed operation. Finally, the parameters of the neural network are learned too, including the hidden layers and the output layer.

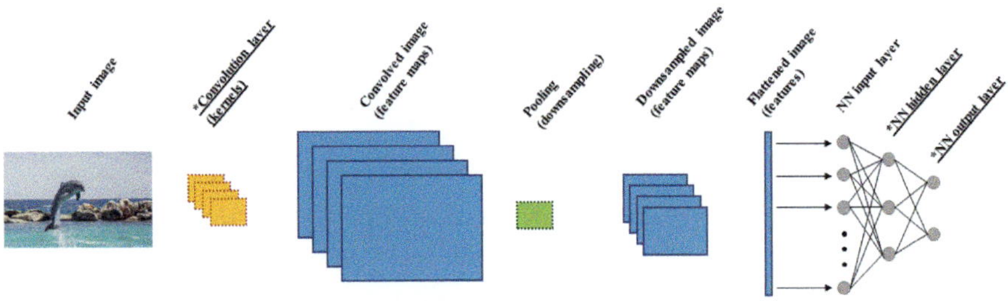

FIGURE 8.26 Simple CNN architecture. An '*' indicates that parameter learning occurs.

One can build more complex CNNs by stacking more convolution layers and pooling operations. By doing so, the level of abstraction increases. For example, the first convolution extracts simple features like horizontal, vertical, diagonal lines, etc. The next convolution could extract more complex features like squares, triangles, and so on. The parameter learning of all layers (including the convolution layers) occurs during the same forward and backpropagation step just as with a normal neural network. Both, the features and the classification task are learned at the same time! During learning, batches of images are forward propagated and the parameters are adjusted accordingly to minimize the error (for example, the average cross-entropy for classification). The same methods for training normal neural networks are used for CNNs, for example, stochastic gradient descent.

Each kernel in a convolution layer can have an associated bias which is also a parameter to be learned. By default, Keras uses a bias for each kernel. Furthermore, an activation function can be applied to the outputs of the convolution layer. This is applied element-wise. ReLU is the most common one.

At inference time, the convolution layers and pooling operations act as feature extractors by generating feature maps that are ultimately flattened and passed to a normal neural network. It is also common to use the first layers as feature extractors and then replace the neural network with another model (Random Forest, SVM, etc.). In the following sections, details about the convolution and pooling operations are presented.

8.6.1 Convolutions

Convolutions are used to automatically extract feature maps from images. A convolution operation consists of a **kernel** also known as a **filter** which is a matrix with real values. Kernels are usually much smaller than the original image. For example, for a grayscale image of height and width of 100x100 a typical kernel size would be 3x3. The size of the kernel is a hyperparameter. The convolution operation consists of applying the kernel over the image starting at the upper left corner and moving forward row by row until reaching the bottom right corner. The **stride** controls how many elements the kernel is moved at a time and this is also a hyperparameter. A typical value for the stride is 1.

The convolution operation computes the sum of the element-wise product between the kernel and the image region it is covering. The output of this operation is used to generate the convolved image (feature map). Figure 8.27 shows the first two iterations and the final iteration of the convolution operation on an image. In this case, the kernel is a 3x3 matrix with 1s in its first row and 0s elsewhere. The original image has a size of 5x5x1 (height, width, depth) and it seems to be a number 7.

In the first iteration, the kernel is aligned with the upper left corner of the original image. An element-wise multiplication is performed and the results are summed. The operation is shown at the top of the figure. In the first iteration, the result was 3 and it is set at the corresponding position of the final convolved image (feature map). In the next iteration, the kernel is moved one position to the right and again, the final result is 3 which is set in the next position of the convolved image. The process continues until the kernel reaches the bottom right corner. At the last iteration (9), the result is 1.

Now, the convolved image (feature map) represents the features extracted by this particular kernel. Also, note that the feature map is a 3x3 matrix which is smaller than the original image. It is also possible

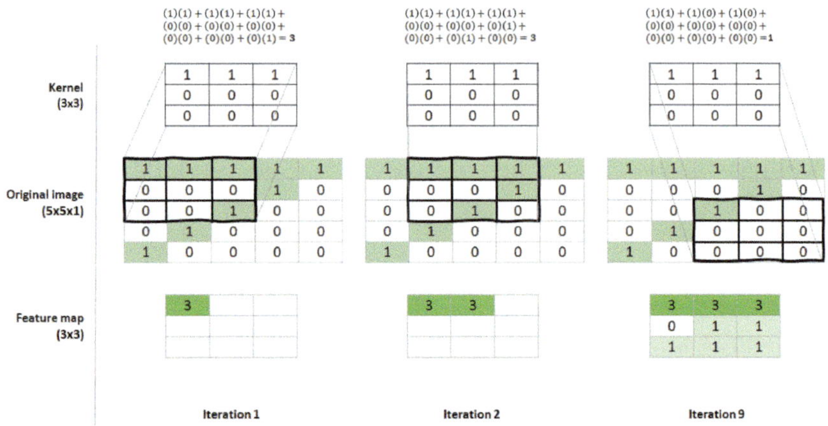

FIGURE 8.27 Convolution operation with a kernel of size 3x3 and stride=1. Iterations 1, 2, and 9.

to force the feature map to have the same size as the original image by padding it with zeros.

Before learning starts, the kernel values are initialized at random. In this example, the kernel has 1s in the first row and it has 3x3 = 9 parameters. This is what makes CNNs so efficient since the same kernel is applied to the entire image. This is known as 'parameter sharing'. Our kernel has 1s at the top and 0s elsewhere so it seems that this kernel learned to detect horizontal lines. If we look at the final convolved image, we see that the horizontal lines were emphasized by this kernel. This would be a good candidate kernel to differentiate between 7s and 0s, for example. Since 0s does not have long horizontal lines. But maybe it will have difficulties discriminating between 7s and 5s since both have horizontal lines at the top.

In this example, only 1 kernel was used but in practice, you may want more kernels, each in charge of identifying the best features for the given problem. For example, another kernel could learn to identify diagonal lines which would be useful to differentiate between 7s and 5s. The number of kernels per convolution layer is a hyperparameter. In the previous example, we could have defined to have 4 kernels instead of one. In that case, the output of that layer would have been 4 feature maps of size 3x3 each (Figure 8.28).

What would be the output of a convolution layer with 4 kernels of size

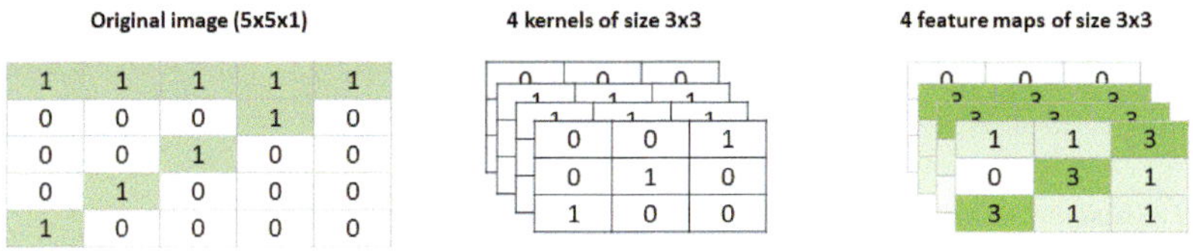

FIGURE 8.28 A convolution with 4 kernels. The output is 4 feature maps.

3x3 if it is applied to an RGB color image of size 5x5x3)? In that case, the output will be the same (4 feature maps of size 3x3) as if the image were in grayscale (5x5x1). Remember that the number of output feature maps is equal to the number of kernels regardless of the depth of the image. However, in this case, each kernel will have a depth of 3. Each depth is applied independently to the corresponding R, G, and B image channels. Thus, each kernel has 3x3x3 = 27 parameters that need to be learned. After applying each kernel to each image channel (in this example, 3 channels), **the results of each channel are added** and this is why we end up with one feature map per kernel. The following course website has a nice interactive animation of how convolutions are applied to an image with 3 channels: `https://cs231n.github.io/convolutional-networks/`. In the next section ('CNNs with Keras'), a couple of examples that demonstrate how to calculate the number of parameters and the outputs' shape will be presented as well.

8.6.2 Pooling Operations

Pooling operations are typically applied after convolution layers. Their purpose is to reduce the size of the data and to emphasize important regions. These operations perform a fixed computation on the image and do no have learnable parameters. Similar to kernels, we need to define a window size. Then, this window is moved throughout the image and a computation is performed on the pixels covered by the window. The difference with kernels is that this window is just a guide but does not have parameters to be learned. The most common pooling operation is **max pooling** which consists of selecting the highest value. Figure 8.29 shows an example of a max pooling operation on a 4x4 image. The window size is 2x2 and the stride is 2. The latter means that the window moves 2 places at a time.

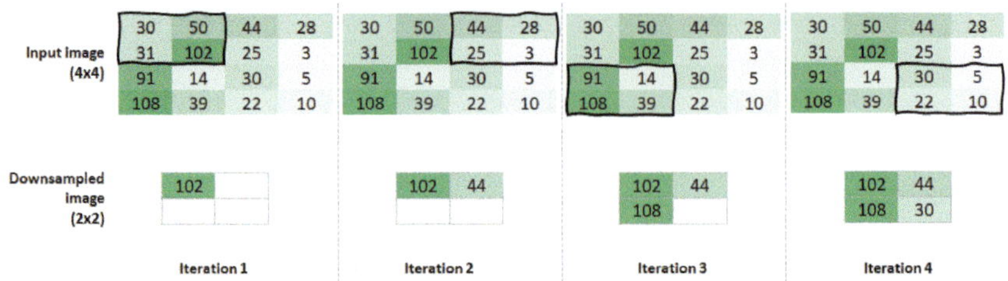

FIGURE 8.29 Max pooling with a window of size 2x2 and stride = 2.

The result of this operation is an image of size 2x2 which is half of the original one. Aside from max pooling, average pooling can be applied instead. In that case, it computes the mean value across all values covered by the window.

8.7 CNNs with Keras

keras_cnns.R

Keras provides several functions to define convolution layers and pooling operations. In TensorFlow, image dimensions are specified with the following order: height, width, and depth. In Keras, the `layer_conv_2d()` function is used to add a convolution layer to a sequential model. This function has several arguments but the 6 most common ones are: `filters`,`kernel_size`,`strides`,`padding`,`activation`, and `input_shape`.

```
# Convolution layer.
layer_conv_2d(filters = 4, # Number of kernels.
              kernel_size = c(3,3), # Kernel size.
              strides = c(1,1), # Stride.
              padding = "same", # Type of padding.
              activation = 'relu', # Activation function.
              input_shape = c(5,5,1)) # Input image dimensions.
                                      # Only specified in first layer.
```

The `filters` parameter specifies the number of kernels. The `kernel_size` specifies the kernel size (height, width). The `strides` is an integer or list of 2 integers, specifying the strides of the convolution along the width and height (the default is 1). The `padding` can take two possible strings: `"same"` or `"valid"`. If `padding="same"` the input image will be padded with zeros based on the kernel size and strides such that the convolved image has the same size as the original one. If `padding="valid"` it means no padding is applied. The default is `"valid"`. The `activation` parameter takes as input a string with the name of the activation function to use. The `input_shape` parameter is required when this layer is the first one and specifies the dimensions of the input image.

To add a max pooling operation you can use the `layer_max_pooling_2d()` function. Its most important parameter is `pool_size`.

```
layer_max_pooling_2d(pool_size = c(2, 2))
```

The `pool_size` specifies the window size (height, width). By default, the strides will be equal to `pool_size` but if desired, this can be changed with the `strides` parameter. This function also accepts a `padding` parameter similar to the one for `layer_max_pooling_2d()`.

In Keras, if the stride is not specified, it defaults to the window size (`pool_size` parameter).

To illustrate this convolution and pooling operations I will use two simple examples. The complete code for the two examples can be found in the script `keras_cnns.R`.

8.7.1 Example 1

Let's create our first CNN in Keras. For now, this CNN will not be trained but only its architecture will be defined. The objective is to understand the building blocks of the network. In the next section, we will build and train a CNN that detects smiles from image faces.

Our network will consist of 1 **convolution layer**, 1 **max pooling layer**,

1 **fully connected hidden layer**, and 1 **output layer** as if this were a classification problem. The code to build such a network is shown below and the output of the `summary()` function in Figure 8.30.

```
library(keras)

model <- keras_model_sequential()

model %>%
  layer_conv_2d(filters = 4,
                kernel_size = c(3,3),
                padding = "valid",
                activation = 'relu',
                input_shape = c(10,10,1)) %>%
  layer_max_pooling_2d(pool_size = c(2, 2)) %>%
  layer_flatten() %>%
  layer_dense(units = 32, activation = 'relu') %>%
  layer_dense(units = 2, activation = 'softmax')

summary(model)
```

```
> summary(model)
________________________________________________________________________________
Layer (type)                      Output Shape                          Param #
================================================================================
conv2d_9 (Conv2D)                 (None, 8, 8, 4)                       40
________________________________________________________________________________
max_pooling2d_8 (MaxPooling2D)    (None, 4, 4, 4)                       0
________________________________________________________________________________
flatten_7 (Flatten)               (None, 64)                            0
________________________________________________________________________________
dense_14 (Dense)                  (None, 32)                            2080
________________________________________________________________________________
dense_15 (Dense)                  (None, 2)                             66
================================================================================
Total params: 2,186
Trainable params: 2,186
Non-trainable params: 0
________________________________________________________________________________
```

FIGURE 8.30 Output of summary().

The first convolution layer has 4 kernels of size 3x3 and a ReLU as the activation function. The padding is set to `"valid"` so no padding will be performed. The input image is of size 10x10x1 (height, width, depth). Then, we apply max pooling with a window size of 2x2. Later, the output is flattened and fed into a fully connected layer with 32 units. Finally, the output layer has 2 units with a softmax activation function for classification.

From the summary, the output of the first Conv2D layer is (None, 8, 8, 4). The 'None' means that the number of input images is not fixed and depends on the batch size. The next two numbers correspond to the height and width which are both 8. This is because the image was not padded and after applying the convolution operation on the original 10x10 height and width image, its dimensions are reduced to 8. The last number (4) is the number of feature maps which is equal to the number of kernels (`filters=4`). The number of parameters is 40 (last column). This is because there are 4 kernels with 3x3 $= 9$ parameters each, and there is one bias per kernel included by default: $4 \times 3 \times 3 \times +4 = 40$.

The output of MaxPooling2D is (None, 4, 4, 4). The height and width are 4 because the pool size was 2 and the stride was 2. This had the effect of reducing to half the height and width of the output of the previous layer. Max pooling preserves the number of feature maps, thus, the last number is 4 (the number of feature maps from the previous layer). Max pooling does not have any learnable parameters since it applies a fixed operation every time.

Before passing the downsampled feature maps to the next fully connected layer they need to be **flattened** into a 1-dimensional array. This is done with the `layer_flatten()` function. Its output has a shape of (None, 64) which corresponds to the $4 \times 4 \times 4 = 64$ features of the previous layer. The next fully connected layer has 32 units each with a connection with every one of the 64 input features. Each unit has a bias. Thus the number of parameters is $64 \times 32 + 32 = 2080$.

Finally the output layer has $32 \times 2 + 2 = 66$ parameters. And the entire network has $2,186$ parameters! Now, you can try to modify, the kernel size, the strides, the padding, and input shape and see how the output dimensions and the number of parameters vary.

8.7.2 Example 2

Now let's try another example, but this time the input image will have a depth of 3 simulating an RGB image.

```
model2 <- keras_model_sequential()

model2 %>%
  layer_conv_2d(filters = 16,
                kernel_size = c(3,3),
                padding = "same",
                activation = 'relu',
                input_shape = c(28,28,3)) %>%
  layer_max_pooling_2d(pool_size = c(2, 2)) %>%
  layer_flatten() %>%
  layer_dense(units = 64, activation = 'relu') %>%
  layer_dense(units = 5, activation = 'softmax')

summary(model2)
```

```
> summary(model2)
________________________________________________________________________________
Layer (type)                       Output Shape                       Param #
================================================================================
conv2d_3 (Conv2D)                  (None, 28, 28, 16)                 448
________________________________________________________________________________
max_pooling2d_3 (MaxPooling2D)     (None, 14, 14, 16)                 0
________________________________________________________________________________
flatten_2 (Flatten)                (None, 3136)                       0
________________________________________________________________________________
dense_4 (Dense)                    (None, 64)                         200768
________________________________________________________________________________
dense_5 (Dense)                    (None, 5)                          325
================================================================================
Total params: 201,541
Trainable params: 201,541
Non-trainable params: 0
________________________________________________________________________________
```

FIGURE 8.31 Output of summary().

Figure 8.31 shows that the output height and width of the first Conv2D layer is 28 which is the same as the input image size. This is because this time we set `padding = "same"` and the image dimensions were preserved. The 16 corresponds to the number of feature maps which was set with `filters = 16`.

The total parameter count for this layer is 448. Each kernel has $3 \times 3 = 9$ parameters. There are 16 kernels but each kernel has a $depth = 3$ because the input image is RGB. $9 \times 16[kernels] \times 3[depth] + 16[biases] = 448$. Notice that even though each kernel has a depth of 3 the output number of feature maps of this layer is 16 and not $16 \times 3 = 48$. This is because as mentioned before, each kernel produces a single feature map regardless of the depth because the values are summed depth-wise. The rest of the layers are similar to the previous example.

8.8 Smiles Detection with a CNN

keras_smile_detection.R

In this section, we will build a CNN that detects smiling and non-smiling faces from pictures from the *SMILES* dataset. This information could be used, for example, to analyze smiling patterns during job interviews, exams, etc. For this task, we will use a cropped [Sanderson and Lovell, 2009] version of the Labeled Faces in the Wild (LFW) database [Huang et al., 2008]. A subset of the database was labeled by Arigbabu et al. [2016], Arigbabu [2017]. The labels are provided as two text files, each, containing the list of files that correspond to smiling and non-smiling faces. The dataset can be downloaded from: `http://conradsanderson.id.au/lfwcrop/` and the labels list from: `https://data.mendeley.com/datasets/yz4v8tb3tp/5`. See Appendix B for instructions on how to setup the dataset.

The smiling set has 600 pictures and the non-smiling has 603 pictures. Figure 8.32 shows an example of one image from each of the sets.

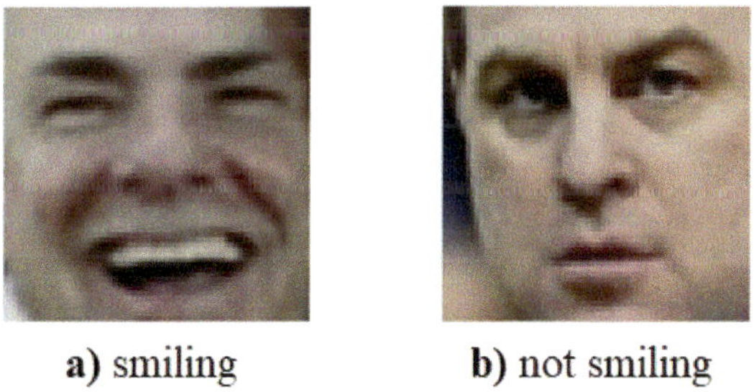

FIGURE 8.32 Example of a smiling and a non-smiling face. (Adapted from the LFWcrop Face Dataset: C. Sanderson, B.C. Lovell. "Multi-Region Probabilistic Histograms for Robust and Scalable Identity Inference." *Lecture Notes in Computer Science (LNCS)*, Vol. 5558, pp. 199-208, 2009. doi: `https://doi.org/10.1007/978-3-642-01793-3_21`).

The script `keras_smile_detection.R` has the full code of the analysis. First, we load the list of smiling pictures.

```
datapath <- file.path(datasets_path,"smiles")
smile.list <- read.table(paste0(datapath,"SMILE_list.txt"))
head(smile.list)
#> V1
#> 1      James_Jones_0001.jpg
#> 2      James_Kelly_0009.jpg
#> 3 James_McPherson_0001.jpg
#> 4       James_Watt_0001.jpg
#> 5      Jamie_Carey_0001.jpg
#> 6       Jamie_King_0001.jpg

# Substitute jpg with ppm.
smile.list <- gsub("jpg", "ppm", smile.list$V1)
```

The SMILE_list.txt points to the names of the pictures in *jpg* format, but they are actually stored as *ppm* files. Thus, the *jpg* extension is replaced by *ppm* with the `gsub()` function. Since the images are in *ppm* format, we can use the `pixmap` library [Bivand et al., 2011] to read and plot them. The `print()` function can be used to display the image properties. Here, we see that these are RGB images of 64x64 pixels.

```
library(pixmap)

# Read an smiling face.
img <- read.pnm(paste0(datapath,"faces/", smile.list[10]), cellres = 1)

# Plot the image.
plot(img)

# Print its properties.
print(img)

#> Pixmap image
#> Type          : pixmapRGB
#> Size          : 64x64
#> Resolution    : 1x1
#> Bounding box  : 0 0 64 64
```

Then, we load the images into two arrays `smiling.images` and `nonsmiling.images` (code omitted here). If we print the array dimensions we see that there are 600 smiling images of size $64 \times 64 \times 3$.

```
# Print dimensions.
dim(smiling.images)
#> [1] 600  64  64   3
```

If we print the minimum and maximum values we see that they are 0 and 1 so there is no need for normalization.

```
max(smiling.images)
#> [1] 1
min(smiling.images)
#> [1] 0
```

The next step is to randomly split the dataset into train and test sets. We will use 85% for the train set and 15% for the test set. We set the `validation_split` parameter of the `fit()` function to choose a small percent (10%) of the train set as the validation set during training.

After creating the train and test sets, the train set images and labels are stored in `trainX` and `trainY`, respectively and the test set data is stored in `testX` and `testY`. The labels in `trainY` and `testY` were one-hot encoded. Now that the data is in place, let's build the CNN.

```
model <- keras_model_sequential()

model %>%
  layer_conv_2d(filters = 8,
                kernel_size = c(3,3),
                activation = 'relu',
                input_shape = c(64,64,3)) %>%
  layer_max_pooling_2d(pool_size = c(2, 2)) %>%
  layer_dropout(0.25) %>%
  layer_conv_2d(filters = 16,
                kernel_size = c(3,3),
                activation = 'relu') %>%
```

```
  layer_max_pooling_2d(pool_size = c(2, 2)) %>%
  layer_dropout(0.25) %>%
  layer_flatten() %>%
  layer_dense(units = 32, activation = 'relu') %>%
  layer_dropout(0.5) %>%
  layer_dense(units = 2, activation = 'softmax')
```

Our CNN consists of two convolution layers each followed by a max pooling operation and dropout. The feature maps are then flattened and passed to a fully connected layer with 32 units followed by a dropout. Since this is a binary classification problem (*'smile'* vs. *'non-smile'*) the output layer has 2 units with a softmax activation function. Now the model can be compiled and the `fit()` function used to begin the training!

```
# Compile model.
model %>% compile(
  loss = 'categorical_crossentropy',
  optimizer = optimizer_sgd(lr = 0.01),
  metrics = c("accuracy")
)

# Fit model.
history <- model %>% fit(
  trainX, trainY,
  epochs = 50,
  batch_size = 8,
  validation_split = 0.10,
  verbose = 1,
  view_metrics = TRUE
)
```

We are using a stochastic gradient descent optimizer with a learning rate of 0.01 and cross-entropy as the loss function. We can use 10% of the train set as the validation set by setting `validation_split = 0.10`. Once the training is done, we can plot the *loss* and *accuracy* of each epoch.

```
plot(history)
```

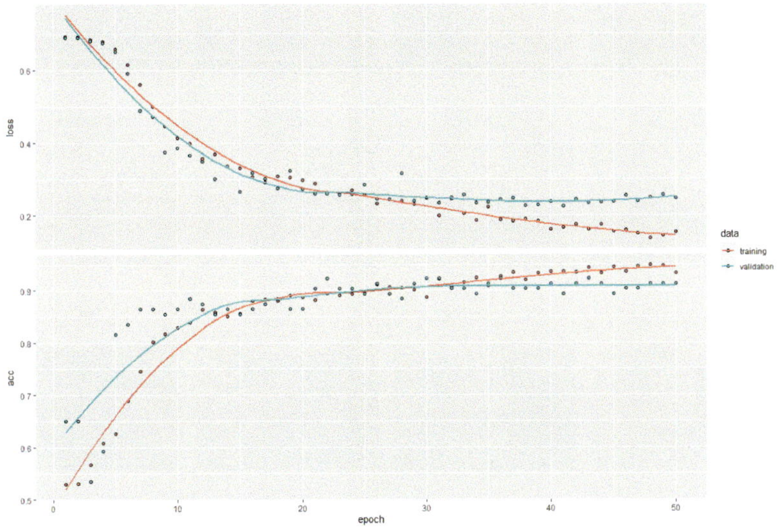

FIGURE 8.33 Train/test loss and accuracy.

After epoch 25 (see Figure 8.33) it looks like the training loss is decreasing faster than the validation loss. After epoch 40 it seems that the model starts to overfit (the validation loss is increasing a bit). If we look at the validation accuracy, it seems that it starts to get flat after epoch 30. Now we evaluate the model on the test set:

```
# Evaluate model on test set.
model %>% evaluate(testX, testY)
#> $loss
#> [1] 0.1862139

#> $acc
#> [1] 0.9222222
```

An accuracy of 92% is pretty decent if we take into account that we didn't have to do any image preprocessing or feature extraction! We can print the predictions of the first 16 test images (see Figure 8.34).

FIGURE 8.34 Predictions of the first 16 test set images. Correct predictions are in green and incorrect ones in red. (Adapted from the LFWcrop Face Dataset: C. Sanderson, B.C. Lovell. "Multi-Region Probabilistic Histograms for Robust and Scalable Identity Inference." *Lecture Notes in Computer Science (LNCS)*, Vol. 5558, pp. 199-208, 2009. doi: `https://doi.org/10.1007/978-3-642-01793-3_21`).

From those 16, all but one were correctly classified. The correct ones are shown in green and the incorrect one in red. Some faces seem to be smiling (last row, third image) but the mouth is closed, though. It seems that this CNN classifies images as *'smiling'* only when the mouth is open which may be the way the train labels were defined.

8.9 Summary

Deep learning (DL) consists of a set of different architectures and algorithms. As of now, it mainly focuses on artificial neural networks (ANNs). This chapter introduced two main types of DL models (ANNs and CNNs) and their application to behavior analysis.

- Artificial neural networks (ANNs) are mathematical models inspired by the brain. But that does not mean they work the same as the brain.
- The **perceptron** is one of the simplest ANNs.
- ANNs consist of an input layer, hidden layer(s) and an output layer.
- Deep networks have many hidden layers.
- **Gradient descent** can be used to learn the parameters of a network.
- Overfitting is a recurring problem in ANNs. Some methods like **dropout** and **early stopping** can be used to reduce the effect of overfitting.
- A Convolutional Neural Network (CNN) is a type of ANN that can process N-dimensional arrays very efficiently. They are used mainly for computer vision tasks.
- CNNs consist of **convolution** and **pooling** layers.

DON'T HURT ME PLEASE!
WHAT DO YOU THINK OF MY NEW SUIT? IT'S CONTROLLED WITH ELECTROMYOGRAPHY.
WOW!, CAN I TRY IT?
I DOUBT IT WILL WORK WITH YOUR BODY UNLESS YOU RETRAIN IT.
I'M EXHAUSTED. HAD TO COLLECT TONS OF TRAINING DATA TO MAKE IT WORK. DON'T TOUCH THE SUIT.
behavior.enriquegc.com
TO BE CONTINUED...

9

Multi-user Validation

Every person is different. We all have different physical and mental characteristics. Every person reacts differently to the same stimulus and conducts physical and motor activities in particular ways. As we have seen, predictive models rely on the training data; and for user-oriented applications, this data encodes their behaviors. When building predictive models, we want them to be general and to perform accurately on new unseen instances. Sometimes this generalization capability comes at a price, especially in **multi-user settings**. A multi-user setting is one in which the results depend heavily on the **target user**, that is, the user on which the predictions are made. Take, for example, a hand gesture recognition system. At inference time, a specific person (the target user) performs a gesture and the system should recognize it. The input data comes directly from the user. On the other hand, a **non multi-user** system does not depend on a particular person. A classifier that labels fruits on images or a regression model that predicts house prices does not depend directly on a particular person.

Some time ago I had to build an activity recognition system based on inertial data from a wrist band. So I collected the data, trained the models, and evaluated them. The performance results were good. However, it turned out that when the system was tested on a new sample group it failed. The reason? The training data was collected from people within a particular age group (young) but the target market of the product was for much older people. Older people tend to walk more slowly, thus, the system was predicting *'no movement'* when in fact, the person was walking at a very slow pace. This is an extreme example, but even within the same age groups, there can be differences between users (*inter-user variance*). Even the same user can evolve over time and change her/his behaviors (*intra-user variance*).

So, how do we evaluate multi-user systems to reduce the unexpected effects once the system is deployed? Most of the time, there's going to

DOI: 10.1201/9781003203469-9

be surprises when testing a system on new users. Nevertheless, in this chapter I will present three types of models that will help you reduce that uncertainty to some extent so you will have a better idea of how the system will behave when tested on more realistic conditions. The models are: **mixed models**, **user-independent models**, and **user-dependent models**. I will present how to train each type of model using a database with actions recorded with a motion capture system. After that, I will also show you how to build **adaptive models** with the objective of increasing the prediction performance for a particular user.

9.1 Mixed Models

Mixed models are trained and validated as ordinary, without considering information about mappings between data points and users. Suppose we have a dataset as shown in Figure 9.1. The first column is the user id, the second column the label we want to predict and the last two columns are two arbitrary features.

userid	label	v1	V2
U1	1	0.52	-1.02
U1	0	0.87	-0.21
U2	0	1.25	0.57
U2	0	-0.55	0.72
U3	1	0.44	1.4
U3	1	1.22	0.82
...	...	...	...

FIGURE 9.1 Example dataset with a binary label and 2 features.

With a mixed model, we would just remove the *userid* column and perform k-fold cross-validation or hold-out validation as usual. In fact, this is what we have been doing so far. By doing so, some random data points will end up in the train set and others in the test set regardless of which data point was generated by which user. The user rows are just *mixed*, thus the *mixed model* name. This model assumes that the data was generated by a single user. One disadvantage of validating a system using a mixed model is that the performance results could be overestimated. When randomly splitting into train and test sets, some data points for a given user could end up in each of the splits. At inference time, when presenting a test sample belonging to a particular user, it is likely that the training set of the model already included some data from that particular user. Thus, the model already knows a little bit about that user so we can expect an accurate prediction. However, this assumption not always holds true. If the model is to be used on a **new user** that the model has never seen before, then, it may not produce very accurate predictions.

When should a mixed model be used to validate a system?

1. When you know you will have available train data belonging to the intended target users.
2. In many cases, a dataset already has missing information about the mapping between rows and users. That is, a *userid* column is not present. In those cases, the best performance estimation would be through the use of a mixed model.

To demonstrate the differences between the three types of models (mixed, user-independent, and user-dependent) I will use the *SKELETON ACTIONS* dataset. First, a brief description of the dataset is presented including details about how the features were extracted. Then, the dataset is used to train a mixed model and in the following subsections, it is used to train user-independent and user-dependent models.

9.1.1 Skeleton Action Recognition with Mixed Models

`preprocess_skeleton_actions.R classify_skeleton_actions.R`

To demonstrate the three different types of models I chose the **UTD-MHAD dataset** [Chen et al., 2015] and from now on, I will refer to it as the *SKELETON ACTIONS* dataset. This database is suitable because it was collected by 8 persons (4 females/4 males) and each file has a subject id, thus, we know which actions were collected by which users. There are 27 actions including: *'right-hand wave'*, *'two hand front clap'*, *'basketball shoot'*, *'front boxing'*, etc.

The data was recorded using a Kinect camera and an inertial sensor unit. Each subject repeated each of the 27 actions 4 times. More information about the collection process and pictures is available in the original dataset website `https://personal.utdallas.edu/~kehtar/UTD-MHAD.html`.

For our examples, I only consider the *skeleton data* generated by the Kinect camera. These data consists of human body joints (20 joints). Each file contains one action for one user and one repetition. The file names are of the form: `aA_sS_tT_skeleton.mat`. The `A` is the action id, the `S` is the subject id and the `T` is the trial (repetition) number. For each time frame, the 3D positions of the 20 joints are recorded.

The script `preprocess_skeleton_actions.R` shows how to read the files and plot the actions. The files are stored in Matlab format. The library `R.matlab` [Bengtsson, 2018] can be used to read the files.

```
# Path to one of the files.
filepath <- "/skeleton_actions/a7_s1_t1_skeleton.mat"

# Read skeleton file.
df <- readMat(filepath)$d.skel

# Print dimensions.
dim(df)
#> [1] 20  3 66
```

From the file name, we see that this corresponds to action 7 (basketball shoot), from subject 1 and trial 1. The `readMat()` function reads the file contents and stores them as a 3D array in `df`. If we print the dimensions we see that the first one corresponds to the number of joints, the second one are the positions (x, y, z), and the last dimension is the number of frames, in this case 66 frames.

We extract the first time-frame as follows:

```
# Select the first frame.
frame <- data.frame(df[, , 1])

# Print dimensions.
dim(frame)
#> [1] 20  3
```

Each frame can then be plotted. The plotting code is included in the script. Figure 9.2 shows how the skeleton looks like for six of the time frames. The script also has code to animate the actions.

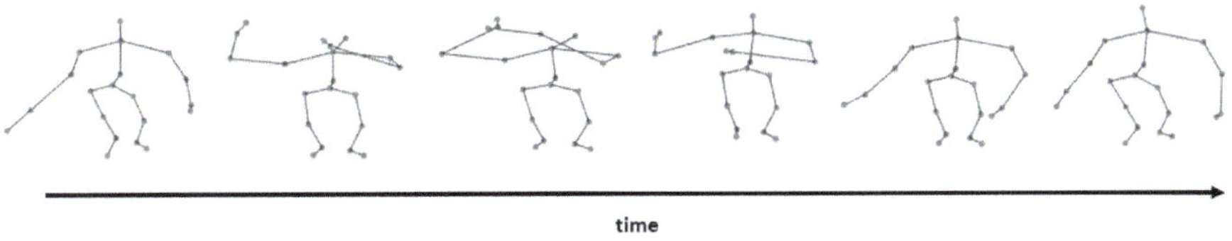

FIGURE 9.2 Skeleton of basketball shoot action. Six frames sampled from the entire sequence.

We will represent each action (file) as a feature vector. The same script also shows the code to extract the feature vectors from each action. To extract the features, a reference point in the skeleton is selected, in this case the spine (joint 3). Then, for each time frame, the distance between all joints (excluding the reference point) and the reference point is calculated. Finally, for each distance, the *mean*, *min*, and *max* are computed across all time frames. Since there are 19 joints (excluding the spine), we end up with $19 * 3 = 57$ features. Figure 9.3 shows how the final dataset looks like. It only shows the first four features out of the 57, the user id and the labels.

The following examples assume that the file *dataset.csv* with the extracted features already exsits in the `skeleton_actions/` directory. To generate this file, run the feature extraction code in the script `preprocess_skeleton_actions.R`.

Once the dataset is in a suitable format, we proceed to **train our mixed model**. The script containing the full code for training the different types of models is `classify_skeleton_actions.R`. This script makes use of the *dataset.csv* file.

First, the auxiliary functions are loaded because we will use the `normalize()` function to normalize the data. We will use a Random Forest for the classification and the `caret` package to compute the performance metrics.

userid	label	meanDist1	meanDist2	meanDist4	meanDist5
s1	a1	0.6097688	0.3756211	0.11980043	0.4278449
s1	a1	0.6020220	0.3818757	0.12027574	0.4331604
s1	a1	0.6004907	0.3734572	0.11724473	0.4357061
s1	a1	0.6019118	0.3750044	0.12217976	0.4263992
s2	a1	0.5907769	0.3891977	0.12354686	0.4096902
s2	a1	0.5754769	0.3830953	0.11769222	0.4044389
s2	a1	0.5700144	0.3820956	0.11841556	0.4044889
s2	a1	0.5668930	0.3813664	0.11645108	0.4046452
s3	a1	0.5387300	0.3529835	0.09848904	0.4042495
s3	a1	0.5362966	0.3523692	0.09610344	0.4118078
s3	a1	0.5321558	0.3512221	0.10050666	0.4041457
s3	a1	0.5329170	0.3534518	0.10855026	0.4025596
s4	a1	0.5383501	0.3564661	0.10706786	0.3988599
s4	a1	0.5402464	0.3554707	0.10908298	0.3969810
s4	a1	0.5394108	0.3533341	0.10190983	0.3996607

FIGURE 9.3 First rows of the skeleton dataset after feature extraction showing the first four features. Source: Original data from C. Chen, R. Jafari, and N. Kehtarnavaz, "UTD-MHAD: A Multimodal Dataset for Human Action Recognition Utilizing a Depth Camera and a Wearable Inertial Sensor", *Proceedings of IEEE International Conference on Image Processing*, Canada, September 2015.

```
source(file.path("..","auxiliary_functions","globals.R"))
source(file.path("..","auxiliary_functions","functions.R"))
library(randomForest)
library(caret)

# Path to the csv file containing the extracted features.
# preprocess_skeleton_actins.R contains
# the code used to extract the features.
filepath <- file.path(datasets_path,
                      "skeleton_actions",
                      "dataset.csv")
# Load dataset.
dataset <- read.csv(filepath, stringsAsFactors = T)

# Extract unique labels.
unique.actions <- as.character(unique(dataset$label))
```

```
# Print the unique labels.
print(unique.actions)
#>  [1] "a1"  "a10" "a11" "a12" "a13" "a14" "a15" "a16" "a17"
#> [10] "a18" "a19" "a2"  "a20" "a21" "a22" "a23" "a24" "a25"
#> [19] "a26" "a27" "a3"  "a4"  "a5"  "a6"  "a7"  "a8"  "a9"
```

The `unique.actions` variable stores the name of all actions. We will need it later to define the levels of the factor object. Next, we generate 10 folds and define some variables to store the performance metrics including the *accuracy*, *recall*, and *precision*. In each iteration during cross-validation, we will compute and store those performance metrics.

```
k <- 10 # Number of folds.
set.seed(1234)
folds <- sample(k, nrow(dataset), replace = TRUE)
accuracies <- NULL; recalls <- NULL; precisions <- NULL
```

In the next code snippet, the actual cross-validation is performed. This is just the usual cross-validation procedure. The `normalize()` function defined in the auxiliary functions is used to normalize the data by only learning the parameters from the train set and applying them to the test set. Then, the Random Forest is fitted with the train set. One thing to note here is that the `userid` field is removed: `trainset[,-1]` since we are not using users' information in the mixed model. Then, predictions on the test set are obtained and the accuracy, recall, and precision are computed during each iteration.

```
# Perform k-fold cross-validation.
for(i in 1:k){

  trainset <- dataset[which(folds != i,),]
  testset <- dataset[which(folds == i,),]

  #Normalize.
  res <- normalize(trainset, testset)
```

```
  trainset <- res$train
  testset <- res$test

  rf <- randomForest(label ~., trainset[,-1])
  preds.rf <- as.character(predict(rf,
                                    newdata = testset[,-1]))
  groundTruth <- as.character(testset$label)
  cm.rf <- confusionMatrix(factor(preds.rf,
                                  levels = unique.actions),
                           factor(groundTruth,
                                  levels = unique.actions))

  accuracies <- c(accuracies, cm.rf$overall["Accuracy"])
  metrics <- colMeans(cm.rf$byClass[,c("Recall",
                                       "Specificity",
                                       "Precision",
                                       "F1")],
                      na.rm = TRUE)
  recalls <- c(recalls, metrics["Recall"])
  precisions <- c(precisions, metrics["Precision"])
}
```

Finally, the average performance across folds for each of the metrics is printed.

```
# Print performance metrics.
mean(accuracies)
#> [1] 0.9277258
mean(recalls)
#> [1] 0.9372515
mean(precisions)
#> [1] 0.9208455
```

The results look promising with an average *accuracy* of 92.7%, a *recall* of 93.7%, and a *precision* of 92.0%. One important thing to remember is that the mixed model assumes that the training data contains instances belonging to users in the test set. Thus, the model already knows a little bit about the users in the test set.

Now, imagine that you want to estimate the performance of the model in a situation where a completely new user is shown to the model, that is, the model does not know anything about this user. We can model those situations using a **user-independent model** which is the topic of the next section.

9.2 User-independent Models

The **user-independent** model allows us to estimate the performance of a system on new users. That is, the model does not contain any information about the target user. This resembles a scenario when the user wants to use a service out-of-the-box without having to go through a calibration process or having to collect training data. To build a user-independent model we just need to make sure that the training data does not contain any information about the users on the test set. We can achieve this by splitting the dataset into two disjoint groups of users based on their ids. For example, assign 70% of the users to the train set and the remaining to the test set.

If the dataset is small, we can optimize its usage by performing **leave-one-user-out cross validation**. That is, if the dataset has n users, then, n iterations are performed. In each iteration, one user is selected as the test set and the remaining are used as the train set. Figure 9.4 illustrates an example of *leave-one-user-out cross validation* for the first 2 iterations.

By doing this, we guarantee that the model knows anything about the target user. To implement this leave-one-user-out validation method in our skeleton recognition case, let's first define some initialization variables. These include the `unique.users` variable which stores the ids of all users in the database. As before, we will compute the *accuracy*, *recall*, and *precision* so we define variables to store those metrics for each user.

```
# Get a list of unique users.
unique.users <- as.character(unique(dataset$userid))

# Print the unique user ids.
```

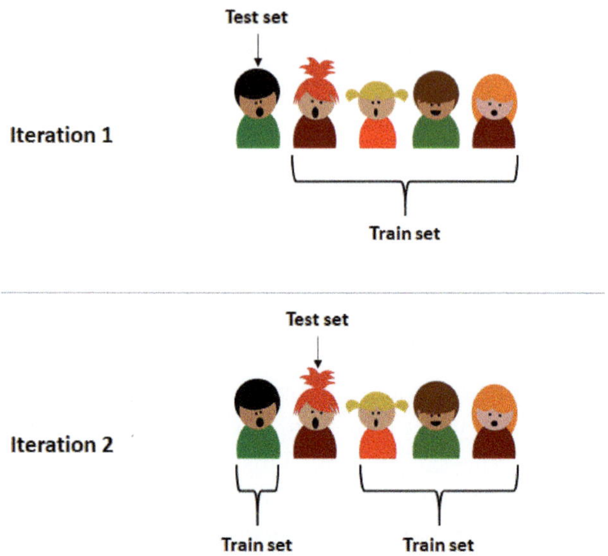

FIGURE 9.4 First 2 iterations of leave-one-user-out cross validation.

```
unique.users
#> [1] "s1" "s2" "s3" "s4" "s5" "s6" "s7" "s8"

accuracies <- NULL; recalls <- NULL; precisions <- NULL
```

Then, we iterate through each user, build the corresponding train and test sets, and train the classifiers. Here, we make sure that the test set only includes data points belonging to a single user.

```
set.seed(1234)

for(user in unique.users){

  testset <- dataset[which(dataset$userid == user),]
  trainset <- dataset[which(dataset$userid != user),]

  # Normalize. Not really needed here since Random Forest
  # is not affected by different scales.
```

```
  res <- normalize(trainset, testset)
  trainset <- res$train
  testset <- res$test

  rf <- randomForest(label ~., trainset[,-1])

  preds.rf <- as.character(predict(rf, newdata = testset[,-1]))

  groundTruth <- as.character(testset$label)

  cm.rf <- confusionMatrix(factor(preds.rf,
                                  levels = unique.actions),
                           factor(groundTruth,
                                  levels = unique.actions))

  accuracies <- c(accuracies, cm.rf$overall["Accuracy"])

  metrics <- colMeans(cm.rf$byClass[,c("Recall",
                                       "Specificity",
                                       "Precision",
                                       "F1")],
          na.rm = TRUE)

  recalls <- c(recalls, metrics["Recall"])

  precisions <- c(precisions, metrics["Precision"])
}
```

Now we print the average performance metrics across users.

```
mean(accuracies)
#> [1] 0.5807805
mean(recalls)
#> [1] 0.5798611
mean(precisions)
#> [1] 0.6539715
```

Those numbers are surprising! In the previous section, our **mixed model** had an accuracy of 92.7% and now the **user-independent model** has an accuracy of only 58.0%! This is because the latter didn't know anything about the target user. Since each person is different, the **user-independent model** was not able to capture the patterns of new users and this had a big impact on the performance.

When should a user-independent model be used to validate a system?

1. When you expect the system to be used out-of-the-box by new users and the system does not have any data from those new users.

The main advantage of the user-independent model is that it does not require training data from the *target users* so they can start using it right away at the expense of lower accuracy.

The opposite case is when a model is trained specifically for the *target user*. This model is called the **user-dependent model** and will be presented in the next section.

9.3 User-dependent Models

A **user-dependent model** is trained with data belonging only to the *target user*. In general, this type of model performs better compared to the *mixed model* and *user-independent model*. This is because the model captures the particularities of a specific user. The way to evaluate user-dependent models is to iterate through each user. For each user, build and test a model only with her/his data. The per-user evaluation can be done using k-fold cross-validation, for example. For the skeleton database, we only have 4 instances per type of action. The number of unique classes (27) is high compared to the number of instances per action. If we do, for example, 10-fold cross-validation, it is very likely that the train sets will not contain examples for several of the possible actions. To avoid this, we will do *leave-one-out cross validation* within each user. This means that we need to iterate through each instance. In each iteration, the selected instance is used as the test set and the remaining ones are used for the train set.

```
unique.users <- as.character(unique(dataset$userid))
accuracies <- NULL; recalls <- NULL; precisions <- NULL
set.seed(1234)

# Iterate through each user.
for(user in unique.users){
  print(paste0("Evaluating user ", user))
  user.data <- dataset[which(dataset$userid == user), -1]

  # Leave-one-out cross validation within each user.
  predictions.rf <- NULL; groundTruth <- NULL

  for(i in 1:nrow(user.data)){

    # Normalize. Not really needed here since Random Forest
    # is not affected by different scales.
    testset <- user.data[i,]
    trainset <- user.data[-i,]
    res <- normalize(trainset, testset)

    testset <- res$test
    trainset <- res$train
    rf <- randomForest(label ~., trainset)
    preds.rf <- as.character(predict(rf, newdata = testset))
    predictions.rf <- c(predictions.rf, preds.rf)
    groundTruth <- c(groundTruth, as.character(testset$label))
  }

  cm.rf <- confusionMatrix(factor(predictions.rf,
                                  levels = unique.actions),
                           factor(groundTruth,
                                  levels = unique.actions))

  accuracies <- c(accuracies, cm.rf$overall["Accuracy"])

  metrics <- colMeans(cm.rf$byClass[,c("Recall",
                                       "Specificity",
                                       "Precision",
```

```
                                           "F1")],
                          na.rm = TRUE)

  recalls <- c(recalls, metrics["Recall"])
  precisions <- c(precisions, metrics["Precision"])
} # end of users iteration.
```

We iterated through each user and performed the leave-one-out-validation for each, independently of the others and stored their results. We now compute the average performance across all users.

```
# Print average performance across users.

mean(accuracies)
#> [1] 0.943114
mean(recalls)
#> [1] 0.9425154
mean(precisions)
#> [1] 0.9500772
```

This time, the average accuracy was 94.3% which is higher than the accuracy achieved with the mixed model and the user-independent model. The average recall and precision were also higher compared to the other types of models. The reason is because each model was targeted to a particular user.

When should a user-dependent model be used to validate a system?

1. When the model will be trained only using data from the target user.

In general, user-dependent models have the best accuracy. The disadvantage is that they require training data from the target user and for some applications, collecting training data can be very difficult and expensive.

Can we have a system that has the best of both worlds between user-dependent and user-independent models? That is, a model that is as accurate as a user-dependent model but requires small quantities of training data from the target user. The answer is *yes*, and this is covered in the next section (*User-adaptive Models*).

9.4 User-adaptive Models

We have already talked about some of the limitations of **user-dependent** and **user-independent** models. On one hand, user-dependent models require training data from the target user. In many situations, collecting training data is difficult. On the other hand, user-independent models do not need data from the target user but are less accurate. To overcome those limitations, models that evolve over time as more information is available can be built. One can start with a user-independent model and as more data becomes available from the target user, the model is updated accordingly. In this case, there is no need for a user to wait before using the system and as new feedback is available, the model gets better and better by learning the specific patterns of the user.

In this section, I will explain how a technique called **transfer learning** can be used to build an **adaptive model** that updates itself as new training data is available. First, in the following subsection the idea of transfer learning is introduced and next, the method is used to build an adaptive model for activity recognition.

9.4.1 Transfer Learning

In machine learning, **transfer learning** refers to the idea of using the knowledge gained when solving a problem to solve a different one. The new problem can be similar but also very unrelated. For example, a model trained to detect smiles from images could also be used to predict gender (of course with some fine-tuning). In humans, learning is a lifelong process in which many tasks are interrelated. When faced with a new problem, we tend to find solutions that have worked in the past for similar problems. However, in machine learning most of the time models are trained from scratch for every new problem. For many tasks, training a model from scratch is very time consuming and requires a lot of effort, especially during the data collection and labeling phase.

The idea of transfer learning dates back to 1991 [Pratt et al., 1991] but with the advent of *deep learning* and in particular, with Convolutional Neural Networks (see chapter 8), it has gained popularity because it has proven to be a valuable tool when solving challenging problems. In 2014 a CNN architecture called VGG16 was proposed by Simonyan and Zisserman [2014] and won the ILSVR image recognition competition. This CNN was trained with more than 1 million images to recognize 1000 categories. It consists of several convolution layers, max pooling operations, and fully connected layers. In total, the network has ≈ 138 million parameters and it took some weeks to train.

What if you wanted to add a new category to the 1000 labels? Or maybe, you only want to focus on a subset of the categories? With transfer learning you can take advantage of a network that has already been trained and adapt it to your particular problem. In the case of *deep learning*, the approach consists of 'freezing' the first layers of a network and only retraining (updating) the last layers for the particular problem. During training, the frozen layers' parameters will not change and the unfrozen ones are updated as usual during the gradient descent procedure. As discussed in chapter 8, the first layers can act as feature extractors and be reused. With this approach, you can easily retrain a VGG16 network in an average computer and within a reasonable time. In fact, Keras already provides interfaces to common pre-trained models that you can reuse.

In the following section we will use this idea to build a **user-adaptive model** for activity recognition using transfer learning.

9.4.2 A User-adaptive Model for Activity Recognition

```
keras/adaptive_cnn.R
```

For this example, we will use the *SMARTPHONE ACTIVITIES* dataset **encoded as images** . In chapter 7 (section: Images) I showed how timeseries data can be represented as an image. That section presented an example of how accelerometer data can be represented as an RBG color image where each channel corresponds to one of the acceleration axes (x, y, z). We will use the file `images.txt` that already contains the activities in image format. The procedure of converting the raw data into this format was explained in chapter 7 and the corresponding code is in the script `timeseries_to_images.R`. Since the input data are images, we will use a Convolutional Neural Network (see chapter 8).

The main objective will be to build an adaptive model with a small amount of training data from the target user. We will first build a **user-independent model**. That is, we will select one of the users as the *target user*. We train the user-independent model with data from the remaining users (excluding the target user). Then, we will apply transfer learning to adapt the model to the target user.

The target user's data will be split into a test set and an **adaptive set**. The test set will be used to evaluate the performance of the model and the adaptive set will be used to fine-tune the model. The adaptive set is used to simulate that we have obtained new data from the target user.

The complete code is in the script `keras/adaptive_cnn.R`. First, we start by reading the images file. Each row corresponds to one activity. The last two columns are the `userid` and the `class`. The first 300 columns correspond to the image pixels. Each image has a size of $10 \times 10 \times 3$ (height, width, depth).

```
# Path to smartphone activities in image format.
filepath <- file.path(datasets_path,
                      "smartphone_activities",
                      "images.txt")

# Read data.
df <- read.csv(filepath, stringsAsFactors = F)

# Shuffle rows.
set.seed(1234)
df <- df[sample(nrow(df)),]
```

The rows happen to be ordered by user and activity, so we shuffle them to ensure that the model is not biased toward the last users and activities.

Since we will train a CNN using Keras, we need the classes to be in integer format. The following code is used to append a new column `intlabel` to the database. This new column contains the classes as integers. We also create a variable `mapping` to keep track of the mapping between integers and the actual labels. By printing the `mapping` variable we see that for example, the *'Walking'* label has a corresponding integer value of 0, *'Downstairs'* 1, and so on.

```
## Convert labels to integers starting at 0. ##

# Get the unique labels.
labels <- unique(df$label)

mapping <- 0:(length(labels) - 1)

names(mapping) <- labels

print(mapping)
#>     Walking Downstairs    Jogging   Standing   Upstairs    Sitting
#>           0          1          2          3          4          5

# Append labels as integers at the end of data frame.
df$intlabel <- mapping[df$label]
```

Now we store the unique users' ids in the `users` variable. After printing the variable's values, notice that there are 19 distinct users in this database. The original database has more users but we only kept those that performed all the activities. Then, we select one of the users to act as the *target user*. I will just select one of them at random (turned out to be user 24). Feel free to select another user if you want.

```
# Get the unique user ids.
users <- unique(df$userid)

# Print all user ids.
print(users)
#> [1] 29 20 18  8 32 27  3 36 34  5  7 12  6 21 24 31 13 33 19

# Choose one user at random to be the target user.
targetUser <- sample(users, 1)
```

Next, we split the data into two sets. The first set `trainset` contains the data from all users but **excluding the target user**. We create two variables: `train.y` and `train.x`. The first one has the labels as integers and the second one has the actual image pixels (features). The second set `target.data` contains data only from the target user.

```
# Split into train and target user sets.
# The train set includes data from all users excluding targetUser.
trainset <- df[df$userid != targetUser,]

# Save train labels in a separate variable.
train.y <- trainset$intlabel

# Save train pixels in a separate variable.
train.x <- as.matrix(trainset[,-c(301,302,303)])

# This contains all data from the target user.
target.data <- df[df$userid == targetUser,]
```

Then, we split the target's user data into 50% test data and 50% adaptive data (code omitted here) so that we end up with the following 4 variables:

1. `target.adaptive.y` Integer labels for the adaptive data of the target user.
2. `target.adaptive.x` Pixels of the adaptive data of the target user.
3. `target.test.y` Integer labels for the test data of the target user.
4. `target.test.x` Pixels of the test data of the target user.

We also need to normalize the data and reshape it into the actual image format since in their current form, the pixels are stored into 1-dimensional arrays. We learn the normalization parameters only from the train set and then, use the `normalize.reshape()` function (defined in the same script file) to perform the actual normalization and formatting.

```
# Learn min and max values from train set for normalization.
maxv <- max(train.x)
minv <- min(train.x)
```

```
# Normalize and reshape. May take some minutes.
train.x <- normalize.reshape(train.x, minv, maxv)
target.adaptive.x <- normalize.reshape(target.adaptive.x, minv, maxv)
target.test.x <- normalize.reshape(target.test.x, minv, maxv)
```

Let's inspect how the structure of the final datasets looks like.

```
dim(train.x)
#> [1] 6399   10   10    3
dim(target.adaptive.x)
#> [1] 124  10  10   3
dim(target.test.x)
#> [1] 124  10  10   3
```

Here, we see that the train set has 6399 instances (images). The adaptive and test sets both have 124 instances.

Now that we are done with the preprocessing, it is time to build the CNN model! This one will be the initial user-independent model and is trained with all the train data `train.x`, `train.y`.

```
model <- keras_model_sequential()

model %>%
  layer_conv_2d(name = "conv1",
                filters = 8,
                kernel_size = c(2,2),
                activation = 'relu',
                input_shape = c(10,10,3)) %>%
  layer_conv_2d(name = "conv2",
                filters = 16,
                kernel_size = c(2,2),
                activation = 'relu') %>%
  layer_max_pooling_2d(pool_size = c(2, 2)) %>%
  layer_flatten() %>%
  layer_dense(name = "hidden1", units = 32,
```

```
                activation = 'relu') %>%
  layer_dropout(0.25) %>%
  layer_dense(units = 6, activation = 'softmax')
```

This CNN has two convolutional layers followed by a max pooling operation, a fully connected layer, and an output layer. One important thing to note is that **we have specified a name for each layer** with the `name` parameter. For example, the first convolution's name is `conv1`, the second one is `conv2`, and the fully connected layer was named `hidden1`. Those names must be unique because they will be used to select specific layers to freeze and unfreeze.

If we print the model's summary (Figure 9.5) we see that in total it has 9,054 **trainable parameters** and 0 **non-trainable parameters**. This means that all the parameters of the network will be updated during the gradient descent procedure, as usual.

```
# Print summary.
summary(model)
```

```
Layer (type)                          Output Shape                    Param #
==============================================================================
conv1 (Conv2D)                        (None, 9, 9, 8)                 104
conv2 (Conv2D)                        (None, 8, 8, 16)                528
max_pooling2d (MaxPooling2D)          (None, 4, 4, 16)                0
flatten (Flatten)                     (None, 256)                     0
hidden1 (Dense)                       (None, 32)                      8224
dropout (Dropout)                     (None, 32)                      0
dense (Dense)                         (None, 6)                       198
==============================================================================
Total params: 9,054
Trainable params: 9,054
Non-trainable params: 0
```

FIGURE 9.5 Summary of initial user-independent model.

The next code will compile the model and initiate the training phase.

```
# Compile model.
model %>% compile(
  loss = 'sparse_categorical_crossentropy',
  optimizer = optimizer_sgd(lr = 0.01),
  metrics = c("accuracy")
)

# Fit the user-independent model.
history <- model %>% fit(
  train.x, train.y,
  epochs = 50,
  batch_size = 8,
  validation_split = 0.15,
  verbose = 1,
  view_metrics = TRUE
)

plot(history)
```

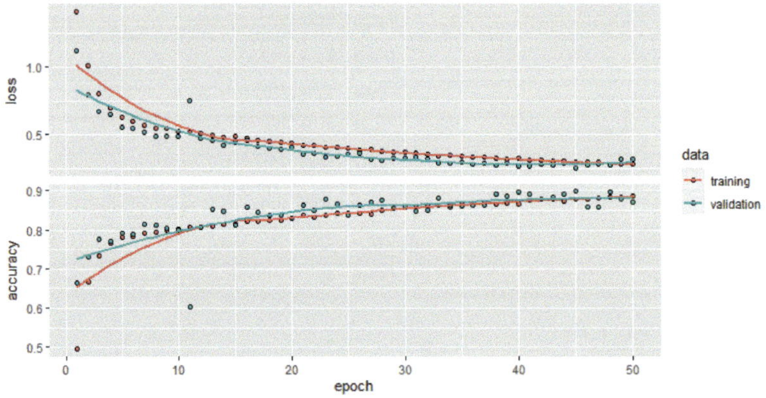

FIGURE 9.6 Loss and accuracy plot of the initial user-independent model.

Note that this time the loss was defined as `loss = 'sparse_categorical_crossentropy'` instead of the usual `loss =`

> 'categorical_crossentropy'. Here, the sparse_ suffix was added. You may have noted that in this example we did not one-hot encode the labels but they were only transformed into integers. By adding the sparse_ suffix we are telling Keras that our labels are not one-hot-encoded but encoded as integers starting at 0. It will then perform the one-hot encoding for us. This is a little trick that saved us some time.

Figure 9.6 shows a plot of the loss and accuracy during training. Then, we save the model so we can load it later. Let's also estimate the model's performance on the target user test set.

```
# Save model.
save_model_hdf5(model, "user-independent.hdf5")

# Compute performance (accuracy) on the target user test set.
model %>% evaluate(target.test.x, target.test.y)
#>      loss  accuracy
#> 1.4837638 0.6048387
```

The overall *accuracy* of this user-independent model when tested on the target user was 60.4% (quite low). Now, we can apply transfer learning and see if the model does better. We will 'freeze' the first convolution layer and only update the second convolution layer and the remaining fully connected layers using the target user-adaptive data. The following code loads the previously trained user-independent model. Then all the CNN's weights are frozen using the `freeze_weights()` function. The `from` parameter specifies the first layer (inclusive) from which the parameters are to be frozen. Here, it is set to 1 so all parameters in the network are 'frozen'. Then, we use the `unfreeze_weights()` function to specify from which layer (inclusive) the parameters should be unfrozen. In this case, we want to retrain from the second convolutional layer so we set it to `conv2` which is how we named this layer earlier.

```
adaptive.model <- load_model_hdf5("user-independent.hdf5")

# Freeze all layers.
freeze_weights(adaptive.model, from = 1)

# Unfreeze layers from conv2.
unfreeze_weights(adaptive.model, from = "conv2")
```

After those changes, we need to compile the model so the modifications take effect.

```
# Compile model. We need to compile after freezing/unfreezing weights.
adaptive.model %>% compile(
  loss = 'sparse_categorical_crossentropy',
  optimizer = optimizer_sgd(lr = 0.01),
  metrics = c("accuracy")
)

summary(adaptive.model)
```

```
________________________________________________________________________________
Layer (type)                        Output Shape                        Param #
================================================================================
conv1 (Conv2D)                      (None, 9, 9, 8)                     104
________________________________________________________________________________
conv2 (Conv2D)                      (None, 8, 8, 16)                    528
________________________________________________________________________________
max_pooling2d (MaxPooling2D)        (None, 4, 4, 16)                    0
________________________________________________________________________________
flatten (Flatten)                   (None, 256)                         0
________________________________________________________________________________
hidden1 (Dense)                     (None, 32)                          8224
________________________________________________________________________________
dropout (Dropout)                   (None, 32)                          0
________________________________________________________________________________
dense (Dense)                       (None, 6)                           198
================================================================================
Total params: 9,054
Trainable params: 8,950
Non-trainable params: 104
```

FIGURE 9.7 Summary of user-independent model after freezing first convolutional layer.

After printing the summary (Figure 9.7), note that the number of **trainable and non-trainable parameters** has changed. Now, the non-trainable parameters are 104 (before they were 0). These 104 parameters correspond to the first convolutional layer but this time they will not be updated during the gradient descent training phase.

The following code will retrain the model using the adaptive data but keeping the first convolutional layer fixed.

```
# Update model with adaptive data.
history <- adaptive.model %>% fit(
  target.adaptive.x, target.adaptive.y,
  epochs = 50,
  batch_size = 8,
  validation_split = 0,
  verbose = 1,
  view_metrics = TRUE
)
```

Note that this time the `validation_split` was set to 0. This is because the target user data set is very small so there is not enough data to use as validation set. One possible approach to overcome this is to leave a percentage of users out when building the train set for the user-independent model. Then, use those left-out users to find which are the most appropriate layers to keep frozen. Once you are happy with the results, evaluate the model on the target user.

```
# Compute performance (accuracy) on the target user test set.
adaptive.model %>% evaluate(target.test.x, target.test.y)
#>        loss  accuracy
#> 0.5173104 0.8548387
```

If we evaluate the adaptive model's performance on the target's user test set, the accuracy is 85.4% which is a considerable increase! ($\approx$ 25% increase).

At this point, you may be wondering whether this accuracy increase was due to the fact that the model was trained for an additional 50 epochs.

To validate this, we can re-train the initial user-independent model for 50 more epochs.

```
retrained_model <- load_model_hdf5("user-independent.hdf5")

# Fit the user-independent model for 50 more epochs.
history <- retrained_model %>% fit(
  train.x, train.y,
  epochs = 50,
  batch_size = 8,
  validation_split = 0.15,
  verbose = 1,
  view_metrics = TRUE
)

# Compute performance (accuracy) on the target user test set.
retrained_model %>% evaluate(target.test.x, target.test.y)
#>      loss  accuracy
#> 1.3033305 0.7096774
```

After re-training the user-independent model for 50 more epochs, its *accuracy* increased to 70.9%. On the other hand, the adaptive model was trained with fewer data and produced a much better result (85.4%) with only 124 instances as compared to the user-independent model ($\approx$ 5440 instances). That is, the 6399 instances minus 15% used as the validation set. These results highlight one of the main advantages of transfer learning which is a reduction in the needed amount of train data.

9.5 Summary

Many real-life scenarios involve multi-user settings. That is, the system heavily depends on the specific behavior of a given target user. This chapter covered different types of models that can be used to evaluate the performance of a system in such a scenario.

- A **multi-user setting** is one in which its results depend heavily on the target user.
- Inter/Intra -user variance are the differences between users and within the same users, respectively.
- **Mixed models** are trained without considering unique users (user ids) information.
- **User-independent models** are trained without including data from the *target user*.
- **User-dependent models** are trained only with data from the *target user*.
- **User-adaptive models** can be adapted to a particular *target user* as more data is available.
- **Transfer learning** is a method that can be used to adapt a model to a particular user without requiring big quantities of data.

behavior.enriquegc.com

10

Detecting Abnormal Behaviors

Abnormal data points are instances that are rare or do not occur very often. They are also called *outliers*. Some examples include illegal bank transactions, defective products, natural disasters, etc. Detecting abnormal behaviors is an important topic in the fields of health care, ecology, economy, psychology, and so on. For example, abnormal behaviors in wildlife creatures can be an indication of abrupt changes in the environment and rare behavioral patterns in a person may be an indication of health deterioration.

Anomaly detection can be formulated as a binary classification task and solved by training a classifier to distinguish between *normal* and *abnormal* instances. The problem with this approach is that anomalous points are rare and there may not be enough to train a classifier. This can also lead to class imbalance problems. Furthermore, the models should be able to detect abnormal points even if they are very different from the training data. To address those issues, several anomaly detection methods have been developed over the years and this chapter introduces two of them: Isolation Forests and autoencoders.

This chapter starts by explaining how Isolation Forests work and then, an example of how to apply them for abnormal trajectory detection is presented. Next, a method (ROC curve) to evaluate the performance of such models is described. Finally, another method called autoencoder that can be used for anomaly detection is explained and applied to the abnormal trajectory detection problem.

DOI: 10.1201/9781003203469-10

10.1 Isolation Forests

As its name implies, an *Isolation Forest* identifies anomalous points by explicitly 'isolating' them. In this context *isolation* means separating an instance from the others. This approach is different from many other anomaly detection algorithms where they first build a profile of normal instances and mark an instance as an anomaly if it does not conform to the normal profile. Isolation Forests were proposed by Liu et al. [2008] and the method is based on building many trees (similar to Random Forests, chapter 3). This method has several advantages including its efficiency in terms of time and memory usage. Another advantage is that at training time it does not need to have examples of the abnormal cases but if available, they can be incorporated as well. Since this method is based on trees, another nice thing about it is that there is no need to scale the features.

This method is based on the observation that anomalies are 'few and different' which makes them easier to isolate. It is based on building an ensemble of trees where each tree is called an Isolation Tree. Each Isolation Tree partitions the features until every instance is isolated (it's at a leaf node). Since anomalies are easier to isolate they will be closer to the root of the tree. An instance is marked as an anomaly if its average path length to the root across all Isolation Trees is short.

A tree is generated recursively by randomly selecting a feature and then selecting a random partition between the maximum and minimum value of that feature. Each partition corresponds to a split in a tree. The procedure terminates when all instances are isolated. The number of partitions that were required to isolate a point corresponds to the path length of that point to the root of the tree.

Figure 10.1 shows a set of points with only one feature (x axis). One of the anomalous points is highlighted as a red triangle. One of the normal points is marked as a blue solid circle.

To isolate the anomalous instance, we can randomly and recursively choose partition positions (vertical lines in Figure 10.1) until the instance is encapsulated in its own partition. In this example, it took 4 partitions (red lines) to isolate the anomalous instance, thus, the path length of this instance to the root of the tree is 4. The partitions were located at

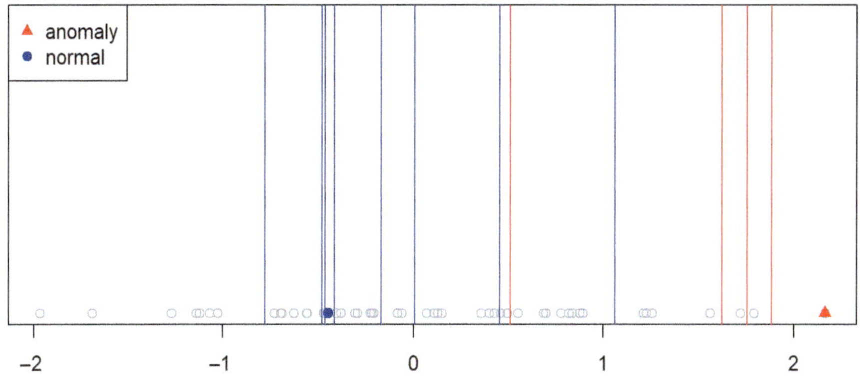

FIGURE 10.1 Example partitioning of a normal and an anomalous point.

0.51, 1.6, 1.7, and 1.8. The code to reproduce this example is in the script `example_isolate_point.R`. If we look at the highlighted normal instance we can see that it took 8 partitions to isolate it.

Instead of generating a single tree, we can generate an ensemble of n trees and average their path lengths. Figure 10.2 shows the average path length for the same previous normal and anomalous instances as the number of trees in the ensemble is increased.

After 200 trees, the average path length of the normal instance starts to converge to 8.7 and the path length of the anomalous one converges to 3.1. This shows that anomalies have shorter path lengths on average.

In practice, an Isolation Tree is recursively grown until a predefined maximum height is reached (more on this later), or when all instances are isolated, or all instances in a partition have the same values. Once all Isolation Trees in the ensemble (Isolation Forest) are generated, the instances can be sorted according to their average path length to the root. Then, instances with the shorter path lengths can be marked as anomalies.

Instead of directly using the average path lengths for deciding whether or not an instance is an anomaly, the authors of the method proposed an anomaly score that is between 0 and 1. The reason for this, is that this score is easier to interpret since it's normalized. The closer the anomaly score is to 1 the more likely the instance is an anomaly. Instances with

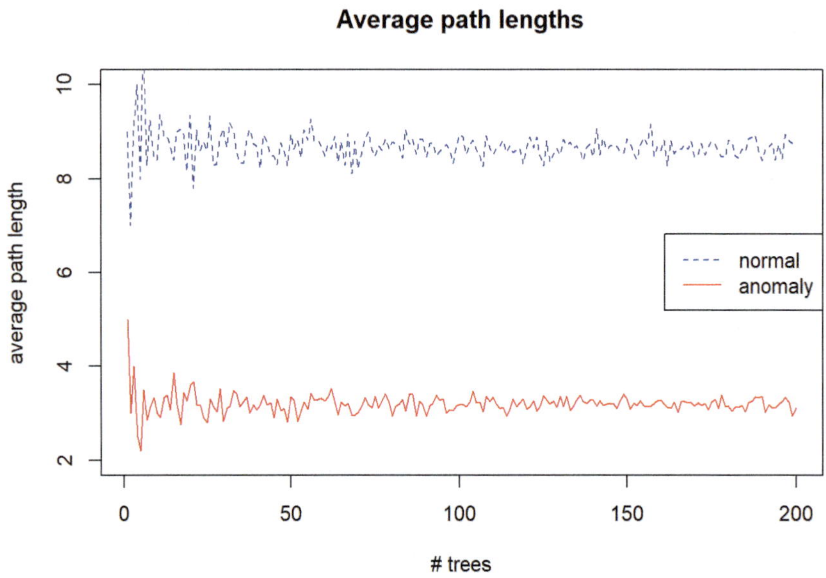

FIGURE 10.2 Average path lenghts for increasing number of trees.

anomaly scores << 0.5 can be marked as normal. The anomaly score for an instance x is computed with the formula:

$$s(x) = 2^{-\frac{E(h(x))}{c(n)}} \tag{10.1}$$

where $h(x)$ is the path length of x to the root of a given tree and $E(h(x))$ is the average of the path lengths of x across all trees in the ensemble. n is the number of instances in the train set. $c(n)$ is the average path length of an unsuccessful search in a binary search tree:

$$c(n) = 2H(n-1) - (2(n-1)/n) \tag{10.2}$$

where $H(x)$ denotes the harmonic number and is estimated by $ln(x) + 0.5772156649$ (Euler-Mascheroni constant).

A practical 'trick' that Isolation Forests use is *sub-sampling without replacement*. That is, instead of using the entire training set, an independent random sample of size p is used to build each tree. The sub-sampling reduces the *swamping* and *masking* effects. *Swamping* occurs when normal instances are too close to anomalies and thus, marked as anomalies.

Masking refers to the presence of too many anomalies close together. This increases the number of partitions needed to isolate each anomaly point.

Figure 10.3 (left) shows a set of 4000 normal and 100 anomalous instances clustered in the same region. The right plot shows how it looks like after sampling 256 instances from the total. Here, we can see that the anomalous points are more clearly separated from the normal ones.

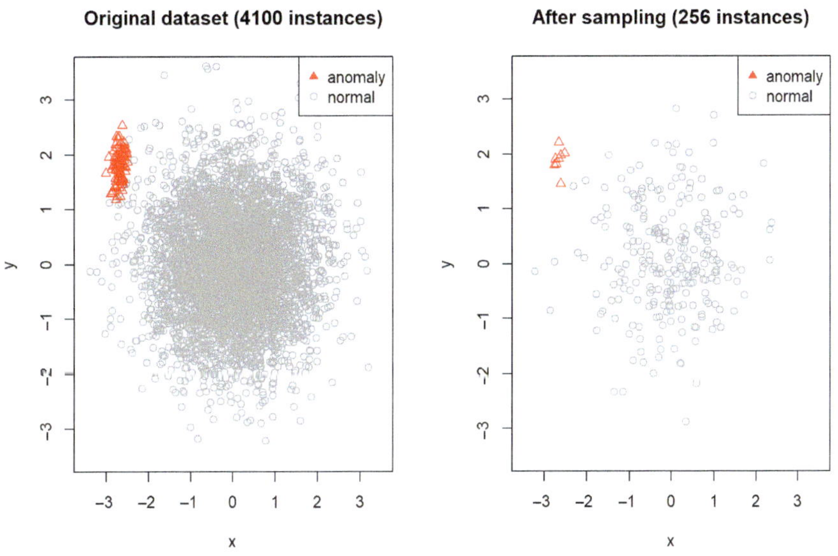

FIGURE 10.3 Dataset before and after sampling.

Previously, I mentioned that trees are grown until a predefined maximum height is reached. The authors of the method suggest to set this maximum height to $l = ceiling(log_2(p))$ which approximates the average tree height. Remember that p is the sampling size. Since anomalous instances are closer to the root, we can expect normal instances to be in the lower sections of the tree, thus, there is no need to grow the entire tree and we can limit its height.

The only two parameters of the algorithm are the number of trees and the sampling size p. The authors recommend a default sampling size of 256 and 100 trees.

At training time, the ensemble of trees is generated using the train data. It is not necessary that the train data contain examples of anomalous instances. This is advantageous because in many cases the anomalous instances are scarce so we can reserve them for testing. At test time, instances in the test set are passed through all trees and an anomaly score is computed for each. Instances with an anomaly score greater than some threshold are marked as anomalies. The optimal threshold can be estimated using an Area Under the Curve analysis which will be covered in the following sections.

The `solitude` R package [Srikanth, 2020] provides convenient functions to train Isolation Forests and make predictions. In the following section we will use it to detect abnormal fish behaviors.

10.2 Detecting Abnormal Fish Behaviors

```
visualize_fish.R extract_features.R isolation_forest_fish.R
```

In marine biology, the analysis of fish behavior is essential since it can be used to detect environmental changes produced by pollution, climate change, etc. Fish behaviors can be characterized by their trajectories, that is, how they move within the environment. A **trajectory** is the path that an object follows through space and time.

Capturing fish trajectories is a challenging task specially, in unconstrained underwater conditions. Thankfully, the Fish4Knowledge[1] project has developed fish analysis tools and methods to ease the task. They have processed enormous amounts of video streaming data and have extracted fish information including trajectories. They have made the fish trajectories dataset publicly available[2] [Beyan and Fisher, 2013].

The *FISH TRAJECTORIES* dataset contains 3102 trajectories belonging to the *Dascyllus reticulatus* fish (see Figure 10.4) observed in the Taiwanese coral reef. Each trajectory is labeled as *'normal'* or *'abnormal'*. The trajectories were extracted from underwater video and stored as coordinates over time.

[1] http://groups.inf.ed.ac.uk/f4k/

[2] http://groups.inf.ed.ac.uk/f4k/GROUNDTRUTH/BEHAVIOR/

FIGURE 10.4 Example of Dascyllus reticulatus fish. (Author: Rickard Zerpe. Source: wikimedia.org (CC BY 2.0) [https://creativecommons.org/licenses/by/2.0/legalcode]).

Our main task will be to detect the **abnormal** trajectories using an Isolation Forest but before that, we are going to explore, visualize, and pre-process the dataset.

10.2.1 Exploring and Visualizing Trajectories

The data is stored in a .mat file, so we are going to use the package R.matlab [Bengtsson, 2018] to import the data into an array. The following code can be found in the script visualize_fish.R.

```
library(R.matlab)

# Read data.
df <- readMat("../fishDetections_total3102.mat"))$fish.detections

# Print data frame dimensions.
dim(df)
#> [1]    7    1 3102
```

We use the dim() function to print the dimensions of the array. From the output, we can see that there are 3102 individual trajectories and each trajectory has 7 attributes. Let's explore what are the contents of a single trajectory. The following code snippet extracts the first trajectory and prints its structure.

```
# Read one of the trajectories.
trj <- df[,,1]

# Inspect its structure.
str(trj)
#> List of 7
#> $ frame.number    : num [1:37, 1] 826 827 828 829 833 834 835 836 ...
#> $ bounding.box.x  : num [1:37, 1] 167 165 162 159 125 124 126 126 ...
#> $ bounding.box.y  : num [1:37, 1] 67 65 65 66 58 61 65 71 71 62 ...
#> $ bounding.box.w  : num [1:37, 1] 40 37 39 34 39 39 38 38 37 31 ...
#> $ bounding.box.h  : num [1:37, 1] 38 40 40 38 35 34 34 33 34 35 ...
#> $ class           : num [1, 1] 1
#> $ classDescription: chr [1, 1] "normal"
```

A trajectory is composed of 7 pieces of information:

1. frame.number: Frame number in original video.
2. bounding.box.x: Bounding box leftmost edge.
3. bounding.box.y: Bounding box topmost edge.
4. bounding.box.w: Bounding box width.
5. bounding.box.h: Bounding box height.
6. class: 1=normal, 2=rare.
7. classDescription: 'normal' or abnormal'.

The bounding box represents the square region where the fish was detected in the video footage. Figure 10.5 shows an example of a fish and its bounding box (not from the original dataset but for illustration purpose only). Also note that the dataset does not contain the images but only the bounding boxes' coordinates.

Each trajectory has a different number of video frames. We can get the frame count by inspecting the length of one of the coordinates.

```
# Count how many frames this trajectory has.
length(trj$bounding.box.x)
#> [1] 37
```

FIGURE 10.5 Fish bounding box (in red). (Author: Nick Hobgood. Source: wikimedia.org (CC BY-SA 3.0) [`https://creativecommons.org/licenses/by-sa/3.0/legalcode`]).

The first trajectory has 37 frames but on average, they have 10 frames. For our analyses, we only include trajectories with a minimum of 10 frames since it may be difficult to extract patterns from shorter paths. Furthermore, we are not going to use the bounding boxes themselves but the center point of the box.

At this point, it would be a good idea to plot how the data looks like. To do so, I will use the `anipaths` package [Scharf, 2020] which has a function to animate trajectories! I will not cover the details here on how to use the package but the complete code is in the same script `visualize_fish.R`. The output result is in the form of an 'index.html' file that contains the interactive animation. For simplicity, I only selected 50 and 10 normal and abnormal trajectories (respectively) to be plotted. Figure 10.6 shows the resulting plot. The plot also includes some controls to play, pause, change the speed of the animation, etc.

The *'normal'* and *'abnormal'* labels were determined by visual inspection by experts. The abnormal cases include events such as predator avoidance and aggressive movements (due to another fish or because of being frightened).

10.2.2 Preprocessing and Feature Extraction

Now that we have explored and visualized the data, we can begin with the preprocessing and feature extraction. As previously mentioned, the database contains bounding boxes and we want to use the center of the boxes to define the trajectories. The following code snippet (from `extract_features.R`) shows how the center of a box can be computed.

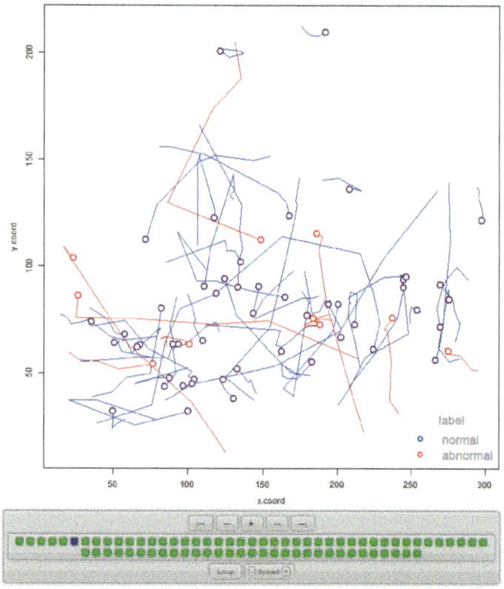

FIGURE 10.6 Example of animated trajectories generated with the anipaths package.

```
# Compute center of bounding box.
x.coord <- trj$bounding.box.x + (trj$bounding.box.w / 2)
y.coord <- trj$bounding.box.y + (trj$bounding.box.h / 2)

# Make times start at 0.
times <- trj$frame.number - trj$frame.number[1]
tmp <- data.frame(x.coord, y.coord, time=times)
```

The x and y coordinates of the center points from a given trajectory `trj` for all time frames will be stored in `x.coord` and `y.coord`. The next line 'shifts' the frame numbers so they all start in 0 (to simplify preprocessing). Finally we store the coordinates and frame times in a temporal data frame for further preprocessing.

At this point we will use the `trajr` package [McLean and Volponi, 2018] which includes functions to plot and perform operations on trajectories. The `TrajFromCoords()` function can be used to create a trajectory object from a data frame. Note that the data frame needs to have a predefined order. That is why we first stored the x coordinates, then the y coordinates, and finally the time in the `tmp` data frame.

```
tmp.trj <- TrajFromCoords(tmp, fps = 1)
```

The temporal data frame is passed as the first argument and the frames per second is set to 1. Now we plot the `tmp.trj` object.

```
plot(tmp.trj, lwd = 1, xlab="x", ylab="y")
points(tmp.trj, draw.start.pt = T, pch = 1, col = "blue", cex = 1.2)
legend("topright", c("Starting point"), pch = c(16), col=c("black"))
```

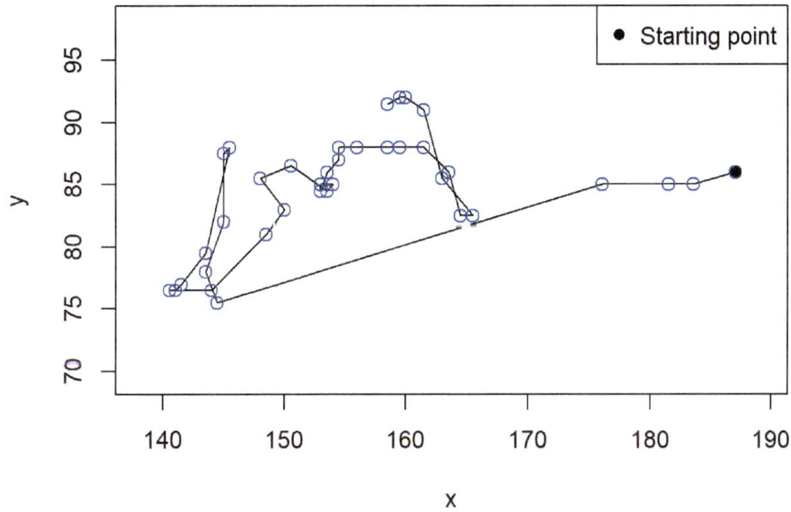

FIGURE 10.7 Plot of first trajectory.

From Figure 10.7 we can see that there are big time gaps between some points. This is because some time frames are missing. If we print the first rows of the trajectory and look at the time, we see that for example, time steps 4, 5, and 6 are missing.

```
head(tmp.trj)
#>          x      y time displacementTime        polar displacement
```

```
#> 1  187.0 86.0    0                  0 187.0+86.0i     0.0+0.0i
#> 2  183.5 85.0    1                  1 183.5+85.0i    -3.5-1.0i
#> 3  181.5 85.0    2                  2 181.5+85.0i    -2.0+0.0i
#> 4  176.0 85.0    3                  3 176.0+85.0i    -5.5+0.0i
#> 5  144.5 75.5    7                  7 144.5+75.5i   -31.5-9.5i
```

Before continuing, it would be a good idea to try to fill those gaps. The function `TrajResampleTime()` does exactly that by applying linear interpolation along the trajectory.

```
resampled <- TrajResampleTime(tmp.trj, 1)
```

If we plot the resampled trajectory (Figure 10.8) we will see how the missing points were filled.

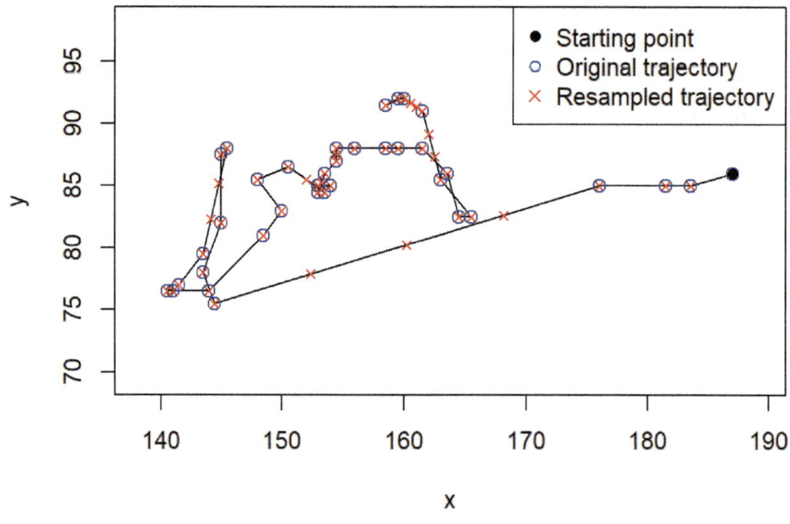

FIGURE 10.8 The original trajectory (circles) and after filling the gaps with linear interpolation (crosses).

Now we are almost ready to start detecting anomalies. Remember that Isolation Trees work with features by making partitions. Thus, we need to convert the trajectories into a feature vector representation. To do that, we will extract some features from the trajectories based on *speed* and *acceleration*. The `TrajDerivatives()` function computes the speed and linear acceleration between pairs of trajectory points.

```
derivs <- TrajDerivatives(resampled)

# Print first speeds.
head(derivs$speed)
#> [1] 3.640055 2.000000 5.500000 8.225342 8.225342 8.225342

# Print first linear accelerations.
head(derivs$acceleration)
#> [1] -1.640055  3.500000  2.725342  0.000000  0.000000  0.000000
```

The number of resulting speeds and accelerations are $n-1$ and $n-2$, respectively where n is the number of time steps in the trajectory. When training an Isolation Forest, all feature vectors need to be of the same length however, the trajectories in the database have different number of time steps. In order to have fixed-length feature vectors we will compute the *mean*, *standard deviation*, *min*, and *max* from both, the speeds and accelerations. Thus, we will end up having 8 features per trajectory. Finally we assemble the features into a data frame along with the trajectory id and the label (*'normal'* or *'abnormal'*).

```
f.meanSpeed <- mean(derivs$speed)
f.sdSpeed <- sd(derivs$speed)
f.minSpeed <- min(derivs$speed)
f.maxSpeed <- max(derivs$speed)

f.meanAcc <- mean(derivs$acceleration)
f.sdAcc <- sd(derivs$acceleration)
f.minAcc <- min(derivs$acceleration)
f.maxAcc <- max(derivs$acceleration)

features <- data.frame(id=paste0("id",i), label=trj$classDescription[1],
                       f.meanSpeed, f.sdSpeed, f.minSpeed, f.maxSpeed,
                       f.meanAcc, f.sdAcc, f.minAcc, f.maxAcc)
```

We do the feature extraction for each trajectory and save the results as a .csv file *fishFeatures.csv* which is already included in the dataset. Let's read and print the first rows of the dataset.

```
# Read dataset.
dataset <- read.csv("fishFeatures.csv", stringsAsFactors = T)

# Print first rows of the dataset.
head(dataset)
#>    id  label f.meanSpeed f.sdSpeed f.minSpeed f.maxSpeed    f.meanAcc
#> 1 id1 normal    2.623236  2.228456  0.5000000   8.225342 -0.05366002
#> 2 id2 normal    5.984859  3.820270  1.4142136  15.101738 -0.03870468
#> 3 id3 normal   16.608716 14.502042  0.7071068  46.424670 -1.00019597
#> 4 id5 normal    4.808608  4.137387  0.5000000  17.204651 -0.28181520
#> 5 id6 normal   17.785747  9.926729  3.3541020  44.240818 -0.53753380
#> 6 id7 normal    9.848422  6.026229  0.0000000  33.324165 -0.10555561
#> f.sdAcc    f.minAcc  f.maxAcc
#> 1  1.839475  -5.532760  3.500000
#> 2  2.660073  -7.273932  7.058594
#> 3 12.890386 -24.320298 30.714624
#> 4  5.228209 -12.204651 15.623512
#> 5 11.272472 -22.178067 21.768613
#> 6  6.692688 -31.262613 11.683561
```

Each row represents one trajectory. We can use the `table()` function to get the counts for *'normal'* and *'abnormal'* cases.

```
table(dataset$label)
#> abnormal   normal
#>       54     1093
```

After discarding trajectories with less than 10 points we ended up with 1093 *'normal'* instances and 54 *'abnormal'* instances.

10.2.3 Training the Model

To get a preliminary idea of how difficult it is to separate the two classes we can use a MDS plot (see chapter 4) to project the 8 features into a 2-dimensional plane.

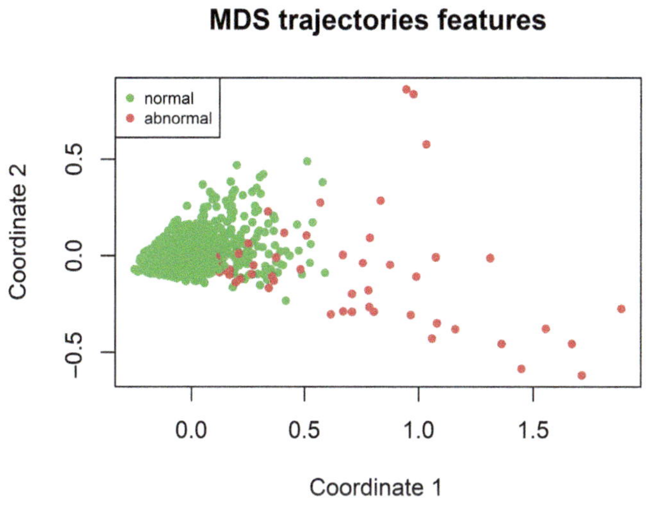

FIGURE 10.9 MDS of the fish trajectories.

In Figure 10.9 we see that several *abnormal* points are in the right hand side but many others are in the same space as the *normal* points so it's time to train an Isolation Forest and see to what extent it can detect the abnormal cases!

One of the nice things about Isolation Forest is that it does not need examples of the abnormal cases during training. If we want, we can also include the abnormal cases but since we don't have many we will reserve them for the test set. The script `isolation_forest_fish.R` contains the code to train the model. We will split the data into a train set (80%) consisting only of normal instances and a test set with both, normal and abnormal instances. The train set is stored in the data frame `train.normal` and the test set in `test.all`. Since the method is based on trees, we don't need to normalize the data.

First, we need to define the parameters of the Isolation Forest. We can do so by passing the values at creation time.

```
m.iforest <- isolationForest$new(sample_size = 256,
                                  num_trees = 100,
                                  nproc = 1)
```

As suggested in the original paper [Liu et al., 2008], the sampling size is set to 256 and the number of trees to 100. The `nproc` parameter specifies the number of CPU cores to use. I set it to 1 to ensure we get reproducible results.

Now we can train the model with the train set. The first two columns are removed since they correspond to the trajectories ids and class label.

```
# Fit the model.
m.iforest$fit(train.normal[,-c(1:2)])
```

Once the model is trained, we can start making predictions. Let's start by making predictions on the **train set** (later we'll do it on the test set). We know that the train set only consists of normal instances.

```
# Predict anomaly scores on train set.
train.scores <- m.iforest$predict(train.normal[,-c(1:2)])
```

The returned value of the `predict()` function is a data frame containing the average tree depth and the anomaly score for each instance.

```
# Print first rows of predictions.
head(train.scores)

#>     id average_depth anomaly_score
#> 1:   1          7.97     0.5831917
#> 2:   2          8.00     0.5820092
#> 3:   3          7.98     0.5827973
#> 4:   4          7.80     0.5899383
#> 5:   5          7.77     0.5911370
#> 6:   6          7.90     0.5859603
```

We know that the train set only has normal instances thus, we need to find the highest anomaly score so that we can set a threshold to detect the abnormal cases. The following code will print the highest anomaly scores.

```
# Sort and display instances with the highest anomaly scores.
head(train.scores[order(anomaly_score, decreasing = TRUE)])

#>       id average_depth anomaly_score
#> 1:   75          4.05     0.7603188
#> 2: 618          4.45     0.7400179
#> 3: 147          4.67     0.7290844
#> 4: 661          4.75     0.7251487
#> 5: 756          4.80     0.7226998
#> 6:   54          5.54     0.6874070
```

The highest anomaly score for a normal instance is 0.7603 so we would assume that abnormal points will have higher anomaly scores. Armed with this information, we set the threshold to 0.7603 and instances having a higher anomaly score will be considered to be abnormal.

```
threshold <- 0.7603
```

Now, we predict the anomaly scores on the **test set** and if the score is > *threshold* then we classify that point as abnormal. The `predicted.labels` array will contain 0*s* and 1*s*. A 1 means that the instance is abnormal.

```
# Predict anomaly scores on test set.
test.scores <- m.iforest$predict(test.all[,-c(1:2)])

# Predict labels based on threshold.
predicted.labels <- as.integer((test.scores$anomaly_score > threshold))
```

Now that we have the predicted labels we can compute some performance metrics.

```
# All abnormal cases are at the end so we can
# compute the ground truth as follows.
gt.all <- c(rep(0,nrow(test.normal)), rep(1, nrow(test.abnormal)))
levels <- c("0","1")

# Compute performance metrics.
cm <- confusionMatrix(factor(predicted.labels, levels = levels),
                      factor(gt.all, levels = levels),
                      positive = "1")

# Print confusion matrix.
cm$table

#>           Reference
#> Prediction   0   1
#>          0 218  37
#>          1   0  17

# Print sensitivity
cm$byClass["Sensitivity"]

#> Sensitivity
#>   0.3148148
```

From the confusion matrix we see that 17 out of 54 abnormal instances were detected. On the other hand, all the normal instances (218) were correctly identified as such. The sensitivity (also known as recall) of the abnormal class was $17/54 = 0.314$ which seems very low. We are failing to detect several of the abnormal cases.

One thing we can do is to decrease the threshold at the expense of increasing the false positives, that is, classifying normal instances as abnormal. If we set `threshold <- 0.6` we get the following confusion matrix.

```
#>           Reference
#> Prediction   0   1
#>          0 206   8
#>          1  12  46
```

This time we were able to identify 46 of the abnormal cases! This gives a sensitivity of $46/54 = 0.85$ which is much better than before. However, nothing is for free. If we look at the normal class, this time we had 12 misclassified points (false positives).

A good way of finding the best threshold is to set apart a validation set from which the optimal threshold can be estimated. However, this is not always feasible due to the limited amount of abnormal points.

In this example we manually tried different thresholds and evaluated their impact on the final results. In the following section I will show you a method that allows you to estimate the performance of a model when considering many possible thresholds at once!

10.2.4 ROC Curve and AUC

The **receiver operating characteristic curve**, also known as **ROC curve** is a plot that depicts how the sensitivity and the false positive rate (FPR) behave as the detection threshold varies. The sensitivity/recall can be calculated by dividing the true positives by the total number of positives TP/P (see chapter 2). The $FPR = FP/N$ where FP are the false positives and N are the total number of negative examples (the normal trajectories). The FPR is also known as the probability of false alarm. Ideally, we want a model that has a high sensitivity and a low FPR.

In R we can use the PRROC package [Grau et al., 2015] to plot ROC curves. The ROC curve of the Isolation Forest results for the abnormal fish trajectory detection can be plotted using the following code:

```
library(PRROC)
roc_obj <- roc.curve(scores.class0 = test.scores$anomaly_score,
                     weights.class0 = gt.all,
                     curve = TRUE,
                     rand.compute = TRUE)
```

```
# Set rand.plot = TRUE to also plot the random model's curve.
plot(roc_obj, rand.plot = TRUE)
```

The argument `scores.class0` specifies the returned scores by the Isolation Forest and `weights.class0` are the true labels, 1 for the positive class (abnormal), and 0 for the negative class (normal). We set `curve=TRUE` so the method returns a table with thresholds and their respective sensitivity and FPR. The `rand.compute=TRUE` instructs the function to also compute the curve of a random model, that is, one that predicts scores at random. Figure 10.10 shows the ROC plot.

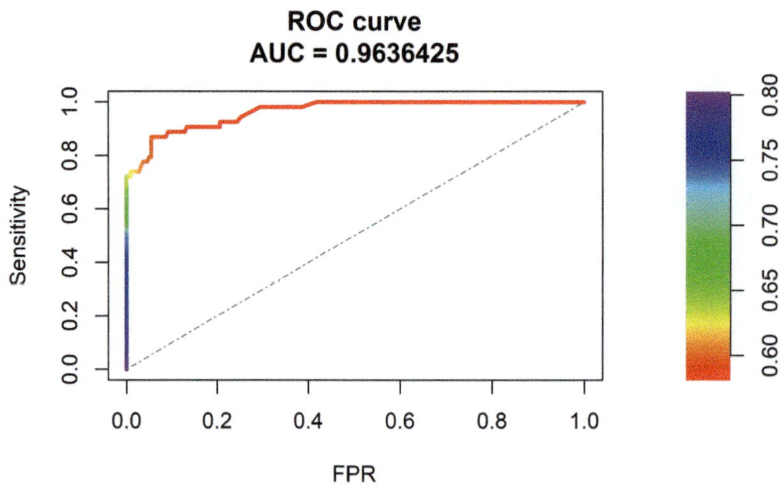

FIGURE 10.10 ROC curve and AUC. The dashed line represents a random model.

Here we can see how the sensitivity and FPR increase as the threshold decreases. In the best case we want a sensitivity of 1 and a FPR of 0. This ideal point is located at top left corner but this model does not reach that level of performance but a bit lower. The dashed line in the diagonal is the curve for a random model. We can also access the thresholds table:

```
# Print first values of the curve table.
roc_obj$curve
```

```
#>          [,1]         [,2]        [,3]
#> [1,]       0 0.00000000 0.8015213
#> [2,]       0 0.01851852 0.7977342
#> [3,]       0 0.03703704 0.7939650
#> [4,]       0 0.05555556 0.7875449
#> [5,]       0 0.09259259 0.7864799
#>   .....
```

The first column is the FPR, the second column is the sensitivity, and the last column is the threshold. Choosing the best threshold is not straightforward and will depend on the compromise we want to have between sensitivity and FPR.

Note that the plot also prints an $AUC = 0.963$. This is known as the **Area Under the Curve (AUC)** and as the name implies, it is the area under the ROC curve. A perfect model will have an AUC of 1.0. Our model achieved an AUC of 0.963 which is pretty good. A random model will have an AUC around 0.5. A value below 0.5 means that the model is performing worse than random. The AUC is a performance metric that measures the quality of a model regardless of the selected threshold and is typically presented in addition to accuracy, recall, precision, etc.

If someone tells you something negative about yourself (e.g., that you don't play football well), assume that they have an AUC below 0.5 (worse than random). At least, that's what I do to cope with those situations. (If you invert the predictions of a binary classifier that does worse than random you will get a classifier that is better than random).

10.3 Autoencoders

In its simplest form, an autoencoder is a neural network whose output layer has the same shape as the input layer. If you are not familiar with artificial neural networks, you can take a look at chapter 8. An autoencoder will try to learn how to generate an output that is as similar as possible to the provided input. Figure 10.11 shows an example of a simple autoencoder with 4 units in the input and output layers. The hidden layer has 2 units.

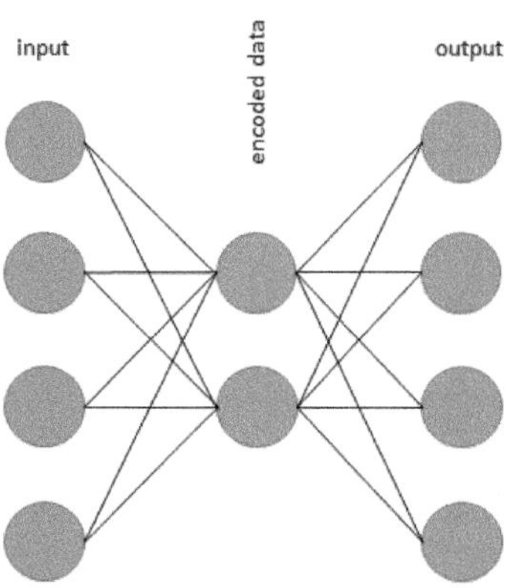

FIGURE 10.11 Example of a simple autoencoder.

Recall that when training a classification or regression model, we need to provide training examples of the form (x, y) where x represents the input features and y is the desired output (a label or a number). When training an autoencoder, the input and the output is the same, that is, (x, x).

Now you may be wondering what is the point of training a model that generates the same output as its input. If you take a closer look at Figure 10.11 you can see that the hidden layer has fewer units (only 2) than the input and output layers. When the data is passed from the input layer to the hidden layer it is 'reduced' (compressed). Then, the compressed data is reconstructed as it is passed to the subsequent layers until it reaches the output. Thus, the neural network will learn to compress and reconstruct the data at the same time. Once the network is trained, we can get rid of the layers after the middle hidden layer and use the 'left-hand-side' of the network to compress our data. This left-hand-side is called the **encoder**. Then, we can use the right-hand-side to decompress the data. This part is called the **decoder**. In this example, the encoder and decoder consist of only 1 layer but they can have more (as we will see in the next section). In practice, you will not use autoencoders to compress files in your computer because there are more efficient methods to do that. Furthermore, the compression is *lossy*, that is, there is no guarantee that the reconstructed file will be exactly the same as the original. However, autoencoders have many applications including:

- Dimensionality reduction for visualization.
- Data denoising.
- Data generation (variational autoencoders).
- Anomaly detection (this is what we are interested in!).

Recall that when training a neural network we need to define a loss function. The loss function captures how well the network is learning. It measures how different the predictions are from the true expected outputs. In the context of autoencoders, this difference is known as the **reconstruction error** and can be measured using the mean squared error (similar to regression).

In this section I introduced the most simple type of autoencoder but there are many variants such as denoising autoencoders, variational autoencoders (VAEs), and so on. The following Wikipedia page provides a good overview of the different types of autoencoders: `https://en.wikipedia.org/wiki/Autoencoder`

10.3.1 Autoencoders for Anomaly Detection

`keras_autoencoder_fish.R`

Autoencoders can be used as anomaly detectors. This idea will be demonstrated with an example to detect abnormal fish trajectories. The way this is done is by training an autoencoder to compress and reconstruct the **normal** instances. Once the autoencoder has learned to encode normal instances, we can expect the reconstruction error to be small. When presented with out-of-the-normal instances, the autoencoder will have a hard time trying to reconstruct them and consequently, the reconstruction error will be high. Similar to Isolation Forests where the tree path length provides a measure of the rarity of an instance, the reconstruction error in autoencoders can be used as an anomaly score.

To tell whether an instance is abnormal or not, we pass it through the autoencoder and compute its reconstruction error ϵ. If $\epsilon > threshold$ the input data can be regarded as abnormal.

Similar to what we did with the Isolation Forest, we will use the *fish-Features.csv* file that contains the fish trajectories encoded as feature vectors. Each trajectory is composed of 8 numeric features based on acceleration and speed. We will use 80% of the normal instances to train the autoencoder. All abnormal instances will be used for the test set.

After splitting the data (the code is in `keras_autoencoder_fish.R`), we will normalize (standardize) it. The `normalize.standard()` function will normalize the data such that it has a mean of 0 and a standard deviation of 1 using the following formula:

$$z_i = \frac{x_i - \mu}{\sigma} \tag{10.3}$$

where μ is the mean and σ is the standard deviation of x. This is slightly different from the 0–1 normalization we have used before. The reason is that when scaling to 0–1 the min and max values from the train set need to be learned. If there are data points in the test set that have values outside the min and max they will be truncated. But since we expect anomalies to have rare values, it is likely that they will be outside the train set ranges and will be truncated. After being truncated, abnormal instances could now look more similar to the normal ones thus, it will be more difficult to spot them. By standardizing the data we make sure that the extreme values of the abnormal points are preserved. In this case, the parameters to be learned from the train set are μ and σ.

Once the data is normalized we can define the autoencoder in keras as follows:

```
autoencoder <- keras_model_sequential()

autoencoder %>%
  layer_dense(units = 32, activation = 'relu',
              input_shape = ncol(train.normal)-2) %>%
  layer_dense(units = 16, activation = 'relu') %>%
  layer_dense(units = 8, activation = 'relu') %>%
  layer_dense(units = 16, activation = 'relu') %>%
```

```
  layer_dense(units = 32, activation = 'relu') %>%
  layer_dense(units = ncol(train.normal)-2, activation = 'linear')
```

This is a normal neural network with an input layer having the same number of units as number of features (8). This network has 5 hidden layers of size $32, 16, 8, 16$, and 32, respectively. The output layer has 8 units (the same as the input layer). All activation functions are RELU's except the last one which is linear because the network should be able to produce any number as output. Now we can compile and fit the model.

```
autoencoder %>% compile(
  loss = 'mse',
  optimizer = optimizer_sgd(lr = 0.01),
  metrics = c('mse')
)

history <- autoencoder %>% fit(
  as.matrix(train.normal[,-c(1:2)]),
  as.matrix(train.normal[,-c(1:2)]),
  epochs = 100,
  batch_size = 32,
  validation_split = 0.10,
  verbose = 2,
  view_metrics = TRUE
)
```

We set *mean squared error* (MSE) as the loss function. We use the normal instances in the train set (`train.normal`) as the input and expected output. The validation split is set to 10% so we can plot the reconstruction error (loss) on unseen instances. Finally, the model is trained for 100 epochs. From Figure 10.12 we can see that as the training progresses, the loss and the MSE decrease.

We can now compute the MSE on the normal and abnormal **test sets**. The `test.normal` data frame only contains normal test instances and `test.abnormal` only contains abnormal test instances.

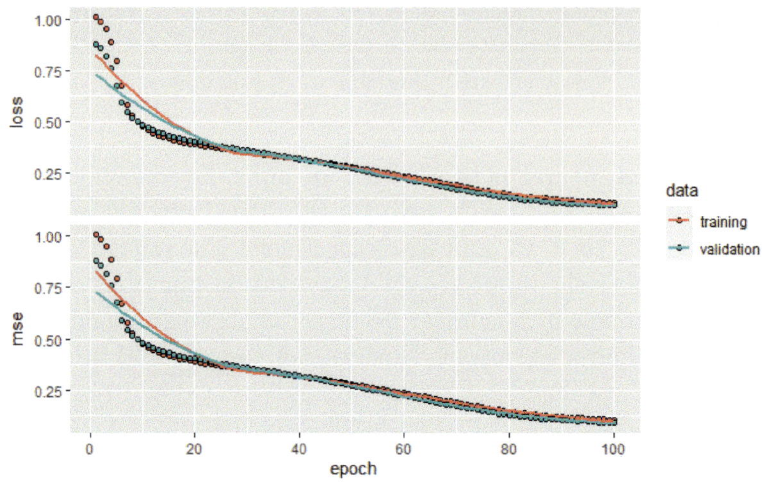

FIGURE 10.12 Loss and MSE.

```
# Compute MSE on normal test set.
autoencoder %>% evaluate(as.matrix(test.normal[,-c(1:2)]),
                         as.matrix(test.normal[,-c(1:2)]))
#>        loss mean_squared_error
#>  0.06147528         0.06147528

# Compute MSE on abnormal test set.
autoencoder %>% evaluate(as.matrix(test.abnormal[,-c(1:2)]),
                         as.matrix(test.abnormal[,-c(1:2)]))
#>       loss mean_squared_error
#>   2.660597           2.660597
```

Clearly, the MSE of the normal test set is much lower than the abnormal test set. This means that the autoencoder had a difficult time trying to reconstruct the abnormal points because it never saw similar ones before.

To find a good threshold we can start by analyzing the reconstruction errors on the **train set**. First, we need to get the predictions.

```
# Predict values on the normal train set.
```

```
preds.train.normal <- autoencoder %>%
  predict_on_batch(as.matrix(train.normal[,-c(1:2)]))
```

The variable `preds.train.normal` contains the predicted values for each feature and each instance. We can use those predictions to compute the reconstruction error by comparing them with the ground truth values. As reconstruction error we will use the squared errors. The function `squared.errors()` computes the reconstruction error for each instance.

```
# Compute individual squared errors in train set.
errors.train.normal <- squared.errors(preds.train.normal,
                                      as.matrix(train.normal[,-c(1:2)]))

mean(errors.train.normal)
#> [1] 0.8113273

quantile(errors.train.normal)
#>          0%         25%         50%         75%        100%
#>   0.0158690   0.2926631   0.4978471   0.8874694  15.0958992
```

The mean reconstruction error of the normal instances in the train set is 0.811. If we look at the quantiles, we can see that most of the instances have an error of <= 0.887. With this information we can set `threshold <- 1.0`. If the reconstruction error is > *threshold* then we will consider that point as an anomaly.

```
# Make predictions on the abnormal test set.
preds.test.abnormal <- autoencoder %>%
  predict_on_batch(as.matrix(test.abnormal[,-c(1:2)]))

# Compute reconstruction errors.
errors.test.abnormal <- squared.errors(preds.test.abnormal,
                                       as.matrix(test.abnormal[,-c(1:2)]))

# Predict labels based on threshold 1:abnormal, 0:normal.
pred.labels.abnormal <- as.integer((errors.test.abnormal > threshold))
```

```
# Count how many abnormal instances were detected.
sum(pred.labels.abnormal)
#> [1] 46
```

By using that threshold the autoencoder was able to detect 46 out of the 54 anomaly points. From the following confusion matrix we can also see that there were 16 false positives.

```
#>           Reference
#> Prediction   0   1
#>          0 202   8
#>          1  16  46
```

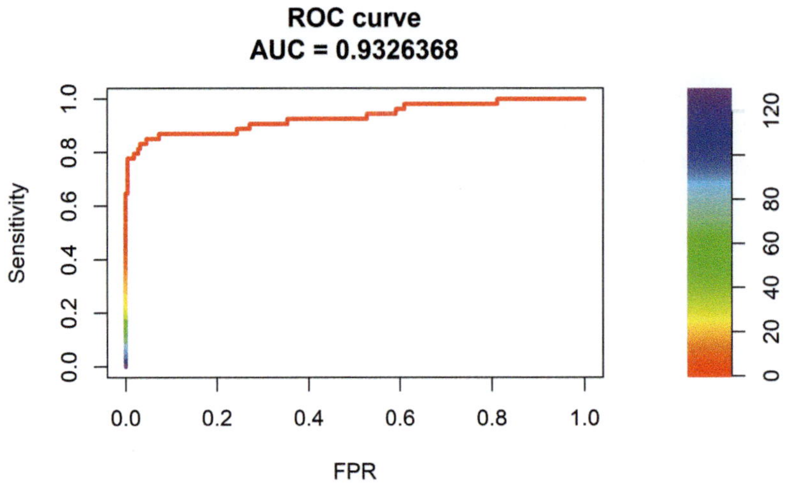

FIGURE 10.13 ROC curve and AUC. The dashed line represents a random model.

From the ROC curve in Figure 10.13 we can see that the AUC was 0.93 which is lower than the 0.96 achieved by the Isolation Forest but with some fine tuning and training for more epochs, the autoencoder should be able to achieve similar results.

10.4 Summary

This chapter presented two anomaly detection models, namely Isolation Forests and autoencoders. Examples of how those models can be used for anomaly trajectory detection were also presented. This chapter also introduced ROC curves and AUC which can be used to assess the performance of a model.

- **Isolation Forests** work by generating random partitions of the features until all instances are isolated.
- Abnormal points are more likely to be isolated during the first partitions.
- The average tree path length of abnormal points is smaller than that of normal points.
- An **anomaly score** that ranges between 0 and 1 is calculated based on the path length and the closer to 1 the more likely the point is an anomaly.
- A **ROC curve** is used to visualize the sensitivity and false positive rate of a model for different thresholds.
- The area under the curve **AUC** can be used to summarize the performance of a model.
- A simple **autoencoder** is an artificial neural network whose output layer has the same shape as the input layer.
- Autoencoders are used to encode the data into a lower dimension from which then, it can be reconstructed.
- The **reconstruction error** (loss) is a measure of how distant a prediction is from the ground truth and can be used as an anomaly score.

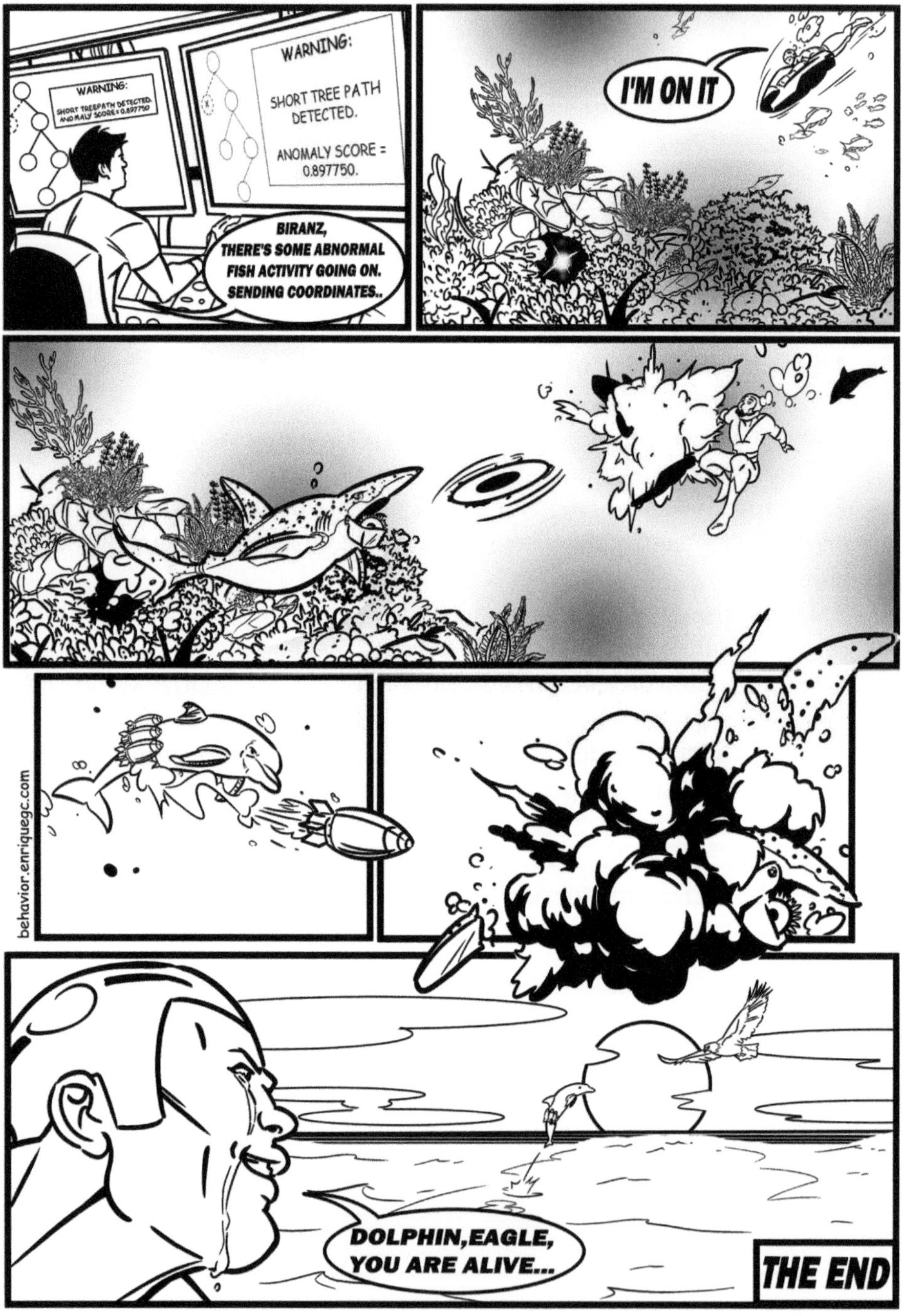
WARNING:
SHORT TREEPATH DETECTED. ANOMALY SCORE = 0.897750
WARNING:
SHORT TREE PATH DETECTED.
ANOMALY SCORE = 0.897750.
BIRANZ, THERE'S SOME ABNORMAL FISH ACTIVITY GOING ON. SENDING COORDINATES..
I'M ON IT
DOLPHIN,EAGLE, YOU ARE ALIVE...
THE END
behavior.enriquegc.com

A

Setup Your Environment

The examples in this book were tested with R 4.0.5. You can get the latest R version from its official website: www.r-project.org/

As IDE, I use RStudio (`https://rstudio.com/`) but you can use your favorite one. Most of the code examples in this book rely on datasets. The following two sections describe how to get and install the datasets and source code. If you want to try out the examples, I recommend you to follow the instructions in the following two sections.

The last section includes instructions on how to install Keras and TensorFlow, which are the required libraries to build and train deep learning models. Deep learning is covered in chapter 8. Before that, you don't need those libraries.

A.1 Installing the Datasets

A compressed file with a collection of most of the datasets used in this book can be downloaded here: `https://github.com/enriquegit/behavior-crc-datasets`

Download the datasets collection file (behavior_book_datasets.zip) and extract it into a local directory, for example, `C:/datasets/`. This compilation includes most of the datasets. Due to some datasets having large file sizes or license restrictions, not all of them are included in the collection set. But you can download them separately. Even though a dataset may not be included in the compiled set, it will still have a corresponding directory with a README file with instructions on how to obtain it. The following picture shows how the directory structure looks like in my PC.

DOI: 10.1201/9781003203469-A

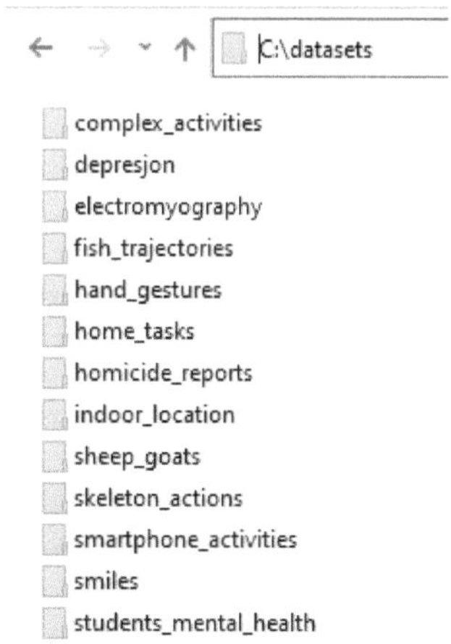

A.2 Installing the Examples Source Code

The examples source code can be downloaded here: `https://github.com/enriquegit/behavior-crc-code`

You can get the code using git or if you are not familiar with it, click on the 'Code' button and then 'Download zip'. Then, extract the file into a local directory of your choice.

There is a directory for each chapter and two additional directories: `auxiliary_functions/` and `install_functions/`.

The `auxiliary_functions/` folder has generic functions that are imported by some other R scripts. In this directory, there is a file called `globals.R`. Open that file and set the variable `datasets_path` to your local path where you downloaded the datasets. For example, I set it to:

```
datasets_path <- "C:/datasets"
```

The `install_functions/` directory has a single script: `install_packages.R`. This script can be used to install all the packages used in the examples (except Keras and TensorFlow which is covered in the next section). The script reads the packages listed in listpackages.txt and tries to install them if they are not present. This is just a convenient way to install everything at once but you can always install each package individually with the usual `install.packages()` method.

When running the examples, it is assumed that the working directory is the same as the actual script. For example, if you want to try `indoor_classification.R`, and that script is located in `C:/code/Predicting Behavior with Classification Models/` then, your working directory should be `C:/code/Predicting Behavior with Classification Models/`. In Windows, and if RStudio is not already opened, when you double-click an R script, RStudio will be launched (if it is set as the default program) and the working directory will be set.

You can check your current working directory by typing `getwd()` and you can set your working directory with `setwd()`. Alternatively, in RStudio, you can set your working directory in the menu bar 'Session' -> 'Set Working Directory' -> 'To Source File Location'.

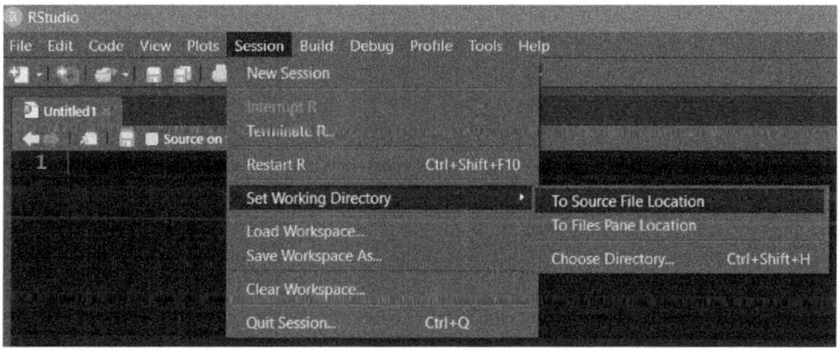

A.3 Running Shiny Apps

Shiny apps[1] are interactive applications written in R. This book includes some shiny apps that demonstrate some of the concepts. Shiny apps file names will start with the prefix `shiny_` followed by the specific file name. Some have an '.Rmd' extension while others will have an '.R' extension. Regardless of the extension, they are run in the same way. Before running shiny apps, make sure you have installed the packages `shiny` and `shinydashboard`.

[1] `https://shiny.rstudio.com/`

```
install.packages("shiny")
install.packages("shinydashboard")
```

To run an app, just open the corresponding file in RStudio. RStudio will detect that this is a shiny app and a 'Run Document' or 'Run App' button will be shown. Click the button to start the app.

A.4 Installing Keras and TensorFlow

Keras and TensorFlow are used until chapter 8. It is not necessary to install them if you are not still there.

TensorFlow has two main versions. a CPU and a GPU version. The GPU version takes advantage of the capabilities of some video cards to perform faster operations. The examples in this book can be run with both versions. The following instructions apply to the CPU version. Installing the GPU version requires some platform-specific details. I recommend you to first install the CPU version and if you want/need to perform faster computations, then, go with the GPU version.

Installing Keras with TensorFlow (CPU version) as backend takes four simple steps:

1. If you are on Windows, you need to install Anaconda[2]. The individual version is free.
2. Install the `keras` R package with `install.packages("keras")`

[2] https://www.anaconda.com

3. Load keras with library(keras)
4. Run the install_keras() function. This function will install TensorFlow as the backend. If you don't have Anaconda installed, you will be asked if you want to install Miniconda.

You can test your installation with:

```
library(tensorflow)
tf$constant("Hello World")
#> tf.Tensor(b'Hello World', shape=(), dtype=string)
```

The first time in a session that you run TensorFlow related code with the CPU version, you may get warning messages like the following, which you can safely ignore.

```
#> tensorflow/stream_executor/platform/default/dso_loader.cc:55]
#> Could not load dynamic library 'cudart64_101.dll';
#> dlerror: cudart64_101.dll not found
```

If you want to install the GPU version, first, you need to make sure you have a compatible video card. More information on how to install the GPU version is available here https://keras.rstudio.com/reference/install_keras.html and here https://tensorflow.rstudio.com/installation/gpu/local_gpu/

B

Datasets

This Appendix has a list with a description of all the datasets used in this book. A compressed file with a compilation of most of the datasets can be downloaded here: `https://github.com/enriquegit/behavior-crc-datasets`

I recommend you to download the datasets compilation file and extract its contents to a local directory. Due to some datasets with large file sizes or license restrictions, not all of them are included in the compiled set. But you can download them separately. Even though a dataset may not be included in the compiled set, it will have a corresponding directory with a README file with instructions on how to obtain it.

Each dataset in the following list, states whether or not it is included in the compiled set. The datasets are ordered alphabetically.

B.1 COMPLEX ACTIVITIES

Included: Yes.

This dataset was collected with a smartphone and contains 5 complex activities: *'commuting'*, *'working, at home'*, *'shopping at the supermarket'* and *'exercising'*. An Android 2.2 application running on a LG Optimus Me cellphone was used to collect the accelerometer data from each of the axes (x,y,z). The sample rate was set at 50 Hz. The cellphone was placed in the user's belt. A training and a test set were collected on different days. The duration of the activities varies from about 5 minutes to a couple of hours. The total recorded data consists of approximately 41 hours. The data was collected by one user. Each file contains a whole activity.

DOI: 10.1201/9781003203469-B

B.2 DEPRESJON

Included: Yes.

This dataset contains motor activity recordings of 23 unipolar and bipolar depressed patients and 32 healthy controls. Motor activity was monitored with an actigraph watch worn at the right wrist (Actiwatch, Cambridge Neurotechnology Ltd, England, model AW4). The sampling frequency was 32 Hz. The device uses the inertial sensors data to compute an activity count every minute which is stored as an integer value in the memory unit of the actigraph watch. The number of counts is proportional to the intensity of the movement. The dataset also contains some additional information about the patients and the control group. For more details please see Garcia-Ceja et al. [2018b].

B.3 ELECTROMYOGRAPHY

Included: Yes.

This dataset was made available by Kirill Yashuk. The data was collected using an armband device that has 8 sensors placed on the skin surface that measure electrical activity from the right forearm at a sampling rate of 200 Hz. A video of the device can be seen here: `https://youtu.be/OuwDHfY2Awg`.

The data contains 4 different gestures: 0-rock, 1-scissors, 2-paper, 3-OK, and has 65 columns. The last column is the class label from 0 to 3. Each gesture was recorded 6 times for 20 seconds. The first 64 columns are electrical measurements. 8 consecutive readings for each of the 8 sensors. For more details, please see Yashuk [2019].

B.4 FISH TRAJECTORIES

Included: Yes.

The Fish4Knowledge[1] [Beyan and Fisher, 2013] project made this database available. It contains 3102 trajectories belonging to the *Dascyllus reticulatus* fish observed in the Taiwanese coral reef. Each trajectory is labeled as *'normal'* or *'abnormal'*. The trajectories were extracted from underwater video. Bounding box's coordinates over time were extracted from the video. The data does not contain the video images but the final coordinates. The dataset compilation in this book also includes a .csv file with extracted features from the trajectories.

B.5 HAND GESTURES

Included: Yes.

The data was collected using an LG Optimus Me smartphone using its accelerometer sensor. The data was collected by 10 subjects which performed 5 repetitions for each of the 10 different gestures (*'triangle'*, *'square'*, *'circle'*, *'a'*, *'b'*, *'c'*, *'1'*, *'2'*, *'3'*, *'4'*) giving a total of 500 instances. The sensor is a tri-axial accelerometer which returns values for the x, y, and z axes. The sampling rate was set at 50 Hz. To record a gesture the user presses the phone screen with her/his thumb, performs the gesture, and stops pressing the screen. For more information, please see Garcia-Ceja et al. [2014].

B.6 HOME TASKS

Included: Yes.

Sound and accelerometer data were collected by 3 volunteers while performing 7 different home task activities: *'mop floor'*, *'sweep floor'*, *'type*

[1] http://groups.inf.ed.ac.uk/f4k/

on computer keyboard', *'brush teeth'*, *'wash hands'*, *'eat chips'*, and *'watch t.v'*. Each volunteer performed each activity for approximately 3 minutes. If the activity lasted less than 3 minutes, another session was recorded until completing the 3 minutes. The data were collected with a wrist-band (Microsoft Band 2) and a cellphone. The wrist-band was used to collect accelerometer data and was worn by the volunteers in their dominant hand. The accelerometer sensor returns values from the x, y, and z axes, and the sampling rate was set to 31 Hz. A cellphone was used to record environmental sound with a sampling rate of 8000 Hz and it was placed on a table in the same room the user was performing the activity. To preserve privacy, the dataset does not contain the raw audio recordings but extracted features. Sixteen features from the accelerometer sensor and 12 Mel frequency cepstral coefficients from the audio recordings. For more information, please see Garcia-Ceja et al. [2018a].

B.7 HOMICIDE REPORTS

Included: Yes.

This dataset was compiled and made available by the Murder Accountability Project, founded by Thomas Hargrove[2]. It contains information about homicides in the United States. This dataset includes the age, race, sex, ethnicity of victims, and perpetrators, in addition to the relationship between the victim and perpetrator and weapon used. The original dataset includes the `database.csv` file. The files `processed.csv` and `transactions.RData` were generated with the R scripts included in the examples code of the corresponding sections to facilitate the analysis.

B.8 INDOOR LOCATION

Included: Yes.

This dataset contains Wi-Fi signal recordings fo access points from different locations in a building including their MAC address and signal strength. The data was collected with an Android 2.2 application running on a LG Optimus Me cell phone. To generate a single instance, the device

[2] `https://www.kaggle.com/murderaccountability/homicide-reports`

scans and records the MAC address and signal strength of the nearby access points. A delay of 500 ms is set between scans. For each location, approximately 3 minutes of data were collected while the user walked around the specific location. The data includes four different locations: *'bedroomA'*, *'beadroomB'*, *'tv room'* and the *'lobby'*. To preserve privacy, the MAC addresses are encoded as integer numbers. For more information, please, see Garcia and Brena [2012].

B.9 SHEEP GOATS

Included: No.

The dataset was made available by Kamminga et al. [2017] and can be downloaded from `https://easy.dans.knaw.nl/ui/datasets/id/easy-dataset:76131`. The researchers placed inertial sensors on sheep and goats and tracked their behavior during one day. They also video-recorded the session and annotated the data with different types of behaviors such as *'grazing'*, *'fighting'*, *'scratch-biting'*, etc. The device was placed on the neck with random orientation and it collects acceleration, orientation, magnetic field, temperature, and barometric pressure. In this book, only data from one of the sheep is used (`Sheep/S1.csv`).

B.10 SKELETON ACTIONS

Included: No.

The authors of this dataset are Chen et al. [2015]. The data was recorded by 8 subjects with a Kinect camera and an inertial sensor unit and each subject repeated each action 4 times. The number of actions is 27 and some of the actions include: *'right hand wave'*, *'two hand front clap'*, *'basketball shoot'*, *'front boxing'*, etc. More information about the collection process and pictures can be consulted on the website `https://personal.utdallas.edu/~kehtar/UTD-MHAD.html`. You only need to download the Skeleton_Data.zip file.

B.11 SMARTPHONE ACTIVITIES

Included: Yes.

This dataset is called WISDM[3] and was made available by Kwapisz et al. [2010]. The dataset includes 6 different activities: *'walking'*, *'jogging'*, *'walking upstairs'*, *'walking downstairs'*, *'sitting'*, and *'standing'*. The data was collected by 36 volunteers with the accelerometer of an Android phone located in the users' pants pocket and with a sampling rate of 20 Hz.

B.12 SMILES

Included: No.

This dataset contains color face images of 64 × 64 pixels and is published here: `http://conradsanderson.id.au/lfwcrop/`. This is a cropped version [Sanderson and Lovell, 2009] of the Labeled Faces in the Wild (LFW) database [Huang et al., 2008]. Please, download the color version (lfwcrop_color.zip) and copy all ppm files into the `faces/` directory.

A subset of the database was labeled by Arigbabu et al. [2016], Arigbabu [2017]. The labels are provided as two text files (SMILE_list.txt, NON-SMILE_list.txt), each, containing the list of files that correspond to smiling and non-smiling faces (CC BY 4.0 `https://creativecommons.org/licenses/by/4.0/legalcode`). The smiling set has 600 pictures and the non-smiling has 603 pictures.

B.13 STUDENTS' MENTAL HEALTH

Included: Yes.

This dataset contains 268 survey responses that include variables related to depression, acculturative stress, social connectedness, and

[3] `http://www.cis.fordham.edu/wisdm/dataset.php`

help-seeking behaviors reported by international and domestic students at an international university in Japan. For a detailed description, please see [Nguyen et al., 2019].

Bibliography

R. Agrawal and R. Srikant. Fast algorithms for mining association rules. In *Proc. 20th int. conf. very large data bases, VLDB*, volume 1215, pages 487–499, 1994.

J. Allaire and F. Chollet. *keras: R Interface to 'Keras'*, 2019. URL https://CRAN.R-project.org/package=keras. R package version 2.2.4.1.

A. Anzulewicz, K. Sobota, and J. T. Delafield-Butt. Toward the autism motor signature: Gesture patterns during smart tablet gameplay identify children with autism. *Scientific reports*, 6(1):1–13, 2016.

O. Arigbabu. *Dataset for Smile Detection from Face Images*, 2017. URL http://dx.doi.org/10.17632/yz4v8tb3tp.5.

O. A. Arigbabu, S. Mahmood, S. M. S. Ahmad, and A. A. Arigbabu. Smile detection using hybrid face representation. *Journal of Ambient Intelligence and Humanized Computing*, 7(3):415–426, 2016.

H. Bengtsson. *R.matlab: Read and Write MAT Files and Call MATLAB from Within R*, 2018. URL https://CRAN.R-project.org/package=R.matlab. R package version 3.6.2.

C. Beyan and R. B. Fisher. Detecting abnormal fish trajectories using clustered and labeled data. In *2013 IEEE International Conference on Image Processing*, pages 1476–1480. IEEE, 2013.

P. Biecek, E. Szczurek, M. Vingron, J. Tiuryn, et al. The r package bgmm: mixture modeling with uncertain knowledge. *Journal of Statistical Software*, 47(i03), 2012.

R. Bivand, F. Leisch, and M. Maechler. *pixmap: Bitmap Images ("Pixel Maps")*, 2011. URL https://CRAN.R-project.org/package=pixmap. R package version 0.4-11.

I. Borg, P. J. Groenen, and P. Mair. *Applied multidimensional scaling* Springer Science & Business Media, New York, New York, 2012.

L. Breiman. Bagging Predictors. *Machine Learning*, 24(2):123–140, 1996. ISSN 0885-6125. doi: 10.1023/A:1018054314350. URL http://dx.doi.org/10.1023/A%3A1018054314350.

L. Breiman. Random forests. *Machine learning*, 45(1):5–32, 2001.

R. F. Brena, J. P. García-Vázquez, C. E. Galván-Tejada, D. Muñoz-Rodriguez, C. Vargas-Rosales, and J. Fangmeyer. Evolution of indoor positioning technologies: A survey. *Journal of Sensors*, 2017:1–22, 2017.

N. V. Chawla, K. W. Bowyer, L. O. Hall, and W. P. Kegelmeyer. Smote: synthetic minority over-sampling technique. *Journal of artificial intelligence research*, 16:321–357, 2002.

C. Chen, R. Jafari, and N. Kehtarnavaz. Utd-mhad: A multimodal dataset for human action recognition utilizing a depth camera and a wearable inertial sensor. In *2015 IEEE International conference on image processing (ICIP)*, pages 168–172. IEEE, 2015.

F. Chollet and J. J. Allaire. *Deep Learning with R.* Manning, Shelter Island, New York, 2018. ISBN 9781617295546.

E. Côme, L. Oukhellou, T. Denoeux, and P. Aknin. Learning from partially supervised data using mixture models and belief functions. *Pattern recognition*, 42(3):334–348, 2009.

A. Cooper, E. L. Smith, et al. *Homicide trends in the United States, 1980-2008.* BiblioGov, 2012.

G. Csardi and T. Nepusz. The igraph software package for complex network research. *InterJournal Complex Systems*:1695, 2006. URL http://igraph.org.

B. Cui. *DataExplorer: Automate Data Exploration and Treatment*, 2020. URL https://CRAN.R-project.org/package=DataExplorer. R package version 0.8.1.

B. De Gelder. Towards the neurobiology of emotional body language. *Nature Reviews Neuroscience*, 7(3):242–249, 2006.

J.-P. Eckmann, S. O. Kamphorst, and D. Ruelle. Recurrence plots of dynamical systems. *EPL (Europhysics Letters)*, 4(9):973, 1987.

R. A. Fisher. The use of multiple measurements in taxonomic problems. *Annals of eugenics*, 7(2):179–188, 1936.

E. A. Garcia and R. F. Brena. Real time activity recognition using a cell phone's accelerometer and wi-fi. In *Workshop Proceedings of the 8th International Conference on Intelligent Environments*, volume 13 of *Ambient Intelligence and Smart Environments*, pages 94–103. IOS Press, 2012. doi: 10.3233/978-1-61499-080-2-94.

E. Garcia-Ceja, R. Brena, and C. Galván-Tejada. Contextualized hand gesture recognition with smartphones. In J. Martínez-Trinidad, J. Carrasco-Ochoa, J. Olvera-Lopez, J. Salas-Rodríguez, and C. Suen, editors, *Pattern Recognition, volume 8495 of Lecture Notes in Computer Science*, pages 122–131. Springer International Publishing, Cham, Switzerland. ISBN 978-3-319-07490-0. doi: doi:10.1007/978-3-319-07491-7_13.

E. Garcia-Ceja, C. E. Galván-Tejada, and R. Brena. Multi-view stacking for activity recognition with sound and accelerometer data. *Information Fusion*, 40:45–56, 2018a.

E. Garcia-Ceja, M. Riegler, P. Jakobsen, J. Tørresen, T. Nordgreen, K. J. Oedegaard, and O. B. Fasmer. Depresjon: A motor activity database of depression episodes in unipolar and bipolar patients. In *Proceedings of the 9th ACM on Multimedia Systems Conference*, MMSys'18. ACM, 2018b. doi: 10.1145/3204949.3208125. URL `http://doi.acm.org/10.1145/3204949.3208125`.

E. Garcia-Ceja, M. Riegler, T. Nordgreen, P. Jakobsen, K. J. Oedegaard, and J. Tørresen. Mental health monitoring with multimodal sensing and machine learning: A survey. *Pervasive and Mobile Computing*, 2018c.

T. Giorgino. Computing and visualizing dynamic time warping alignments in r: the dtw package. *Journal of statistical Software*, 31(7): 1–24, 2009.

J. C. Gower. Some distance properties of latent root and vector methods used in multivariate analysis. *Biometrika*, 53(3-4):325–338, 1966.

J. Grau, I. Grosse, and J. Keilwagen. Prroc: computing and visualizing precision-recall and receiver operating characteristic curves in r. *Bioinformatics*, 31(15):2595–2597, 2015.

M. Hahsler. arulesViz: Interactive visualization of association rules with R. *R Journal*, 9(2):163–175, December 2017. ISSN 2073-4859. URL https://journal.r-project.org/archive/2017/RJ-2017-047/RJ-2017-047.pdf.

M. Hahsler. *arulesViz: Visualizing Association Rules and Frequent Itemsets*, 2019. URL https://CRAN.R-project.org/package=arulesViz. R package version 1.3-3.

M. Hahsler, C. Buchta, B. Gruen, and K. Hornik. *arules: Mining Association Rules and Frequent Itemsets*, 2019. URL https://CRAN.R-project.org/package=arules. R package version 1.6-4.

M. Halkidi, Y. Batistakis, and M. Vazirgiannis. On clustering validation techniques. *Journal of Intelligent Information Systems*, 17(2):107–145, 2001.

T. Hastie, R. Tibshirani, and J. Friedman. *The elements of statistical learning: data mining, inference, and prediction.* Springer Science & Business Media, New York, New York, 2009.

G.-B. Huang. Learning capability and storage capacity of two-hidden-layer feedforward networks. *IEEE Transactions on Neural Networks*, 14(2):274–281, 2003.

G. B. Huang, M. Mattar, T. Berg, and E. Learned-Miller. Labeled faces in the wild: A database forstudying face recognition in unconstrained environments. 2008.

R. J. Hyndman and G. Athanasopoulos. *Forecasting: principles and practice.* OTexts, Melbourne, Australia, 2nd edition, 2018. URL https://otexts.com/fpp2/. Accessed on 09-2020.

J. W. Kamminga, H. C. Bisby, D. V. Le, N. Meratnia, and P. J. Havinga. Generic online animal activity recognition on collar tags. In *Proceedings of the 2017 ACM International Joint Conference on Pervasive and Ubiquitous Computing and Proceedings of the 2017 ACM International Symposium on Wearable Computers*, pages 597–606, 2017.

N. S. Keskar, D. Mudigere, J. Nocedal, M. Smelyanskiy, and P. T. P. Tang. On large-batch training for deep learning: Generalization gap and sharp minima, 2016.

R. Kolde. *pheatmap: Pretty Heatmaps*, 2019. URL https://CRAN.R-project.org/package=pheatmap. R package version 1.0.12.

I. Kononenko and M. Kukar. *Machine learning and data mining.* Horwood Publishing, 2007.

J. R. Kwapisz, G. M. Weiss, and S. A. Moore. Activity recognition using cell phone accelerometers. In *Proceedings of the Fourth International Workshop on Knowledge Discovery from Sensor Data (at KDD-10), Washington DC.*, 2010.

Y. LeCun, L. Bottou, Y. Bengio, and P. Haffner. Gradient-based learning applied to document recognition. *Proceedings of the IEEE*, 86(11): 2278–2324, 1998.

A. Liaw and M. Wiener. Classification and regression by randomforest. *R News*, 2(3):18–22, 2002. URL `https://CRAN.R-project.org/doc/Rnews/`.

F. T. Liu, K. M. Ting, and Z. Zhou. Isolation forest. In *2008 Eighth IEEE International Conference on Data Mining*, pages 413–422, 2008.

D. J. McLean and M. A. S. Volponi. trajr: An r package for characterisation of animal trajectories. *Ethology*, 124(6), 2018. doi: 10.1111/eth.12739. URL `https://onlinelibrary.wiley.com/doi/abs/10.1111/eth.12739`.

D. Meyer, E. Dimitriadou, K. Hornik, A. Weingessel, and F. Leisch. *e1071: Misc Functions of the Department of Statistics, Probability Theory Group (Formerly: E1071), TU Wien*, 2019. URL `https://CRAN.R-project.org/package=e1071`. R package version 1.7-3.

S. Milborrow. *rpart.plot: Plot 'rpart' Models: An Enhanced Version of 'plot.rpart'*, 2019. URL `https://CRAN.R-project.org/package=rpart.plot`. R package version 3.0.8.

C. Molnar. *Interpretable Machine Learning. A Guide for Making Black Box Models Explainable.* Leanpub, 2019.

F. M. Neves, R. L. Viana, and M. R. Pie. Recurrence analysis of ant activity patterns. *PLOS ONE*, 12(10):1–15, 10 2017. doi: 10.1371/journal.pone.0185968. URL `https://doi.org/10.1371/journal.pone.0185968`.

M.-H. Nguyen, M.-T. Ho, Q.-Y. T. Nguyen, and Q.-H. Vuong. A dataset of students' mental health and help-seeking behaviors in a multicultural environment. *Data*, 4(3), 2019. ISSN 2306-5729. doi: 10.3390/data4030124. URL `https://www.mdpi.com/2306-5729/4/3/124`.

R. Peng. *Exploratory data analysis with R.* Leanpub.com, 2016. Accessed on 11-08-2021.

L. Y. Pratt, J. Mostow, C. A. Kamm, and A. A. Kamm. Direct transfer of learned information among neural networks. In *Aaai*, volume 91, pages 584–589, 1991.

J. R. Quinlan. *C4.5: programs for machine learning*. Morgan Kaufmann Publishers, San Mateo, California, 2014.

L. Rabiner and B.-H. Juang. *Fundamentals of speech recognition*. Prentice hall, Englewood Cliffs, New Jersey, 1993.

F. Rosenblatt. The perceptron: a probabilistic model for information storage and organization in the brain. *Psychological review*, 65(6): 386, 1958.

P. J. Rousseeuw. Silhouettes: a graphical aid to the interpretation and validation of cluster analysis. *Journal of computational and applied mathematics*, 20:53–65, 1987.

A. Rushworth. *inspectdf: Inspection, Comparison and Visualisation of Data Frames*, 2019. URL `https://CRAN.R-project.org/package=inspectdf`. R package version 0.0.7.

H. Sakoe, S. Chiba, A. Waibel, and K. Lee. Dynamic programming algorithm optimization for spoken word recognition. *Readings in speech recognition*, 159:224, 1990.

N. F. Samatova, W. Hendrix, J. Jenkins, K. Padmanabhan, and A. Chakraborty. *Practical graph mining with R*. CRC Press, Boca Raton, Florida, 2013.

C. Sanderson and B. C. Lovell. Multi-region probabilistic histograms for robust and scalable identity inference. In *International conference on biometrics*, pages 199–208, Berlin, Heidelberg, 2009. Springer.

H. Scharf. *anipaths: Animation of Observed Trajectories Using Spline-Based Interpolation*, 2020. URL `https://CRAN.R-project.org/package=anipaths`. R package version 0.9.8.

T. Segaran. *Programming collective intelligence: building smart web 2.0 applications*. "O' Reilly Media, Inc." , Sebastopol, California, 2007.

M. Shoaib, S. Bosch, O. D. Incel, H. Scholten, and P. J. Havinga. A Survey of Online Activity Recognition Using Mobile Phones. *Sensors*, 15(1):2059–2085, 2015. ISSN 1424-8220. doi: 10.3390/s150102059. URL `http://www.mdpi.com/1424-8220/15/1/2059`.

J. Silge and D. Robinson. *Text mining with R: A tidy approach.* "O'Reilly Media, Inc.", 2017.

K. Simonyan and A. Zisserman. Very deep convolutional networks for large-scale image recognition. *arXiv preprint arXiv:1409.1556*, 2014.

K. S. Srikanth. *solitude: An Implementation of Isolation Forest*, 2020. URL `https://CRAN.R-project.org/package=solitude`. R package version 1.1.1.

N. Srivastava, G. Hinton, A. Krizhevsky, I. Sutskever, and R. Salakhutdinov. Dropout: A simple way to prevent neural networks from overfitting. *Journal of Machine Learning Research*, 15(56):1929–1958, 2014. URL `http://jmlr.org/papers/v15/srivastava14a.html`.

D. Steinberg and P. Colla. Cart: classification and regression trees. *The top ten algorithms in data mining*, 9:179, 2009.

T. Therneau and B. Atkinson. *rpart: Recursive Partitioning and Regression Trees*, 2019. URL `https://CRAN.R-project.org/package=rpart`. R package version 4.1-15.

N. Tierney, D. Cook, M. McBain, and C. Fay. *naniar: Data Structures, Summaries, and Visualisations for Missing Data*, 2019. URL `https://CRAN.R-project.org/package=naniar`. R package version 0.4.2.

K. M. Ting and I. H. Witten. Issues in stacked generalization. *Journal of artificial intelligence research*, 10:271–289, 1999.

I. Triguero, S. García, and F. Herrera. Self-labeled techniques for semi-supervised learning: taxonomy, software and empirical study. *Knowledge and Information Systems*, 42(2):245–284, 2013. ISSN 0219-3116. doi: 10.1007/s10115-013-0706-y. URL `http://dx.doi.org/10.1007/s10115-013-0706-y`.

M. van der Loo. *simputation: Simple Imputation*, 2019. URL `https://CRAN.R-project.org/package=simputation`. R package version 0.2.3.

D. Vanderkam, J. Allaire, J. Owen, D. Gromer, and B. Thieurmel. *dygraphs: Interface to 'Dygraphs' Interactive Time Series Charting Library*, 2018. URL `https://CRAN.R-project.org/package=dygraphs`. R package version 1.1.1.6.

H. Williams, E. Shepard, M. D. Holton, P. Alarcón, R. Wilson, and S. Lambertucci. Physical limits of flight performance in the heaviest soaring bird. *Proceedings of the National Academy of Sciences*, 2020.

D. H. Wolpert. Stacked generalization. *Neural networks*, 5(2):241–259, 1992.

X. Xi, E. Keogh, C. Shelton, L. Wei, and C. A. Ratanamahatana. Fast time series classification using numerosity reduction. In *Proceedings of the 23rd international conference on Machine learning*, pages 1033–1040, 2006.

K. Yashuk. *Classify gestures by reading muscle activity: a recording of human hand muscle activity producing four different hand gestures*, 2019. URL `https://www.kaggle.com/kyr7plus/emg-4`.

J. P. Zbilut and C. L. Webber. Embeddings and delays as derived from quantification of recurrence plots. *Physics Letters A*, 171(3):199 – 203, 1992. ISSN 0375-9601. doi: https://doi.org/10.1016/0375-9601(92)90426-M. URL `http://www.sciencedirect.com/science/article/pii/037596019290426M`.

Index